JESUS THE CHRIST

JESUS THE CHRIST

WALTER KASPER

BURNS & OATES

PAULIST PRESS

First published in Great Britian in 1976 by
Burns and Oates Limited, Wellwood,
North Farm Road, Tunbridge Wells,
Kent TN2 3DR, England
and in the USA by
Paulist Press, 997 Macarthur Blvd., Mahwah, New Jersey 07430.
Original German text *Jesus der Christus*
copyright © 1974 Matthias-Grunewald-Verlag,
Mainz, Federal Republic of Germany

This translation was made by V. Green
Copyright ©1976 Search Press Limited

New Edition (Paperback) 1977
Reprinted 1978, 1980, 1982, 1985

ISBN (UK) 0 86012 058 9
ISBN (USA) 0-8091-2081-X
Library of Congress Catalog Card
Number 76-20021

Printed and bound in the
United States of America

CONTENTS   *Page*

ABBREVIATIONS

This list does not include biblical and other well-known abbreviations.

DS   H. Denzinger and A. Schönmetzer, *Enchiridion Symbolorum, Definitionum et Declarationum de Rebus Fideli et Morum* (33rd edition, Freiburg-im-Breisgau, 1965).

ET   English translation.

HTG   *Handbuch theologischer Grundbegriffe*, ed., H. Fries (Munich, 1962 ff.)

LTK   *Lexikon für Theologie und Kirche*, 10 vols. + index, eds., J. Höfer and K. Rahner (2nd rev. ed., Freiburg-im-Breisgau, 1957-67).

MS   *Mysterium Salutis. Grundriss heilsgeschichtlicher Dogmatik*, eds., J. Feiner and M. Löhrer (Einsiedeln, 1965 ff.).

NR   J. Neuner and H. Roos, *Der Glaube der Kirche in den Urkunden der Lehrverkündigung*, eds., K. Rahner and K.-H. Weger (8th edition, Regensburg, 1971).

RAC   *Reallexikon für Antike und Christentum*, ed., T. Klauser (Stuttgart, 1941 ff.)

RGG   *Die Religion in Geschichte und Gegenwart. Handwörterbuch für Theologie und Religionswissenschaft*, 6 vols. + index ed. K. Galling (3rd rev. ed., Tübingen, 1956-65).

SM   *Sacramentum Mundi. Theologisches Lexikon für die Praxis*, 4 vols., eds., K. Rahner *et al.* (Freiburg-im-Breisgau, 1965-8). ET: *Sacramentum Mundi: An Encyclopedia of Theology*, 6 vols. (London, 1968-70).

TW   *Theologisches Wörterbuch zum Neuen Testament*, ed. G. Kittel, continued by G. Friedrich (Stuttgart, 1933 ff.). ET: *Theological Dictionary of the New Testament* (London, 1964 ff.).

W   Works.

FOREWORD

The first pages of this book were written more than ten years ago when I had to give my first lecture in the winter term at the University of Münster. Since then I have given that course on Jesus Christ and his life's work a number of times: first in Münster, then in Tübingen, and finally (in 1974) at the Gregorian University in Rome. I revised it thoroughly on each occasion, so that in each instance the new hardly resembled the old version. In its present published form, too, it is intended primarily as a stimulus to further thought on the subject. Jesus Christ is one of those figures with whom you are never finished once you have begun to explore his personality.

I only agreed to publication after a long delay and on the insistence of many friends and students. After the numberless, to some degree turbulent, theological disputes and dissensions of the last ten years there is an unmistakable interest in a treatment of central theological topics which examines the state of discussion critically yet offers at the same time a responsible account of scholarship. I have written this book for all those who read and study theology as well as for clergy and laity in the service of the Church. But I also intend it for the very many Christians for whom participation in theological debate is now part of their faith. I hope too that this book will help the increasingly large number of people outside the churches who are interested in Jesus Christ and all that concerns him.

Methodologically this book is indebted to the Catholic Tübingen School, and in particular the Christological approaches of Karl Adam and Joseph Rupert Geiselmann. Their theology focussed on a study of the origins of Christianity in Jesus Christ. In contradistinction, however, to many contemporary works on Jesus, they had no doubt that that origin, which is still normative for us, was accessible only through biblical and ecclesiastical tradition. They knew that we could dispense with that tradition only at the cost of a severe impoverishment of our resources. They differed from the neoscholastic theology of their time in their parallel conviction that tradition had to be handed on as something living; that is, in conjunction and confrontation with the comments and questions of a particular time. That idea of a contemporary transmission of an inheritance from the past and of a responsible commentary on tradition can also act as a support and an encouragement to us in the present transitional state of Christianity.

Therefore this book is not a repetition of old and sterile material; nor is it an attempt at a grand, exhaustive précis of the almost impossibly large number of new studies of exegetical, historical and dogmatic cruces. There is no lack of detailed investigations and encyclopaedic summaries. What then is needed is an unrelentingly profound and systematic reflection on the principal themes of tradition and of novel contemporary approaches; a study and investigation of those themes; and an attempt at a new, systematic treatment which responsibly confronts modern thought with the riches of tradition and the results of ongoing debate.

All this would have proved impossible without effective and selfless support from my colleagues. My graduate Assistants at Tübingen, Dr Arno Schilson and Thomas Pröpper, have made many valuable suggestions. I would also like to thank Anne Buck, Giancarlo Collet, Hans-Bernhard Petermann, Albrecht Rieder, Gerhard Glaser, Dr Jakob Laubach, and my sister Hildegard for their help.

Tübingen, 1974-5   WALTER KASPER

PREFATORY NOTE

The translation of the Bible used in this work is the Revised Standard Version: Old Testament copyright © 1946, 1952; New Testament copyright © 1946, 1971; Apocrypha copyright © 1957 by Division of Christian Education of the National Council of the Churches of Christ in the United States of America. In exceptional cases the translator and author have made their own version of the original text. Wherever possible and appropriate, reference is made to the standard English translations of German and other foreign language texts. In some cases, however, in order to preserve the author's emphasis. the original text has been translated and/or cited. The translator wishes to thank the following for their help in producing the English version: Rev. E. Quinn, W. J. O'Hara, Francis McDonagh, Rosaleen Ockenden.

I. JESUS CHRIST TODAY

I. THE PROBLEMATICS OF CONTEMPORARY CHRISTOLOGY

I. THE PROBLEMATICS OF CONTEMPORARY CHRISTOLOGY

1. THE POSITION OF CHRISTOLOGY TODAY

Theological discussion in the last decade, among Catholics at least, has been largely devoted to the renewal of the Church proposed by the second Vatican Council. The question of the Church, its nature, its unity and its structures, and the problem of the relation of the Church to present-day society, have been at the forefront of interest. Ecumenical theology, the theology of the world, political theology, and theologies of secularization, of development, of revolution, and of liberation have dominated the discussion. The associated problems however are by no means resolved. And they clearly cannot be resolved on the level of ecclesiology.

With its programme of *aggiornamento* the Church runs the risk of surrendering its unambiguousness for the sake of openness. Yet whenever it tries to speak straightforwardly and clearly it risks losing sight of men and their actual problems. If the Church worries about identity, it risks a loss of relevance; if on the other hand it struggles for relevance, it may forfeit its identity. Moltmann has described this identity-involvement dilemma most effectively.[1]

If we are to find a way out of this impasse and the related polarizations in the Church we have to reflect more profoundly on the real basis and meaning of the Church and its task in the modern world. The basis and meaning of the Church is not an idea, a principle, or a programme. It is not comprized in so many dogmas and moral injunctions. It does not amount to specific church or social structures. All these things are right and proper in their setting. But the basis and meaning of the Church is a person. And not a vague person, but one with a specific name: Jesus Christ. The many churches and communities and groups within the Church, however much they differ among themselves, agree on one thing: their claim to represent the person, word and work of Jesus Christ. Even if their results are controversial, they have one starting-point and one centre. The churches can solve the problems that beset them only from that centrepoint, and only by reference to it.

The question is: Who is Jesus Christ? Who is Jesus Christ for us today? Jesus Christ is not an ordinary Christian name and surname, like John Smith, for instance, but an acknowledgement and a confession that Jesus is the Christ.[2] The assertion 'Jesus is the Christ' is the basic statement of Christian belief, and Christology is no more than the conscientious elucidation of that proposition. When we say that Jesus is the Christ, we maintain that this unique, irreplaceable Jesus of Nazareth is at one and the same time the

Christ sent by God: that is, the Messiah anointed of the Spirit, the salvation of the world, and the eschatological fulfilment of history. Therefore belief in Jesus Christ is provocatively exact and individual on the one hand, and uniquely universal on the other. A profession of faith in Jesus Christ establishes the exactness, uniqueness and distinctness of all that Christ is about and at the same time its universal openness and global relevance. The unresolved questions of ecclesiology can be answered only within a renewed Christology, and only a renewed Christology can enable the Church to regain its universality and catholicity (in the original sense of the word), without denying the foolishness of the cross and surrendering the unique provocation of Christianity.

The split between faith and life in the contemporary Church has an extensive background in cultural and social history, examined above all by Hegel in his early writings. For Hegel, the dichotomy between faith and life is only a form of the alienation characteristic of the whole modern era. The emancipation in modern times of the (human) subject reduced the external world increasingly to the status of mere object: the dead material for man's ever more unrelenting domination of the world, a domination achieved with the aid of modern science and technology. External reality was increasingly demythologized and desacralized. Religion however withdrew more and more into the individual; it became a characterless, empty longing for the infinite. 'Religion raises its temples and altars in the heart of the individual, and these sighs and prayers search for the God whose vision is refused because that danger of the understanding is present which would perceive what is envisioned as a thing, and the wood as trees.'[3] Ultimately however, there is a yawning gulf on both sides — the objective and the subjective. The outer world turns neutral and banal; the inner world of the individual becomes hollow and empty. A meaningless nothingness arises from both aspects. As Jean Paul, Jacobi, Novalis, Fichte, Schelling, Hegel and German Romanticism as a whole suggested, as Nietzsche relentlessly asserted, and as Heidegger has summarily confirmed, the road travelled by the modern spirit leads to nihilism. The Church's crisis of identity has as its background the entire crisis of meaning of modern society.

It is here that Christology wins a relevance beyond the narrower theological context. The doctrine of the Incarnation has to do with the reconciliation of God and the world. Since the oneness of God and man, as it occurred in Jesus Christ, cancels neither the distinction between them nor the autonomy of man, but realizes that oneness and that distinction, reconciliation occurs in Jesus as liberation, and liberation as reconciliation — at one and the same time. Here God is not, as modern atheistic humanism asserts, a restriction but the condition and basis of human freedom. Christology can approach and tackle the legitimate concern of the modern era and resolve its problem. That, to be sure, is possible only on the basis of a decision: the basic decision between belief and unbelief. Liberating reconciliation, as it occurs in and through Jesus Christ, is primarily a divine gift and only secondarily a human

16

task. Here precisely is the border line between Christian theology and ideologies or utopias (which nevertheless retain traces of Christian influence). The decisive option is the sword or faith (Albert Camus), promise or achievement.

Christianity sees the indicative of a granted liberation and reconciliation as giving rise to the imperative of henceforth devoting oneself wholly to liberation and reconciliation in the world. But the real choice before us can be escaped only at the cost of the Christian identity. And there is no involvement, no relevance, without identity.

Christology, in which identity and relevance, existence and meaning, are revealed in a unique and complete manner, is the task of theology today. Thinking about Christology discloses the help which is needed at the moment and which theologians (who are certainly not the whole Church) can give modern society and the Church in their search for an identity.

2. THE BASIC TRENDS IN CONTEMPORARY CHRISTOLOGY

The first wave of modern Christological thought[4] in the second half of this century began twenty-five years ago — fifteen centuries after the Council of Chalcedon (451-1951). Karl Rahner's article on Chalcedon as end or beginning set the tone.[5] Rahner stated that every conciliar definition signified the end and the result of a discussion, the victory and the unambiguousness of truth, but that it was also a beginning for new questions and deeper insights. He spoke of the self-transcendence of all formulas. They must constantly be rethought, not because they are false, but because they are true. They remain alive insofar as they are elucidated. Significant new interpretations of the dogma of Chalcedon were offered by (to name only leading writers) Rahner himself, Bernhard Welte, F. Malmberg and Edward Schillebeeckx.[7] Piet Schoonenberg also belong to this group,[8] even though his interpretation led to a reversal of the Chalcedonian formula and consequently (as I shall show later) to a departure from its context.

The main concern of all those efforts was to show how the dogma 'true God and true man in one person' was to be understood in faith today, and how it could be interpreted and adapted with the aid of modern philosophical methods and categories (which at that time meant existential philosophy). The question, therefore, was how a unique man could also be God and consequently lay a claim to universal, absolute and henceforth insurpassable significance. That can be demonstrated in various ways. There are at present three major Christological approaches.

The oldest but constantly recurrent approach sees belief in Christ in a cosmological perspective. This view was already present in the *Logos*-Christology of the second-century apologists. They found *logoi spermatikoi*, fragments of the one *Logos*, at work everywhere in the world. Nature and history manifested particles of the one *Logos* who appeared in his fulness in Jesus Christ. The main exponent of that cosmological interpretation of faith in Christ in our own century was Teilhard de Chardin,[9] who offered a particularly inspired version of the approach. Of course Teilhard does not start from a static but from an evolutionary world-view, and tries to show how cosmogenesis and anthropogenesis find fulfilment in Christogenesis. In that view Jesus Christ would be evolution fully (self-) realized.

A second approach is not cosmological but anthropological. It tries to confront the challenge of modern atheistic humanism: namely, that God must be dead if man is to be truly free. The appropriate Christological viewpoint is that man is the being who is open for and to reality as a whole. He is an impoverished reference to a mystery of fulness. From this starting-point Karl Rahner[10] (principally) sees the Incarnation of God as the unique and highest instance of the essential completion of human reality. For him Christology is the absolute expression of anthropology, the study of man. Rahner maintains the once-for-all nature and underivability of the Christ-event. Other commentators, however, take this anthropological interpretation to the point of an anthropological reductionism. Then Jesus Christ becomes a mere cypher and just a model for an authentic human existence (F. Buri, S. Ogden, D. Sölle, P.M. van Buren); Christology is yet another reading of anthropology.

A third approach begins with the assumption that there is no such thing as man 'pure and simple', 'as such', but that man as he actually is confronts us only within a complex of physiological, biological, economic, social, cultural and intellectual influences; this ensures that every individual human being is involved in human solidarity: he is woven as it were into the whole complex historical fabric of humankind. The question of the meaning and salvation of man then becomes the question of the meaning and salvation of history as a whole. The result is Christology in the perspective of universal history. This approach has been taken up principally by Pannenberg[11]. He interprets Jesus Christ as the predetermined end of history. Moltmann has adopted the notion but with a new emphasis — that of justice.[12] In his view, the history of human suffering ultimately has to do with justice. In this case, Christology is discussed within the framework of theodicy. This historical approach, which I shall shortly examine in greater detail, is able to cite the scriptural stress on salvation history, and that tradition in theology which strongly emphasizes its importance. But it can and must also connect with the Hegelian philosophy of history. Consequently it has to confront the historical ideology of Marxism.

Hans Urs von Balthasar has been prominent in pointing out the immanent danger of all these approaches.[13] The problem in his view is that in them Jesus Christ is set in a predetermined scheme of reference, and that the eventual result of the consequent cosmological, anthropological or world historical diminution of faith is a mere philosophy or ideology.

The second wave in the modern rethinking of Christology[14] has been influenced by the rediscovery of the 'quest of the historical Jesus', with which Bultmann's pupils (E. Käsemann, E. Fuchs, G. Bornkamm, H. Conzelmann, J. Robinson, and so on) ushered in the post-Bultmannian era. Catholic theology very soon took up the new problematics and approach (J.R. Geiselmann, A. Vögtle, H. Schürmann, F. Mussner, J. Blank, R. Pesch, H. Küng, and so on). It recognized that a renewed Christology does not consist solely in the interpretation and re-interpretation of traditional kerygmatic or dogmatic formulas of belief. That would be no more than scholasticism in the bad sense. The language of the confession and profession of faith is, like all human discourse, meaningful language and not ideology only so long as it conceives reality in its words and proves itself against reality. The Christological formulas of belief intend nothing other than the expression of the being and significance of the person and work of Jesus Christ. Their practical criterion is to be found in Jesus. If Christological profession had no connexion with the historical Jesus, then belief in Christ would be no more than ideology: a general world-view without any historical basis. Metz took the rejection of a purely argumentative Christology to the point of a projected narrative theology and Christology.[15]

Of course that kind of novel approach is rarely free from cul-de-sacs and banal side issues. One of those dead-end approaches of the last few years is the concentration on 'Jesus' cause'.[16] The inherently attractive though essentially ambiguous and equivocal idea of 'Jesus' cause' started with W. Marxsen. But when it is extended as a fundamental programme, it very often leads in practice to a reduction to the earthly Jesus and his 'cause', and what can be made of that in terms of contemporary historical methodology. It also ends in a hermeneutics strongly influenced by a fashionable neo-Marxism. Belief in the risen and exalted Christ is allowed at best the function of confirming the existence of the historical Jesus. A flat-footed theology can justify neither the uniqueness nor the universality of Christian faith. Both the invocation of *this* Jesus of Nazareth and the affirmation of his universal and ultimate significance must in the end appear arbitrary in the perspective of a theology of that kind. In this view Jesus is reduced ultimately to a universally exchangeable symbol and model of certain ideas, or a certain form of practice, which itself can claim only a relative significance. J. Nolte has expressed those conclusions most emphatically.[17]

If we exclude both a unilateral kerygma- and dogma-Christology, and a Christology exclusively orientated to the historical Jesus, the right way of re-establishing Christology can only be to take both elements of Christian faith with equal seriousness, and to ask how, why and with what justice the proclaimed and believed-in Christ developed from the Jesus who proclaimed; and how that historically unique Jesus of Nazareth relates to the universal claim of belief in Christ. In the present century the Tübingen dogmatic theologian J.R. Geiselmann has already tried to reestablish Christology along those, lines in his book *Jesus the Christ*.[18] Even though the detailed exegeses of his approach have been outdated since then, his fundamental perspective is still valid. Today, though on other premises, W. Pannenberg, J. Moltmann, and E. Jüngel try to construct Christology from the correlation of the historical Jesus and the proclaimed Christ.

3. THE TASKS OF CHRISTOLOGY TODAY

The approach consistent with the profession that 'Jesus is the Christ' and our summary account of the contemporary Christological debate, reveal three major fundamental tasks for Christology at the present time.

1. *An historically determined Christology.* The approach accordant with the belief that 'Jesus is the Christ' is a Christology orientated to a quite specific history and a unique life and destiny. It is derivable neither from human nor social needs; neither anthropologically nor sociologically. Instead it has to preserve a real and actual unique memory, and to represent it here and now. It has to narrate a real and actual story — history — and to bear testimony to it. It has to ask, in other words: Who was this Jesus of Nazareth? What did he want? What was his mission and message, his behaviour, his destiny? What was (despite the dangers of the term) his 'cause'? How did this Jesus, who proclaimed not himself but the imminent Rule of God, become the proclaimed and believed-in Christ?

This kind of historically-orientated Christology has a respectable tradition behind it. Until the era of baroque scholasticism, the theology of the mysteries of Jesus' life played a major rôle in Christology.[19] But if we wish to approach and answer these questions in accordance with a modern problematics today, we must face problems that are complex and thorny, and at first even scandalous for many Christians. They are the problems of modern historical research: the quest for the historical Jesus, the quest for the origins of the Easter faith, and the quest for the earliest Christological formulation of belief. These questions raised by H.S. Reimarus, D.F. Strauss, W. Wrede, A. Schweitzer, and R. Bultmann are neither mere sophistries of unbelief, nor wholly external and irrelevant to belief in Jesus Christ and systematic Christology. The historical questions have to be answered if the scandalous reality of faith in Christ is to be taken seriously. As soon as one tries to do that, there is no such thing as a trouble-free area — some kind of belief pure and simple, or a 'simple' Christian faith. It is not enough to examine these questions purely from an historical angle. We have to inquire into the theological relevance of the historical aspect.

2. *A universally responsible Christology.* Even though Christology cannot be derived *from* human or social needs, its universal claim demands that it is considered and represented *in the light of* human questions and needs, and in accordance (analogy) with the problems of the age. Remembrance of Jesus and the Christological tradition must be understood as a living tradition, and must be preserved in creative loyalty. That is the only way in which a living faith can arise. The Christian should be able to give account of his hope (cf 1 Pet 3. 15). For that reason we cannot pit a narrative Christology against an argumentative Christology, even though Metz has recently tried to do just that.

The universal claim of Christological belief can be represented appropriately only against the most extensive horizon conceivable. That brings

20

Christology into encounter and confrontation with philosophy and, more exactly, with metaphysics. Christology inquires not just into this or that existent, but into existence in general. A Christian is so to speak compelled to become a metaphysician on account of his faith. He cannot escape that compulsion by recourse to the social sciences, sociology itself for instance, even though the importance of such assistance is not to be underestimated. That does not mean that he must follow some particular version of metaphysics, for instance the Aristotelian-Thomistic variety. A pluralistic approach to philosophies and theologies is not only legitimate but necessary. But, fundamentally, Christology cannot be inserted into any predetermined philosophical system. And there is no question of applying predetermined philosophical categories within Christology. On the contrary, faith in Jesus Christ is a radical questioning of all closed systems of thought. It is specifically ideology-critical. It claims that the ultimate and most profound means of reality as a whole has been revealed only in Jesus Christ, in a unique and at the same time finally valid way. Here then the meaning of being, of existence, is decided in a quite real, and once-for-all, actual and concrete human history.

That implies a quite specific understanding of reality; one which is obviously not subject to a naturally-defined philosophy of existence, but under the primacy of an historically and personally defined ontology. Here Christology has to criticize its own tradition. The appropriate debate about the hellenization and de-hellenization of belief must not of course (as often happens) start from a fundamentally anti-metaphysical attitude. There is no question of playing off an ontologically determined Christology of tradition against a non-ontological, usually 'functional' Christology. It is a matter of developing a Christologically determined historical and personal ontology.

The task with which we are faced goes deeper than that, however. The question is how we are to see the relation between Christology and philosophy. In this respect we find old denominational controversies on the relationship between nature and grace, or law and Gospel, recurring in new guises. Two initial standpoints are possible in this matter. One either sees, as Rahner requires, Christology as lying within the God-world relation,[20] or like Karl Barth, one explains the God-world relation within Christology. In the first case there is at least the danger of theology becoming philosophy, an objection that B. van der Heijden has raised against Rahner.[21] In the second case, we are faced with a Christological overlap, as Balthasar objects against Barth.[22] Wiederkehr therefore refers in his *Project for a Systematic Christology* to an ellipse with two focal points.[23] What he says is more true of the traditional Catholic teaching of analogy. This complex of questions shows once again that in Christology we are ultimately concerned with the Christian understanding of reality in the broadest sense of the word. Christology has to do at least in rudimentary terms with the relation between Christianity and culture, politics and so forth.

21

3. *A soteriologically determined Christianity.* I would combine this third viewpoint with the two others in a higher unity. The foregoing shows that the person and history of Jesus are inseparable from their universal significance; and, equally, that the significance of Jesus is inseparable from his person and history. Christology and soteriology (that is, the doctrine of the redemptive meaning of Jesus Christ) form a whole. That whole can be unilaterally divided from two aspects.[24] Medieval scholasticism separated the doctrine of the person of Jesus Christ, his divinity and his humanity and the unity of both, from the doctrine of the work and offices of Christ. Christology became an isolated and abstract teaching on the divine-human constitution of Christ. The question was incessantly posed of the being-in-itself, the virtual being, of the true divinity and humanity of Jesus; it became increasingly less evident to men what all this meant for them and their life. The indifference of many people to Christianity is a reaction to this development, which is not part of the tradition of the early Church. It can be shown that there are soteriological motives behind all the Christological pronouncements of the early Church. Both the defence of the true divinity and that of the true humanity are intended to ensure the reality of Redemption. This more historical argument should be accompanied by a further, fundamental viewpoint. We know the nature of a thing only by way of its appearance: from, that is, its being for an other, and therefore from its meaning for, and effect on, an other. The actual meaning of a profession of faith in Jesus Christ and of Christological teaching is only apparent if we inquire into the liberating and redemptive meaning of Jesus. For that reason the scholastic separation between Christology and soteriology has to be cancelled.

The opposite extreme is the reduction of Christology to soteriology. In relation against the scholastic teaching of the being of Christ 'in himself', Luther stressed the *pro me* of the saving action of Christ. In so doing, Luther never departed from the 'objective' meaning of Christological belief. Yet even Melanchthon gave the *pro me* principle a one-sided emphasis. In his introduction to the *Loci Communes* of 1521, there is the famous sentence 'Hoc est Christum cognoscere beneficia eius cognoscere, non, quod isti docent, eius naturas, modos incarnationis contueri'.[25] This principle became the basis of Schleiermacher's Christology, and via Schleiermacher, of 'neo-Protestantism'. Schleiermacher argues from the present experience of Redemption back to the Redeemer.[26] That incurs the danger that all Christological propositions will become an expression of Christian self-consciousness, and that Jesus Christ will be reduced to the primary model of the religious man.

Schleiermacher's influence today can be discerned in Tillich and, apart from him, in Bultmann and his school. In his criticism of the Christological creed of the World Council, Bultmann answered the question whether faith in Jesus Christ as God and Saviour accords with the New Testament thus: 'I do not know'. He means by this that faith is not unambiguous. The question is: 'Does the designation of Christ as "God" describe his nature, his metaphysical essence, or his meaningfulness? Is the statement soteriological or cosmological in nature, or both?' For him, the decisive question is 'whether and how far the titles intend to say something about the nature of Jesus; how far they describe him objectively in his so to speak being-in-himself; or whether and how far they talk about him in his significance for man, for belief? Do they have something to say about his *physis* . . . or are they talking about Christ *pro me?* How far is a Christological statement about me? Does it help me that he is the Son of God, or is he the Son of God because he helps me?'[27] Bultmann himself allows no room for doubt that the New Testament statements on the divinity of Jesus are not in his opinion intended to be statements about the nature but only the significance of Jesus. Consequently Christology is ultimately no more than a variant of anthropology (H. Braun).

The main opponent of the use of Luther's *pro me* as a methodological principle has been H.J. Iwand.[28] He confirms that here we have a confusion of Luther's idea of Jesus' sacrifice for us with Kant's subjectivity of experiental knowledge. Kant was the first to elicit a dualism between the thing-in-itself *(Ding-an-sich)* and the appearance of things for us. The basic contradictoriness of his position has often been noted. For although Kant at first explains the in-itself, the inherently essential entity of things, as unknowable, he nevertheless ascribes to it the ability to affect our consciousness. Essentially, therefore, he grounds knowledge in being. If we reject that grounding of meaning in being, then theology necessarily approaches Feuerbach's theses, according to which all our religious ideas are only projections of human needs and wishes for redemption and divinization. The Incarnation is then only the appearance of man divinized. For Feuerbach it is a question of the reversal of theology. God-become-man is the appearance of man become God, for the descent of God to man necessarily precedes the elevation of man to God.[29]

This complex of problems takes us once again to the situational description. With the abovementioned dichotomy between being and meaning, Christology for its part shares in the spiritual and cultural destiny of modern times. Analogously to the general alienation of subject and object, Christological faith and dogma appear unassimilable; they are external and alien. Faith reverts to the realm of pure subjectivity and inwardness. Hence it is a question of an opposition between the content of faith (*fides quae creditur*) and the expression of faith (*fides qua creditur*). On the one hand the Christological formulations appear in their hard objectivity as a reification of 'individual' personal faith, or as dead ballast for Christian practice. On the other hand, the attempts at a subjective appropriation of belief seem to dissolve faith into an insecure subjectivity. Orthodoxy and orthopractice are opposed. Yet orthodox supranaturalism and modernistic immanentism are only the two separated halves of one whole.

Being and meaning are indissolubly joined in the confession that 'Jesus is the Christ'. What is believed can be known only in the exercise of belief. The exercise of belief, however, is meaningless if it is not directed to a something which is to be believed. The choice between an ontological and a functional Christology is therefore, theologically speaking, illusory and a position into which theology must not allow itself to be manoeuvred. That means that today the Church cannot secure its identity by sheer presumption of orthodoxy, or by a reversion to the exercise of faith and orthopractice. Present-day problems must be tackled from the foundations. We must ask how both are revealed in Jesus Christ. Only when that is clear, is it possible to explain how in the Church today concern for Christian identity can accord with concern for relevance and involvement. The question we have to ask is therefore: Where and how do we meet Jesus Christ today?

Notes

[1] Cf. J. Moltmann, *Der gekreuzigte Gott, Das Kreuz Christi als Grund und Kritik christlicher Theologie* (Munich, 1972), pp. 12-33. ET: *The Crucified God* (London, 1974).

[2] Cf. O. Cullmann, *Die Christologie des Neuen Testaments* (4th ed. Tubingen, 1966, pp. 134-61, ET: *The Christology of the New Testament* (London, 1971); F. Hahn, *Christologische Hoheitstitel. Ihre Geschichte im frühen Christentum* (3rd ed., Gottingen, 1966), pp. 218-25, ET: *The Titles of Jesus in Christology: Their History in Early Christianity* (New York, 1969); W. Grunmann, *et al.*, art. *chrio*, in: TW IX, pp. 482-576, esp. 518 ff.

[3] G.W.F. Hegel, 'Glauben und Wissen', in: W I (ed. Glockner) (3rd ed., Stuttgart, 1958), pp. 281 ff.

[4] Cf. the following reports on the relevant literature: A. Grillmeier, 'Zum Christusbild der heutigen katholischen Theologie,' in: J. Feiner, J. Trutsch, F. Böckle (eds.), *Fragen der Theologie heute* (Einsiedeln, 1957), pp. 265-99; R. Lachenschmid, 'Christologie und Soteriologie,' in: H. Vogrimler, R. Van der Gucht (eds.), *Bilanz der Theologie im 20. Jahrhundert*, vol. 3 (Freiburg, 1970), pp. 82-120; J. Pfammatter, F. Furger (eds.), *Theologische Berichte II. Zur neueren christologischen Diskussion* (Zürich, 1973); K. Reinhardt, 'Die Einzigartigkeit der Person Jesu Christi: Neue Entwurfe,' in: *Internationale katholische Zeitschrift* 2 (1973, pp. 206-224; W. Kasper, 'Jesus im Streit der Meinungen,' in: *Theologie der Gegenwart* 16 (1973), pp. 233-41; A. Schilson, W. Kasper, *Christologie im prasens. Kritische Sichtung neuer Entwerfe* (Freiburg, 1974).

[5] Cf. K. Rahner, 'Chalkedon − Ende oder Anfang?' in: *Das Konzil von Chalkedon*, eds. A. Grillmeier and H. Bacht, vol. 3 (Würzburg, 1954), pp. 3-49 (see also Schriften I; ET: *Theological Investigations*, vol 1 (London, 1966).

[6] *Op. cit.* pp. 3 ff.

[7] Cf. B. Welte, '*Homoousios hemin.* Gedanken zum Verstandnis der theologischen Problematik der Kategorien von Chalkedon', in: *Das Konzil von Chalkedon*, pp. 3, 51-80 F. Malmberg, *Uber den Gottmenschen* (QD, vol 9) (Freiburg 1960); E. Schillebeeckx, 'Die Heiligung des Namens Gottes durch die Menschenliebe Jesu des Christus,' in: *Gott in Welt* Festschrift for K. Rahner, eds., J.B. Metz, *et al* vol 2 (Freiburg, 1964), 43-91; *idem*, 'De persoonlijke openbaringsgestalte van de Vader', in: *Tijdschrifte voor Theologie* 6 (1966), pp.274-288; *idem* 'De Toegang tot Jezus van Nazaret,' in: *Tijdschrift voor Theologie* 13 (1973), pp. 145-166.

[8] Cf. p. Schoonenberg, *Hij is een God van mensen* (Den Bosch, 1969). ET: *A God for Man* (London, 1970).

[9] For the Christology of Teilhard de Chardin see mainly the following: *Let Me Explain* (London, 1970); *Le Milieu Divin* (London, 1960); *Science and Christ* (London, 1968).

[10] For literature, see *infra* ch. III.

[11] Cf. W. Pannenberg, *Grundzüge der Christologie*, (3rd ed., Gütersloh, 1969).

[12] Cf. J. Moltmann, *Der gekreuzigte Gott, op. cit.*; ET: *The Crucified God.*

[13] H. Urs von Balthasar, *Glaubhaft ist nur Liebe* (Einsiedeln, 1963).

[14] On the present state of Jesus research, see F. J. Schierse (ed.), *Jesus von Nazareth* (Mainz 1972); P. Feidler, L. Oberlinner, *Jesus von Nazareth. Ein Literaturbericht,* in: BuL 12 (1972), p. 52-74; G. Schneider, Jesus-Bücher und Jesus-Forschung 1966-1971,' in: ThPQ 120 (1972), pp. 155-160; H. Schürmann, 'Zur aktuellen Situation der Leben-Jesu-Forschung,' in: GuL 46 (1973), pp. 300-110; J. Roloff, 'Auf der Suche nach einem neuen Jesusbild,' in: ThLZ 98 (1973), pp. 561-172; K. Kertelge, (ed.), *Rückfrage nach Jesus* (QD, 63) (Freiburg, 1974).

[15] Cf. J. B. Metz, 'Kleine Apologie des Erzählens,' in: *Concilium* 9 (1973); ET: 'A Short Apology of Narrative' in *Concilium* 9 (1973); *idem,* 'Erlösung und Emanzipation,' in: L. Scheffczyk (ed.), *Erlösung und Emanzipation* (QD, vol 61), (Freiburg, 1973), pp.120-140; *idem* 'Erinnerung', in: *Handbuch philosophischer Grundbegriffe* I (Munich, 1973), pp. 368-96.

[16] See, J. Nolte, 'Dei Sache Jesu und die Zukunft der Kirche. Gedanken zur Stellung von Christologie und Ekklesiologie,' in: F.J. Schierse (ed.), *Jesus von Nazareth,* pp. 214-133; for a critical account, see 'Die Sache Jesu und Grenzen eines Interpretationsversuches,' in: *Her Korr* 26 (1972), pp. 185-9.

[17] Cf. J. Nolte, ' "Sinn" oder "Bedeutung" Jesu?,' in: *Wort und Wahrheit* 28 (1973), pp. 322-8.

[18] J.R. Geiselmann, *Jesus der Christus* (Stuttgart, 1951); *idem., Jesus der Christus,* I. *Die Frage nach dem historischen Jesus* (Munich, 1965).

[19] Cf. MS III/2, pp. 1-326.

[20] Cf. K. Rahner, Probleme der Christologie heute,' in: *Schriften* I; *Theological Investigations* vol. 1.

[21] Cf. B. van der Heijden, *Karl Rahner, Darstellung und Kritik seiner Grundpositionen* (Einsiedeln, 1973).

[22] H. Urs von Balthasar, *Karl Barth. Darstellung und Deutung seiner Theologie* (2nd ed., Cologne, 1962).

[23] D. Wiederkehr, 'Entwurf einer systematischen Christologie,' in: MS III/1; pp. 500 ff.

[24] See W. Pannenberg, *Grundzüge*, pp. 32 ff.

[25] Ph. Melanchthon, *Loci communes* (1521) in: II/1 (ed. R. Strupperich) (Gütersloh, 1952), p. 7.

[26] Cf. F. Schleiermacher, *Der christliche Glaube* (ed. M. Redeker), vol. 2 (Berlin, 1960).

[27] R. Bultmann, 'Das christologische Bekenntnis des Ökumenischen Rates,' in: GuV II (5th ed., Tübingen, 1968) pp. 246-81.

[28] Cf. H. J. Iwand, 'Wider den Missbrauch des *pro me* als methodisches Prinzip in der Theologie.' in: ThLZ 79 (1954), pp. 453-8.

[29] Cf. L. Feuerbach, *Das Wesen des Christentums (The Essence of Christianity),* ed. W. Schuffenhauer, vol. 1, (Berlin, 1956), p. 104.

II. THE HISTORICAL QUEST FOR JESUS CHRIST

II. THE HISTORICAL QUEST FOR JESUS CHRIST

1. THE STARTING-POINT IN CONTEMPORARY BELIEF IN JESUS CHRIST

Jesus Christ is an historical figure of world-historical importance. Jesus of Nazareth lived in Palestine sometime between 7 BC and 30 AD.[1] His appearance gave rise to a series of events which fundamentally altered the world not only religiously but spiritually, intellectually, and socially. This effective history of Jesus Christ extends beyond Christ and the Christian community, the churches and their communities, to our historical present. But there is also an effective history of Jesus outside 'official' Christianity and in our entire western civilization. Therefore Jesus of Nazareth and his work have been directly present up to now in a universal historical sense. The historical quest for Jesus of Nazareth, that is, the quest undertaken with present-day historical methods, for any details we can discover of his life, appearance, message and death, is only of direct interest because of its repercussions on contemporary Christianity, the churches today, and the entire civilization and culture directly or indirectly codetermined by Christianity. If that were not the case, most people would be interested in Jesus as much and as little as they are interested in Socrates, Buddha and Lao Tse. In a universal-historical perspective, the starting-point of our quest for and our interest in Jesus of Nazareth is present-day Christianity.

That is even more the case if we pose the question of access to Jesus Christ from a specifically theological perspective. The sources which report on Jesus of Nazareth are the Scriptures of the New Testament. What we can learn about Jesus from the scanty exta-Christian sources is hardly worth discussion. The New Testament writings are only there because Jesus received a faith extending beyond his death, and because the first believers collected together, handed on and finally set down in writing, the reports on Jesus, for the needs of their communities: for their liturgy, their religious instruction, and for missionary preaching, and to introduce order into their churches, and to exhort and edify them. If it were not for that interest of the first Christian communities, we should know as much and as little about Jesus of Nazareth as about other itinerant preachers of his time. Therefore we can join modern form-criticism[2] in saying: the 'Sitz im Leben', or existential location, of the writings of the Jesus tradition in the New Testament is the Church. The gospels, even though they contain much detailed and authentic historical material, are not historical witnesses in the modern sense. They are rather testimonies of faith. It is the Christological credo of the early Church that we find in the writings of the New Testament. Therefore Jesus of Nazareth is accessible for us only by way of the faith of the first Christian churches.

If we wish to understand the testimonies of the New Testament today, that is possible only by reading ourselves into the same life context from which they arose. No linguistic statement can be understood outside the complex of the situation in which it was uttered. We should not remove the Jesus tradition from the context of proclamation, liturgy and parish practice of the Christian churches. Only where the message of Jesus Christ is alive and believed, where that same Spirit is alive who enlivens the writings of the New Testament, can the testimony of the New Testament be understood as a living witness. Even today, therefore, the community of the Church is the proper location of the Jesus tradition and encounter with Christ.

But the thesis of the Church as the existential location of belief in Jesus Christ introduces a highly emotional complex of problems. Many see what they think of as institutionally ossified churches as having practically nothing to do with Jesus Christ and what he intended. They say: 'Jesus, yes — the Church, no!' What interests them is not the Christ whom the churches proclaim. They are interested in Jesus himself and his 'cause'. What attracts them is not the ecclesiastical belief in Christ and Son of God but the faith of Jesus himself and his unqualified surrender of self for the sake of men. Such mistrust of the churches and institutions as a whole is reasonable. Even the churches run the risk of succumbing to what threatens all institutions: the danger of institutional rigidity, of institutional self-interest, of power, manipulation and abuses for the sake of the authority and self-interest of the institutions themselves. Those dangers have seized the churches often enough in their history. For that reason a lot of people think that it is no longer possible to discern any trace of the original Spirit of Jesus in the churches.

To meet that objection, we have to demonstrate both the justice and the limit of our starting-point in the faith of the Church. The modern theory of institutionalization[3] helps us to go a little further in establishing the correctness of our starting-point. The modern theory indicates that the subjectivity of the individual is always restricted; that it cannot master the existing multitude of phenomena and viewpoints. There are cognitive advantages in a 'system' in which experiences of other and earlier generations are 'stored' and objectified in the form of morals, customs, traditions, and so forth. The relative stability which such institutional phenomena enjoy has the advantage that they remove the fundamental values of a community from subjective whim and even the arbitrariness of the 'dominant' powers. In this sense we can join J.A. Möhler and the whole Catholic Tübingen school of the nineteenth century in describing the Church as the objectification of Christianity. In the Church, Christian faith has so to speak taken on flesh and blood. This embodiment in a social setting, its traditions and institutions, is already, viewed in purely human terms, the strongest protection for, and the best guarantee of, continuity. As history shows, Christian belief can most readily regenerate itself from the basis of such an heritage.

To be sure, if that institutional viewpoint is stated onesidedly, there is the danger of the truth being functionalized and relativized in the interest of the survival of the individual and of the social 'system'. In practical terms: there is then the danger that Jesus Christ will be subsumed in the Church, and that the Church will take the place of Jesus. The Church does not proclaim and testify to Jesus Christ, if that is the case, but becomes its own witness and testimony. Then Christology is an ideological insurance for ecclesiology. But that deprives both Christology and ecclesiology of their essential meaning. As the community of the faithful, the Church must never be understood as a self-reliant entity. The Church must always be on its way towards Jesus Christ. For that reason, it has continually to reconsider its origins. It has to think back to Jesus Christ, to his word and deeds, to his life and destiny. Most of the renewal movements within the Church have begun from that kind of consideration. We have only to think of the meaning of the earthly Jesus for Francis of Assisi, and the meaning of the meditations on the earthly life of Jesus in the Exercises of Ignatius of Loyola. Church renewal today has to go in the same direction of reconsideration of its origins in Jesus.

The foregoing can be summarized in a double thesis: The starting-point of Christology is the phenomenology of faith in Christ; faith as it is actually believed, lived, proclaimed and practised in the Christian churches.[4] Faith in Jesus Christ can arise only from encounter with believing Christians. The proper content and the ultimate criterion of Christology is however, Jesus Christ himself: his life, destiny, words and work. In this sense we can say too that Jesus Christ is the primary, and faith of the Church the secondary, criterion of Christology. Neither of the two criteria can be pitted against the other. The question is of course how the two criteria are to be joined together. That is one of the fundamental questions of modern theology. It is posed with special emphasis in modern research into the life of Jesus.

2. THE JUSTICE AND LIMITS OF MODERN RESEARCH INTO THE LIFE OF JESUS

An especially historically-significant stimulus to reconsideration of the origins was the sixteenth-century Reformation. The Reformers wanted to renew the Church on the basis of primitive testimony: the witness of the New Testament. In Scripture, however, the Reformers were concerned only with what 'moved Christ'. Their basic principle of *sola Scriptura* was essentially a *solus Christus*. Therefore the Reformers, despite all their undoubted achievements in exegesis, were not yet concerned with historico-critical biblical research in the modern sense. Their concern was the *viva vox Evangelii*, the living voice of the Gospel: the preached word of God. Biblical theology in its own right, in distinction and partly in opposition even to dogmatic theology, only came about when Christian tradition was no longer a direct self-evident, directly convincing authority. Historico-critical thought presupposes a distance from tradition, and the experience of a gulf between them.[5] Only if history is no longer directly present, is it possible to consider it objectively and critically. This break with tradition was prepared by

Pietism, which in contradistinction to church life of the time and the existing scholastic theology, tried to reach a practical, personal, simple, and biblical theology. After that preliminary stage, the German Enlightenment developed an autonomous biblical theology in which exegesis was established as a critical yardstick over against ecclesiology.[6]

The most important area in modern biblical theology is research into the life of Jesus. A. Schweitzer, its greatest historiographer, calls it the 'greatest achievement of German theology'.[7] 'It represents the most powerful achievement that religious self-examination has ever ventured and accomplished.[8] It did not however begin from 'pure historical interest, but sought out the Jesus of history as an ally in the struggle for freedom from dogma'.[9] With their demonstration that the Jesus of history was not the Christ of church faith, that he claimed no divine authority, the critics intended to remove the basis of the Church's claim to authority. R. Augstein recently put that intention as follows: 'They wished to show exactly how justified the churches were in invoking a Jesus who never existed, a teaching which he never taught, an authority he never extended, and a divine Sonhood which he himself never held to be possible and which he never claimed.[10] Behind the historical quest of Jesus there was on the one hand the interest of faith and the renewal of faith, but on the other the Spirit of the Enlightenment. Both were so to speak godparents at the baptism of the new biblical theology, and therefore of research into the life of Jesus. This has also to be seen in the larger context of the modern criticism of ideology and the emancipation from predetermined authorities and traditions. This tension makes the quest attractive and fruitful, even though up to now it has provoked numerous misunderstandings and disputes.

That can easily be demonstrated from the history of research into the life of Jesus. It began in 1774-8 when G.E. Lessing published the 'Wolfenbüttel Fragments' of the Hamburg Professor of Oriental Languages, Hermann Samuel Reimarus. Reimarus had drawn an essential distinction between the teaching of Jesus, the first *systema,* and the teaching of the apostles, the second *systema.*[11] According to Reimarus, Jesus himself taught 'no lofty mysteries or points of belief'[12] but 'only moral teachings and everyday duties'.[13] His proclamation of the Kingdom of God cannot be distinguished from the ideas of contemporary Judaism. He preached the coming of an messianic kingdom in an earthly and a secular and political sense. In the 'overture' (Schweitzer) of Reimarus we hear all the themes of the future Jesus-research programme: the distinction between the Jesus of history and the Christ of faith, the eschatological character of Jesus' message, and the associated problem of the delayed *parousia,* the theme of the political Jesus and the problem of the later spiritualization of his message. Lessing summarized the result exactly when he called the religion of Christ and the Christ of religion 'two quite different things'.[14]

With his radical theses, Reimarus discredited the most progressive theology of his time. The other master of historical theology, Salomo Semler, tried to save what was left. He explained the difference between the earthly and the spiritual understanding of Jesus as accommodation to the level of comprehension of his contemporaries. That announced a further persistent theme. Whether one, like J.G. Herder, understands the idea concealed in the outwardly historical aspect more in an aesthetico-symbolic manner, or, like the rationalist H.E.G. Paulus, views it more rationalistically and pragmatically, matters little in principle. It was some time before the next great surge of interest. That was the two-volume *Life of Jesus* published by D.F. Strauss in 1835-6. It provoked the second great storm and a virtual flood of replies.[15] The old supranatural explanation of Jesus was according to Strauss untenable, yet the modern rationalistic interpretation was too external. Strauss tried to find a third way: mythic interpretation. Here he entered a tradition of academic debate since Heyne and Eichhorn.[16] However Strauss' mythic interpretation does not deny the historical core. He even maintained it as an 'irrefutable fact' that Jesus had announced his conviction that he was the Messiah.[17] Yet Strauss distinguishes between the historical core and the associated mythic interpretation, between the Christ of faith and the Jesus of history. For Strauss that distinction was identical with the distinction between the 'historical Christ and the ideal image, that is, the primal image of human reason, the picture of how Christ ought to be'. But that means the 'extension of the religion of Christ as a religion of humanity'.[18] Strauss had to answer No to the question 'Are we still Christians?'

With this dilemma between the historical Jesus and his ideal interpretation, theology is no more than participating in the general spiritual complex of spiritual problems characteristic of the modern era.[20] The emancipation of the human subject in respect to reality had the necessary result of reducing that reality to the status of mere object, to a technically controlled and scientifically deciphered world of things and labour. Hence the dualism of the human and natural sciences, *res cogitans* and *res extensa* (Descartes), the logic of reason and the logic of the heart (Pascal), of existential-personal and objective relations, is constitutive of the evolution of modern times. This methodological dualism was translated into terms proper to theology, and there — with the distinction between the historical Jesus and the Christ of faith — led to a dual form of access to Jesus: an historico-critical, rational mode, and an inward, higher, mental-spiritual, existential-personal, faithful mode. That dualism is our spiritual and intellectual inheritance. Strauss posed questions that are not yet answered.

After the unity of the Jesus of history and the Christ of faith was broken, it was vitally incumbent on theology to restore it. The attempt was made by the life-of-Jesus research of the nineteenth century. The main names in this regard are F. Schleiermacher, K.H. Weizsäcker, H.J. Holtzmann, T. Keim, K. Hase, W. Beyschlag, and B. Weiss. These theologians were drawn by apologetical interest. Since they wanted to practise their theology in a specifically modern way, they had to use historical methods to ground faith in Christ. But it was principally Schleiermacher who from 1819 to 1832 was the first to give regular lectures on the life of Jesus, who put theological and not biographical interest to the forefront. He was interested not in the destruction and substitution of Christological dogma, but in its historical interpretation.[21] A new way of access to belief was to be disclosed to modern man by virtue of 'mature' historical research. That necessitated the characteristic modern emphasis on the individual as subject. An ontology of Christ gave way to a psychology of Christ.[22] The mental life of Jesus was so to speak the mirror in which his divinity was reflected. It was Schleiermacher's concern so to present the human aspect in Jesus 'that we perceive it as the expression or effect of the divine which was within him'.[23] It is a question of 'the self-manifestation of God in him for others'.[24] The distinctive thing about Christ is 'the constant strength of his God-consciousness, which was a very indwelling of God in him'[25] and into which he takes us too in faith. Clearly it was no longer possible in this perspective of a 'Christology from below' to understand the message and work of Jesus politically, but only spiritually, inwardly and morally. Hence Harnack can say: 'Everything dramatic in the external world-historical sense has now vanished. The entire external hope in the future has also disappeared'. It is a question only of 'God and the soul, of the soul and its God'.[26]

The cause of liberal life-of-Jesus research is now for the most part lost. Three things contributed to its collapse.

Firstly, A. Schweitzer in his *History of Research into the Life of Jesus* pointed out that what was represented as the historical Jesus was no more than the reflection of the individual authors' ideas. 'And so each subsequent epoch in theology found its own ideas in Jesus, and could find no other way of bringing him to life. Not only epochs found themselves in him. Each individual recreated him in the image of his own personality'.[27] Rationalists describe Jesus as a moral preacher; idealists as the inclusive concept of humanity; aesthetes praise him as a genius of oratory; socialists as the friend of the poor and a social reformer; and numberless pseudo-scientists turn him into a sheer figure of romance.[28] But ultimately people had to acknowledge: 'The Jesus of Nazareth who appeared as Messiah, proclaimed the morality of the Kingdom of God, established the Kingdom on earth and died in order to consecrate his work, never existed. He is a phantom of rationalism, enlivened by liberalism and clothed in historical dress by modern theology'.[29] Jesus as he really was is not a modern man but something 'alien and mysterious'.[30] He resists all attempts at modernization. He did not want to improve the world, but proclaimed instead the coming of a new world. At the centre of his message is the Kingdom of God which does not come through human efforts. It is not the highest moral good but the action of God. Schweitzer says: 'Research into the life of Jesus has developed oddly. It set out to find the historical Jesus and thought it could place him just as he is, as Teacher and Saviour, in our time. It undid the bonds with which he had been tied for centuries to the rock of ecclesiastical dogma, and rejoiced when life and movement re-entered the figure, and the historical man Jesus was seen to come into his own. He did not stay there, however, but bypassed our age and returned to his own'.[31]

We owe a second insight to modern form-criticism. It has shown that the gospels are not historical sources in the modern sense but are instead testimonies to the faith of the early churches. They are not primarily interested in the Jesus of history, but are concerned with the Christ who is present in proclamation, liturgy and the whole life of the churches. The only trace which Jesus has left behind is the faith of his disciples. He takes effect in history only by virtue of that faith. If it is true that he is an historical personality who is subsequently effective in history then we must join M. Kähler, the first great critic of research into the life of Jesus, in saying: 'The real Christ is the Christ who is preached'.[32] To make the Christianity of Christ (which is an historical discovery, and which had no significance for primitive Christianity) the criterion, is for F. Overbeck (who was certainly no church apologist) to put oneself outside the Christian religion'.[33]

Here we come to a third, more hermeneutical viewpoint. Ultimately, historical criticism is like an endless screw, and faith cannot take a foothold if it must continually change and move ground.[34] It would then be like an army which marches without security and therefore can be surprised by the smallest enemy force and constantly plunged into danger.[35] Karl Adam is wholly justified when he says: 'A Christianity that had to live in continual fear of a sentence of death that criticism might pronounce any day would be useless'.[36] An historically competent theologian who can survey the whole field and see the values of the various methods and the presuppositions, may decide that, all in all, the picture is not so bad. But what are the 'simple faithful' to do other than to believe this or that professor more than another? A theologians' Church would be something quite different from a Church of mature Christians — it would have to establish quite different claims to authority.

In this century, between the two world wars, and directly after World War II, these and other considerations led to a renewal of ecclesial-dogmatic Christology. On the Catholic side, the main figure in this respect is Karl Adam; on the Protestant side, Karl Barth. Bultmann rejected a dogma-Christology, but evolved an analogous kerygma-Christology which started from the presence of Christ in proclamation. To some extent the corresponding venture among Catholics was the mysteries-theology of O. Casel, which centred on the presence of Christ in the mysteries and his redemptive work in the celebration of the liturgy. This renewed Catholic Christology was accompanied on the Catholic side by a renewal of ecclesiology. In the neo-romanticism of the nineteen-twenties and thirties there was a reversion to the Tübingen school of the nineteenth century, and especially to the notions of J.A. Möhler: the idea of the Church as the body of Christ was rediscovered. According to Möhler, Christ is still effective and lives on in the Church, and in this perspective, the visible Church is 'the Son of God continually apparent among men in human form, always renewing himself, always rejuvenating himself, the permanent Incarnation of God, just as the faithful in Holy Scripture are called the Body of Christ.'[37] On the Protestant side, D. Bonhoeffer spoke of 'Christ existing as the church community'.[38] Others spoke of an awakening of the Church in the souls of men (Romano Guardini), and yet others prophesied a century of the Churches (W. Stählin).

The second Vatican Council took up these ideas and initially justified the expectations in question. But subsequently things turned out rather differently. It was obvious that the questions raised by the Enlightenment and modern criticism had not been resolved and had not vanished. They recurred principally in the writings of Bultmann and his school. The study and treatment of the modern complex of problems is therefore one of the most important tasks of contemporary theologians. The question of the theological relevance of the historical aspect, and hence of research into the life of Jesus, has still to be resolved.

3. THE THEOLOGICAL RELEVANCE OF THE HISTORICAL ASPECT

The penultimate, contemporary stage of Christological thought began when in 1953 Ernst Käsemann gave a lecture in Marburg on 'The problem of the historical Jesus', in which he asked for the old liberal quest for the historical Jesus to be resumed on the changed theological premises of the present age.[39] This proved to be the stimulus of a veritable flood of commentaries. E. Fuchs, G. Bornkamm, H. Conzelmann. H. Braun, J. Robinson, G. Ebeling, F. Gogarten, W. Marxsen and others immediately took up the quest. On the Catholic side the problem was tackled by J.R. Geiselmann, A. Vögtle, H. Schürmann, F. Mussner, R. Schnackenburg, H. Küng, J. Blank, R. Pesch, and others. The theological relevance of the historical aspect has become an acute and decisive though essentially unresolved problem.

Not only fundamental theological but historico-exegetical reasons were behind the new emphasis. In historico-exegetical terms, the situation was not so hopeless; instead 'the Synoptics contain much more authentic traditional material than the other side will allow'. The Gospels give us no reason for resignation and scepticism. Rather they. allow us to see the historical figure of Jesus in all his power, though in quite a different way from chronicles and historical narratives'.[40] It is characteristic of the gospels to mix message and report. Obviously they have to face the problem of the mythization of history, but also that of the historicization of a myth.

That brings us to the theological emphases proper.

Firstly, it is a question of the rejection of myth. The eschatological process is 'not a new idea and not a culminating-point in a process of development',[41] but happens once and for all. This historical contingency reflects the freedom of divine action. It also grounds the new *kairos*, the great turning-point, the new historical possibility of our decision. On the other hand: it is a question of the rejection of Docetism and of the conviction that the Revelation occurs 'in the flesh'. Therefore everything focusses on the identity of the exalted

Lord with the earthly Jesus. It is a question of the reality of the Incarnation and of the salvific meaning of the true humanity of Jesus. Ultimately, it is a question of the rejection of enthusiasm and of a purely contemporary understanding of salvation. The reference is to 'the *extra nos* of salvation as the presumption of faith'. A faith which refers only to the kerygma becomes in the end faith in the Church as bearer of the kerygma. In the quest for the historical Jesus, on the other hand, what has to be elicited is 'the non-assignability of salvation, the *prae* of Christ before his own, the *extra nos* of proclamation, the necessity of the exodus of the faithful from themselves'. [42] It is a question of the primacy of Christ before and over the Church.

The new quest for the historical Jesus does not intend with these arguments to return to the province of liberal theology. That is why reference is made to the *new* quest for the historical Jesus. The new aspect of the new quest for the historical Jesus is that the quest is undertaken not in bypassing the kerygma, but through the medium of the primitive Christian message. According to Käsemann,[43] interpretation and tradition are fundamentally inseparable. Therefore it is not a question of getting behind the kerygma or even of a reduction of the Gospel to the historical Jesus. That pursuit of the Enlightenment has shown itself to be a will o' the wisp. History cannot be pressed into the service of legitimation of the kerygma. 'It is not a matter of grounding faith historically. But it is a matter of critically distinguishing true from false proclamation.'[44] E. Fuchs has reduced this methodological procedure to a precise formula: 'If earlier on we interpreted the historical Jesus with the aid of the primitive Christian kerygma, today we interpret that kerygma with the aid of the historical Jesus – both directions in interpretation complement each other'.[45]

The new quest for the historical Jesus therefore maintains the hermeneutical circle, which is valid for all elucidation and understanding. It proceeds from the premiss of present belief, and measures that faith by its content: Jesus Christ. It understands Jesus Christ in the light of church belief, and it interprets church belief from Jesus. Christological dogma and historical criticism would seem (though in a very critical way) to be reconciled. But only seemingly. In reality this attempt, from which we have a lot to learn in certain respects, contains certain presuppositions and options which have first to be elucidated theologically.

The first presupposition is philosophical in nature. The word 'history' is of course ambiguous. The history to which the New Testament kerygma refers is something else: the earthly Jesus as he really was, as he moved and lived. The historic Jesus is something less again, when we consider him as that Jesus whom we take from the kerygma by a complicated method of subtraction, and with the aid of modern historical methodology. Troeltsch has shown that this modern historical method is anything but presuppositionless. It presupposes the standpoint of modern subjectivity, and stands for an entire world-view. In historical research, in other words, the mature individual subject tries to discern history 'objectively', and also to naturalize and neutralize it. Historical criticism starts from the assumption of the similarity in principle of all events; it perceives everything according to the law of analogy and presupposes a general correlation of all events.[46] That means that everything is conceived under the primacy of universality. The category of singularity and that of the underivable-and-new has no place here. The future can only be understood in terms of the past.[46] But that has direct theological consequences: Eschatology, the centre of Jesus' proclamation, has to be excluded or obviated in some way.

The second presupposition is theological in nature. But it is closely related to the abovementioned philosophical premiss. It is taken for granted that the reality of Jesus is the reality of the earthly or the historical Jesus. The quest — or the new quest — for the historical Jesus is therefore: What happens to the Resurrection? Is it only the legitimation of the earthly Jesus, the presupposition or essential notion of the continuation of his 'cause', or is it something wholly new and never-before-present, which not only confirms the earthly Jesus, but simultaneously continues his 'cause' in a *new* way? But if the Resurrection has more than a legitimating meaning, and is also a redemptive event with its own 'content', then the kerygma too, in addition to the proclamation and cause of the earthly Jesus, must have a 'more' and a 'new' aspect. It is not then a question of making the earthly Jesus or the historical Jesus, in a one-dimensional way, the criterion for belief in Christ. The content and primary criterion of Christology is the earthly Jesus *and* the risen, exalted Christ. That takes us to a Christology of complementarity — of the earthly Jesus *and* the risen and exalted Christ.

Within such a Christology of reciprocity between the earthly Jesus and the exalted Christ, under the conditions of the modern notion of understanding, the historical aspect becomes essential. Historical research not only has to afford *dicta probantia* for the later Christ-faith of the Church. The church belief instead has in the earthly Jesus, as he is made accessible to us through historical research, a relatively autonomous criterion, a once-and-for all yardstick by which it must continually measure itself. Nevertheless it is impossible to make the historical Jesus the entire and only valid content of faith in Christ. For Revelation occurs not only in the earthly Jesus, but just as much, more indeed, in the Resurrection and the imparting of the Spirit. Jesus today is living 'in the Spirit'. Hence we are granted not only an historically mediated, but a direct mode of access to Jesus Christ 'in the Spirit'. If we had only an historical way of reaching Jesus Christ, then Jesus would be a dead letter for us — indeed, a stultifying and enslaving law. He is the Gospel that makes us free only in the Spirit (cf 2 Cor 3. 4-18). There is a dialectic of regressive movement and standardization at the beginning on the one hand, and of progressive movement and historical development on the other hand. That dialectic was disclosed by the later Möhler. He showed that Jesus Christ can be a living presence to us only in that way, if we are not to surrender to a loose enthusiastic dogmatism of the kind that Möhler deprecated at the time in F.C. Baur.[48]

This project of a Christology of reciprocity of the earthly Jesus and the risen Christ of faith resumes under present-day notions and understanding, the oldest of all Christological approaches: the so-called two-stages Christology.[49] It already exists in the formula in Rom 1.3 f which Paul had taken from tradition: '. . . who was descended from David according to the flesh and designated Son of God in power according to the Spirit of holiness by his Resurrection from the dead'. This schema of a double assessment of Jesus Christ 'according to the flesh' (*kata sarxa*) and 'according to the Spirit' *(kata pneuma)* recurs in 1 Tim 3.16 and 1 Pet 3.18. The two-stage Christology is found at its fullest development (with the addition of pre-existence) in the Christ-hymn in Phil 2. 5-11. Here the whole Christology is one great drama of debasement and exaltation. He who was obediently reduced to the state of a servant is exalted by God as the *Pantocrator.*

This schema was taken much further by the Fathers of the first three centuries. F. Loofs has shown that the double assessment of Christ is the most ancient Christological schema.[50] With Tertullian the two-stage Christology is already the teaching of two *status* in Christ, which was then extended to become a two-natures Christology. The Council of Chalcedon understood this two-natures Christology as an interpretation of the historically concrete two-stage Christology. The Christology of two stages or of two states was never wholly suppressed in subsequent centuries. The tradition of the Middle Ages and baroque scholasticism still features a detailed two-state doctrine, which increasingly lost its function for Christology as a whole, and finally fell for the most part into desuetude.[51] It was different in the Protestant tradition. There the two-state doctrine played an increasingly important role. In the seventeenth and nineteenth centuries it was extended to become '*kenosis*-Christology'. It made — an ultimately unsuccessful — attempt to interpret the two-natures Christology as a dynamic process of debasement and exaltation, in such a way that the *Logos* emptied himself of his divinity. Only Karl Barth succeeded by a stroke of genius in systematically reuniting the two-states and the two-natures Christologies.[52] The inadequate aspect of his approach is of course that he includes no reference to the earthly Jesus. Recently E. Jüngel made an interesting attempt to extend the basic principles of Barth's Christology, and to include the quest for the historical Jesus in the total dogmatic project of his Christology.[53]

With that the circle has been closed. The original correspondence of the earthly Jesus and the risen Christ, which was at first developed dogmatically in the form of the two-stages, and later in the two-natures and two-states Christologies, has caught up with these subsequent interpretations. That makes the way open in principle ahead of the present new quest for the historical Jesus. The approach of the classical two-natures and two-states Christology is ready for a new synthesis.

Summary:

The approach and problems of Christology
1. The starting-point is the confession of faith of the church community. Ultimately Christology is no more than the exposition of the confession that 'Jesus is the Christ'. This starting-point, the framework, is not the entire content. The church confession is not self-enclosed. Its content and pre-given standard lie in the history and activity of Jesus. The Christological professions and dogmas must be understood in reference to that point and from it. What is true of language in general is true analogously in this regard: Concepts without perception are empty; perception without concepts is blind (Kant). Whenever theology is no more than interpretation of traditional formulas and notions, then it is scholastic in the bad sense. Then doctrine is reduced to the breath of the voice. That leads us to a bipartite structure of Christology: 1. The history and activity of Jesus Christ; 2. The mystery of Jesus Christ.

2. The centre and content of a Christology which claims to be an interpretation of the confession of faith that 'Jesus is the Christ' is the cross and Resurrection of Jesus. This is where the transition takes place from the Jesus of history to the exalted Christ of faith. The identity between the earthly Jesus and the exalted Christ includes however a difference, or rather, something totally new — a *novum*. A unilateral Jesusology as much as a unilateral kerygma Christology does not go far enough. Where the cross and Resurrection become the mid-point, that also means however an adjustment of a one-sided Christology orientated to the Incarnation. If the divine-human person Jesus is constituted through the Incarnation once and for all, the history and activity of Jesus, and above all the cross and the Resurrection, no longer have any constitutive meaning whatsoever. Then the death of Jesus would be only the completion of the Incarnation. The Resurrection would be no more than the confirmation of his divine nature. That would mean a diminution of the whole biblical testimony. According to Scripture, Christology has its centre in the cross and the Resurrection. From that midpoint it extends forward to the *Parousia* and back to the Pre-existence and the Incarnation. That does not imply an abandonment of faith in the Incarnation, but instead its transformation into a total interpretation of the history and activity of Jesus, so that it states that God assumed not only a human nature but a human history, and in that way introduced the fulfilment of history as a whole.

3. The basic problem of a Christology with its midpoint in the cross and Resurrection is the relation of the Resurrection and Exaltation Christology expressed in it to the descent-Christology expressed in the notion of Incarnation. Both are biblically grounded. For that reason, neither can be set against the other. To be sure their relation is not easy to determine. In descent-Christology, the divine-human being of Jesus is the ground of his history; in ascent-Christology his being is constituted in and through his history.

At this point, Christology faces us with one of the most fundamental problems of all thought: namely, the question of the relation of being and time. Christology is not concerned solely with the nature of Jésus Christ, but with the Christian understanding of reality in general. The historical quest for Jesus Christ becomes a question about history as a whole. Only in that universal perspective can the historical quest for Jesus Christ be considered appropriately.

Notes

[1] On the history of Jesus see esp. W. Trilling, *Fragen zur Geschichtlichkeit Jesu,* (2nd ed., Dusseldorf, 1967); and H. Windisch, 'Das Probleme der Geschichtlichkeit Jesu,' in: *Theol. Rundschau* NF 1 (1929), pp. 266-188 (Lit); A Vögtle, Art. 'Jesus Christus,' in: LTK V, pp. 922-5; F Hahn, *Das Verstandnis der Mission im Neuen Testament* (Neukirchen, 1963) pp. 47-6; J. Blank, *Jesus von Nazareth. Geschichte und Relevanz* (Freiburg, 1972), esp. pp. 20 ff.

[2] See M. Dibelius, *Die Formgeschichte des Evangeliums* (Tübingen, 1919); ET: *From Tradition to Gospel* (London, 1933); K. L. Schmidt, *Der Rahmen der Geschichte Jesu* (Berlin, 1919); R. Bultmann, *Die Geschichte der synoptischen Tradition* (Göttingen, 1921); ET: *The History of the Synoptic Tradition* (Oxford, 1963); E. Fascher, *Die formgeschichtliche Methode. Eine Darstellung und Kritik,* (Geissen, 1924); K. H. Schclkle, *Die Passion Jesu in der Verkündigung des Neuen Testaments. Ein Beitrag zur Formgeschichte und zur Theologie des Neuen Testaments* (Heidelberg, 1949). See the recent critical account of E. Güttgemanns: *Offene Fragen zur Formgeschichte des Evangeliums. Eine methodologische Skizze der Grundlagenproblematik der Form-und Redaktiongeschichte* (Munich, 1970).

[3] See esp. N. Luhmann, *Zweckbegriffe und Systemrationalität. Über die Funktion von Zwecken in sozialen Systemen* (Tübingen, 1959); J. Habermas, N. Luhmann, *Theorie der Gesellschaft oder Sozialtechnologie − Was leistet die Systemforschung?* (Frankfurt, 1971); N. Luhmann, 'Religion als System. Religiöse Dogmatik und gesellschaftliche Evolution,' in: K.-W. Dahm, N. Luhmann, D. Stoodt, *Religion − System und Sozialisation* (Darmstadt-Neuwied, 1972), pp. 11-132.

[4] See K. Rahner, 'Grundlinien einer systematischen Christologie,' in: *idem,* W. Thüsing, *Christologie − systematisch und exegetisch. Arbeitsgrundlagenfür eine interdisziplinäre Vorlesung* (QD vol 55) (Freiburg, 1972) p. 18.

[5] On the origins of historical theology, cf. esp. K. Scholder, *Ursprünge und Probleme der Bibelkritik im 17. Jahrhundert. Ein Beitrag zur Enstehung der historisch-kritischen Theologie* (Munich, 1966); and G. Hornig, *Die Anfänge der historisch-kritischen Theologie. J. S. Semlers Schriftverständnis und seine Stellung zu Luther* (Göttingen, 1961); H. J. Kraus, *Geschichte der historisch-kritischen Erforschung des Alten Testaments,* 2nd ed. (Neukirchen-Vlyun, 1969).

[6] Cf., eg,. A. F. Büsching, *Gedanken von der Beschaffenheit und dem Vorzug der biblisch-dogmatischen Theologie vor der alten und neuen scholastischen* (Lemgo, 1958); J. Ph. Gabler, *Oratio de iusto discrimine theologica biblicae et dogmaticae, regundisque recte utriusque finibus* (Altdorf, 1787); G. Ph. Kaiser, *Die Biblische Theologie oder Judaismus und Christianismus nach der grammatisch-historischen Interpretationsmethode und nach einer freimütigen Stellung in die kritisch vergleichende Universalgeschichte der Religionen und in die universale Religion* (Erlangen, 1813/14); F. Chr. Baur, *Vorlesungen über neutestamentliche Theologie,* F. F. Baur (Leipzig, 1864). Recent survey in, H.J. •Kraus, *Die biblische Theologie. Ihre Geschichte und Problematik* (Neukirchen-Vlyun, 1970).

[7] A. Schweitzer, *Geschichte der Leben-Jesu-Forschung,* (2nd ed. Tübingen, 1913).

[8] *Ibid;* p. 2.

[9] *Ibid;* p. 4.

[10] R. Augstein, *Jesus Menschensohn* (Gütersloh, 1972), p. 7.

[11] Fragment "Von dem Zwecke Jesu und seiner Jünger", in: G. E. Lessing, W XIII, ed. K. Lachmann, F. Munker (Leipzig, 1897) p. 226. The seven fragments Lessing published were taken from an early stage of Reimarus' work. This was published in its final form in 1972: H. S. Reimarus, *Apologie oder Schutzschrift für die vernünftigen Verehrer Gottes,* ed. G. Alexander, 2 vols. (Frankfurt, 1972).

[12] Ebd.

[13] *Op. cit. 269* ff.

[14] G. E. Lessing, 'Die Religion Christi,' in: W XVI (Leipzig, 1902), p. 518.

[15] See the summary in A. Schweitzer,*Geschichte*, pp. 98-123. See also J. E. Kuhn, *Das Leben Jesu wissenschaftlich bearbeitet* (Frankfurt, 1968) (= Mainz, 1838).

[16] Cf. C. Hartlich, W. Sachs, *Der Ursprung des Mythosbegriffe in der modernen Bibelwissenschaft* (Tübingen, 1952).

[17] Cf. D. F. Strauss,*Das Leben Jesu, kritisch bearbeitet*, vol. 1 (Tübingen, 1835), p. 499.

[18] *Idem, Das Leben Jesu für das deutsche Volk* (6th ed. Bonn, 1891), pt. 2, p. 387.

[19] *Idem, Der alte und der neue Glaube* (6th ed. Bonn, 1873), p. 94.

[20] Cf. J. Moltmann, 'Exegese und Eschatologie der Geschichte,' in: *idem, Perspektiven der Theologie* (Munich, 1968), pp. 57-62.

[21] R. Slenczka, *Geschichtlichkeit und Personsein Jesu Christi. Studien zur christologischen Problematik der historischen Jesusfrage* (Göttingen, 1967).

[22] J. Ternus, 'Das Seelen- und Bewusstseinsleben Jesu. Problemgeschichtlich-systematische Untersuchung,' in: *Das Konzil von Chalkedon*, vol. 3, pp. 158.

[23] F. Schleiermacher, *Das Leben Jesu*, in: W, sect. 1. vol. 6 (Berlin, 1864), p. 35.

[24] *Idem.*

[25] *Der christliche Glaube*, vol. 2, p. 43.

[26] A. von Harnack, *Das Wesen des Christentums* (Munich, 1964), p.45.

[27] A. Schweitzer, *Geschichte*, op.cit., p.4.

[28] J. Jeremias, 'Der gegenwartige Stand der Debatte um das Problem des historischen Jesus,' in: H. Ristow, K. Matthiae (eds.), *Der historische Jesus und der kerygmatische Christus. Beiträge zum Christusverständnis in Forschung und Verkündigung* (Berlin, 1960), p. 14.

[29] A. Schweitzer, *Geschichte, op. cit.,* p. 631

[30] *Ibid.*

[31] *Op.cit*, pp. 631 ft.

[32] M. Kähler, *Der sogenannte historische Jesus und der geschichtliche, biblische Christus,* ed. E. Wolf (4th ed., Munich, 1969), p.44.

[33] F. Overbeck, *Über die Christlichkeit unserer heutigen Theologie* (3rd ed., Darmstadt, 1963), p. 75.

[34] M. Kähler, *Der sogenannte historische Jesus, op. cit.,*pp. 89, 91.

[35] A. Schweitzer, *Geschichte*, p. 512.

[36] K. Adam, *Der Christus der Glaubens. Vorlesungen über die kirchliche Christologie* (Düsseldorf, 1954), p. 17.

[37] J.A. Möhler, *Symbolik oder Darstellung der dogmatischen Gegensätze der Katholiken und Protestanten nach ihren öffentlichen Bekenntnisschriften*, ed J.R. Geiselmann (Cologne 1958), p. 389.

[38] D. Bonhoeffer, *Sanctorum communio. Eine dogmatische Untersuchung zur Soziologie der Kirche* (Munich, 1954), pp. 92 *seq.*

[39] E. Käsemann, 'Das Problem des historischen Jesus,' in: *idem, Exegetische Versuche und Besinnungen* I (6th ed, Göttingen, 1970, pp. 187-214. See also: *Rückfrage nach Jesus,* ed. K. Kertelge (QD, vol. 63) (Freiburg, 1974).

[40] G. Bornkamm, *Jesus von Nazareth* (9th ed, Stuttgart, 1971) p. 21.

[41] E. Käsemann, *Problem*, p. 200.

[42] '*Sackgassen im Streit um den historischen Jesus,'* in: *idem, Exegetische Versuche und Besinnungen* II (3rd ed., Gottingen, 1970), p. 67.

[43] *Idem Problem,* pp. 190-5.

[44] *Idem, Sackgassen,* p. 55.

[45] E. Fuchs, *Zur Frage nach dem historischen Jesus* (2nd ed., Tübingen), 1965, VII.

[46] E. Troeltsch, 'Über historische und dogmatische Methode in der Theologie,' in: idem, W II (Aalen, 1962) (=Tübingen, 1913), pp. 729-53.

[47] cf. M. Heidegger, *Holzwege* (3rd ed., Frankfurt a. M., 1957), p. 76.

[48] J.A. Möhler, *Neue Untersuchungen der Lehrgegensätze zwischen den Katholiken und Protestanten,* ed. P. Schanz (Regensburg, 1900).

[49] See: R. Schnackenburg, *Christologie des Neuen Testaments,* in: MS III/1, 264-271, 309-322.

[50] F. Loofs, *Leitfaden zum Stadium der Dogmengeschichte,* ed. K. Aland (Tübingen 1959), pp. 69-72, 74f, 108f.

[51] M. J. Scheeben, *Handbuch der katholischen Dogmatik* V/2 = W VI/2 (Freiburg, 1954) pp. 108-56.

[52] K. Barth, *Die Kirchliche Dogmatik* IV/1 (Zollikon-Zürich, 1953), pp. 140-70.

[53] E. Jüngel, 'Jesu Wort and Jesus als Wort Gottes. Ein hermeneutischer Beitrag zum christologischen Problem,' in: *idem, Unterwegs zur Sache. Theologische Bemerkungen* (Munich, 1972), pp. 126-44.

III. THE RELIGIOUS QUEST FOR JESUS CHRIST

III. THE RELIGIOUS QUEST FOR JESUS CHRIST

1. THE CHALLENGE FROM A SECULARIZED WORLD

The confession that 'Jesus is the Christ' is the answer to the question of salvation and redemption. That question was widespread at the time of Jesus. Expectations of salvation were universal among Jews and pagans then. In the age of Augustus those expectations crystallized in hope for a kingdom of freedom and justice. In his famous fourth eclogue, Vergil expresses that longing most poignantly. The new realm of peace and justice is expected in the birth of a child.[1] There is no mention of who is meant by the child. Probably Vergil was not thinking of any specific child; instead 'child' was a symbol of salvation and nothing more. Similar prognostications of salvation are to be found in Judaism.[2] The history of Palestinian Judaism at the time was a history of blood and tears. The apocalyptics reacted to the inward and outward stress of circumstances with visions of the future filled with expectation of the coming of a heavenly kingdom of God. The Zealots on the other hand carried on a kind of guerrilla war against the heathen powers — the occupation troops — and tried by force of arms to establish the Kingdom of God as an earthly theocracy. The primitive Christian proclamation of Jesus the Christ (that is, the redeemer and liberator sent by God) could be taken then as a direct answer to *the* question of the age. The question, 'Are you he who is to come, or shall we look for another?' (Mt 11.3) was to be heard everywhere.

But what about that same question today? Is the problem of salvation and redemption still an issue for us now? How do *we* experience the Christ news as a saving and liberating answer? Does it really mean anything to us?

The contemporary world is often described as secularized. Terms like 'secularization', 'desacralization', 'demythologization' and even 'de-ideologization' are used as magic amulets or universal terms for the entire present-day situation.[3] But quite diverse phenomena can be concealed in portmanteau words of this kind. In a tentative, still very general, way we can say, however, that in the process of secularization man and society escape the tutelage of models of thought and behaviour with a Christian and religious emphasis.

Man wants to assess the world and treat it in a worldly way. He wants to reach a rational insight into the immanent objective structures of politics, economics, science, and so on, and to orientate his activity accordingly. The 'absolute' and ultimate questions which cannot be solved in this way are largely counted as meaningless and as best set aside in favour of the soluble problems which — so it is claimed — accord with actual needs.

The modern secularization process is to be understood only against the background of the basic principle of modern thought: the principle of subjectivity. Subjectivity means that man posits himself as the starting-point and measure for understanding reality as a whole. It is not to be confused with subjectivism — which might be defined as an obdurate insistence of the individual subject on his limited perspective and on his special interests. Subjectivity is not a matter of that particular, but of a wholly universal, perspective.[4] This so-called anthropological turning-point began, after the preliminaries of mysticism and Nicholas of Cusa, with the Cartesian *cogito ergo sum*. From that point on, man no longer understood himself in terms of the total context of a reality encompassing him and determining his notions of measure and order. Instead he himself became the reference-point of reality. Where man makes himself the lord of reality in that way, reality becomes a mere object to be comprehended through the sciences and controlled by technology. Of course it still contains a mass of unsolved problems, but no real mysteries. Man believes that he is in the process of increasingly understanding the real causes of things, and that he is coming more and more to master and control them. God is dispensable as a cognitive and working hypothesis, and the world is demythologized and desacralized. The demythization of the objective world naturally results in the de-objectification of the image of God and of religious ideas. The Enlightenment and Romanticism, natural science and mysticism in the modern era, have often been but the two aspects of a single movement. (It would be naive to say that the problems posed by the secularization process of modern times are going to be resolved by the present — however fortunate — 'religious wave').

Behind this modern development there is ultimately the emotive phenomenon of freedom and of liberation from objective pressures. Emancipation is therefore a kind of epochal catchword for our contemporary experience of reality, and an historico-philosophical category used to characterize the processes of enlightenment and liberation in the modern era (Metz).[5] But what exactly does that mean?

The notion of emancipation[6] originated in legal thought. In Roman law it refers to the benevolent though guaranteed release of a slave or the release of a son who has come of age from the authority of his father. That original understanding of emancipation can of course have a properly theological meaning. Paul understands Christian redemption as liberation from 'powers', and there is no doubt that Christianity enjoys an important place in the history of freedom in western civilization. It was Christianity that first recognized the dignity and worth, grounded in freedom, of every man irrespective of race, origin, position and sex. In this perspective it is possible to see the modern era to some extent as the historical expression of Christianity. It would however be a simplification if we were for that reason to understand the whole process of development in modern times as 'anonymously' or 'structurally' Christian.

The notion of emancipation as a benevolently granted freedom gave way to the modern conception of man's autonomous self-liberation. That was the decisive impulse of the Enlightenment, which Kant defined as the emergence of man from the immaturity he had incurred through his own fault, and as the courage to apply his own understanding and to make open use of it.[7] The liberation of the individual in that way became a social process, in which entire social groups freed themselves from spiritual, legal, social or political tutelage or disadvantage, or from a domination of lords and masters which they experienced as injustice. We speak therefore of the liberation of the peasants, of the emancipation of the bourgeoisie, of the proletariat, of the Jews, of the blacks, of women, and of former colonial possessions. The common goal of these movements became increasingly clearer as a removal of all discrimination and as open privileges: in other words, the emancipated society. The first legal and later political concept of emancipation increasingly became an ideological holistic category. In that total sense, Marx offers this definition: 'All emancipation is the reference of the human world and of conditions to man himself'.[8] This totalized emancipation expressly excludes (for Marx) any mediation by any kind of mediator.[9] For Marx, therefore, emancipation from religion is the prime condition and presupposition of all other forms of emancipation.[10]

Emancipation is to be seen as a kind of epochal catchword for our present experience of the world and as an historico-philosophical category for the process of enlightenment and freedom in the modern era, in the circumstances (and not just the conditions) of which we have to articulate and represent the Christian message of redemption (Metz). In that case it is a fundamental question for modern Christology to decide the relation between redemption understood in a Christian perspective and emancipation understood as the modern age understands it.

An answer to these questions is attempted in Bultmann's theology of demythologization, and in Karl Rahner's anthropologically-orientated theology. Ultimate questions and fundamental alternatives occur in the process; in the process, that is, in which theology and the modern theology of emancipation can and must learn from one another. We are faced with nothing less than a question of the destiny of faith and theology.

2. THE DEMYTHOLOGIZATION OF BELIEF IN CHRIST

When human freedom and maturity become the dominant midpoint and criterion of thought, traditional religious ideas and convictions must appear mythological. The traditional faith in Jesus Christ has also incurred the suspicion of being mythological. Can we honestly and sincerely continue to hold and pass on the message that God came down from heaven, assumed human form, was born of a virgin, walked about working miracles, descended to the dead after his death, rose again on the third day, was exalted to the right hand of God, and now is present and effective from heaven through the Spirit in the proclamation and sacraments of the Church? Surely all that is the language and substance of an out-of-date mythic world-view? Surely, out of intellectual honesty and for the sake of a more genuine idea of God, we have to demythologize the whole thing?

That question cannot be answered if we do not first make clear what we mean by mythology and demythologization.[11] I shall restrict myself here to the understanding of myth and mythology predominant in the history of religions, or comparative religious studies, and in the associated theology of demythologization.[12] According to that view, myth is the form of understanding proper to an out-of-date epoch of human history: the primitive era, or childhood, of mankind. In that epoch, man was not yet aware of the real causes of things, and therefore he saw supramundane and divine powers at work everywhere in the world and in history. Mythology is accordingly the mode of thought and imagination which understands the divine in a worldly form, and the worldly in a divine form. God is the gap-filler, the *deus ex machina*, who replaces natural causes with miraculous and supernatural interventions. The divine and the mundane are intermingled and form a whole, the one cosmos. The divine is so to speak the numinous dimension of depth in the world. It can be experienced everywhere and directly in everything. All reality can become a symbol in which the divine can be experienced.

The demythologization programme tries to accord with man's changed understanding of reality. But the intention behind demythologization is not, as the word seems at first to imply, a process of elimination; it is *interpretation*. Its essential concern is positive, not negative. Demythologizers want to keep the remaining objective core which was present as a mythological cypher in the traditional profession of faith. They want to reveal the lasting content and intention in a way appropriate to the modern mind.

The demythologization project is not new. It was already apparent among the English Deists. Some of them (Locke for instance) wanted a rational Christianity, and some a religion without mystery (Toland). Spinoza anticipated in essence the entire modern debate. On the basis of his panentheistic philosophy, he is convinced that the divine wisdom has taken a human form in Christ. But the divine wisdom shows itself in Christ only so that it stands out with exceptional clarity against nature and the human spirit. Scripture teaches nothing that offends against reason. Its authority does not concern questions of truth but questions of conversion; of alteration of a way of life and of virtue — what we would call practice. Significantly, Spinoza entitled his work *Tractatus theologico-politicus.* Similarly, though from other premisses, Kant wished to see all statuary laws and all positive historical ecclesiastical belief as a means and vehicle for the encouragement and extension of a religion of morality. Otherwise, in his view, it was no more than superstition and foolish subservience, religious fanaticism, and idol worship. The first major discussion of the problem of mythology in Christology occurred, however, when D.F. Strauss published his epoch-making two-volume *Life of Jesus,* and explained faith in Christ as the unintentional outcome of a myth in literary form.[13] He too wished to make the religion of Christ a religion of humanity. For '. . . the humanity is the union of the two natures, the God become man, the infinite God self-emptied to the point of infinity, and the finite Spirit remembering his infinity . . .' 'Conceived in an individual, a God-man, the qualities and functions which the teaching of the Church ascribes to Christ contradict one another . . .'[14] Nevertheless, Strauss maintained that there was an historical core to the Christ-event. He did not hold the untenable thesis which A. Drews proposed at the turn of the century with something approaching missionary fervour. Drews maintained that Jesus had been a myth and had never really existed. Similarly, for B. Bauer and A. Kalthoff, Jesus was only a symbol of the ideas of the early Church.[16] The discussion of 'these contraband pathways to the heights of thought'[16] was resumed by E. Troeltsch and W. Bousset.[17] For them Jesus is symbolic of the cult of the early Church. Of course a cultic symbol is only effectual and effective if there is a real man behind it. But historical facts serve Troeltsch only 'for illustration and not for demonstration'.

Bultmann's demythologization project is comprehensible against this background. Bultmann sees as mythological (in the tradition of Bousset's history of religions) 'that mode of thought in which the unworldly, the divine, appears as worldly, and human, and the other-worldly appears as this-worldly'.[20] But Bultmann takes a different view of the cult. Bousset saw it as at the centre of interest, whereas for Bultmann that position is occupied by proclamation. This gives his presentation a more enlightened aspect. For him mythology is almost the counter-concept of our modern scientific world-view, which according to him operates with a closed context of cause-and-effect, whereas for mythic thought the world is open to the intervention of other-worldly powers. For us today that way of thinking is no longer possible. That does not mean, of course, that Bultmann wants the New Testament kerygma dissolved.

He is more concerned to disclose the understanding of existence concealed in the myth, and in that way to reveal the specific intention of the biblical writings. Myth shows man as a being who is not in control of himself. In contact with the kerygma of Jesus Christ he attains to a new understanding of existence. The notion of demythologization is not, as far as Bultmann is concerned, the negative formulation of what he sees as the positive meaning of the existential interpretation. It is not intended to dissolve the indispensable content and the scandal of Christian faith (namely, that it is God who is acting in Jesus Christ), but to demonstrate precisely that content and scandal while at the same time freeing the message from false, time-conditioned impedimenta.

A number of his critics think Bultmann is sitting on the fence. Surely, they say, any talk of the decisive action of God in Jesus Christ must also be treated as mythical. Bultmann's answer is No. 'For the redemptive event of which we are speaking is not a miraculous, supranatural occurrence; it is historical occurrence in space and time'.[21] Others, and especially K. Jaspers, W. Kamlah, F. Buri and S. Ogden, see that too as a persistent mythological spatialization and chronologization of God. 'The redemptive event does not consist in . . . a once and for all saving event in Christ, but in the fact that it is possible for men to understand themselves in their uniqueness just as the myth of Christ expresses it'.[22] In that view, Jesus Christ is the especially impressive manifestation of a possibility man has of being an authentic human being. Christology is the cypher for a specific anthropology, a symbol for a successful human existence, a kind of common humanity or a stimulus to a new way of acting that will change the world.

In the meantime attempts to demythologize faith in Christ have also gained entry to Catholic circles. Hubertus Halbfas in his *Fundamental Catechetics* conceives the history of man's self-discovery as insurpassably expressed in Jesus Christ. The revelation of God in Jesus of Nazareth is not 'something categorically different from exta-biblical revelations' but the 'law of evolution fulfilling itself'.[23] Even more radically, J. Nolte sees in the person of Jesus the Fact, Meaningful Image, True Sign and Bearer of Significance of a freedom determined by love — which does not exclude the possibility of other Facts, Meaningful Images, True Signs, and Bearers of Significance. 'Accordingly, the Christ-matter has to be radically relativized and seen merely as an intermediate, didactic and symbolic concretion of a permanent truth-value'. 'God is greater than what is called "God" in the figure of Jesus and in Christianity'.[24] Edward Schillebeeckx is much more careful and reticent. In the Jesus narrative he sees 'the great parable of God himself and at the same time the paradigm of the humanity of our human being', 'a new, unheard of possibility of existence thanks to the God who is intent on humankind'.[25]

Whatever detailed criticism may have to be made of these attempts to demythologize faith in Christ, we must always remember that demythologization is not unjustifiable in its critical or in its positive aspects. There is a time and a place for demythologization. It is undeniable that in generally current ideas of Christianity, Jesus Christ is often thought of more or less as a god descending to earth whose humanity is basically only a kind of clothing behind which God himself speaks and acts. Extreme notions of that kind see God dressed as a Father Christmas, or slipping into human nature like someone putting on dungarees in order to repair the world after a breakdown. The biblical and church doctrine that Jesus was a true and complete man with a human intellect and human freedom, does not seem to prevail in the average Christian head. Therefore demythologization is not only permissible but necessary; precisely in order to disclose the authentic meaning of belief in Christ.

Demythologization is also acceptable in its positive aspect, as, that is to say, existential or anthropological interpretation. Relevation uses human language, which only reveals something when it reaches the hearer: when, that is, he understands it. Furthermore, in Jesus Christ human existence as a whole becomes the 'grammar' of God's self-expression. Christological statements: statements about man. Conversely, the knowledge and study of man must give us an initial understanding of what has happened in Jesus Christ. But here, surely, we have only touched on the real problem. We have to ask whether and how far theological discourse and discussion are really possible and meaningful. Perhaps hermeneutically orientated theology is itself mythological. After all, it too contains 'something' which in the end cannot be stated or demonstrated.

46

My answer will be given in stages. The first stage is a description of the problems and difficulties which have beset the emancipation, enlightenment and demythologization movement of recent years. The Frankfurt school of sociology and social psychology and philosophy offered a detailed critique — or, rather, self-critique — of the modern critical attitude under the general heading of the 'dialectic of enlightenment' (Horkheimer and Adorno in, especially, the book of that title). They wished to show that the rational approach ran the risk of succumbing to irrationalism by itself becoming irrational. If man tries to explain, organize and manipulate everything rationally, he is sure to become a victim of that very planning and manipulation. When everything is seen from the angle of profitability, man too becomes a number without human features. That kind of rational mastery of reality is only possible by means of the rationalized and organized cooperation of a large number of people. And that leads, almost inevitably, to the 'administered world', and in extreme cases to a totalitarian state. Freedom is caught in the very net that it has cast and made. The sorcerer's apprentice cannot control the spirits he has summoned up.

The dialectic of enlightenment is most clearly evident in that when reason elevates itself into an absolute, it almost always creates a new myth. Then (as Feuerbach noted) politics becomes religion.[26] But surely a man who elevates himself as an absolute (for that is what the foregoing implies) surrenders the title of human being and becomes inhuman? Perhaps politics which has turned into religion must necessarily make totalitarian claims and end in a general deprivation of liberty.

The unfortunate consequences of the modern subjectivity principle take us back to the starting-point. The basic premiss of the Enlightenment is to make human reason the yardstick and reference-point for all understanding and all behaviour. The Enlightenment argues from the essentially rational nature of reality as a whole and — since it wants to consider everything in the light of the same rational principles — from the essential similarity of all activity. But if we do follow enlightenment principles and assume the essential similarity and comparability — the sameness — of everything that happens, we not only have to abandon the idea of a specific history of salvation, but have to admit that basically there is nothing new under the sun. The primacy of the general and the universal means the subjugation of everything spare, strange and original. The unique and special becomes mere vehicle, function, cypher, symbol, interpretament and, ultimately, the particular instance of a universal. Then Christology too must be a mere vehicle, function, cypher, symbol, interpretament and, ultimately, a particular instance of anthropology.

We cannot turn the clock back. The best way of solving the problem is to take up the theme which explodes the abstract philosophy of equalization from within. That is most effective with the fundamental modern Enlightenment topic: its desire to make human dignity and freedom the ultimate value. Schelling, with characteristic vision, observed that to make freedom the centrepoint of the system meant a more drastic change than with any previous revolution.[27]

Freedom denies the primacy of the universal over the particular. Freedom in any real sense is possible only on the premiss that reality as a whole is determined by freedom, for that is the only condition which allows freedom room for action within reality. To conceive reality under the rule of freedom means that reality is to be seen not as an enclosed but as a basically open system with room for the unique, new and original. But surely then the Enlightenment tradition, which denies God in the name of liberty, contradicts itself in the end. How can we conceive reality as existing under the primacy of freedom without a universal guarantee of divine freedom? We are right to ask whether a second Enlightenment (an enlightenment, that is, of the Enlightenment about itself) cannot, though in a new way, reassert belief in God as deciding the very possibility of freedom.

These questions take us to the border line between permissible and impermissible demythologization. Demythologization is permissible if it helps us to show Jesus Christ as the location of divine and human freedom. It is impermissible when it cancels the underivable originality and novelty of Jesus Christ, and makes Christology a kind of anthropology. If we cross that barrier between an acceptable anthropological interpretation and an unacceptable anthropological reduction, then demythologization converts dialectically into its opposite and Jesus of Nazareth becomes man mythologized.

3. CHRISTOLOGY WITH AN ANTHROPOLOGICAL EMPHASIS

Karl Rahner has done us an immense service in showing how Christology can be pursued in a new way on the presuppositions (not the conditions) of the modern movement.[28] He has opened a new road to Christian belief for a great number of people and has established a bridgehead between Catholic theology and the hermeneutical discussion of recent years.

Rahner invokes the permissible aspect of demythologization and usually starts with an unrelenting attack on the common mythological idea of what belief in Christ entails. That misunderstanding reduces human nature to a mere uniform, and degrades the mediator to a means. Rahner sees that a non-mythological understanding of Christ is only possible if Jesus' humanity is thought of as a real symbol of God. In his later works Rahner calls that a 'Christology from below'.[29] This approach wishes to show that the divine Incarnation takes away nothing of man's autonomy and originality, but is the unique highest instance of the essential realization of human reality.[30] Therefore it starts from a seeking and anonymous Christology which man practises whenever he absolutely recognizes and wholly accepts his humanness.[31] Christology from below can appeal to the other and ask him whether what he is looking for in his life in the most profound sense isn't something which has already been fulfilled in Jesus, who has the words of eternal life, and who is the only one to whom we can turn (Jn 6.5,8).[32]

48

Rahner's Christology from below extends the approach of what has always been a transcendental Christology. That approach is often misunderstood, as if Rahner wished to derive the content of Christology *a priori* from human thought and from human existence as it is lived. But Rahner's transcendental method may not be made to approximate to Kant's. Rahner in fact warns us against the illusion that a transcendental Christology could be made to work by methodological abstraction from the historical Jesus Christ.[35] Only as a second step does he consider the transcendental conditions of this perception, and then as a third step reveals the Christ-idea as the objective correlative of the transcendental structure of man and his knowledge.

On such premises, then, Rahner develops his transcendental Christology from below in three steps[36]:

1. Man experiences himself in every categorical act of cognition and freedom as referred beyond himself and every categorical object to an inconceivable mystery. It is only possible to recognize that the finite is finite if one has a preconception of an infinite; and freedom is possible only when that is the case. By his nature, then, man is a self-realizing but undefined, incomplete but gradually self-comprehending reference to a mystery of fulness.[37]

2. In his most daring moments, man hopes that mystery does not bear and support existence merely as the asymptotically orientated guarantee of an unending movement which remains forever in the finite world. He hopes instead that the mystery offers itself as the fulfilment of human existence. But that kind of divine self-communication has to be historically mediated, which brings in the concept of the absolute redemptive event and the absolute Redeemer in whom man experiences his nature as truly acknowledged and confirmed by God through his absolute and irreversible self-surrender. God's self-communication presupposes man's free acceptance.

3. The foregoing takes us to the very principle of the Incarnation, towards which — by virtue of his human nature — man is always on his way. But when Rahner says that the Incarnation is therefore the unique, highest instance of the realization of the essential nature of human reality,[38] he does not mean that such a possibility is to be realized in every man. Man's transcendence produces his openness to the self-communication of absolute mystery. We cannot conclude however that a fulfilment of that kind is necessary. The problem is not that something like that does in fact happen, but how, where and when the One is present of whom all that can be asserted.

This transcendental Christology leads Rahner to formulate Christology as a self-transcendent anthropology, and that anthropology in its turn as a deficient Christology.[39] This might well be termed the basic formula of all Rahnerian theology, and the one on which he grounds his theory of the anonymous Christian.[40] If Christology represents the unique fulfilment of anthropology, it follows that everyone who fully accepts his life as a human being has thereby also implicitly accepted the Son of man. Hence, according to Rahner, such an individual has already encountered Jesus Christ without knowing however that he had met with the person whom Christians justly call Jesus of Nazareth.[41] With his theory of anonymous Christianity, Rahner is able to make the universality of belief in Christ and the salvation offered by Jesus Christ theologically comprehensible in a new way, and without demythologizing historical Christianity to the point of almost nothingness. Nevertheless, at this point (which is so characteristic of Rahnerian theology) the critical questions really stand out. We have to ask whether, if we adopt so anthropologically orientated a theology and Christology, we are not unilaterally 'metaphysicizing' historical Christianity, and cancelling by philosophical speculation the scandal of its specific reference.

The criticism most often directed against Rahner[42] is that his approach to human subjectivity means an attenuation of intersubjectivity as a phenomenon. There is no such thing as 'man' pure and simple; there are men who exist only and always within the network of I-you-we relations. Man exists so to speak only as a *plurale tantum.* A child's consciousness is awakened with its mother's smile; the freedom of the individual arises from an encounter with the freedom of other individuals. The clearest sign of this intersubjectivity is the phenomenon of human language, the medium in which all spiritual and intellectual processes happen and are fulfilled. That means that being addressed, being approached, being asked to respond comes first, and not — as Rahner suggests — questioning. Even the finely-nuanced transcendental problematics of modern philosophy is not a 'self-evident' starting-point, for it is mediated through the entire history of western philosophy and the history of Christianity.

In his later writings, Rahner examines that historical mediation and tries to define the reciprocal influence of transcendentality and history.[43] He shows that a stronger emphasis on intersubjectivity and history would not necessarily destroy his transcendental approach as such. It is essentially true that man exists only in and through language; it is also true that language and the condition of being addressed presuppose a susceptibility and receptivity to being addressed. It is not the transcendental approach as such which deserves criticism but the fact that Rahner plays down the formal nature of that approach. In his later writings, history is essentially the categorical material in and through which transcendental freedom is realized. Rahner takes too little notice of the fact that the true reality of history implies a determination of the transcendental conditions affecting the possibility of understanding. It is a determination which is not derivable from and not wholly conceivable in terms of those conditions.

This constitutive tension between historical reality and transcendental possibility discloses the basic problem of Rahner's approach. We might put it in thesis form by saying that Rahner's approach is still largely within the bounds of the idealistic philosophy of identity and its identification of being and consciousness. Hence he argues directly from the undoubted openness of the human spirit to the infinite to the reality of that infinite. But surely a distinction has to be made here? In his reaching out to infinity — precisely, indeed, in that — man remains finite. Is it really possible for him as a finite being to conceive the infinite? Surely his way of knowing it must deny its true nature? Can he have more than a negative notion of the infinite? Isn't that the point where man touches on the ultimate ground of his existence, and therefore comes up against an inevitable mystery? What that infinite really is remains open, ambiguous and ambivalent. It can be interpreted in numberless ways. We can call it the pantheistic ground of all reality; but we can also understand it as the expression of an ultimate absurdity of existence. We can interpret it sceptically and we can practise due self-restraint in revering in it that which resists exploration. We can also understand it theistically. Each of these approaches implies an option. The ultimate ground of our human being means an inescapable tension between being and consciousness. It implies that in his questioning, thinking and longing, man is on the one hand greater than reality, because in questioning, thinking and longing he overreaches reality. On the other hand reality is demonstrably greater than man; ultimately man cannot overtake reality. Man therefore is faced with an irremovable mystery. He himself, in fact, is an impenetrable mystery of that very kind. The lines of his being and nature cannot be seized in words.

If we take this highly problematic or aporetic situation of humanity seriously, then the main lines of man's real nature cannot be produced until they reach a certain point called Jesus Christ. The most that we can show is a certain degree of convergence of the lines of human existence on Christ. Man has to acknowledge that in Jesus Christ everything which he hopes for is indeed fulfilled, but in an ultimately underivable way. That takes us, in contradistinction to Rahner, to a new definition of the relationship between anthropology and Christology, which I offer mainly in the tradition of J.E. Kühn, the most impressive speculative theologian of the Catholic Tübingen school of the nineteenth century.[44] Christology is a substantial determination of anthropology which as such must remain open. In the sense of the classical notion of analogy, we have to say that however great the similarity between anthropology and Christology, the dissimilarity is still greater. Anthropology is so to speak the grammar which God uses to express himself. But the grammar as such is still available for a great number of pronouncements. It is concretely decided only through the actual human life of Jesus. If this distinction is not maintained, then fundamentally not very much that is new can happen in salvation history in contradistinction to the human transcendental consciousness beyond the mere fact that the idea of the absolute Redeemer is made actual in Jesus of Nazareth, and nowhere else.

If we abandon this substantial underivability of the Christ-event, we have to relativize the fact that the idea of the absolute Redeemer has been realized in Jesus of Nazareth. For if the underivability consists only of the 'that' but not at the same time of the 'what', we have to join Hans Urs von Balthasar in asking whether the absolute surrender and openness which Rahner attributes to Christ could not also be attributed to Mary.[45] We could go further and follow D.F. Strauss in asking whether the nature of the idea is to expend its fulness in a single instance, or whether it is not more consonant with it to extend its riches in a multitude of complementary instances.[46] We can deduce neither the content of the Christ idea nor the realization of that content in a single individual. We can do no more than acknowledge the fact that what we hope for in the deepest part of our being and nature has been fulfilled in Jesus Christ in a way which surpasses all expectation. Only if the category of the New is taken seriously, in that way, can we begin to see things historically, as in fact we have to pose the question and conduct the quest for Jesus Christ today.

4. THE QUEST FOR SALVATION IN AN HISTORICIZED WORLD

The Second Vatican Council sees humanity as standing at the beginning of a new age in its history. After the Council it is undergoing, with great hopes but also in profound crises, 'a transition from a more static understanding of the order of reality as a whole to a more dynamic and evolutionary understanding.'[47] This transition is experienced nowadays in a vast number of ways. It is almost commonplace to remark that at present everything is subject to dissolution and change, and that there is hardly anything solid left to hold onto; hardly anything on whose firmness and validity we can build. We also constantly hear how the quest for the eternal salvation which only God can give us is increasingly changing into a quest for a temporal well being which we ourselves plan, organize, devise and fight for. But the philosophical and theological quest goes deeper. If history is the most inclusive horizon of all human understanding and behaviour, then the Absolute too can be expressed fundamentally only in history. We can also ask how it is possible in any meaningful way to continue the quest for the Absolute, for redemption and salvation, for God and his Kingdom, in an historicized world. How in present circumstances are we to speak meaningfully of Jesus Christ and the salvation he brought?

To answer that question, we must first of all ask: What is history? History is not simply a sequence of days, hours, years. And history is not exactly the same thing as development and evolution. There is history only where there is freedom. Augustine recognized that the flow of time is to be experienced only in the human spirit, in the intellect of man who by reason of his freedom can stand back from the individual moment and extend himself through memory into the past and by anticipation into the future. This past and future tension of the human spirit (its *distentio animae*) enables us to comprehend at one and the same time what no longer exists and what does not as yet exist.[48] External time and history then are grounded only in a synthesis which the human spirit makes on the basis of its inner sense of history and understanding of time.

In that sense, inward historicity enjoys the primacy over outward history. On the other hand the historicity grounded in human freedom is always actual freedom. It arises from the freedom of others, and is conditioned too by historical circumstances and by the whole tradition of freedom. History therefore is a human synthesis, and not one constructed by some abstract man, but a synthesis attempted by an actual man, and an actual freedom. Hence we may say: History is a process of reciprocity between subject and object, a mediation of world and man, in which the world determines man and man the world.[49]

The question therefore is how can we go on speaking about God and something absolute inside that kind of historical framework of thought? If reality is defined as a process of reciprocity, then everything is in flux. Nothing seems firm. Everything is relative. Surely then the assumption of an absolute in history is essentially contradictory? Can Christian hope be sustained within an historical view? I shall try to answer these questions from three viewpoints. None of these three arguments claims to be a proof in the strict sense. Any historical view of man requires man's ultimate destiny to be open *and* highly-nuanced and complex, and that it should be ultimately defined only through personal decision. Yet that decision cannot and must not be arbitrary. Wherever the ultimate meaning of existence is in question, the decision can be made only on a basis of ultimate responsibility. The following arguments are not intended to show that every man must logically become a Christian or must necessarily be already unconsciously and anonymously a Christian. All I wish to show is how the decision of faith can be supported in all intellectual honesty. Whoever proves more in this instance, actually proves less. No proof would make faith possible as faith; it would cancel it.

1. As a reciprocity of man and world, history is permeated with the dialectics of power and impotence.[50] On the one hand, by reason of his freedom, man overreaches all that is. He lives by wishful thoughts and images of a successful existence. He tries to found a new and better order in culture, politics, art and religion. He overreaches all facts and asks about the meaning of existence, about the one and entire significance of reality. He can know all that is finite as actually finite only in anticipation of an infinite horizon. He conceives the individual existent only in foreknowledge of existence as a whole. That anticipation, which he undertakes implicitly in every act of cognition, gives him distance from any particular instance of existence and offers space for freedom, decision and venture. Therefore man is greater than reality. He always enjoys a greater possibility than reality, and that possibility is the stage for his freedom of action. On the other hand reality is bigger than man. Man is already pregiven to himself in his freedom. He cannot already deduce the pure fact of his existence. The wonder that something exists at all and not nothing is the primal experience of philosophizing. Reality therefore inconceivably precedes man. It is ultimately inconceivable mystery. Therefore man is always frustrated by reality. And that frustration

finds its ultimate poignancy in death. The human corpse is still reality without any possibility. Reality encompasses man again at the end. Reality surrounds; it is greater than him.

Therefore we have a reciprocal restriction of facticity and transcendence, freedom and necessity, reality and possibility, power and impotence, the grandeur and poverty of man. We can go further. We can see that limitation more inwardly. The power and impotence of man in history are not two adjacent areas. Precisely in the fact that he reaches out in knowledge and desire beyond all that is, precisely in his greatness, man recognizes his finiteness and his poverty. Precisely in his transcendence he continually experiences his immanence. He continually experiences his immanence in his transcendence. But the converse is also true. In his poverty his greatness is shown in that he knows about his poverty and suffers from it. For he could not suffer from his poverty if he did not have at least an inkling of his greatness, and therefore knew that everything could and must be different.[51]

Nietzsche often remarked that the possible depth of human suffering almost determined the social hierarchy.[52] In suffering man experiences his own existential situation. Here he experiences himself as that being that exceeds itself for the sake of an infinite, and in that very process experiences its finiteness. His finiteness becomes his indication, sign and symbol of transcendence. Yet he has only a negative concept of that transcendence. If man as a finite being wished to conceive the infinite, he would have to devitalize it in the very same movement. At this point all dialectics is frustrated.[53] In the end man remains an open question to which he has no answer. He touches on an impenetrable mystery; he himself, indeed, is such a mystery. Man experiences transcendence as the constitutive non-inclusion of his existence in history.

The question is: How is human existence possible in this aporetic historical situation? Are ancient and modern tragedy, ancient and modern scepticism, to have the last word? Is man no more than a fragment, a torso? Against that, of course, we ask: Can man ever come to terms with that aporia? Is human existence, as a defiant venture, in view of the meaninglessness of reality, ultimately tenable? If Prometheus is excluded as a symbol of human existence, is Sisyphus to have the last word? Can we really stand up to history without any hope in the meaningfulness of history? Or does the exclusion of hope mean that all other human moral efforts are meaningless? Perhaps an 'as if' remains and we can behave as if there were some meaning in history (W. Schulz). But does that help us to suffer the experiences of life and history?

Here a thought of Kant's is relevant,[54] which Fichte, Schelling and Hegel developed, each in his own way. According to them, human freedom is possible only if — ultimately - freedom rules in reality as a whole.

Only if initially 'dead' nature and reality (impenetrable for and inconceivable by man) are wholly determined by freedom, and are a location and world of freedom, can human freedom become ultimately meaningful and human existence really succeed. But that all-determinative freedom cannot be the finite freedom of mankind. What we are concerned with here is an infinite freedom which is master of the factors which condition reality; that reality which is always beyond human grasp. But that means: Only if God exists as absolute creative Freedom is the world a possible realm of freedom for men. Kant calls that seeing the world as the Kingdom of God in which nature and freedom are reconciled. Of course Kant conceives this Kingdom of God as a moral and not as a messianic kingdom.[53] Yet he still recognizes the non-deducibility and mysteriousness of freedom. But as soon as the non-deducibility of freedom is taken seriously, the realm of freedom cannot be deduced as a necessary postulate of freedom. The realm of freedom is itself possible only in and through freedom. It must either be hoped for as an historically underivable entity, or conceived as a gift. The coming of the kingdom of freedom is not to be postulated; it can only be asked for: 'Thy kingdom come'. God's freedom, therefore, contrary to the conception atheistic humanism has of it, is not revealed as the boundary of human freedom, but as its ultimate ground. The hope of mankind is not that God is dead, but that he is a living God of history.

2. The dialectics of power and impotence in history is further refined by the phenomenon of evil. Historically, evil is certainly an empirically accessible reality. But at the same time it is an impenetrable mystery. Where does evil come from? Neither dualistic nor monistic philosophies have offered an acceptable answer. If human nature or history as such is conceived as absolutely evil, then we cannot explain our longing for good, and our suffering under evil. But if human nature is good of itself, how did it come to be perverted? Initially, all we can say when faced with these difficult questions is: Evil has its essential possibility in the basic structure of man and history as I have already described it.[56] Finite freedom is possible only within a horizon of infinity. It is not something hard and fast, but is so to speak in suspense, pending. That is why it can go doubly wrong. It can absolutize its impotence and its finiteness *(acedia)*; it can become comfortable, dull and indolent, petty-bourgeois, sceptical, dispirited and faint-hearted. It can also absolutize its power and dynamism to infinity *(superbia)*, and turn supercilious, proud and presumptuous. Both forms of error, haughty and pusillanimous behaviour, cannot support the tension which is constitutive for man: the *mean* which is being human. Evil therefore may be described not merely as a lack of being but as a perversion of being: as the perversion of the meaning of existence. Evil is either the humiliation or the violation of man. It brings man to the point of self-contradiction. For that reason, evil is absolute meaninglessness and perversion.

A man who finds that he is contradicting himself cannot merely come to terms with the reality of evil. If he is unwilling to surrender his human nature, he has to protest against the reality of evil and commit himself to a better order of things. Yet as soon as we begin to pit ourselves against existing injustice for the sake of more justice, we notice that in this endeavour too we are subject to the trammels of evil. If we try to oppose an unjust use of force, we are ourselves compelled to use force. And so we carry into the new order for which we are striving the seeds of further disorder and embitterment. We find ourselves in a perpetual vicious circle of guilt and revenge, violence and counter-violence. If hope is to prove possible in spite of the power of evil, and if human existence and history are to succeed, that can happen only on the basis of a qualitatively new beginning which is not derivable from history. Horkheimer talks in this connexion of 'longing for what is wholly other'. Adorno says: 'The only form of philosophy which could be justified in the face of despair, is the attempt to see everything in the perspective of redemption. Knowledge has no light other than that which shines from redemption onto the world. Everything else is empty and imitative, sheer technical effects.'[57]

Whenever man refuses to despair in the meaning of history, and instead hopes against all hope for a meaning of his human existence, he is supported by a pre-comprehension of salvation and redemption. Ultimate hope is possible in history only on the basis of a qualitatively new beginning which is not derivable from history itself. And that new start is the outward worldly form of what the Christ message means by redemption, grace and salvation.

3. The two negative phenomena of finiteness and evil mean that history cannot fulfil itself of itself. Ultimately it is an open question to which it can give no answer. But who says that there is any answer? Perhaps everything is empty and meaningless in the end? Is everything that has been said about hope up to now no more than an empty postulate? It would be, if there were no signs of hope being answered — signs which in their turn point beyond themselves and allow us to hope in a new and greater fulfilment. The New Testament writers and the Fathers of the Church saw such signs of pre-fulfilment mainly in the prophecies and miracles of the Old Testament. In another, essentially weaker and more ambiguous way they discerned fragmentary traces of the *Logos* (who appeared in Jesus Christ in his fulness) in the entire history of religions, in human philosophies and cultures. They tried in that way to decypher all reality in a perspective that looked to and from Christ. That is the only way in which the declaration 'Jesus is the Christ' can be made truly plausible.

The question is how we in an evolutionary world-order are to make Jesus Christ's eschatological claim 'understandable'. Teilhard de Chardin did more than anyone in that direction. He tried to describe a clear line from cosmogenesis to anthropogenesis and thence to Christogenesis. But his theory is bound up with a number of scientific questions in which a theologian is not directly competent. Therefore Karl Rahner has — with a similar result — offered a more philosophical and theological interpretation, which is valid quite apart from its transcendental-philosophical presuppositions. Rahner starts from the premiss[58] that it is characteristic of evolution that the lower will always give rise to the higher. What is said to take place is not only a process of becoming different, but one of becoming *more* and *new*: the achievement of a greater fulness of being. But that *more* is no mere addition to what is already there. On the one hand it is effected by what has been up to now, but on the other hand it is a real increase of being. 'That means however that coming to be, if it is to be taken seriously, has to be conceived as actual self-transcendence, self-surpassing, active retrieval of its fulness by emptiness'.[59] This phenomenon of self-transcendence is to be found not only at individual points of the process of evolution, at say the origin of the first man, but fundamentally at the genesis of each new man. Something in the physiologico-biological act of generation which is more than mere *physis* and mere *bios*: a spirit-person. The occurrence of each new man is a miracle.

How is something like that possible? In the act of evolution and procreation reality becomes not only ecstatically self-transcendent but at the same time creative. Its movement of transcendence is not an empty wish and promise but is accompanied by fulfilment. But if the notion of self-transcendence 'does not make nothingness the ground of being, emptiness as such the source of fulness, if in other words the metaphysical principle of causality is preserved, then that self-transcendence . . . can be conceived only as happening by the power of the absolute fulness of being'.[60]

The miracle of becoming something more and something new can only be explained through participation in a creative fulness of being. This absolute fulness of being cannot be an essential constituent of the finite active, for if that finite already possessed the absolute fulness of being as its very own, it would no longer be capable of real becoming in time and history. Nevertheless that does not mean that it is to be thought of as an external intervention, for otherwise not evolution but something positively new would arise but not through mediation with existing reality. Therefore that absolute fulness of being must inwardly enable what takes effect finitely to reach the point of really active self-transcendence. In conceiving active self-transcendence, the notion of 'self' and the concept of 'transcendence' are to be taken seriously if the phenomenon of becoming, of coming to be, is to be explained. We have to take into account extraordinary events which are not miracles in the sense of occurrences which violate the natural order.

For those who have eyes to see the world is both filled with instances of hope and replete with examples of fulfilment. Wherever the New becomes and comes to be, some part of meaning and fulfilment is revealed which allows us to hope in ultimate meaning. History is not only moved by the quest and hope for salvation but contains signs of salvation which alone give meaning to hope in an ultimate meaning and a universal salvation in history. These signs of salvation are to be found wherever the underivably new comes into being. Wherever new life originates hope breaks forth. (As for Vergil in his fourth eclogue, for us today the child is the sign and symbol of salvation).

This interpretation becomes problematic as soon as we construct a great teleological process of evolution which − to be sure not necessarily, but clearly not quite by accident − comes to a point in man and finally in Christ. Here I must part company with Teilhard de Chardin and Karl Rahner. That kind of accommodation of Christology to an evolutionary world-order is not only theologically dubious; it does not accord with the facts. We can observe and demonstrate only a few steps in evolution; we can never see the evolutionary process as a whole. The individual stages are always in some way tentative, trivial and even futile. There is no such thing as one ascending evolutionary process. There are signs and pointers to meaning *in* the world; but there are no signs of a meaning *of* the world: of an all-inclusive context of meaning with its ultimate crown in Jesus Christ. The signs of meaning and fulfilment are opposed by signs of meaninglessness, non-fulfilment, futility, and an inexplicable creaturely suffering. Are we justified in describing those merely as by-products and waste-products of development? We cannot conceive a meaning of reality but we have reason to *hope for* such a thing. We can go further and say: Jesus Christ can only fulfil all reality if he also accepts the ultimately distressing — the agonal — aspects of reality. That means, if he is not merely to be set in a pure history of ascent, passing as it were over the dead bodies of time on its way up. The compelling and convincing aspect of Jesus Christ is that in him both the greatness and the inadequacy of mankind are accepted, and accepted infinitely. In *that* sense, Jesus Christ is the fulfilment of history.

We have moved gradually away from the modern idea of subjectivity. The alternative however came out of the inner dialectic of modern thought itself: from the idea of human freedom. The category of the unique and the new is characteristic of freedom. In his freedom man forever transcends himself. In so doing he is a question for himself — a question to which he knows no answer. In his freedom a man is placed in the world in solidarity with all other men. There is no such thing as 'man' pure and simple, man as such. Man exists only in the context of a circumambient historical whole. The experience of the constitutive finiteness of man veers away from the modern approach to human subjectivity. Together, both viewpoints give rise to a new form of experience of transcendence, which from the start refutes the charge that it is flight from the world. It is neither flight above nor flight ahead. If the borders of finiteness and the reality of evil are to be taken seriously, both those roads are closed. But if man refuses to give in, in spite of all finiteness and all evil, if he opts for meaning and fulfilment in history, then history is to be deciphered and understood as symbolic. In that symbol, we see something like a negative image of the quest and hope for salvation. There are countless signs of that hope in history. It will always be assailed by doubt, but it will live in expectation of an unambiguous sign.

Questioning, seeking for meaning, justice, freedom and life, hope turns to Jesus Christ and asks: 'Are you he who is to come, or shall we look for another?' (Mt 11.3).

Notes

[1]P. Vergilius Maro, Ecloga IV, in: *idem, Opera,* ed. F.A. Hirtzel (Oxonii, 1963) (=1900); cf M. Seckler, *Hoffnungsversuche* (Freiburg, 1972), pp. 27-32.

[2] M. Hengel, *Judentum und Hellenismus. Studien zu ihrer Begegnung unter besonderer Berücksichtigung Palästinas bis zur Mitte des 2. Jahrhunderts vor Christus* (Tübingen, 1969); ET: *Judaism and Hellenism* (London, 1975); *idem, Die Zeloten. Untersuchungen zur jüdischen Freiheitsbewegung in der Zeit von Herodes I. bis 70n. Chr.* (Leiden-Cologne, 1961).

[3] F. Gogarten, *Verhängnis und Hoffnung der Neuzeit. Die Säkularisierung als theologisches Problem* (Stuttgart, 1953); D. Bonhoeffer, *Widerstand und Ergebung. Briefe aus der Haft*, ed. E. Bethge (Munich, 1958); *ET: Letters and Papers from Prison* (London, 1971); H. Lübbe, *Säkularisierung. Geschichte eines ideenpolitischen Begriffs* (Freiburg, 1965); J.B. Metz, 'Versuch einer positiven Deutung der bleibenden Weltlichkeit der Welt', in: HPTh II/2, pp. 239-67; *idem, Zur Theologie der Welt*, (Mainz, 1968); *ET: Theology of the World* (London, 1969); H. Blumenberg, *Die Legitimität der Neuzeit* (Frankfurt a. M. 1966); J. Matthes, *Religion und Gesellschaft. Einführung in die Religionssoziologie* I, (Reinbek, 1967), esp. pp. 74ff; H. Bartsch (ed.), *Probleme der Entsakralisierung* (Munich-Mainz, 1970); H. Mühlen, *Entsakralisierung. Ein Epochales Schlagwort in seiner Bedeutung für Zukunft der christlichen Kirchen* (Paderborn, 1971).

[4] 'At first subjectivity is only formal, but it is the real possibility of substantiality. Subjectivity in and for itself – intrinsic subjectivity – consists in the subject determining to fulfil its universality, to realize it in positing itself as identical with substance'. G.W.F. Hegel, *Einleitung in die Geschichte der Philosophie (Introduction to the History of Philosophy)*, ed., J. Hoffmeister (3rd ed., Hamburg, 1959), p. 244.

[5] Cf J.B. Metz, *Erlösung und Emanzipation, op. cit., p. 121.*

[6] M. Greiffenhagen, 'Emanzipation', in: *Historisches Wörterbuch der Philosophie* II, ed., J. Ritter (Darmstadt, 1972), pp. 448ff; G. Rohrmoser, *Emanzipation und Freiheit* (Munich, 1970); R. Spaemann, 'Autonomie, Mündigkeit, Emanzipation', in: *Kontexte 7 (Stuttgart-Berlin, 1971), pp. 94-102.*

[7] Kant, *Beantwortung der Frage: Was ist Aufklärung? (An Answer to the Question: What is Enlightenment?)*, in: W. vol. 6, ed., W. Weischedel (Darmstadt, 1964), pp. 53, 55.

[8] K. Marx, *Zur Judenfrage (On the Jewish Question)*, in: Karl-Marx-Studienausgabe, vol. I (Darmstadt, 1971), p. 497.

[9] Cf *ibid.*, p. 459.

[10] *Ibid.*, p. 453.

[11] H. Fries, 'Mythos-Mythologie', in: SM III; *ET:* 'Myth' in *Sacramentum Mundi*, vol. 4, pp. 152-6; J. Sloke *et al.*, 'Mythos und Mythologie', in: RGG IV, pp. 1263-84.

[12] Cf C. Hartlich, W. Sachs, *Der Ursprung des Mythosbegriffes, op. cit.*

[13] D.F. Strauss, *Das Leben Jesu (The Life of Jesus)*, vol. I, p. 750.

[14] *Op. cit.*, vol. 2, pp. 734ff.

[15] Cf A. Schweitzer, *Geschichte*, pp. 444ff.

[16] *Ibid.*, p. 519.

[17] *Ibid.*, p. 522.

[18] E. Troeltsch, *Die Bedeutung der Geschichtlichkeit Jesu für den Glauben* (Tübingen, 1911), p. 9.

[19] R. Bultmann, 'Neues Testament und Mythologie', in: *Kerygma und Mythos* I, ed., H. W. Bartsch (Hamburg-Bergstedt, 1967) pp. 15-48; *idem*, 'Zur Frage der Entmythologisierung', in: KuM III (Hamburg-Volksdorf, 1952), pp. 179-208; *idem*, 'Zum Problem der Entmythologisierung', in: GuV IV, (Tübingen, 1967), pp. 128-137; *idem*, 'Jesus Christus und die Mythologie', in GuV IV, pp. 141-89; 'New Testament and Mythology' in: *Kerygma and Myth* (London, 1953), pp. 102-23; *Jesus Christ and Mythology* (New York, 1958); 'The case for Demythologizing: A Reply to Karl Jaspers' in: *Myth and Christianity: An Inquiry into the Possibility of Religion without Myth* (New York, 1958), pp. 57-71; *Existence and Faith* (London, 1961).

[20] R. Bultmann, 'Neues Testament und Mythologie', *op. cit.*, p. 22, n. 2.

[21] *Ibid.*, p. 48.

[22] F. Buri, 'Entmythologisierung oder Entkerygmatisierung der Theologie', in: *Kerygma*

und Mythos II, (Hamburg-Volksdorf, 1952), p. 97.

[23] H. Halbfas, *Fundamentalkatechetik. Sprache und Erfahrung im Religionsunterricht* (Stuttgart, 1968); *ET: Fundamental Catechetics* (New York, 1970).

[24] J. Nolte, *'Sinn' oder* 'Bedeutung' Jesu?, op. cit., p. 327.

[25] E. Schillebeeckx, 'Der "Gott Jesu" und der "Jesus Gottes". in: *Concilium* 10 (1974); 'The "God of Jesus" and the "Jesus of God" in: *Concilium,* vol. 3, No. 10 (1974), pp. 110-26.

[26] Cf L. Feuerbach, 'Notwendigkeit einer Veränderung' ('The Need for a Change') (1842/43), in: Kleine Schriften (Frankfurt a. M., 1966), p. 225.

[27] Cf F.W.J. Schelling, *Philosophische Untersuchungen über das Wesen der menschlichen Freiheit und die damit zusammenhängenden Gegenstände (Philosophical Investigations into the Nature of Human Freedom)* (1809), in: W IV, ed. M. Schröter (Munich, 1958), p. 243.

[28] See in this regard Karl Rahner's various essays on Christ and Christology in *Schriften,* I, III, IV, V, VII, VIII, IX, X; *ET: Theological Investigations,* vols, 1, 3, 4, 5, 7, 8, 9, 10. See also K. Rahner, *Ich glaube an Jesus Christus* (Einsiedeln, 1968); art. 'Jesus Christus' in SM II; *ET:* 'Jesus Christ: IV' in: *Sacramentum Mundi,* vol. 3, pp. 192-209; K. Rahner, W. Thüsing, *Christologie - systematisch und exegetisch* (QD, vol. 55) (Freiburg, 1972).

[29] Cf *idem, Christologie,* pp. 47, 65-8; *idem, Schriften X: ET: Theological Investigations,* vol. 10; *idem,* 'Gnade als Mitte menschlicher Existenz', *in: HerKorr* 28 (1974), p. 87.

[30] *Idem, Schriften* IV; *ET: Theological Investigations,* vol. 4.

[31] Cf *idem, Christologie,* p. 60.

[32] Cf *ibid.*

[33] *Idem, Schriften* I; *ET: Theological Investigations,* vol. 1.

[34] On the following, see p. Eicher, *Die anthropologische Wende. Karl Rahners philosophischer Weg vom Wesen des Menschen zur personalen Existenz* (Fribourg, 1970), pp. 55-64.

[35] Cf K. Rahner, *Christologie, op. cit.,* pp. 18ff.

[36] On the following, see *idem, Schriften* IV; TI, vol. 4; *idem, Christologie,* pp. 20ff, 65ff.

[37] Cf *idem, Schriften* IV; *ET: TI* vol. 4.

[38] *Ibid.*

[39] *Idem, Schriften* I; *ET; TI* vol. 1.

[40] See Rahner's essays on world history and salvation history, Christianity and the non-Christian religions, ecclesiastical piety in *Schriften* V. *ET: Theological Investigations,* vol. 5; on anonymous Christians in S VI, TI 5; on atheism and implicit Christianity in S IX, TI 8; on anonymous Christianity in S IX, TI 9 and SX, TI 10. See also A. Röper, *Die anonymen Christen* (Mainz, 1963); K. Riesenhuber, 'Der anonyme Christ nach Karl Rahner', in: ZkTh 86 (1964), pp. 286-303.

[41] Cf K. Rahner, *Schriften* IV; *ET* TI, vol. 4.

[42] On the debate with Rahner, see especially H. Urs von Balthasar, *Karl Barth. Darstellung und Deutung seiner Theologie* (Cologne, 1962), pp. 302-12; E. Simons 'Philosophie der Offenbarung' in *Auseinandersetzung mit "Hörer des Wortes" von Karl Rahner* (Stuttgart, 1966); A. Gerken, *Offenbarung und Transzendenzerfahrung. Kritische Thesen zu einer künftigen Dialogischen Theologie* (Düsseldorf, 1969); B. van der Heijden, *Karl Rahner. Darstellung und Kritik seiner Grundpositionen* (Einsiedeln, 1973); C. Fabro, *La svolta antropologica di Karl Rahner* (Torino, 1974); K.P. Fischer, *Der Mensch als Geheimnis. Die Anthropologie Karl Rahners* (Freiburg, 1974).

[43] K. Rahner, *Christologie, op. cit.,* pp. 20ff.

[44] Cf J.E. Kuhn, *Katholische Dogmatik* I (2nd ed., Tübingen, 1859), pp. 228 ff.

[45] H. Urs von Balthasar, *Herrlichkeit. Eine theologische Ästhetik,* vol. III/2, part 2 (Einsiedeln, 1969), p. 147.

[46] Cf D.F. Strauss, *Das Leben Jesu, kritisch bearbeitet (Life of Jesus),* vol. 2, p. 734.

[47] Vatican II, Pastoral Constitution *Gaudium et Spes,* 5.

[48] Augustine, *Confessions* XI.

[49] This dialectical notion of reality is offered by W. Schulz, *Philosophie in der veränderten Welt* (Pfullingen, 1972), pp. 10, 143f, 470, 472, 602-9, 841-54.

[50] See, on the following R. Spaemann, 'Gesichtspunkte der Philosophie', in: H.J. Schultz (ed.), *Wer ist das eigentlich – Gott?* (Munich, 1969), pp. 59-65; *idem*, 'Die Frage nach der Bedeutung des Wortes "Gott"', in: *Internationale katholische Zeitschrift* I (1972), pp. 54-72.

[51] Cf Pascal, *Pensèes*, various editions.

[52] F. Nietzsche, *Jenseits von Gut und Böse (Beyond Good and Evil)*, in: W vol. 2, ed., K. Schlechta (7th ed., Darmstadt, 1973), p. 744.

[53] That was acknowledged mainly by the later Schelling. Cf W. Kasper, *Das Absolute in der Geschichte. Philosophie und Theologie in der Spätphilosophie Schellings* (Mainz, 1965). Therefore I do not follow Rahner, Bouillard, and so on, in preferring the Blondel tradition in this respect. Instead I adhere to the apologetical emphasis which derives from Pascal.

[54] Kant, *Kritik der praktischem Vernunft (Critique of Practical Reason)*, A 223-237, in: W IV, pp. 254-64.

[55] Cf *idem, Die Religion innerhalb der Grenzen der blossen Vernunft (Religion within the Bounds of Pure Reason)*, B208, in: W IV, p. 803.

[56] Cf B. Welte, *Über das Böse. Eine thomistische Untersuchung* (QD, vol. 6) (Freiburg, 1959).

[57] T.W. Adorno, *Minima Moralia. Reflexionen aus dem beschädigten Leben* (Frankfurt a. M., 1970), p. 333.

[58] Cf K. Rahner, 'Die Christologie innerhalb einer evolutiven Weltanschauung', in: Schriften V (Einsiedeln, 1962) pp. 183-221; *ET: 'Christology within an Evolutionary View of the World' in: Theological Investigations*, vol. 5 (London, 1966), pp. 157-92; K. Rahner, P. Overhage, *Das Problem der Hominisation. Über den biologischen Ursprung des Menschen* (QD, vol. 12/13) (Freiburg, 1961); *ET: Hominization* (Freiburg and New York, 1965).

[59] K. Rahner, *Schriften* V, p. 191; *ET: Theological Investigations*, vol. 5, *op. cit.*, p. 164.

[60] *Ibid.*, p. 191; *ET:* p. 165.

II. THE HISTORY AND DESTINY OF JESUS CHRIST

I. JESUS' ACTIVITY

A. THE EARTHLY JESUS

I.THE ACTIVITY OF JESUS (A SUMMARY)

In the early years of this century, various theses were propounded which all assert that Jesus never lived, and that the story of Jesus is a myth or legend. These claims have long since been exposed as historical nonsense. There can be no reasonable doubt that Jesus of Nazareth lived in Palestine in the first three decades of our era, probably from 6-7 BC to 30 AD.[1] That is a fact. 'The manger, the carpenter's son, the orator among ordinary people, the gallows at the end, all this is the stuff of history, and not the gilding of legend'.[2] We may therefore confidently begin from the premises that Jesus was born in the reign of the Emperor Augustus (23 BC — 14 AD; cf Lk 2.1), and carried out his ministry during the reign of Tiberius (14 — 37 AD); that at the same time Herod, whom he calls a fox (Lk 13.32), was tetrarch of Galilee (4 BC — 39 AD; cf Lk 3.1); and that Jesus died under the Roman procurator Pontius Pilate (Mk 15.1 etc.). In addition, we can point to a general consensus among exegetes (who, in the last ten years particularly, have concentrated on the question of the historical Jesus), that the characteristics of the activity and preaching of Jesus stand out with relative clarity from the darkness of history. The Jesus we have as a result is a figure of unparalleled originality. Attempts to maintain the opposite can safely be left to amateur theologians.

Biblical scholars also agree that the state of the sources makes it impossible to write a biography of Jesus. The New Testament accounts mention the historical background only in passing, if at all, and the extra-biblical sources are more than inadequate. We are told nothing about any experience by Jesus of a call. We know just as little about his physical presence and looks, and even less about his psychology. The gospels are less interested in the actors at the front of the stage of history and in historical relations than in the fulfilment in history of God's plan. The gospels are intended as witnesses to faith in the earthly and risen Jesus. They present their evidence in the form of a narrative; and they interpret that narrative in the light of their faith. An understanding of this point does not justify any exaggerated scepticism about the historical basis of the New Testament narrative, but it does rule out any uncritical, pseudo-biblical fundamentalism.

In particular the infancy narratives, or stories of Jesus' childhood in Matthew and Luke offer very little material for tracing the course of his life. They describe Jesus' early life on Old Testament models, especially by analogy with the story of Moses.[4] Their concern is more theological than biographical; their purpose is to say: 'Jesus is the fulfilment of the Old Testament.' There is also uncertainty about the course and length of Jesus' public activity. According to the three synoptic gospels the scene of Jesus' public activity was mainly Galilee and the cities about the Lake of Genesareth. From the period of the public ministry the synoptics report only one visit of Jesus to Jerusalem, during which he was imprisoned and sentenced to death. If we had only the synoptics we would have to assume that Jesus' public activity lasted only about a year. John, on the other hand, says that Jesus spent three passover feasts in Jerusalem (2.13; 6.4;11.55) and that he made a total of four journeys between Galilee and Jerusalem (2.13; 5.1; 7.10; 12.12). According to the fourth gospel, the scene of events is mainly Jerusalem. From this it would seem that we must allow for two or three years of public activity by Jesus. The synoptics also imply that there had been conflicts (Mt 23.37-38), even before the last great collision, which resulted in Jesus' death. The fourth gospel's presentation of events, according to which Jesus attracted the hostility of the Jewish hierarchy by successive visits to Jerusalem and several confrontations, makes his fate more intelligible. It seems that Jesus' activity in Galilee there commenced with a relatively successful period. As Jesus was increasingly faced with the bitter hostility of the official representatives of contemporary Judaism, he retired into the narrower circle of his disciples, until he was taken prisoner and sentenced to death on the cross during his last stay in Jerusalem.[5]

We are on slightly firmer historical ground in regard to the beginning and end of Jesus' public life, which began with John's baptism of Jesus in the Jordan and ended with the death on the cross in Jerusalem. Jesus' public life can be fitted fairly well between these two fixed points.

John's baptism of Jesus is reported by all four evangelists (Mk 1.9-11 par). This report cannot be seen as pure theology of the Early Church, with no historical core; for the early Christian communities it was more of a hindrance than a help to their preaching of Christ.[6] For John's supporters, the fact that Jesus had submitted to baptism by John could have been a valuable support for the claim that Jesus himself had submitted to John, and that not Jesus but John was the crucial eschatological figure. We may therefore assume that John's baptism of Jesus is an historical fact. Hence we may assume that Jesus had been a member of John's baptismal movement, and accepted its leader's eschatological message. According to Matthew, John preached in terms similar to those used later by Jesus: 'Repent, for the Kingdom of heaven is at hand' (Mt 3.2). But Jesus began a ministry of his own, which made even John curious, excited and uncertain (Mt 11.2-6). Whereas in John's preaching the coming of God's rule is marked by judgment, Jesus proclaims it with the stress on God's love and compassion for sinners. Jesus' theme is 'Blessed are you. . . ' (Mt 5.3-12; 13.16-17 and passim). Jesus' message is a message of joy: God's final and definitive offer of grace.

The new and surprising thing about Jesus' message appears above all in his behaviour. Jesus' association with sinners and the ritually impure (Mk 2.16 etc.), his breaking of the Jewish Sabbath commandment (Mk 2.23-28 etc.) and the regulations on purity (Mk 7.1-13 etc.) are among the best-attested features of his life. It seems that quite early a satirical jingle was made up about him: 'a glutton and a drunkard, a friend of tax collectors and sinners' (Mt 11.19). Jesus' behaviour in this regard drew attention and even aroused anger, but how little it had to do directly with what is normally thought of today as social concern or revolution can be seen from the fact that the tax collectors were in no sense the exploited, but the exploiters, who collaborated with the Roman occupying power. Jesus had come for them too; his message of God's love was also for them. Jesus' behaviour can only be understood in connexion with his message of the rule of God and the will of God. God is a God of people, people of all sorts, and his commandment exists for the sake of people (Mk 2.27; 3.4). The essence of God's will is therefore love of God and other people (Mk 12.30-31 par.). Its claim on a person is absolute and total. It cannot be contained in a set of casuistic laws. It is not a heroic human achievement, but an answer to the boundless compassion and forgiveness of God's love, which makes the sun rise on the evil and on the good (Mt 5.45). Jesus' miracles and his exorcisms, which cannot be denied a historical basis,[7] also belong in this context. They also illustrate the way in which the coming of God's kingdom in Jesus means men's salvation in body and soul, and that that salvation is offered unconditionally to anyone who repents and believes.

From the beginning, Jesus' activities obviously aroused wonder, fascination and enthusiasm, and at the same time muttering, rejection, anger and hatred. Nothing like this had ever been seen or heard before. To a pious Jew that sort of behaviour and message were tantamount to scandal, even blasphemy (Mk 2.7 etc.). The message about a God whose love was directed even to sinners challenged the Jewish conception of divine holiness and righteousness. It very soon won Jesus the enmity and hatred of the official representatives of the judaism of the day. His revolutionary new message about God had to make him seem a false prophet. The penalty for that in Jewish law was death. (Dt 18.20). Jesus' violent end was written into the logic of his work.

With Jesus' death on the cross we reach the second fixed point in his life. The historicity of the inscription on the cross, reported by all four evangelists, can hardly be questioned.[8] It records the reason for his condemnation: 'King of the Jews' (Mk 15.26 par.). Jesus was executed as a messianic pretender. It is very unlikely that he described himself as Messiah, but his eschatological preaching clearly aroused messianic hopes and started a messianic movement. Messianic claims were not a capital offence in Jewish law, but the messianic movement which Jesus inspired could be used as a pretext for denouncing him to the Roman procurator Pontius Pilate as a political agitator and thus involving the Roman penalty for agitators, which was crucifixion. The result was Jesus' crucifixion by the Romans as a political rebel.

This fact has often led to speculation that Jesus held a purely political, theocratic, idea of Messiahship, that he was a political troublemaker, perhaps even something of guerilla leader.[9] That is out of the question. Jesus' message of love, in particular his commandment to love our enemies (Mt 5.39-48) rules out such an interpretation. Jesus wanted to heal wounds, not to inflict them. He did not take the path of violence but the way of non-violence and service. Love, as it were, entraps evil and by doing so it overcomes it and creates the possibility of a new start. Jesus brought about a much more radical revolution than a political upheaval could have produced. By the cross '. . .what was counted most lowly was made most high. That is a direct expression of complete revolution against the status quo, against current opinion. When the dishonouring of existence is made the highest honour, all ties of human association are fundamentally attacked, shaken and dissolved.'[10] The revolution Jesus brings is the revolution of unrestricted love in a world of egotism and power.

Who was Jesus of Nazareth? On the one hand he is regarded as the messianic bringer of salvation, on the other as a blasphemer and false prophet or as a rebel. Herod derides him as a fool (Lk 23.6-12) and his closest relatives regard him as mad (Mk 3.21). In public opinion the most widely varied reports about him seem to be in circulation. It was said that he was John the Baptist risen from the dead, the risen Elijah, the long-awaited eschatological prophet (cf Mk 6.14-16; 8.28 par.). Later history has added similar judgments. The Life of Jesus library and the Image of Jesus gallery are packed and wide-ranging. Even today efforts are made to extend it: Jesus the moral preacher, the humanist, the social reformer and revolutionary, the demagogue, the superstar, the nonconformist, the free man. In fact it was most of all the Lord's own Spirit which was reflected in Jesus. All the labels capture individual aspects, but never the whole phenomenon of Jesus of Nazareth. Jesus cannot be superficially modernized. He is a Jew living in the world of the Old Testament, and his intellectual roots reach back into that world. Ultimately, however, Jesus fits into no categories; he is the man who destroys all categories.

Jesus is different from John the Baptist. He does not lead a life of withdrawn asceticism apart from the world. He does not cut himself off and retreat into a monastery like the Qumran sect. He approaches people and lives among them. In one sense he could be said to be an enlightened secular man. To him the world is God's good creation; and its things are good gifts to mankind. He is not too proud to eat with the rich or to be supported by pious women (Lk 8.2-3). Nor, on the other hand, is he a 'liberal' like the Sadducees. He does not think he can satisfy his religious obligations by the correctness of the orthodox, and specific cultic and ritual observances. The will of God takes him over totally. Many of his sayings reveal a total claim and fundamental seriousness. He is concerned about everything. This 'abandoning all' leads him to a break with his family (Mk 3.20-21; 31-35), makes him homeless in this world (Mt 8.20). But he is no zealot or fanatic. His zeal is never brutish. And he is different from the Pharisees. He is not pious in the average meaning of the word. He teaches neither religious technique nor moral casuistry. He calls God his Father, whose love breaks down all categories and frees people from anxiety (Mt 6.25-34).

God's love claims Jesus totally for others. He wants nothing for himself, but everything for God and others. Among his disciples he is like a servant; he does not disdain even the most menial slave's work (Lk 22.26-27). He did not come to be served but to serve (Mk 10.45). He does not belong to the establishment, but comes from humble origins and retains a feeling for the everyday distress and troubles of the poor (Mt 9.36). His respect for women is striking in a man of the ancient world. He does not look on poverty and disease as punishments from God; the poor and sick are particular objects of God's love. He goes after the lost (Lk 15). Most striking of all, even at the time, was that he brought even sinners and misfits, the ritually impure and the outcasts, into his company. He even invites them to eat with him. But there is no sign of hatred or envy of the rich. He gets along even with exploiters, the tax collectors; he summons one or two of them into the immediate circle of his disciples (Mk 2.13-17). Class-war slogans find no direct support in Jesus. His fight is not against political authorities, but against the daemonic powers of evil. He neither leads a guerrilla war nor organizes an agrarian reform movement. He does not systematically heal all the sick. Jesus has no programme. There is nothing planned or organized about his career. He does the will of God as he recognizes it here and now. Everything else he leaves with childlike trust to God, his father. It is in prayer to the Father that he has his deepest roots (Mk 1.35; 6.46 etc.). The final end of his service to others is that men should recognize the goodness of God and praise him (Mk 2.12 etc.). He is not just the man for others, but the man from God and for God.

In his outward activity Jesus has some similarity with the scribes. Like a rabbi, he teaches and is surrounded by a circle of disciples; he argues about the interpretation of the law and is approached for legal decisions (Lk 12.13). However, he lacks theological study and ordination – the basic qualifications for being a scribe. Jesus is not a trained theologian. He speaks simply, vividly and directly. When he is addressed as 'Rabbi' (cf Mk 9.5 etc.), that is not a theologian's title like 'Professor', but a normal form of polite address. Ordinary people very soon see the difference between Jesus and theological experts and lawyers. Jesus teaches with authority (Mk 1.22, 27). The best description for him is 'prophet'. This was the common judgment of him (Mk 6.15; 8.28 etc.). His disciples regarded him as a prophet (Lk 24.19). And he placed himself in the line of the prophets (Mk 6.4; Lk 13.33; Mt 23.31-39). He was charged and condemned as a false prophet. But if, as Jesus said, the Baptist himself was more than a prophet and yet the least in the kingdom of God was greater than the Baptist (Mt 11.9-11), who was this who so lightly set himself above the Baptist? Not even the category of prophet can adequately describe the phenomenon of Jesus of Nazareth. Ultimately his claim can be comprised only in formulas of intensification: 'more than Jonah', more than Solomon' (Mt 12.41-42).

This 'more' has an eschatological ring. Jesus is not just one in the line of the prophets, but the eschatological one: the last, definitive, all-transcending prophet. He brings God's final word, his definitive will. He is filled with the Spirit of God (Mk 3.28-29; Mt 12.28 etc). In contemporary Jewish thinking, the Spirit of God had died out after the time of the prophets. The idea of the quenching of the Spirit expresses an awareness of God's distance. God is silent. All that can be heard now is the 'echo of his voice' (*bat-kol*). Not until the last times is the Spirit expected again. When Jesus is seen as a charismatic and a prophet of the last times, that means that the time has come. The painful period of God's absence is over. God has broken his silence. He lets his voice be heard again. He performs works of power among his people. The time of grace has dawned. But it was a very offputting dawn – quite different from what had been generally expected. Could a handful of uneducated and quite dubious people be the turning-point of world history? And Jesus' appearance was highly offensive to a pious Jew. Could anyone be a true prophet if he broke the law and went about with sinners? Was that how God spoke and acted? Jesus was accused of having an evil spirit (Mk 3.22-23). From the very beginning, he was caught in a conflict of opinions. He forced people to choose. The choice involved the foundations of Judaism and the Old Testament. In Jesus we finally come face to face with God. His life is the answer to the question 'Who is God?'.

Jesus does not fit into any category. Neither ancient nor modern, nor Old Testament categories are adequate to understand him. He is unique. He is and remains a mystery. He himself does little to illuminate this mystery. He is not interested in himself at all. He is interested in only one thing, but interested in it totally: God's coming rule in love. He is interested in God and human beings, in God's history with human beings. That is his mission. We get closer to the mystery of his person only when we look into that mission. The theological perspective is the only one which does not falsify the person and work of Jesus.

Notes

[1] On the problems of the chronology of Jesus' life, see W. Grundmann, *Die Geschichte Jesu Christi* (Berlin, 1957); H. U. Instinsky, *Das Jahr der Geburt Christi. Eine geschichtswissenschaftliche Studie* (Munich, 1957); A. Jaubert, *La date de la Cène. Calendrier biblique et liturgie chrétienne* (Paris, 1957); J. Jeremias, *Die Abendmahlsworte Jesu* (Göttingen, 3rd. ed., 1960); ET: *The Eucharistic Words of Jesus* (2nd rev. ed., London, 1966); E. Ruckstuhl, *Die Chronologie des letzten Mahles und des Leidens Jesu* (Einsiedeln, 1963); J. Blinzler, *Der Prozess Jesu* (4th ed., Regensburg, 1969); W. Trilling, *Fragen zur Geschichtlichkeit Jesu* (Düsseldorf, 1966).
[2] E. Bloch, *Das Prinzip Hoffnung* (Frankfurt am Main, 1959), p. 1482; *idem, Philosophy of the Future* (New York, 1970).
[3] On this, see *supra*, pp. 18, n.14, and 27, n.1, and references.
[4] See H. Schürmann, *Das Lukasevangelium,* Part 1 (Freiburg, 1969), pp. 18-145; R. Laurentin, *'Structure et théologie de Luc I-II', Etudes Bibliques* (1957); A. Vögtle, *Messias und Gottessohn. Herkunft und Sinn der matthäischen Geburts - und Kindheitsgeschichte* (Düsseldorf, 1971); K. H. Schelkle, *Theologie des Neuen Testaments,* vol. 2 (Düsseldorf, 1973), pp. 168-82.
[5] See F. Mussner, 'Gab es eine "galiläische Krise"?', in P. Hoffman (ed.), *Orientierung an Jesus. Zur Theologie der Synoptiker. Festschrift für J. Schmid* (Freiburg, 1973), pp. 238-52.
[6] See R. Bultmann, *Geschichte der synoptischen Tradition* (1921); ET: *The History of the Synoptic Tradition,* (Oxford, 2nd ed., Göttingen, 1968); M. Dibelius, *Formgeschichte op. lit.,* pp. 270ff.; F. Lentzen-Deis, *Die Taufe Jesu nach den Synoptikern,* Frankfurter Theologische Studien, 4 (Frankfurt, 1970).

[7] See below, ch. III, pp. 104ff.

[8] M. Dibelius, 'Das historische Problem der Leidensgeschichte', *Botschaft und Geschichte*, vol I (Tübingen, 1953), pp. 256, 282-3; N. A. Dahl, 'Der gekreuzigte Messias', in: H. Ristow and K. Matthiae (eds.), *Der historische Jesus*, pp. 159-60; F. Hahn, *Hoheitstitel*, p. 178; W. Trilling, *Fragen zur Geschichtlichkeit Jesu*, p. 134; H. Kessler, *Die theologische Bedeutung des Todes Jesu. Eine traditionsgeschichtliche Untersuchung* (Düsseldorf, 1970), p. 231.

[9] See the interpretations of R. Eisler, *Jesous basileus ou basileusas* (Heidelberg, 1929-39); J. Klausner, *Jesus von Nazareth. Seine Zeit, sein Leben und seine Lehre* 3rd ed., Jerusalem, 1952); J. Carmichael, *The Death of Jesus* (London, 1963); S. G. F. Brandon, *Jesus and the Zealots* (Manchester, 1967); also M. Hengel, *War Jesus Revolutionär?* (Stuttgart, 1970); ET: *Was Jesus a Revolutionist?* (Philadelphia, 1971); O. Cullman, *Jesus und die Revolutionären seiner Zeit. Gottesdienst, Gesellschaft, Politik* (Tübingen, 1970); E. Grässer, '"Der politisch gekreuzigte Messias". Kritische Anmerkungen zu einer politischen Hermeneutik des Evangeliums', *Text und Situation. Gesammelte Aufsätze* (Gütersloh, 1973), pp. 302-30.

[10] G. W. F. Hegel, *Vorlesungen über die Philosophie der Religion*, II/2, ed. Lasson (Hamburg, 1929), p. 161; ET: G. W. F. Hegel, *Lectures on the Philosophy of Religion* (London, 1895), p. 130.

II. JESUS' MESSAGE

II. JESUS' MESSAGE

1. THE MAIN THEME: THE COMING OF THE KINGDOM OF GOD

Mark sums up the content of Jesus' Gospel thus: 'The time is fulfilled, and the Kingdom of God is at hand; repent, and believe in the gospel' (Mk 1.15).[1] The general opinion now is that in this verse Mark is not reproducing an original saying of Jesus, but is offering his own summary. Nevertheless, there is no doubt that that summary correctly reproduces the heart of Jesus' message. Matthew's reference to the Kingdom of 'the heavens' instead of the Kingdom of God (cf Mt 4.17) is a common Jewish circumlocution for the name of God. Mark and Matthew summarize Jesus' message in the same way. The centre and framework of Jesus' preaching and mission was the approaching Kingdom of God. The Kingdom of God was what it was about.

Jesus nowhere tells us in so many words *what* that Kingdom of God is. He only says that it is near. He presupposes in his hearers a familiarity and an expectation which in our time can no longer be taken for granted. And even in his time expectations of the Kingdom of God differed widely. The Pharisees imagined it to be the complete fulfilment of the Torah; the Zealots thought of a political theocracy which they thought they would install by force of arms; and the apocalyptics looked forward to the coming of the new eon, the new heaven and the new earth. Jesus cannot be easily attached to any of these groups. His way of talking about the kingdom of God is remarkably open.

The openness of Jesus' Kingdom message has given scope in the course of history for the most varied interpretations. In older Catholic writing the Church was often seen as the historical instantiation of the kingdom of God. Since the Enlightenment the most influential interpretation has been the liberal view, going back to Kant, of the Kingdom of God as a highest Good, the kingdom of the spirit and freedom. It was only with Albert Schweitzer[2] and Weiss[3] that the consistent eschatological theme of Jesus' message was rediscovered. According to these scholars, Jesus did not want a better world; he wanted the new world: the new heaven and the new earth. However, their 'consistent eschatology' was in fact never wholly consistent because they regarded this eschatological and apocalyptic view as impossible to implement in the present, and so returned to an ethical view. This has recently reappeared in a different form in the various notions of political theology. Political theology says that Jesus' message of the Kingdom of God is a political and social utopia, to be created by kindness and brotherly love. Ultimately this dissolves God and his Kingdom into the kingdom of freedom, and the idea of the Kingdom of God loses its original meaning.

Today we can get at this original meaning of the concept of the Kingdom or Rule of God only with great difficulty. We relate the concept of rule to that of servitude. It has far too authoritarian a ring. We think of a theocracy which suppresses human freedom, and for us theocracy and theonomy are in direct contradiction to human freedom. In the ancient world it was completely the opposite. For the Jews of Jesus' time the Kingdom of God was the essence of the hope for the establishment of the ideal of a just ruler which was never fulfilled on earth. In that ancient Middle Eastern conception, justice did not consist primarily in impartial judgments, but in help and protection for the helpless, weak and poor. The coming of the Kingdom of God was expected to be the liberation from unjust rule and the establishment of the justice of God in the world. The Kingdom of God was the main element of the hope for salvation. And lastly its coming coincided with the establishment of the eschatological *shalom*, peace between nations, between individuals, within the individual and in the whole universe. Paul and John therefore correctly interpreted Jesus' intention when they spoke, not of the Kingdom of God, but of his justice or of life. In other words, Jesus' message of the coming of the Kingdom of God must be seen in the context of mankind's search for peace, freedom, justice and life.

To understand this connexion between mankind's fundamental hopes and the promise of the coming of the Kingdom, we must start from the fact that, in a view common to the whole Bible, man is seen as incapable of possessing peace, justice, freedom and life through his own unaided resources. Life is constantly threatened, freedom suppressed and sold, justice trampled under foot. This abandonment is so great that man cannot free himself by his own power. He cannot pull himself out of the swamp by his own bootlaces. This force which pre-exists the freedom of every individual and of the whole race, and keeps them from reaching freedom, is called by Scripture 'the demons'. The Bible sees man's alienation, slavery and abandonment, as the action of 'principalities and powers'.[4] The ideas on these matters which appear in many parts of the Bible are often influenced by mythology or superstition, but these mythological or superstitious statements express a fundamental human experience, which the biblical faith does no more than reinterpret. This experience is that things which are in origin created can develop into powers hostile to man. They determine human freedom in advance of every decision and therefore human beings can never be completely aware of them, let alone overcome them. They are responsible for the conflicts which characterize reality and for the tragic character of many situations.

It is only against this background that it becomes fully clear why a new, completely fresh start (which only God, as Lord of life and history, can give) is necessary. This new element, which did not exist before, which could not have been imagined, could not have been developed from what was before. It was simply impossible. This thing which God alone can provide, which God ultimately himself is, is what is meant by the Kingdom of God. It involves the meaning of God's being God and Lord, which at the same time means the humanity of human beings and the salvation of the world because it means liberation from the forces of evil which are hostile to creation, and reconciliation in place of the implacable antagonisms of the present world. That is the fundamental theme of Jesus' message and – as I shall try to show later – the basic mystery of his person. This means that the message of the imminent Kingdom of God is a fundamental concept of Christology. The task now is to explain and argue this view in detail.

2. THE ESCHATOLOGICAL CHARACTER OF THE KINGDOM OF GOD

The biblical hope for the coming of the kingdom of God is not just wishful thinking or a dream of utopia, nor does it derive from an insight into physical or historical laws or trends and tendencies in world development. It has its own source in Israel's particular historical experience. In the history of Israel, and especially in the exodus from Egypt and the journey through the wilderness, God revealed himself as a God who leads, who knows the way, as the Lord who can be relied upon absolutely and whose power knows no limits. At the point at which Israel came into contact with the great powers of the time, they had to develop their belief in Yahweh as Lord of history into one in Yahweh as Lord of the world. Only if God was the Lord of all nations could he deliver the people from their historical oppression in exile.

In the Old Testament the hope for the coming of the Kingdom of God grows out of these ideas about the Kingdom of Yahweh over Israel and the whole world. The statements about God as Lord and king are associated particularly with worship. The enthronement psalms celebrate Yahweh's present lordship with the cry: 'The LORD reigns' (or 'The LORD has become king', Ps 91.1; 96.10; 97.1; 99.1). This ritual acclamation soon acquired a universal dimension: 'Sing praises to our God, sing praises! Sing praises to our King, sing praises! For God is the King of all the earth; sing praises with a psalm! God reigns over the nations; God sits on his holy throne. The princes of the peoples gather as the people of the God of Abraham.' (Ps 47.6-9). 'Thy kingdom is an everlasting kingdom, and thy dominion endures throughout all generations' (Ps 145.13). The idea of the dominion of God is a late Jewish abstraction from the older credal formula 'God is Lord' or 'God is King'. It implies that God's dominion consists, not primarily in a kingdom in the sense of an area ruled by God, but in the establishment and recognition of God's Lordship in history.

In the course of its history, however, Israel learned through painful experience that the belief in the Lordship of God contrasted sharply with the world as it was. The result, particularly from the time of the great writing prophets, was a definite eschatologization of that belief. All the great saving acts of the past such as the making of the covenant and the exodus are now expected in intensified form in the future.[5] There now develops the hope of a new covenant and a new exodus. The coming of the Kingdom of God is also

74

now expected in the future. This hope is developed by apocalyptic in the expectation of a new age (*olam ha-ba*). In contrast to the royal Lordship of God, which is looked for as a historical event, the new age represents a transcendental reality. The process whereby the eschatological hope becomes transcendental first appears explicitly in the book of Daniel. Daniel also includes the vision of the four empires which succeed each other and which are crushed 'by no human hand' (Dan 2.34,35) in an instant (cf 2.35), after which God 'will set up a kingdom which shall never be destroyed, nor shall its sovereignty be left to another people' (2.44).

This examination of the development of the biblical idea of the kingdom of God shows that eschatological hope is not concerned with anticipatory reports of future events. More importantly, it is a word of comfort and hope in a situation of distress. Eschatological and apocalyptic statements transpose an experienced and hoped for salvation into a mode of fulfilment. They have to do with the certainty of the belief that at the end God will reveal himself as the absolute Lord of all the world.[6]

Jesus gives yet another twist to this hope. He proclaims that the eschatological hope is being fulfilled *now*. The transition from the old age no longer lies in the unattainable future, but is immediately at hand. 'The time is fulfilled, and the Kingdom of God is at hand' (Mk 1.14-15; Mt 4.17; cf Mk 10.7; Lk 10.9,11). The moment for which so many generations have waited is now here. The eyewitnesses can be told: 'Blessed are the eyes which see what you see! For I tell you that many prophets and kings desired to see what you see, and did not see it' (Lk 10.23-4). In his 'inaugural sermon' in Nazareth, Jesus can say, after the reading of the lesson from the prophet, 'Today this scripture has been fulfilled in your hearing' (Lk 4.21). The time to which the prophets' promise referred has come: 'The blind receive their sight and the lame walk, lepers are cleansed and the deaf hear, and the dead are raised up, and the poor have good news preached to them. (Mt 11.5; cf Is 35.5). All this is happening now and comes about in the words and actions of Jesus, which is why he adds: 'Blessed is he who takes no offence at me' (Mt 11.6).

Offence might well be taken. An unknown rabbi from a remote corner of Palestine with a handful of uneducated disciples and surrounded by a disreputable rabble — tax collectors, prostitutes, sinners — was this the new age, the Kingdom of God? The hard facts seemed, and still seem, to disprove Jesus' preaching. From the very beginning he was met with amazement and incredulous questions. Even his closest relatives thought he was mad (cf Mk 3.21). In this situation Jesus began to talk about the kingdom of God in parables. The Kingdom of God is like a grain of mustard seed, which is the smallest and most inconspicuous of all seeds but out of which comes a great tree (cf Mk 4.30-2 par.), or like a piece of leaven which is enough for three measures of flour (cf Mt 13.33). What is mightiest is hidden and active in what is most humble. The Kingdom of God comes in obscurity and failure. It is like seed which falls on stony, briar-choked ground and brings forth plentiful fruit (cf Mk 4.1-9 par.). The modern reader or hearer of these parables immediately thinks of organic growth, but the idea of natural development was alien to people of the ancient world. Between seed and fruit they saw, not continuous development, but contrast, and recognized a divine miracle. The parable is therefore not a purely external, accidental form, a purely illustrative aid to put over a lesson quite independent of it. It is clearly the appropriate form for talking about the Kingdom of God. The parable is the vehicle of the Kingdom of God which is itself a parable.[7] That is to say, it is hidden, but not in the way the apocalyptics meant, hidden away in heaven, but here and now in the most ordinary events of the present whose real significance no one can see. The 'secret of the Kingdom of God' (Mk 4.11) is nothing 'but the hidden dawn of the Kingdom of God itself in a world which to human eyes gives no sign of it'.[8]

The fact that the Kingdom of God is hidden for the present is reflected in the tension between present and future in the sayings of Jesus. We find two series of statements. One set talks about the appearance of the Kingdom in the here-and-now, whereas in the other the coming of the Kingdom is something to be looked forward to and prayed for. 'Thy kingdom come', runs the second petition of the Our Father (Mt 6.10; Lk 11.2).

This tension has in the past received very different interpretations.[9] One which will not stand is the psychological view which believes that as a result of inspirational ecstasy or of a specific prophetic attitude Jesus saw present and future as interwoven. Equally untenable is the solution proposed by tradition criticism, which attributes only statements about the present to Jesus, and tries to ascribe those about the future to the later community and its apocalyptic outlook. Both these interpretations fail to see that the tension of present and future belongs to the essence of the Kingdom of God preached by Jesus. Other solutions which disqualify themselves for the same reason are those which either stress only the future statements (the consistent eschatology or consistent future view held by scholars such as J. Weiss, Albert Schweitzer, and Werner), or recognize as valid only the statements about the present (C.H. Dodd's theory of realized eschatology). Both are in conflict with both the findings of historians and the data. When the tension is taken seriously concepts such as eschatology in tension (Kümmel), a self-realizing eschatology (Jeremias) or a salvation-history eschatology (Cullmann) are introduced.

The real question is what we are to make of this interweaving and tension between present and future. Liberal theology, and notably A. Ritschl, tried to present the Kingdom of God, along the lines of Kant's doctrine of the highest Good, as the common goal of all human moral strivings. The objection to this view is that it ignores the time perspective and historical character which are essential elements in the Kingdom. The Kingdom of God is not the supra-temporal goal of ethical endeavour, but happens, takes place, here and now. Hence it was initially an advance when Weiss and Schweitzer rediscovered the eschatological character of the Kingdom, though both immediately began systematically to obscure their exegetical insight. They regarded Jesus' eschatology as temporal, and Schweitzer therefore wanted to replace Jesus' eschatological ethics with an ethical eschatology. He regarded the Kingdom of God as belief in the irresistible power of the moral spirit and a symbol for the idea of the moral perfection of the world.[10] The main voice raised against this ethical interpretation was that of Karl Barth. In the second edition of his *Epistle to the Romans* (1921) he argued that 'if Christianity be not totally and without remainder eschatology, there remains in it no relation whatever with Christ'.[11] Barth neutralized eschatology, however, by interpreting it within the framework of the time-eternity dialectic. For him, eternity is an absolute simultaneity, an eternal moment and an eternal Now, equally close to all moments in time: 'Every moment in time bears within it the unborn secret of revelation, every moment can become the *special* moment. . . Being the transcendent meaning of all moments, the eternal 'Moment' can be compared with no moment in time.'[12] Rudolf Bultmann's attempt to demythologize Jesus' eschatological statements was carried out within the framework, not of a dialectic of time and eternity, but that of a specific human existential dialectic. According to Bultmann, Jesus' eschatological message is based on a particular view of man. Man is always having to make choices; it is always the last minute. He is asked whether he chooses his past or the open and uncontrollable future. 'Every moment contains the possibility that it is the eschatological moment, it is up to you to awaken it from its slumber'.[13]

In other words, Bultmann interpreted the eschatological character of the *basileia* in terms of the orientation of human existence towards the future. Yet another view was put forward by Paul Tillich. For him the 'Kingdom of God' was a symbol, which he interpreted as an answer to the search for the meaning of history.[14]

All these interpretations eliminate the temporal and historical character of the tensions between the statements about the present and those about the future. A correct interpretation must not start from the philosophical dialectic of time and eternity, but from the specifically biblical view of time. The first characteristic of the biblical view of time and history is that it does not regard time as *purely* quantitative. It is not a continuous and homogeneous sequence of days and hours, but qualitative.[15] Time is measured by its content; it depends what it is time for. 'For everything there is a season, and a time for every matter under heaven'. 'There is a time for planting and a time for uprooting, a time to weep and a time to laugh, a time for mourning and a time for dancing, a time for silence and a time for speech, a time for war and a time for peace' (cf Eccles 3.1-8). In the context of this view of time as dependent on its content, Jesus' message of the Kingdom that is now in the future becomes more intelligible. What is being said is that now is the time for the coming of God's kingdom; that is, the present is modified by the fact that the coming of the Kingdom has begun and faces men with a choice. The Kingdom, in other words, is the power which controls the future. It is now forcing a choice, and in this way is active in the present and totally determines it. 'Hence in Jesus' preaching, speaking of the present means speaking of the future, and vice versa. The future of God is *salvation* to the man who apprehends the future as God's present, and as the hour of salvation. The future of God is *judgment* for the man who does not accept the "now" of God but clings to his own present, his own past, and also to his own dreams of the future. . . God's future is God's call to the present, and the present is the time of decision in the light of God's future.'[16] Nevertheless, an interpretation of Jesus' message which uses this substantial biblical view of time cannot eliminate the distinctly other and future character of the Kingdom of God from his sayings. There can be no doubt that Jesus talked about a change taking place in the immediate future and about the Kingdom's coming soon. This immediate expectation creates a difficult and much-discussed problem. Was Jesus then wrong in his immediate expectations? If that were so, it would have far-reaching consequences both for his personal claim to authority and for the truth and validity claimed for his whole message. That is not a subsidiary and unimportant question, but one which involves the core of his message.

The answer to this difficult question begins to appear when we remember a second characteristic of the biblical view of time and history. The tension between immediate expectation and the delay of the *parousia* is not just a New Testament problem, but pervades large sections of the Old Testament.[17] This is connected with what Martin Buber called 'active history'.[18] Buber said that history does not simply follow a plan, whether human or divine, but takes place in dialogue between God and men. God's promise opens up a new possibility for human beings, but the particular realization of the possibility depends on human decisions, on their faith or unbelief. God's Kingdom, in other words, does not bypass human faith, but comes where God is recognized in faith as Lord.

This dialogal character of active history helps us to understand the tension between immediate expectation and the delay of the *parousia*. Jesus' message about the approaching Kingdom of God is God's firm and final offer, and demands a decision. This offer is serious; it is not an act on God's part. At the same time, however, the offer is left to man's free choice; it makes the present situation the eschatological situation of choice. When it was rejected by Israel as a whole, God did not withdraw the promise made once and for all, but he now took a different course to achieve his aim of establishing his Kingdom. This course led, as we shall see, through the death and Resurrection of Jesus. That means that Jesus' message about the coming of the Kingdom of God contains an excess of promise; it creates a hope which is still unfulfilled after the message has been proclaimed. The hope will not be fulfilled until God is finally 'all in all' (cf 1 Cor 15.28). This eschatological tension must leave its mark on every Christology. Its implications must be worked out in terms of human hope.

3. THE THEOLOGICAL CHARACTER OF THE KINGDOM OF GOD

In the tradition of the Old Testament and of Judaism the coming of the Kingdom of God means the coming of God. The centre of eschatological hope was the 'Day of Yahweh', the day appointed and brought to pass by God, the day on which God would be 'all in all', on which God's Godhead would be fully asserted. When Jesus proclaims, 'The Kingdom of God is at hand', he is saying, 'God is at hand'. Both statements often appear together in the gospels. Even on the level of terminology, therefore, the eschatological statements in the preaching of Jesus appear in a relationship of tense co-existence and concentricity. The Kingdom of God, in other words, does not primarily imply a realm, but God's lordship, the manifestation of his glory, God's Godhead. It implies a radical interpretation of the first commandment and a demonstration of it which changes the course of history: 'I am the LORD your God. . . You shall have no other gods before me' (Ex 20.2-3).

The idea of God's Lordship was given universal extension in the Old Testament in the doctrine of creation, the meaning of which is that God is in an absolute sense the Master of all reality. The article of the creed about the creation of the world out of nothing is merely the negative formulation of the belief that the world in itself is nothing and in its entirety is from God, in other words, that it only exists because God wills its existence and supports it. This idea, that everything that exists comes, as it were, at every moment new from the hand of God, recurs in the preaching of Jesus. Jesus does not teach a doctrine of creation, but his preaching is sharply distinct from the late Jewish idea of a purely transcendent God who comes into contact with man only through the mediation of the Law. Jesus' God is the God who is near, who cares for the grass of the field (Mt 6.30) and feeds the sparrows (Mt 10.31). This makes it possible to understand how everyday things, the farmer's sowing, the housewife's baking, can become a parable of God's coming in the Kingdom of God.

But the idea of God's closeness is deepened in the preaching of Jesus to a level which goes far beyond the Old Testament statements on creation. Jesus almost reinterprets the Kingdom and the Lordship of God. For him, God's Lordship consists in the sovereignty of his love. His coming and his nearness mean the coming of the Kingdom of his love. This reinterpretation is expressed most noticeably in the way Jesus speaks of God as his Father (*abba*) and addresses him as Father.[20] The way Jesus uses the term combines the dominative and authoritarian aspects of fatherhood in the ancient world with its other side, the familiar, the intimate, the affectionate. The term 'Father' crystallized in a special way Jesus' view of God's kingdom as God's rule in love.

That becomes clear when Jesus' use of the word 'Father' is compared with its use by other thinkers. The idea of the fatherhood of God is current in numerous variants in almost all ancient religions, and the invocation of the deity as 'Father' is one of the commonest phenomena in religious research. The original basis was probably the apotheosis of the master of the house and the idea of the father of the family as the image of a deity. The Stòics gave the idea a universal scope and a basis in natural philosophy, and the idea that participation in the same Logos makes men a single race, and all men brothers, is an idea which appears in Paul's sermon on the Areopagus (Acts 17.28). This mythological and pantheistic background helps to explain why the Old Testament is very reluctant to describe God as Father. Use of a biological term defines the relationship with the Deity with great emphasis as a generative blood relationship, and neglects the distance between God and creature. For that reason, when Israel talks about God as *like* a father and describes the people (Ex 4.22; Is 1.2; 30.1) or the king (2 Sam 7.14; Ps 2.7; 89.27) as a son, the idea in the background is not the biological one of procreation, but the theological one of election.

It was the gradual development of an idea of creation which first made it possible for the Old Testament to describe God as father in a new way (Dt 32.6; Is 64.7; Sir 23.1).

Even before that, however, the Old Testament had used the concept of fatherhood to describe more than remoteness of God (Mal 1.6; Sir 23.1); from as early as Hosea (11.1,9) the idea of compassion and paternal love was also significant (cf Is 63.15-6; Jer 31.20). The recollection that God was the 'father of orphans' (Ps 68.6) became an important symbol of consolation and trust (Ps 27.20; 89.27; Sir 51.10). In late Judaism the description of God as father became more frequent. Behind it was not the idea of divine generation, still less that of God as a cosmic principle, but the belief that God has the attitude of a father. In the synagogue 'Father' was for this reason the most affectionate of all titles for God. Nevertheless it 'seems to be, as it were, stuck on top of a quite different system, a legalistic view'. The title does not go all that deep. 'The materials are there, but the spirit of true faith in the Father is still lacking.'[21]

In the Gospels the situation is quite different. Here we find God called 'Father' no less than a hundred and seventy times. Underlying this is a clear tendency in the tradition to put this usage in the mouth of Jesus, but this undoubted fact is still no reason for scepticism. There can be scarcely any doubt that Jesus himself described God as Father, and indeed that the way he did so seemed new and remarkable. The tendency of the tradition has a basis in Jesus himself. This can be shown most clearly in the case of the use of *abba* to address God. This form of address is directly attested only in Mk 14.36 (but cf Mt 6.9; Lk 11.2; Mt 11.25; Lk 10.21; Mt 26.42; Lk 23.34,46). However, the fact that, according to Gal 4.6 and Rom 8.15, even Greek-speaking communities preserved the Aramaic form as a liturgical invocation supports the view that this form of address to God was held up in the primitive communities as a unique and characteristic recollection of Jesus. That we have to do here with the very words of Jesus cannot be doubted.

The novelty of Jesus' language is that he does not merely describe God as Father, as Judaism did, but addresses him as father. The reluctance of Jewish liturgical literature to use this form of address can easily be understood when we know that *abba* is in origin a children's onomatopoeic word (something like 'Daddy'). It was not, however, (unlike 'Daddy') restricted to children's language, but was used by older children in addressing their fathers. In addition, it was used to other people (as well as fathers) to whom respect was due. *Abba* was, then, children's language, ordinary language and a polite title. Jesus' contemporaries felt that it was not sufficiently respectful to address God with this familiar word. Jesus nevertheless used it, and did so because he was proclaiming in a unique way the nearness of God, a nearness in which human beings could feel confident of being accepted. As a father, God knows what his children need (Mt 6.8; Lk 12.30); his kindness and care have no limits (Mt 5.45 par.). His care includes even the sparrows (Mt 10.29). But being a child of God is not strictly a gift of creation, but an eschatological gift of salvation (Mt 5.9,45; Lk 6.35; 20.36). To be a child is itself the mark of the kingdom. 'Unless you turn and become like children, you will never enter the kingdom of heaven' (Mt 18.3). Calling God *abba* reveals what is new about Jesus' understanding of God: God is close to men in love.

The real theological meaning of this use of *abba* appears only when it is seen in connexion with Jesus' message of the Kingdom of God. It then

80

becomes clear that calling God 'Father' is not a banal, almost automatic intimacy. Nor is it an interiorized message of fatherhood, as liberal theology interpreted it. The phrase 'Father in heaven' (Mt 5.9,16,45,48; 6.1; 7.11; etc.) and the mention of the perfection of the Father (Mt 5.48) indicate the difference between God and man. That is why Jesus forbids his disciples to let themselves be called 'Father', 'for you have one Father who is in heaven' (Mt 23.9). In the 'Our Father', the invocation 'Father' is connected with the prayer 'hallowed be thy name. Thy kingdom come. Thy will be done' (Mt 6.9-10; Lk 11.2). The dignity, sovereignty and glory of God are in this way preserved, but they are imagined in a different way: God's lordship is lordship in love. God's lordship shows itself in his sovereign freedom to love and to forgive. That is what shows that he is God and not man (cf Hos 11.9). It was not without cause that Luke interpreted the perfection of the Father in heaven as mercy (Lk 6.36). His perfection is not, as in the Greek system, a fulness of moral goodness, but a creative goodness which makes others good, a contagious love. God's paternal love goes out to the lost, and even restores to life what was dead (Lk 15.24). When God begins his reign as Father, it is the new creation. The old has passed away; all things are made new in the blaze of his love, all things are possible (Mk 14.36; 10.27; Mt 19.26; Lk 18.27).

The implication of this total reinterpretation of the idea of the Kingdom of God is that the Kingdom is totally and exclusively God's doing. It cannot be earned by religious or moral effort, imposed by political struggle, or projected in calculation. We cannot plan for it, organize it, make it or build it, we cannot invent or imagine it. It is given (Mt 21.43; Lk 12.32), 'appointed' (Lk 22.29). We can only inherit it (Mt 25.34). This is what comes out most clearly from the parables of Jesus: the coming of the Kingdom of God is, notwithstanding all human expectations, opposition, calculations and plans, God's miracle, God's doing, God's lordship in the truest sense of the word.

The coming of the Kingdom of God is, then, the revelation that God is God in love, but this does not imply quietism on the human side. Even though we human beings cannot build the Kingdom of God by our actions, whether conservative or progressive, evolutionary or revolutionary, pure passivity is the last thing we are condemned to. What is demanded of us is repentance and faith (Mk 1.15 par.). Repentance does not mean ascetic rigorism, nor faith the surrender of the intellect. Either of these would simply be one more human effort designed to please God. This belief in one's own capabilities is what Jesus, and before him the Baptist, want to destroy. The positive side of repentance is shown by faith. Expressions of faith appear mainly in connexion with reports of miracles, that is, in situations in which human possibilities have been exhausted. Faith means ceasing to rely on one's own capabilities, admitting human powerlessness. It is the recognition that human beings cannot help themselves by their own efforts and with their own resources, and cannot provide the basis for their own existence and its salvation. This means that faith is open to something other, something new, something to come. Because a believer no longer expects anything from himself, he expects everything from God, to whom all things are possible (Mk 10.27 par.). But when someone allows God to act in this way, the saying becomes true: 'All things are possible to him who believes' (Mk 9.23). It is a description of the essence of faith to say: faith is participation in the omnipotence of God.

Believing means trusting and building on the power of God which is at work in Jesus, making God the foundation of existence. It means letting God act, letting God go into action, letting God be God, giving him glory, recognizing his rule. Where people believe in this way, God's rule becomes reality in the ordinary events of history. Faith is like a mould in which the Kingdom of God takes shape. Naturally, this is not the doing or achievement of faith. Faith is an answer to the news of the coming of God and his Kingdom, and this answer is only possible in the power and the light of this news. Nevertheless, it is only in this answer that the word of God acquires its ultimate meaning; this answer brings it to full development. That sort of faith is also not a private or interior matter. Because it is the reply to God's love it is at the same time love for God and neighbour (Mk 2.29-31 par).

By now Jesus' use of *abba* or 'Father' to talk to God has become so familiar to us that is is cliché-like. It is hard for us to see what is revolutionary about it. Part of the blame for this lies with theology, which has failed to consider the implications of the message of the Kingdom of God for the way we think of God. Instead of making Jesus' preaching of the Kingdom of God the framework for developing a Christian view of God, traditional theology has tended to take over the Greek philosophical view of God and so failed to emphasize the difference and the novelty of Jesus' view of God. Greek philosophy got to God as a result of a deductive process. God was the ultimate source of the unity, meaning and existence of all things. This meant that God had to be unchanging and eternal, 'resting entirely in himself'.[23] Schelling referred sarcastically to the 'God at the end'.[24] This God appears at the end of a return to the origins, but he is also at the end of the line in another sense. Because he never changes he can never do anything, no life goes out from him, he is dead. Nietzsche's 'God is dead' is therefore only the final implication of this form of Western metaphysics.

The way Jesus talked about God is very different. His God is defined not as the unmoved mover and unchangeable source but as the living God of love. To Jesus, as to the Old Testament, God is a God of history, who creates and carries through a new beginning. He is the power of the future. God and time go together, but this does not mean that God develops and reaches his full growth in time. He is the power of the future, and therefore is not bound by the laws of time; he is the Lord of time and of the future. That, however, is the definition of freedom. Freedom means the ability to do things on one's own initiative, the ability to create one's own future. This freedom of God's is ultimately his transcendence, because it means that God cannot be manipulated or controlled, that he is incalculable. But though it may be incalculable, the future is not blank fate and God's freedom is not incalculable arbitrariness. God's freedom is his freedom in love. Love means freedom and loyalty, unity, closeness and intimacy, distinctness and difference. Hegel described this dialectic of love in a commentary on the statement 'God is love' (1 Jn 4.8,16): 'Love is a distinction between two who are nevertheless not distinct for one another. The consciousness, the feeling of that identity, to be this, outside myself and in the other, is love: I have my self-consciousness not in myself but in the other, but this other. . . insofar as he also is outside himself, has his self-consciousness only in me, and both are only this consciousness of their being without themselves and their identity. ... that is love, and it is empty talk to speak of love without knowing that it is the discernment and cancellation of difference'.[25] God's divinity consists in the sovereignty of his love. That means that he can give himself without losing himself. He is himself precisely when he enters into that which is other than himself. It is by surrendering himself that he shows his divinity. Concealment is therefore the way in which God's glory is revealed in the world.

It is easy to see how these ideas could completely transform the image of God and also how they give new relevance to the idea of creation. The belief that the world is a creation means that an adequate source of its existence and nature does not lie within itself. It means that the world is nothing in itself but depends totally on God, that it owes its being completely and utterly to God's generous love. In other words, love is not only the ultimate meaning, but also the origin of all reality. But that source is not just there. Love does not exist. It is constantly appearing in new forms, constantly on the way. It is constantly reasserting itself in the face of egotism and selfishness. Jesus' message of the coming of God's Kingdom in love means that the ultimate source and meaning of all reality is now becoming reality in a new and final form. The final decision in history about the meaning of reality is now being made. With the entry of the Kingdom of God the world enters into salvation.

4. THE SOTERIOLOGICAL CHARACTER OF THE KINGDOM OF GOD

For John the Baptist the approach of the Kingdom of God means a threatening judgment, but for Jesus the offer of salvation. Jesus' preaching is not a message of fear, but one of joy. For that reason the synoptic Gospels often use the term 'good news' (*euangelion:* Mk 1.14; 14.9; Mt 4.23; 9.35; 24.14; cf Lk 16.16). This phrase points to an essential feature of Jesus' preaching. The change Jesus made was to make the concept of the Kingdom of God not just important, but the central element in the concept of salvation. By his preaching of the Kingdom he promised the fulfilment of all human hopes, expectations and longings for a fundamental transformation of the order of things and a completely new start. There was an ancient hope, which appears in the early myths and was taken over by the Old Testament prophets, that in the time of redemption, when God's Kingdom came, all suffering, all tears and all distress would be ended. Jesus too adopts this hope: the blind are to see, the lame walk, the lepers are to be cleansed, the deaf hear, the dead are to be raised up and the poor have the good news preached to them (Lk 7.22-23; Mt 11.5-6).

The approaching reversal of the whole order of the world is expressed particularly in the greeting 'Blessed are you. . .' which is characteristic of Jesus' preaching (Mt 5.3-11; Lk 6.20-22; Mt 11.6; Lk 7.23; Mt 13.16; Lk 10.23). These beatitudes are a fixed form in Greek and Jewish wisdom literature (see Sir 25.7-10), but Jesus uses the same form in a very different way. Greek and Jewish wisdom literature describes as blessed the man who has obedient children, a good wife, faithful friends, is successful, and so forth. Jesus' beatitudes are different. They do not derive from common human wisdom, but are prophetic sayings, appeals and promises. In contrast with the Greek beatitudes, all worldly blessings and values recede before the good fortune of sharing in the Kingdom of God. All values are reversed. Those who are called blessed are not the propertied, the happy and the successful, but the poor, the hungry, the mourners, the despised and the persecuted. Jesus, in his 'inaugural sermon' in Nazareth can take up a saying of the prophet Isaiah (61.1), and say that he has been sent to preach the good news to the poor, to proclaim release to the captives and recovery of sight to the blind, to set at liberty the oppressed and to proclaim the acceptable year of the Lord (Lk 4.18-19).

Who are the poor to whom the Kingdom of God is promised? (Lk 6.20; Mt 5.3). Matthew and Luke preserve this saying in different forms and give it different interpretations. Matthew refers to the 'poor in spirit', which implies a religious interpretation of poverty in the sense of humility, poverty before God. Luke thinks of the really poor, but not just those without material goods, but those who suffer on account of their discipleship (cf Lk 6.22-23). Jesus himself talks about the poor in the context of a series of parallel expressions; he also calls blessed the broken-hearted, the oppressed, the hated, and the mourners. 'Poor' is taken in a very broad sense: it includes the helpless, those without resources, the oppressed, those in despair, the despised, the ill-treated, the abused. Jesus' partiality for the poor is in complete harmony with the attitude of the Old Testament, similar in style to the prophet Amos's criticism of social injustice and oppression (Am 2.7; 4.1; 5.11), or the way the psalms invoke and celebrate Yahweh as the protector and helper of all who are persecuted and powerless.

The Old Testament never completely rejects prosperity — it accepts it gratefully as a gift of God — and equally it never romanticizes poverty. It knows that poverty may be deserved as a result of idleness (Prov 6.9-11; 24.30-34) or pleasure-seeking (Prov 21.7). The New Testament's attitude here is also completely realistic: 'You always have the poor with you' (Mk 14.7). Jesus refuses to be an arbitrator or adjudicator (Lk 12.14). He shows no trace of deep-seated hatred of the rich, but receives and accepts their invitations. Jesus' glorification of the poor is not related to any social stratum and implies no social programme. He does not make poverty a claim, a sort of inverted greed. His poor are those 'who have nothing to expect from the world, but who expect everything from God. They look towards God, and also cast themselves upon God'.[26] They have been driven up against the limits of the world and its possibilities; they are outwardly and inwardly so poor that they cannot even start a revolution any more. They have discovered their own and all men's true situation. They are beggars before God. Only from him can they expect help.

Jesus' attitude corresponds to his preaching. His sympathy and solidarity are with the humble (Mk 9.42; Mt 10.42; 18.10,14) and simple (Mt 11.25 par.), the toilers and heavy-laden (Mt 11.28). The people with whom he associates are often contemptuously called tax-collectors and sinners (Mk 2.16 par.; Mt 11.19 par.; Lk 15.1) or tax-collectors and harlots (Mt 21.32) or simply sinners (Mk 2.17; Lk 7.37,39; 15.2; 19.7); that is, godless. The godless included people who notoriously ignored the commandments of God and were held up to public contempt. The category included particular professions which in the public mind were associated with temptation, not only tax-collectors and prostitutes but shepherds. The whole lot were lumped together as *ha-aretz*, the poor uneducated people who either did not know the complicated provisions of the Law or, if they did, could not keep them and were consequently despised by the pious. This bad company was Jesus' choice, and he gained the reputation of being the friend of tax-collectors and sinners (Mt 11.19; Lk 7.34). He took the part of these *déclassés*, outcasts who lived a despised existence on the edge of society, who because of circumstances, their own fault, or social prejudice, had no place in this world. Their fate was made much worse because under the Jewish dogma of retributive punishment they were obliged to regard their situation as a punishment from God, and had no chance of altering their state. They could therefore expect nothing either from man or from God. These were the people Jesus called 'blessed'.

But what is this salvation? It is striking that Jesus concentrates all the varied expectations of salvation into a single theme, participation in the Kingdom of God. This, for him, is identical with life (Mk 9.43,45; 10.17; Lk 18.18). It would be a misunderstanding of this concentration, however, if we were to see it as a spiritualizing process or the offer of consolation in an indefinite future or another world beyond the grave. For Jesus the time of salvation is being revealed and made reality here and now. This is what Jesus' deeds of power and miraculous healings are meant to show; in them the Kingdom of God reaches into the present to save and heal. They show that the salvation brought by the Kingdom of God is the well-being of the whole individual, body and soul. The parables of the two debtors (Lk 7.41-43), the hard-hearted servant (Mt 18.23-35), the lost son (Lk 15.11-32) show that the saving message of the coming of the Kingdom of God includes a cancellation of obligations. The findings of what was lost brings joy (Lk 15.4-10; 22-24;

31-32). This is why the message of salvation is also a message of joy. The salvation brought by the Kingdom of God consists in the first instance of the forgiveness of sins and rejoicing at having encountered the boundless and unmerited mercy of God. Experiencing God's love means experiencing that one has been unreservedly accepted, approved and infinitely loved, that one can and should accept oneself and one's neighbour. Salvation is joy in God which expresses itself in joy in and with one's neighbour.

Another sign of the salvation of the Kingdom is that the love of God is established in power among men. If God remits an enormous debt of ours, which we would never have been able to pay, we too must be prepared to release our fellow men from their petty debts to us (Mt 18.23-24). God's forgiveness gives us the capacity for limitless forgiveness (Lk 17.3-4). Willingness on our part to forgive is also the condition (Mk 11.25; Mt 6.12) under which and the measure in which (Mk 4.24; Mt 7.2; Lk 6.38) God forgives us. Salvation is promised to the merciful (Mt 5.7). Since this salvation is now upon us, there is no more time, there can be no more delay (Lk 12.58-59). The age of the coming Kingdom of God is the age of love, which requires us to accept each other unconditionally. Such love, which does not answer back and never says no, ensnares evil in the world (Mt 5.39-40; Lk 6.29). It smashes the vicious circle of violence and counter-violence, guilt and revenge. Love is the new start. It is the visible presence of salvation. In union with our fellow men we will share in God's joy at the return of sinners (Lk 7.36-47; 15.11-32; 19.1-10). The all-surpassing love of God makes itself felt in the acceptance of human beings by each other, in the dismantling of prejudices and social barriers, in new unrestricted communication among men, in brotherly warmth and the sharing of sadness and joy.

The full implications of these statements do not appear until we see that the coming of the Kingdom of God means the overcoming and the end of the demonic forces (Mt 12.28; Lk 11.20). Jesus' confrontation with the demonic powers cannot, as we shall see, simply be removed from the gospels. The salvation of the Kingdom of God means the overcoming of the destructive forces of evil which are hostile to creation and the coming of a new creation. The marks of this new creation are life, freedom, peace, reconciliation and love.

We can summarize that as follows: The salvation of the Kingdom of God means the coming to power in and through human beings of the self-communicating love of God. Love reveals itself as the meaning of life. The world and man find fulfilment only in love.

In practice, however, human beings have separated themselves from the love of God by sin and put themselves at the service of egotism, self-seeking, self-will, self-advantage and self-importance. Everything falls apart in meaningless isolation and a general battle of all against all. In place of unity come loneliness and isolation, and the isolated individual or entity inevitably falls victim to meaninglessness. But when the ultimate source of all reality, God's love, re-establishes itself and comes to power, the world is restored to order and salvation. Because each individual can feel himself accepted and approved without reserve, he becomes free to live with others. The coming of the Kingdom of God's love therefore means the salvation of the world as a whole and the salvation of every individual. Everyone can now know that love is the ultimate, that it is stronger than death, stronger than hatred and injustice. The news of the coming of the Kingdom of God is therefore a promise about everything that is done in the world out of love. It says that, against all appearances, what is done out of love will endure for ever; that it is the only thing which lasts for ever.

Such a starting-point has obvious consequences for a Christian attitude to the world. It opens up possibilities which avoid the alternative of transforming the world by violence and escaping the world in pacifism: namely, the transformation and humanizing of the world through the violence of love. Love is no substitute for justice. It is more akin to the supreme perfection of justice. After all we are not doing justice to another person when we merely give him whatever he has a right to; we have to accept him as a person and approve of him, when we give him ourselves. Love includes the demands of justice. It is a passionate commitment to justice for everyone, but at the same time it goes beyond justice and by so doing accomplishes it. Love is the power and the light which enables us to recognize the demands of justice in changing situations, and to meet them appropriately. In that sense, love is the soul of justice. Love is the answer to the search for a just and human world, the solution to the riddle of history. It is the wholeness of man and the world.

Notes

[1] In addition to the articles *'Basileia'*, 'Reign of God' and 'Kingdom of God' in the theological dictionaries and reference books, see esp. H. Kleinknecht, G. von Rad and H. G. Kuhn, K. L. Schmidt, article *'Basileia'*, etc., TDNT I, cols 564-93; E. Staehelin, *Die Verkündigung des Reiches Gottes in der Kirche Jesu Christi. Zeugnisse aus allen Konfessionen*, 7 vols. (Basle, 1951-65); N. Perrin, *The Kingdom of God in the Teaching of Jesus* (London, 1963); R. Schnackenburg, *Gottes Herrschaft und Reich. Eine biblischtheologische Studie* (4th ed., Freiburg, 1965); ET: *God's Rule and Kingdom* (London, 1968); C. Bornkamm, *Jesus von Nazareth, op. cit.*, 58-87.
[2] See A. Schweitzer, *Das Messianitäts- und Leidensgeheimnis. Eine Skizze des Lebens Iesu* (1901; 3rd ed. Tübingen, 1956), ET: *The Mystery of the Kingdom of God. The Secret of Jesus' Messiahship and Passion* (London, 1925).
[3] See J. Weiss, *Die Predigt Jesu vom Reich Gottes* (Göttingen, 1892).
[4] See H. Schlier, *Mächte und Gewalte im Neuen Testament* (Freiburg, 1958); ET: *Principalities and Powers in the New Testament* (London, 1960).
[5] G. von Rad, *Theologie des Alten Testaments*, vol. 2 (4th ed., Munich, 1965); ET: *Old Testament Theology*, vol. 2 (from the 3rd Ger. ed., London and Edinburgh, 1965) pp. 116-19.
[6] On how to interpret eschatological statements, see K. Rahner, 'Theologische Prinzipien der Hermeneutik eschatologischer Aussagen', *Schriften zur Theologie*, vol. IV, pp. 401-28; ET: 'The Hermeneutics of Eschatological Assertions', in: *Theological Investigations, IV* (London, 1966), pp. 323-46; H. Urs von Balthasar, 'Umrisse der Eschatologie', in: *Verbum Caro* (2nd ed., Einsiedeln, 1960), pp. 276-300.

[7] See E. Jüngel, *Paulus und Jesus* (2nd ed., Tübingen, 1964), pp. 139ff.

[8] Bornkamm, *Jesus von Nazareth*, *op. cit.*, pp. 14ff; ET: *Jesus of Nazareth*, *op. cit.*, p. 71.

[9] See the survey in Schnackenburg, *Gottes Herrschaft*, *op. cit.*; ET: *God's Rule and Kingdom*, *op. cit.*

[10] See A. Schweitzer, *Geschichte*, *op. cit.*, pp. 634ff; ET: *Quest of the Historical Jesus* pp. 219-21.

[11] K. Barth, *Der Römerbrief* (9th ed., Zollikon-Zürich, 1954); ET: *The Epistle to the Romans* (London, 1933), p.498 (translation slightly altered).

[12] Barth, *op. cit.*, pp. 498-9 (translation slightly altered).

[13] R. Bultmann, *Geschichte und Eschatologie* (Tübingen, 1958), p. 194; ET: *History and Eschatology* (Edinburgh, 1957), p. 194.

[14] See P. Tillich, *Systematische Theologie*, vol. 3 (Stuttgart, 1966).

[15] On the biblical understanding of time, see C. H. Ratschow, 'Anmerkungen zur theologischen Auffassung des Zeitproblems', ZTK 51 (1954), pp. 360-87; T. Boman, *Das hebräische Denken im Verleich mit dem Griechischen* (5th ed., Göttingen, 1968), pp. 109ff.; W. Eichrodt, 'Heilserfahrung und Zeitverständnis im Alten Testament', ThZ 12 (1956), pp. 103-25; von Rad, *Theologie des alten Testaments*, vol. 2, *op. cit.*, pp. 108ff; ET: *Old Testament Theology*, vol. 2, pp. 102-10.

[16] Bornkamm, *Jesus von Nazareth*, *op. cit.*, p. 85; ET: *Jesus of Nazareth*, p. 93.

[17] See G. Fohrer, 'Prophetie und Geschichte', THLZ 89 (1964), pp. 481-500.

[18] See M. Buber, W II (Munich-Heidelberg, 1964), pp. 1031-6.

[19] See H. Schürmann, 'Das hermeneutische Hauptproblem der·Verkündigung Jesu. Eschatologie und Theologie im gegenseitigen Verhältnis', in: *Gott in Welt. Festgabe für Karl Rahner*, vol. 1 (Freiburg, 1964), pp. 579-607.

[20] See J. Jeremias, 'Abba', *Abba. Studien zur neutestamentlichen Theologie und Geistesgeschichte* (Göttingen, 1966), pp. 15-67; W. Marchel, *Abba, Père! La prière du Christ et des chrétiens (Analecta Biblica*, vol. 19 A (Rome, 1971).

[21] Schrenk, art. 'Pater', TDNT, vol. V, p. 982.

[22] G. Ebeling, *Wort und Glaube* I, (3rd ed., Tübingen, 1967); ET: 'Jesus and Faith', in: *Word and Faith* (London, 1963), p. 242.

[23] See W. Pannenberg, 'Die Aufnahme des philosophischen Gottesbegriffs als dogmatisches Problem der frühchristlichen Theologie', *Grundfragen systematischer Theologie* (Göttingen, 1967), pp. 296-346; ET: 'The Appropriation of the Philosophical Concept of God as a Dogmatic Problem of Early Christian Theology', in: *Basic Concepts in Systematic Theology*, vol. 2 (London, 1971), pp. 119-83.

[24] See F. W. J. Schelling, 'Geschichte der neueren Philosophie', W X, pp. 216ff.; 'Philosophie der Offenbarung', W XIII, pp. 71-2.

[25] G. W. F. Hegel, *Vorlesungen über die Philosophie des Religion* II/2, *op. cit.*, p. 75. There is some danger, however, in taking Hegel's dialectic of love into theology, since Hegel regards the other as an essential part of self-hood, which is just what cannot be said of God's love in relation to man. In theology, Hegel's dialectic of love must be conceived of as a 'dialogic' of love.

[26] Bornkamm, *Jesus von Nazareth*, *op. cit.*, p. 69; ET: *Jesus of Nazareth*, p. 100.

III. JESUS' MIRACLES

III. JESUS' MIRACLES

1. THE PROBLEMATICS OF JESUS' MIRACLES

Jesus did not work by words alone, but with actions. He did more than talk; he did things.[1] His message was part of his general approach and attitude, in particular his provocative readiness to eat with sinners. But there is one aspect of Jesus' activity which, above all else (for modern men at least), makes it so remarkable and hard to understand. That odd and mysterious aspect is his miracles. The miracle tradition of the gospels cannot be wished away. It is in the earliest strata. Mark in fact builds his gospel almost exclusively on the miracle stories. No effective discussion of Jesus can ignore those reports.

Goethe called miracles 'faith's favourite children', but nowadays they are faith's problem-children. The growth of critical thought and its interest in proven, applicable knowledge brought about a concentration on general and uniform aspects of reality. However, when particulars receive their definition primarily from analogy and correlation with everything else, the sense of the incalculable, the unique, the once-for-all, disappears. Extraordinary events are no longer regarded with astonishment. They are reduced to the general level of what can in theory be explained. If modern men and women experience any wonder, it is likely to be provoked by the regularity and order of nature. On the other hand, they regard history as the area in which they fulfil themselves. If people talk in this context about miracles, an economic miracle perhaps, or the wonders of technology, this is a very different use of the word; it now describes human achievements.

As regards the miracles of Jesus, this transformation of our experience of the world and history since the Enlightenment has created two sorts of problems, historical problems and scientific ones. Historical scepticism with regard to the miracle reports requires us to examine them with great care, and the scientific approach calls for a fundamental reconsideration of the whole concept of miracle.

Critical historical study of the miracle tradition has had three main results:

1. Literary criticism reveals a tendency to intensify, magnify and multiply the miracles. According to Mk 1. 34, Jesus healed many sick; in the parallel Mt 8.16 he heals them all. In Mark Jairus's daughter is on the point of death; in Matthew she is already dead. The healing of one blind man and one possessed becomes the healing of two blind men and two possessed. The feeding of the 4000 becomes the feeding of the 5000, and the seven baskets left over become twelve. If this tendency to develop, multiply and intensify can be found in the gospels themselves, then naturally it must also be presumed to have existed in the period before our gospels were compiled. This reduces the material on which the miracle reports are based very considerably.

2. A further reduction results from a comparison with rabbinic and hellenistic miracle stories. The New Testament accounts of miracles are analogous to, or use, themes familiar to us from other ancient sources. There are for example, rabbinic and hellenistic miracle stories of cures, expulsions of demons, raisings from the dead, quellings of storms, and so on. Numerous parallels exist in the case of Jesus' contemporary, Apollonius of Tyana, and many healings are reported in particular from the sanctuary of Asclepius at Epidaurus. One gets the impression that the New Testament is transferring non-Christian symbols to Jesus in order to emphasize his greatness and authority. There is even a clearly recognizable style in miracle stories, a fixed three-part pattern into which the accounts are fitted. First the failure of previous efforts is described, and the severity of the disease is noted, to intensify the power of the miracle. There follows the account of the miraculous event, and finally we are given the names of the witnesses who saw the miracle and confirmed it (the choral ending). There are also, of course, significant differences between the miracles of Jesus and others reported in antiquity: Jesus does not work miracles for money, to punish, or for display. Nevertheless, in view of the parallels which remain, it is hardly possible to reject all the rabbinical and hellenistic miracle reports as unhistorical lies and deceit, while accepting the New Testament accounts at face value as historical.

3. A number of miracle stories turn out in the light of form criticism to be projections of the experiences of Easter back into the earthly life of Jesus, or anticipatory representations of the exalted Christ. Among these epiphany stories we should probably include the stilling of the storm, the transfiguration, Jesus' walking on the lake, the feeding of the four (or five) thousand and the miraculous draught of fishes. The clear purpose of the stories of the raising from the dead of Jairus's daughter, the widow's son at Naim and Lazarus is to present Jesus as Lord over life and death. It is the nature miracles which turn out to be secondary accretions to the original tradition.

The result of all this is that we must describe many of the gospel miracle stories as legendary. Legends of this sort should be examined less for their historical than for their theological content. They say something, not about individual facts of saving history, but about the single saving event which is Jesus Christ. To show that certain miracles cannot be ascribed to the earthly Jesus does not mean that they have no theological or kerygmatic significance. These non-historical miracle reports are statements of faith about the significance for salvation of the person and message of Jesus.

It would nevertheless be wrong to conclude from this view that there are no historically authenticated miracles of Jesus. The opposite is the case. There can scarcely be a single serious exegete who does not believe in a basic stock of historically certain miracles of Jesus. The most important arguments for this position are:

1. The miracle tradition of the Gospels would be completely and utterly inexplicable if Jesus' earthly life had not left behind a general impression and a general recollection of a sort which later made it possible to proclaim Jesus as a miracle-worker.

2. The miracle tradition can be examined by the same criteria that are generally used to establish the historical Jesus. That would mean accepting as historical those miracles whose transmission cannot be explained by reference to either Judaism or Hellenistic literature. Those are miracles which have an explicitly anti-Jewish bias. This applies above all to the Sabbath healings, and the confrontations these provoked about the Sabbath commandment (of Mk 1. 23-28; 3. 1-6; Lk 13. 10-17). Reports of Jesus driving out demons (that is, performing exorcisms) also belong in this context. That is true

particularly of the saying Mt 12.28, 'but if it is by the Spirit of God that I cast out demons, then the kingdom of God has come upon you' (of Lk 11. 20). The context of this saying is Jesus' defence against the accusation that he is in alliance with the devil (Mk 3.22; Mt 9.34; Lk 11.15). This hideous charge can scarcely be pure invention, and it also shows that Jesus' miracles could not be denied by his opponents.

3. Many reports of miracles are connected with striking accounts of individual incidents whose lack of tendentiousness shows them to be original (Mk 1.29-31). The saying in Mt 11. 20-22 about miracles in Chorazin and Bethsaida must also be old, since there is no other reference to any activity by Jesus in Chorazin.

Even a critical historical consideration of the gospel miracle tradition leads to the conclusion that a historical core of the miracle tradition cannot be disputed. Jesus performed extraordinary actions, which amazed his contemporaries. These included curing various diseases and symptoms which at the time were thought to be signs of possession. On the other hand, the probability is that we need not take the so-called 'nature miracles' as historical.

However, proving the existence of a basic stock of extraordinary acts of Jesus does not take us very much further. It is generally accepted that facts themselves are ambiguous, and only acquire a meaning from the context in which they are put by the language of interpretations. This applies with particular force to Jesus' miracles. Even during his lifetime there are signs of a dispute about the meaning of his mighty deeds. Some saw them as signs of God's action, while Jesus' opponents called them demonic illusions, deceit and chicanery (cf Mk 3. 22-30). In our times attempts are made to 'explain' cures of fever, lameness and leprosy (a term used for various skin diseases) as 'psychological'. Some commentators propose that Jesus' miracles should be seen as 'suggestion therapy'. That would give us the possibility of interpreting the miracles of Jesus theologically as acts of God while at the same time giving them a psychological interpretation in terms of the charismatic power which went out from Jesus and the faith he inspired. This raises the question of the mode of reality to which we are to allocate the events the miracle accounts relate. That question takes us from the historical problems to the much more fundamental set of problems: the scientific problems raised by miracles. The question here is: What is a miracle of this sort? What is going on?

A miracle was understood traditionally as a perceivable event outside the possibilities of nature; one brought about by God's almighty power in contravention or at least circumvention of natural causality, for the purpose of confirming verbal revelation. That apologetic concept of the miracle was obviously constructed in direct opposition to modern scientific attitudes and to the idea of a system of causality and determinism with no gaps. On closer inspection, however, this concept of the miracle turns out to be empty. By these criteria miracles could only be firmly established if we really had a complete knowledge of all the laws of nature and could inspect their operation in every individual case. Only then could we show that an event had to be regarded as produced directly by God. In fact, such a complete knowledge of all possible combinations of conditions, which is a necessary condition for such a proof, is probably never available to us. Apart from this, there are serious theological objections to this concept of the miracle. God can never replace this-worldly causality. If he were on the same level as this-worldly causes, he would no longer be God but an idol. If God is to remain God, even his miracles must be thought of as mediated by created secondary causes. They would otherwise be like a meteor from another world: an alien body completely unassimilable to our world. It is questionable whether such an event is conceivable at all: can we imagine something happening in the world without being subject to natural laws? Quite apart from that, however, a miracle which was unrelated to any this-worldly context of meaning and could still be clearly proved to be a divine intervention, would be no profit to theology either. A miracle of this sort would compel belief, and would remove its character of free choice.

These and other difficulties have led theologians more or less to abandon the apologetically-based concept of miracle and to rely on the original biblical meaning of miracle. In describing the miracles of Jesus the Bible never uses just the normal ancient term *térata*, which always had the undertone of the miraculous, but interprets this term by means of two others, 'acts of power' *(dunameis)* and 'signs' *(séméia)*. These signs are extraordinary, unexpected events which provoke amazement and wonder. Attention in this process is not directed at nature and its laws – the concept of a law of nature is alien to the people of the ancient world. A miracle turns people's eyes upwards, towards God. Biblical man does not look at reality as nature, but as creation. To him, all reality is ultimately miraculous. The problems presented by miracles for scripture are therefore not scientific, but religious and theological. They concern belief in God and his glorification. What this realization means can be shown by a simple example. According as one says: 'A depression is producing an east wind'; or 'God is bringing up an east wind', one is operating on two quite different levels of discourse and reality. The first statement stays in the realm of determinable causes, while the second points into the realm of transcendental causes and the religious significance of these determinable events. In the two cases one and the same event is being talked about in completely different ways and in a completely different context. Consequently, neither statement can be used against the other, and neither can be confused with the other. The question of miracles can only be properly discussed by taking account of their religious context and of the theological 'language game' from which they cannot be isolated.

Theologians have often been too ready to adopt this approach and have either extended the concept of miracle so far that it included almost any event considered from a religious point of view, or have interpreted in a purely inward and spiritual sense as a miracle of faith and forgiveness. The first approach left out the extraordinary and symbolic aspects which the Bible claims to be part of the miraculous, and there is a danger of a reversion into mythology. At this point, however, new difficulties appear.

Must we not attribute to God not only nature miracles but natural disasters, which kill thousands of people? The second course leaves out the physical dimension which is part of the biblical concept. If the biblical view of miracles is demythologized and spiritualized in this way, we are forced to ask whether belief in miracles is not finally an empty assertion? If 'miracle' does not include the idea of a 'thing' in the realm of the reality which confronts man, we have to ask whether belief in miracles is not ultimately a mere ideology. As long as there is no clarity about which mode of reality this 'thing' belongs to, talk of God's signs and acts of power will remain, as Seckler has rightly said, a theological cryptogram, preventing us from looking at the 'hard' core of the problem of miracles, the question of the reality to which the belief in miracles is addressed.[3] The question is this. Are miracles events in which God acts no differently from the way he acts in all other events, but by which men feel themselves particularly addressed? The immediate question is, of course: What does this feeling of being addressed consist of? Is it no more than an interpretation of faith, or does this interpretation correspond to 'something' in reality? Does the unique feature of the miraculous occurrence exist only on the level of interpretation, or does it also exist on the level of the reality we encounter? Is a miracle no more than an interpretation produced by faith, or is it a reality over against faith and affecting it? If so, what is the nature of this pecularity of reality if it does not exist on the level of observable phenomena?

Valuable as consideration of the biblical understanding of miracles is in enabling us to appreciate the original theological meaning of miracles, it is not the complete answer. Unlike the people of biblical times, we cannot avoid the task of clarifying not only the different levels of language and reality involved in scientific and theological statements, but – if the concept of a miracle is not to lose all reality for us – the relation of the two. The task of coming to terms with the modern understanding of reality as represented primarily by the natural sciences faces us once more in a new form on a new theoretical level.

The premiss of the scientific approach is a wholly law-bound determination of all events. The unique, the particular and the extraordinary are also covered by this postulate, even if in practice they cannot (yet) be completely explained. In scientific theory there is no room for a miracle in the sense of an event with no physical cause and therefore no definable origin. If the attempt is made nonetheless, as it sometimes is, to locate the miraculous in the practical impossibility of tracing the causes of certain events, that leads to a dragging rearguard action against the advance of scientific knowledge and robs preaching and theology of all credibility. On the other hand, science now accepts that it cannot even in principle encompass the totality of all determining factors. This is to say that the human mind can never get to the source of the facticity of reality. In other words, every event is completely contingent and also completely determined. And because that tension between the contingent nature of the particular and the general nature of its determination is fundamental, it is not possible to find a place for miracles in the over-determination of the particular as opposed to the general.[4] There are also theological objections to any such attempt. The theological question about miracles is only well-formed when it does not look for a 'gap' within physical causality as it has been discovered, but asks about the general system of causality. In scientific terms, however, problems about the nature of this system of causality can only be described as a never-ending task and a question which in principle cannot be answered by scientific methods. The question of the ultimate nature of this system of causality is therefore not a scientific question, but the philosophical and theological question of the meaning of existence as such.

Natural science alone cannot settle the question of miracles one way or the other, because this is a question which involves the meaning not just of this or that event, but the meaning of reality as symbolized in a particular event. This means that the encounter between theology and natural science does not ultimately take place in the area of observable facts. It takes place at a point which involves the ultimate presuppositions of natural science, the transcendental question, the question of the whole of reality and its meaning. This is a question about the meaning of the data of natural science.

The question of the mode of reality to which miracles belong turns finally into the question of what the ultimate meaning of reality as a whole is. Is it pure chance, blind fate, a universal regularity which allows no room for freedom, or an all-determining freedom which we call God? If we choose the religious interpretation of reality (in which case the grounds for this choice must themselves be examined), the question of miracles becomes the problem of correctly defining the relationship between God and the world. Is God just a kind of world architect who gives the world once-and-for-all laws in accordance with which it now functions? That is deism. Does God work uniformly in all events? Or is he the living God of history to whom the Bible testifies: that is, the God who in constantly original ways offers his love to human beings in and through the events of the world? This God uses the laws of nature which he created, and which he therefore wills and respects, and in and through them shows men by means of effective signs that he is near to help and hold them. That view holds that when God makes an event a special sign of his saving work, his choice of it gives it its full secular autonomy. We may therefore postulate as the basic law of the biblical relationship between God and the world that the unity of God and the world and the autonomy of creation are not inversely but directly proportional.

The foregoing is a tentative account of a possible theological theory of miracles. An adequate theology of miracles meeting all contemporary demands is admittedly in large part still an ideal, and it is too much to expect the lack to be supplied here. To summarize the discussion:

1. On the phenomenal level, miracles involve the extraordinary, the unusual and the amazing. So far these characteristics are capable of many interpretations. Precise definition is given to them only by the preaching which accompanies them and which is received in faith. Vatican II describes this relationship of word and act thus: 'This plan of revelation is realized by deeds and words having an inner unity: the deeds wrought by God in the history of salvation manifest and confirm the teaching and the realities signified by the words, while the words contain the deeds and clarify the mystery contained in them' (Dogmatic Constitution *Verbum Dei*, 2).

2. On the religious level made accessible by the word, a miracle is the result

of a personal initiative of God. The characteristic feature of a miracle is to be found on the level of a personal communication and claim by God, a communication and claim which show their power by taking symbolic physical form.

3. Historically, this assumption of a physical form always comes about through the action of created secondary causes. A divine intervention in the sense of a directly visible action of God is theological nonsense. Part of the very meaning of the coming of the Kingdom of God is that the revelation of God's divinity frees human beings to be human and the world to be secular. The same is true of miracles. The intensity of creation's independence grows in direct and not inverse ratio to the intensity of God's action.

4. Because of the rôle of creation and history, a miraculous event in itself can have many interpretations. This polyvalence is also the scope of faith's freedom of choice. A miracle can only be seen as the act of God by faith. It does not force faith, but challenges it and makes it credible. This brings us back to our Christological problem. The question is now: What is the significance of Jesus' miracles for faith? In what way do they reveal the meaning of reality?

2. THE THEOLOGICAL SIGNIFICANCE OF JESUS' MIRACLES

Mark reports the first miracles immediately after his summary of the message of the approach of the Kingdom (Mk 1.21ff). Jesus' miracles are signs of the arrival of the Kingdom of God. Their coming means the beginning of the end of Satan's Kingdom. The two go together: 'But if it is by the Spirit of God you cast out demons, then the Kingdom of God has come upon you' (Mt 12.28). A feature of the kingdom of demons is its hostility to creation. The alienation of man from God results in the alienation of man from himself and from nature. When fellowship with God is restored, when the Kingdom of God is established, things go 'back to normal' and the world becomes well again. The miracles say something about this well being; they tell us that it is not just a spiritual state, but affects human beings as a whole, including their bodies. The miracles of Jesus are signs that the well-being the Kingdom of God brings has already arrived. They are an expression of the physical and visible dimension of the Kingdom of God.

The Kingdom of God is an eschatological phenomenon, pointing to the future, and so also are the miracles of Jesus. They are *signa prognostica,* a first sight, the dawn of the new creation, a taste of the future inaugurated by Christ. They are therefore guarantees of man's hope for the liberation of himself and his world from its bondage to decay (Rom 8.21). They can only be understood against the background of the basic human hope for something totally different and totally new, for the coming of a new and reconciled world. It is to that hope in man, and not to his observing and recording intellect, that the miracles speak. The hope for the unprecedented and unparalleled new is essential to man. To deny the possibility of miracles would be to abandon this basic human hope. Certainly for the biblical conception of the Kingdom a faith with no room for miracles would be hollow. Jesus' miracles mean the penetration of the Kingdom of God into our ordinary, physical world, and because of this they are signs of hope for the world. For the same reason, Jesus' miracles cannot be defined as mere breaches of the laws of nature. Quite apart from the fact that this would be to reduce God's incomparable actions to the level of physical causality, this purely negative description would make miracles always seem arbitrary. The real significance of miracles is as a sign that the whole reality of the world has been taken into God's historical economy. Only in this context are the miracles 'intelligible' and meaningful. They show our world to be a dynamic, developing world, 'moving towards hope'.

This view rules out the interpretations of miracles put forward by Rudolf Bultmann.[5] He sees the miraculous as the forgiveness of sins and faith. No-one indeed would deny that the forgiveness of sins and faith are a miracle, but it would be wrong to ignore the hope present in both the Old and New Testaments for the salvation of the body in the world. This hope resists any simple spiritualization. It is too important an element in Scripture to be simply eliminated as a marginal element or demythologized. It does not, however, follow that the meaning of Jesus' miracles should be limited to this secular aspect. That is occasionally argued at the moment, sometimes in reaction to a purely spiritual interpretation; and Jesus' exorcisms are demythologized and updated by being presented as the breaking down of taboos, the unmasking and overthrowing of worldly absolutes and idols such as pleasure, technology, and so on; they show the destruction of discrimination and prejudice. The healing miracles, for their part, show Jesus as the man for others. All this certainly has some truth in it, but it does not exhaust the meaning of Jesus' miracles. An important feature of them is the absence of any planned or systematic attempt to improve the world. Jesus did not systematically heal all the sick or drive out all the demons; he simply gave isolated signs, which cannot be separated from the total context of his work, the message of the coming Kingdom of God. Jesus is not interested in a better world, but in the new world. But according to his message, man and the world can only become really human when they have God as their Lord. Anything else would not be human, but would lead to superhuman efforts and very easily to inhuman results.

The miracles that show the entry of the Kingdom of God into the world are also miracles performed by Jesus: If it is by the finger of God that 'I' cast out demons, then the Kingdom of God has come upon you' (Lk 11.20). In other words, the miracles have as a second function to attest the eschatological *exousia* of Jesus (Mt 7.29; 9.6, 8 etc.). The miracles are signs of Jesus' mission and authority. He is not only the Messiah of words, but also the Messiah of action. He brings the kingdom by word and work. But Jesus does not perform these acts of power merely to demonstrate his messianic authority. He explicitly rejects spectacular miracles (cf Mt 12.38ff; 16.1-2; Lk 11.29ff; Mk 8. 11-12). Consequently the miracles are also a sign of the way Jesus wanted his eschatological authority to be understood. To put it negatively – not like worldly power, outward show or glory. Jesus is not in show business! The positive meaning of Jesus' miracles from this point of view can be clarified further under three headings:

1. Jesus' miracles are claimed to be the fulfilment of the Old Testament. That is particularly true of the summary in Mt 11. 5-6: 'The blind receive their sight and the lame walk, lepers are cleansed and the deaf hear, and the dead are raised up and the poor have good news preached to them'. With two exceptions these are quotations from Isaiah (29. 18-19; 35. 5-6; 61.1). Through his miracles Jesus recapitulates the Old Testament; in them the justice of God promised in the Old Testament prevails. With these miracles Jesus places himself under God's will as revealed in the Old Testament. His miracles are therefore also an act of obedience. That distinguishes them from magic and the miracles of the hellenistic wonder-workers.

2. In Jesus' miracles God's power appears in human lowliness, concealment, ambiguity and scandalousness: 'Blessed is he who takes no offence at me' (Mt 11.6). The miracles can also be seen as the work of the devil (Mk 3.22; Mt 12.27); in themselves they are completely and utterly open, and taken on their own are never a proof of the divinity of Jesus but, on the contrary, a sign of the lowliness of God in Christ. The tangible human history of Jesus in this way becomes the scene of the hidden epiphany of God's power. This aspect is particularly developed by the gospel of Mark.

3. The miracles of Jesus are meant to release men for discipleship. The casting out of demons is meant to release men to follow Jesus and share in the Kingdom of God. Discipleship also means mission, and Jesus therefore gives his disciples not only authority in word but authority in action: that is, to work miracles (Mk 6.7; Mt 10.1; Lk 9.1). In this way Jesus' miracles bring about the eschatological gathering together of the people of God. This gathering together concerns particularly the lost, the poor, the weak and the rejected. They are here and now to experience symbolically the salvation and love of God so that they can bear witness of it to others.

There is a third important aspect. The miracles of Jesus are signs for faith. Miracles and faith go closely together. This can be shown even by simple word-counts: the words *pistis* and *pisteuein* appear mostly in connexion with reports of miracles. These reports constantly end with the words, 'Your faith has made you well' (Mk 5.34; 10.52; Mt 9.22; Lk 17.19). Where Jesus finds this faith wanting, he cannot perform miracles (Mk 6.5-6; Mt 13.58). On a closer view there turns out to be a double connexion between faith and miracles:

1. The purpose of the miracle is to lead to faith; that is, it is to provoke the question 'who is this?' (Mk 4.41; Mt 12.23; of Mk 1.27). The purpose of miracles is to awaken the basic human attitude of wonder, and thus enlighten people. They are meant to make people ask questions and shake their

certainties. In other words Jesus' miracles act like an 'alienation technique', a dramatic distancing. It is true that the answers to these questions cannot be given with certainty. Whether these remarkable, question-provoking events are miracles in the theological sense (that is, acts of God) cannot be proved. The gospels themselves say that they can be given a different interpretation, namely as the work of the devil (cf Lk 11.15). That rules out the view that miracles are such extravagant prodigies that they simply bowl men over, 'steamroller' them, force them to their knees. If miracles did that, paradoxically they certainly would not lead to faith, which of its essence is beyond proof, but would make it impossible. God does not 'steamroller' people. He wants a free answer. For this reason miracles can never be a sufficient basis for faith.

2. Seeing and recognizing miracles as miracles, that is, as acts of God, presupposes faith. Miracles are signs for faith. Faith here is not yet, as in the post-Easter kerygma, faith in Jesus Christ, but confidence in Jesus' miraculous power, a very limited calculation and trust that God's power does not end when human possibilities are exhausted. The miracles are an answer to petitions seen as an expression of faith. The believer in the Gospels often has to struggle before his request is granted; the miracles are Jesus' answer to the movement of a will towards him, his answer to human prayer. But when we say that faith and miracle are related as prayer and answer, that does not mean that faith and prayer create the miracle. It is the mark of faith that it expects everything from God and nothing of itself. The believer ultimately has no confidence in himself. The saying 'Lord, I believe; help my unbelief' (Mk 9.22b-24) applies here. Only in this final openness does faith become capable of receiving miracles from God. Then it becomes true of the believer that all things are possible to him (Mk 9.22-23; Mt 17.20). This faith shares in God's almighty power;[6] that is why miracles are promised to it.

Discussion of the New Testament miracle reports bring us back to our starting-point. Belief in miracles is not belief in prodigies, but trust in God's almighty power and providence. The real object of this belief is not various extraordinary phenomena, but God. What Jesus' miracles are ultimately saying is that in Jesus God was carrying out his plan, and that God acted in him for the salvation of mankind and the world.

Notes

[1] On the miracles of Jesus and the problems they raise, see Bultmann, *History of the Synoptic Tradition*, pp. 223-60; 'Zur Frage des Wunders', *Glauben und Verstehen*, vol. 1 (5th ed., Tübingen, 1964), pp. 214-28: ET: Faith and Understanding, UR I (New York, 1969); Dibelius, *Formgeschichte, op. cit.;* H.J. Held, 'Matthäus als Interpret der Wundergeschichten', in: G.Bornkamm *et al.* (ed.), *Überlieferung und Auslegung im Matthäusevangelium* (2nd ed., Neukirchen, 1963), pp. 155-287; W.Herrmann, *Die Wunder in der evangelischen Botschaft* (Berlin, 1961); L.Monden, *Theologie des Wunders* (Freiburg, 1961), pp. 103-25; F.Mussner, *Die Wunder Jesu* (Gütersloh, 1967); R.H.Fuller, *Interpreting the Miracles* (London, 1966); F. Lentzen-Deis, 'Die Wunder Jesu. Zur neueren Literatur und zur Frage nach der Historizität', ThP 43 (1968), pp. 392-402; K.Gutbrod, *Die*

Wundergeschichten der NT dargestellt nach den ersten drei Evangelien (Stuttgart, 1968); A.Kolping, *Wunder und Auferstehung Jesu Christi* (Bergen-Enkheim, 1969); K.Kertelge, *Die Wunder Jesu im Markus Evangelium* (Munich, 1970); R.Pesch, *Jesu ureigene Taten? Ein Beitrag zur Wunderfrage* (Freiburg, 1970), Quaestiones Disputatae, vol. 52 (bibliography); R.Pesch, 'Zur theologischen Bedeutsamkeit der Machtaten Jesu'. ThQ 152(1972), pp. 203-13; H.Küng, 'Die Gretchenfrage des christlichen Glaubens? Systematische Überlegungen zum neutestamentlichen Wunder', ThQ 152 (1972), pp. 214-23; K.Kertelge, 'Die Überlieferung der Wunder Jesu und die Frage nach dem historischen Jesus', *Rückfrage nach Jesus*, pp. 174-93.

[2] On the general problem of miracles see Bultmann, *op. cit.*, n.1, *supra;* C.S.Lewis, *Miracles* (London, 1960); G.Söhngen, 'Wunderzeichen und Glaube', *Die Einheit in der Theologie* (Munich, 1952), pp. 265-85; R.Guardini, *Wunder und Zeichen* (Würzburg, 1959); E.Käsemann, 'Zum Thema der Nichtobjektivierbarkeit', 6th ed., *Exegetische Versuche und Besinnungen*, vol. I (Göttingen, 1970), pp. 224-36; K.Rahner, 'Heilsmacht und Heilungskraft des Glaubens', in: *Schriften zur Theologie* vol. V (1962); ET: 'The Saving Force and Healing Power of Faith', in:*Theological Investigations* vol. 5 (London, 1966), pp. 460-7; H. Fries, 'Zeichen/Wunder! Geschichtlich und systematisch' HThG II, pp. 886-96; J.B.Metz, 'Wunder, VI. Systematisch', LTK X, pp. 1263-65; W.A. de Pater, *Theologische Sprachlogik* (Munich, 1971); M.Seckler, 'Plädoyer für Ehrlichkeit im Umgang mit Wundern', TQ 151 (1971), pp. 337-45; B.Weissmahr, 'Gibt es von Gott gewirkte Wunder? Grundsätzliche Überlegungen zu einer verdrängten Problematik', StdZ 191 (1973), pp. 47-63; *Gottes Wirken in der Welt. Ein Diskussionsbeitrag zur Frage der Evolution und des Wunders*, Frankfurter Theologische Studien, Vol. 15 (Frankfurt, 1973).

[3] See Seckler, *op. cit.*

[4] See esp. the works by Weissmahr listed above.

[5] See Bultmann, 'Zur Frage des Wunders', *art. cit.*, pp. 221 ff.

[6] See Ebeling, *'Jesus und Glaube', op. cit.*, pp. 238 ff; ET: 'Jesus and Faith', *Word and Faith, op. cit.*, p. 242.

IV. JESUS' CLAIM

IV. JESUS' CLAIM

1. JESUS' HIDDEN CLAIM

In spite of all that I have said about the message and miracles of Jesus, the question remains: 'Where is the Kingdom of God? Where can it be seen?' Jesus himself tells us that you cannot point to it and say 'here' or 'there'. In some mysterious way it is already among us (Lk 17.21). It appears wherever people surrender to God and his love, even when they never explicitly mention God or Jesus (Mt 25.35ff). The Kingdom of God is a hidden reality. It can be talked about only in parables. Parables as Jesus used them are more than a way of illustrating a quite separate thing – what is to be taught. The Kingdom of God can be appropriately described and announced only in parables. There is a mist of uncertainty over the message of the coming of the Kingdom of God. Jesus talks of the mystery of the Kingdom (Mk 4.11). What is that mystery which alone makes everything else clear and intelligible?

The idea of a mystery is important particularly in apocalyptic, in Qumran, and with Paul and his disciples.[1] It refers to the decree of God hidden from human eyes; the decree only revealed by revelation and which will become fact at the end of time. Knowing about the mystery of the Kingdom means knowing about the fact of its appearance. If the disciples know the mysteries of the Kingdom, this means that their eyes have been opened to see the dawn of the messianic age (Mt 13.16-17). That dawn takes place in the words and work of Jesus; his coming means the coming of the Kingdom of God. He is the mystery of the Kingdom in person. Hence eyewitnesses can be told: 'Blessed are the eyes which see what you see! For I tell you that many prophets and kings desired to see what you see, and did not see it, and to hear what you hear, and did not hear it' (Lk 10.23-24). That is why, at his 'inaugural sermon' in Nazareth, Jesus can follow the reading of the passage from the prophets with the claim, 'Today this scripture has been fulfilled in your hearing' (Lk 4.21). When Jesus casts out demons by the finger (or through the Spirit) of God, it means that the Kingdom of God has come (Lk 11.20; Mt 12.28). The moment which prophets promised has arrived: 'The blind receive their sight and the lame walk, lepers are cleansed and the deaf hear, and the dead are raised to life, and the poor have good news preached to them'. This takes place now through Jesus, and so he adds: 'Blessed is he who takes no offence at me' (Mt 11.5-6).

In the coming of Jesus, the Kingdom of God is arriving in a hidden way. Origen described this situation by saying Jesus was the *autobasileia* – the Kingdom in person.[2] To be more precise, we would have to say that Jesus is

100

the Kingdom of God in the form of concealment, lowliness and poverty. In him the meaning of his message is made visible and tangible; in him is made manifest what God's kingdom is. In his poverty, his obedience and his homelessness: the visible exegesis of God's will. In him we see what God's divinity and man's humanity mean.

Person and 'cause' cannot be separated in Jesus. He is cause in person. He is the physical embodiment and personal form of the coming of the Kingdom of God. Because of that, the whole preaching of Jesus about the coming Kingdom of God, his manner and actions, contain an implicit or indirect Christology which after Easter was put into an explicit and direct creed.[3] The only thing wrong with this description is that it could imply that the explicit and direct post-Easter Christology is only a more or less logical analysis produced by human minds. But since the coming of the Kingdom of God is completely the act of God and completely the free answer of faith, this Christological development must also be completely the act of God and completely the answer of faith. It cannot be just an analysis. We must admit something new. We have to think in terms of two forms or levels of the coming of the Kingdom: the hidden and the glorified.

The detailed exposition of this Christology concealed in the appearance, word and work of Jesus can take different forms. I shall start with the appearance and behaviour of Jesus.

Normally Jesus performed the duties of a pious Jew; he prayed and went to the synagogue on the Sabbath. But he also broke the Jewish interpretation of the sabbath commandment (Mk 2.23-3.6 etc.), the law of fasting (Mk 2.18-22), and the regulations regarding purity (Mk 7.1-23). He shared meals with sinners and tax collectors, and associated with the ritually unclean, who in his time were called 'godless'. Because of this he was called the friend of sinners and tax-collectors (Mt 11.19). This behaviour had no more than an indirect connexion with criticism of society and social change. Its full meaning is apparent only in connexion with Jesus' message of the coming of the Kingdom of God in love. In the east, even today, to share a meal with someone is a guarantee of peace, trust, brotherhood and forgiveness; the shared table is a shared life.[4] In Judaism fellowship at table had the special meaning of fellowship in the sight of God. Each person at the table ate a piece of broken bread and thus received a share in the blessing spoken by the master of the house over the whole loaf. Finally, every meal is a sign of the coming eschatological meal and the eschatological fellowship with God. 'Thus Jesus' meals with the publicans and sinners, too, are not only events on a social level, not only an expression of his unusual humanity and social generosity and his sympathy with those who were despised, but had an even deeper significance. They are an expression of the mission and message of Jesus (Mk 2.17), eschatological meals, anticipatory celebrations of feasts in the end-time (Mt 8.11 par.), in which the community of saints is already being represented (Mk 2.19). The inclusion of sinners in the community of salvation, achieved in table-fellowship, is the most meaningful expression of the message of the redeeming love of God.'[5] There is also another crucial point. Jesus, by taking sinners into fellowship with him, takes them into fellowship with God. This means that he forgives sins. The enormity of this claim was obviously felt from the beginning: 'It is blasphemy!' (Mk 2.7). Forgiving sins is something only God can do. Jesus' attitude to sinners implies an unprecedented Christological claim. Jesus acts here like someone who stands in the place of God.[6] In and through him God's love and mercy become fact. It is not far from this to the saying in John: 'He who has seen me has seen the Father' (Jn 14.9).

Jesus' preaching also includes an implicit Christology. At first sight Jesus comes on the scene like a rabbi, a prophet or a teacher of wisdom, but closer inspection reveals characteristic differences between him and all three other groups. The difference was noticed by Jesus' own contemporaries, who asked in amazement: 'What is this? A new teaching, and one proclaimed with authority' (cf Mk 1.27). Jesus did not teach like a rabbi who simply explained the Law of Moses. It is true that he used a phrase which the rabbis also employed: 'but I say to you' (Mt 5.22,28 etc.). The rabbis used this phrase in doctrinal discussions and debates to distinguish their own views sharply from those of their opponents. All these discussions, however, remained on the common ground of the Jewish Law. Jesus went beyond the Law (at least in the first, second and fourth paradoxes of the Sermon on the Mount, which are original) and in so doing exceeded the bounds of Judaism. He placed his word, not against, but above, the highest authority in Judaism, the word of Moses. And behind the authority of Moses was the authority of God. The passive formula 'it was said to the men of old' is no more than a circumlocution to avoid the name of God. In other words, Jesus' 'but I say to you' makes a claim to say God's last word, a word which brings the word of God in the Old Testament to its transcendent fulfilment.

Jesus also speaks in a different way from a prophet. All the prophet does is transmit the word of God. He points back from his word to the word of God: 'Thus says the LORD', 'A saying of Yahweh'. There is no trace of any such phrase in Jesus' teaching. He makes no distinction between his word and God's. He speaks from his own authority (Mk 1.22, 27; 2.10 etc.) It makes no difference whether he claimed in so many words to be the Messiah. The only category which does justice to such a claim is that of Messiah. In Judaism, the Messiah was expected not to abolish the Torah but to interpret it in a new way. Jesus fulfilled that expectation, and in such an unexpected way that he destroyed all previous models. His way went so far beyond previous anticipations that Judaism as a whole rejected Jesus' claim. It cannot be put in any other way: Jesus regarded himself as God's mouth, as God's voice. His contemporaries understood his claim very well, even in rejecting it. They said: 'It is blasphemy!' (Mk 2.7).

There is a third way of tracing an implicit Christology in Jesus' earthly career: in his call for a choice and his call to discipleship.[7] Through his appearance and his preaching Jesus summoned his people to a final decision, and linked that decision to accept or reject the kingdom of God specifically to the decision for or against himself, his word and his work. The link is particularly clear in Mk 8.38, which must be a substantially authentic saying: 'Whoever is ashamed of me and of my words . . . of him will the Son of man also be ashamed'. The eschatological choice is presented in the appearance and preaching of Jesus; in relation to him we make a choice about God. Such a summons to choose implies a whole Christology.

This observation receives further confirmation when we look at Jesus' call to discipleship. That Jesus gathered a circle of disciples round him, and in particular that the choice of the Twelve goes back to him, can hardly be doubted. In this Jesus behaved initially much like a Jewish rabbi gathering disciples around him. Nevertheless it is inaccurate to talk simply about the 'Rabbi Jesus'. You could not ask Jesus, as you could another rabbi, for admission as a disciple. Jesus chose, freely and without pressure, 'those whom he desired' (Mk 3.13). His call, 'Follow me', (Mk 1.17) is not a question, inducement, invitation or offer; it is a command. It is more than that. It is a creative word which makes disciples of those to whom it is spoken (Mk 1.17; 3.14). The way one becomes a disciple already reveals something about the authority of Jesus. This becomes clearer still as we look at what this discipleship involves. We never hear of Jesus and his disciples conducting learned disputations like the rabbis. The purpose of discipleship is not the transmission of tradition, but sharing in the proclamation of the Kingdom of God. This means sharing in Jesus' authority to announce the coming of the Kingdom of God with authority and to drive out evil spirits (Mk 1.17; 3.14; 6.7 etc). Lastly, unlike the rabbinic master-teacher relationship, it is not temporary, something persisting until the former pupil himself becomes a teacher. There is only one teacher (Mt 10.24-25; 23.8). Hence the link between the disciples and Jesus covers more than among the rabbis. Jesus called his disciples 'to be with him' (Mk 3.14). They shared his wanderings, his homelessness, his dangerous fate. They entered a shared life and a shared fate, for better or worse. The choice of discipleship also means a break with all other ties, 'leaving everything' (Mk 10.28). Ultimately, it means risking life and limb (cf Mk 8.34). This sort of radical and inseparable discipleship is equivalent to a confession of faith in Jesus. There is a factual continuity in the profession of faith between the periods before and after Easter, but there is also a sociological continuity between the pre- and post-Easter group of disciples.[8]

The implied Christology of the earthly Jesus contains an unprecedented claim which breaks down all previous schemes. In him we meet God and his glory. In him we come into contact with God's grace and God's judgment. He is God's kingdom, God's word and God's love in person. That claim is greater and more exalted than any honorific titles can express. Therefore when Jesus, as we are about to see, was very reluctant to accept those titles, that was not because he claimed to be less, but because he said he was more than they could express. Who he is can only be expressed by means of intensifying formulas: 'something greater than Jonah . . . something greater than Solomon is here' (Mt 12.41-2). And yet that claim, raised to the highest power, presents itself to us in Jesus without any signs of greatness or any arrogance, without any of the trappings we associate with power, influence, wealth and fame. He is poor and homeless. He is among his disciples like one who serves (Lk 22.27). The question comes up again: Who is this?

2. THE PROBLEM OF JESUS' TITLES (MESSIAH, SON OF MAN, SON OF GOD)

Jesus' appearance and miracles as well as his preaching prompt the question: 'Who is this?' Who does he say he is?' The question is old. We know that it goes back to the first group of disciples of Jesus and their disputes; their answers were very varied (cf Mk 6.14-15; 8.27ff). Since then the question has been asked repeatedly. The problem of the person and meaning of Jesus is the fundamental Christological question even in the New Testament. It dominates the development of dogma in the early Church and in modern theology.

If this question is asked about the earthly Jesus, it runs initially: Did Jesus claim to be the Christ: that is, the Messiah? The title Messiah or Christ was regarded even in the New Testament as so central that it finally became a proper name of Jesus. This is the supreme Christological title. In the New Testament it was becoming a sort of crystallization point for other important New Testament statements on Christology; at a very early stage it was combined with the saying about the Son of man (cf Mk 8.29, 31; 14.61, 62) and with the reference to the son of God (cf Mt 26. 63; Jn 20.31). In Christology, therefore, a great deal hangs on the question: Did Jesus himself know he was the Messiah? or, better: Did Jesus himself claim to be the Messiah?

At the time of Jesus the expectation of a Messiah could mean many things. In the Old Testament hope was originally directed not towards a particular bringer of salvation, but towards God himself and the coming of his kingdom. The transition to the expectation of a Messiah was brought about by the Old Testament idea of the king. The king was regarded, alongside the priests, and later the prophets, as the anointed (1 Sam 10.1; 16.3; 2 Sam 2.4;5.3) and as Yahweh's earthly representative. As a result, on his accession a promise of universal dominion was made to him. For the ruler of a tiny principality, wedged between the great powers, this was an immense claim. Naturally the question arose: 'Are you he that is to come, or must we wait for another;[10] The prophecies of Nathan (2 Sam 7.12-16) are the first trace of such a promise of future power connected with the house of David. The words are 'I will be his father, and he shall be my son' (7.14). The promise of a future heir of David who will be the bringer of salvation appears later in very different forms (see Amos 9,11; Is 9.6-7; 11.1; Mic 5. 2-4; Jer 33.15-17; Ezek 37.22-24; Hag 2.20ff). In Second Isaiah the bringer of salvation is the suffering servant of God (Is 42.1-7; 49.1-9; 50.4-9; 52.13-53. 12), in Daniel the Son of man (Dan 7.13), while in Zechariah there are two messianic figures, a king and a high priest (Zech 4.11-14). A similar picture comes from Qumran. In the time of Jesus there was an enormous range of expectations of the Messiah, from the nationalistic political hopes of the Zealots to the rabbinic expectation of a new teacher of the Law. Other shapes taken by the expected Messiah were the eschatological high priest, the prophet, Elijah returned, the son of man and the servant of God. The title 'Messiah' was undefined, even unclear. It was capable of many interpretations and of misinterpretation.

In this situation it is no surprise that in the Gospels the title Messiah is never found in the mouth of Jesus. It could have too many meanings, and was too liable to misunderstanding to be a clear description of his mission. The title is always applied to Jesus by others, and he corrects or even criticizes it (of Mk 8.29-33).

This fact has given rise to very different interpretations. Reimarus believed that Jesus remained within the Jewish perspective, regarded the Kingdom of God as a political entity and himself as a political Messiah. According to Reimarus, that meant that right up to his death his disciples placed their hopes in him as a secular redeemer. Only after his death did they modify their previous 'systema' and develop the idea of a suffering spiritual redeemer of the whole human race. Liberal theology took a very different view of the biblical data. In the liberal view, Jesus transformed the outward political expectation of the Messiah in Judaism and made it inward and purely spiritual. In the liberal outlines of the life of Jesus, he is an intellectual and moral liberator of his people who set out to bring about moral renewal and found a kingdom of the mind. This Jesus went willingly to death in the knowledge that death too was part of the triumph of his kingdom. Liberal theologians also provided an anthropological explanation of this view: namely, that there is a natural human belief in victory after conflict, and a passage from disfigurement to transfiguration. Here Jesus is, in effect, being made a symbol for a general idea and a moral principle. Albert Schweitzer remarked neatly that from its psychological interpretation of the first three Gospels liberal research into the life of Jesus had produced an ideal fourth gospel which it substituted for the historical Fourth Gospel. The liberal psychologizers failed to see that there was no trace of any of that in Mark. [11]

The literary-critical solution proposed by W. Wrede was of more lasting value. Wrede argued that the idea of the Messiah in the gospels derives from Christian rather than Jewish sources, and represents a dogmatic addition of early church theology.[12] Wrede started from the observation that the Jesus of Mark's gospel constantly insists on silence about his status as Messiah (Mk 3.11-12; 8.30). Those who are miraculously cured are told not to spread the news of Jesus' miracles (1.44; 5.43; 7.36; 8.26). At the same time Jesus works miracles without any concealment. What is the solution of the contradiction? Wrede claimed that Jesus' life had no messianic features, and was not presented in the light of the messianic faith until after Easter. Mark's theory of secrecy was his way of covering up the discrepancy. On this view, Jesus' Messiahship is not a historical proposition, but a dogmatic proposition formulated by Mark and the tradition on which he drew. For this reason Martin Dibelius labelled Mark's gospel 'the book of secret epiphanies'.[13] Bultmann especially adopted Wrede's theory. As a result, in spite of all the modifications it has undergone, it has been an important influence on contemporary theology.

The most thorough-going criticism of Wrede's and Bultmann's theory about the un-messianic life of Jesus has come from Albert Schweitzer.[14] If we treat the life of Jesus as un-messianic, argues Schweitzer, it is no longer possible to explain why he was executed. On the other hand, all four gospels agree in their description of the title over Jesus' cross: 'Jesus of Nazareth, the King of the Jews' (Mk 15.26 par.).[15] There can be little doubt that this report, which gives the ground of the sentence, is historically authentic. This means that Jesus was executed by the Romans as a would-be Messiah and political agitator. If we want to explain this as a mere misunderstanding, Jesus' career must at least have given occasion for a political and messianic interpretation. This leads into Schweitzer's second objection: how could the community come to a belief in the Messiahship of Jesus if the life of Jesus did not contain at least messianic and eschatological indications? 'It is not easy to eliminate the messianic aspect from the "life of Jesus", especially from the Passion. But it is more difficult still . . . to reinsert it into early church theology later on.' 'Why should not Jesus be just as capable of thinking dogmatically and actively "making history" as a poor evangelist who, required to do so by the theology of the early Church", has to do the same thing on paper.'[16] To what extent can 'appearances of the Risen One make the disciples think the crucified teacher was the Messiah?' The messianic-eschatological interpretation of the resurrection experiences somehow or other presupposes a messianic eschatological reference made by the earthly Jesus.

The starting-point for any discussion of Jesus' messianic claims is the scene at Caesarea Philippi (Mk 9.27-33 par.).[17] On the way to Jerusalem, Jesus asks 'Who do men say that I am?' The answers are very varied: 'John the Baptist; and others say, Elijah; and others one of the prophets.' Simon Peter declares, 'You are the Christ.' Jesus replies with a command of silence, and contrasts Peter's declaration with a saying about the sufferings of the Son of man. When Peter tries to remonstrate with him over this, Jesus calls him Satan and brushes him off. Rudolf Pesch has recently given strong arguments for regarding the core of this story as historical.

According to Pesch, even before Easter there existed among the disciples a recognition of Jesus as the Christ, that is the Messiah. This recognition, however, differed from current popular opinions, and therefore did not imply a political Messiahship. It is true that the group of disciples included some who might have been Zealots or who at least were close to the movement, but Jesus had always rejected a nationalistic or political interpretation of his activity. Peter's declaration does not therefore connect with political theories of the Messiah, but with the prophetic tradition of the anointed. In this strand of the tradition, the Messiah is the prophet of the last times who is anointed with the holy Spirit. This view fits perfectly into the framework outlined above of Jesus as the messenger and embodiment of God's last word, who demands absolute obedience. At this point, however, it too is transcended. Jesus indirectly rejects Peter's view of the Messiah, or rather develops it in his saying about the divinely ordained necessity for suffering. While there may be traces of such ideas in the Jewish tradition, they are foreign to Peter, not only here in Caesarea Philippi, but also on Good Friday. This is the reason for Jesus' refusal to adopt this view of the Messiah. He bans it, an action which made sense for other reasons; messianic expectations could give rise to political mis-interpretations, and the messianic movement this might set off among the people could lead to accusation and condemnation.

This brings us to a second text which has an important bearing on this question. This is Jesus' declaration before the Sanhedrin (Mk 14. 61-62 par.). The report cannot be based on a record of the trial, since none of Jesus' disciples was present. Jesus' declaration also shows signs of later Christological reflection in its combination of the title Messiah with that of Son of man. Nevertheless the question of the Messiah must have played an important part in the trial, since all four evangelists report that Jesus was condemned as 'King of the Jews' (Mk 15. 26 par.), i.e. as a messianic pretender. There can be little doubt of the authenticity of the inscription on the cross, and this allows conclusions about the course of the trial. Jesus could not simply deny messianic claims without giving up his eschatological claim. If he had simply denied the messianic character of his work, he would have called his mission in question. It can be concluded with fair probability, therefore, that before the Council Jesus was forced to declare himself the Messiah. This was made more feasible by the situation. In Jesus' helplessness the title of Messiah had lost its liability to political misinterpretation and had acquired a new meaning. Jesus now became the suffering Messiah, the Messiah of the cross.

This conclusion is confirmed by the fact the the epithet 'Christ' first appears in the Passion kerygma and within the Passion tradition (1 Cor 15.3-5). This means that the earliest tradition regards Jesus as the Messiah of the cross. Correspondingly, the older tradition also holds that God only made Jesus Messiah through his death and resurrection (Acts 2.36). If we want to talk about Jesus as the Messiah, we cannot take as a basis any of the ideas of the Messiah current in Jesus' time. Our premiss must be that, while the primitive community took over a Jewish title, it gave it a Christian interpretation. Even if it is admitted that the title was not used by the historical Jesus, what the primitive Christian preaching did was not to re-Judaize the message of Christ, but to give a legitimate answer to his claim to be the eschatological fulfilment of Israel. In its use of the title Messiah, the primitive community was maintaining that Jesus was a fulfilment which went beyond all expectations.

The conclusion is clear. Jesus is the fulfilment of the Old Testament because he bursts asunder all previous hopes. If he had followed the Jewish model of the Messiah, he would have identified his adversary as a political force, but instead he identified it as the Satanic power of evil. He did not seek power or an apparatus of repression, but thought of his activity as a service. 'If dominion is a mark of the Messiah, Jesus' dominion takes the form of service. If the Messiah's path to dominion leads through struggle and victory, Jesus' path points towards suffering and defeat . . . In the dominion of service which includes suffering, which comes from thinking God's thoughts, . . . we begin to see the new understanding of Messiahship which prevented Jesus from letting himself be called Messiah, since that title would only have encouraged misunderstanding of his mission.'[18]

The sayings about the Son of man tell us more about what Jesus claimed than the titles Messiah and Christ.[19] Unfortunately, they are one of the most difficult New Testament problems, and scholarship is still a long way from reaching anything like a clear and agreed interpretation of either their origin or their meaning. I can only put forward a reasoned hypothesis, which largely follows E. Schweizer's views.

Whereas the title Messiah or Christ is always found in the mouths of others and never in the mouth of Jesus, the New Testament Son of man sayings occur, with one exception (Acts 7.56), in the mouth of Jesus. The title is used in all eighty times. It is generally recognized that in many cases the reference to the Son of man is a secondary addition, in other words, that there is a tendency in the New Testament to put this title in the mouth of Jesus. However, the fact that it is always Jesus himself who talks about the Son of man is the strongest argument for taking this as a historical recollection, and holding that Jesus himself talked about the Son of man. Certainly, all other assumptions raise more problems than they solve. This is true, for example of Vielhauer's arguments, according to which Jesus cannot have talked at one and the same time of the Kingdom of God and the Son of man because the two ideas are fundamentally unrelated, and in fact mutually exclusive. Vielhauer claims that the Kingdom is exclusively the work of God and so excludes an eschatological bringer of salvation. It may be asked, however, whether the important and original feature of Jesus' work and preaching was not that with him his person and his 'cause', the coming of the Kingdom of God, were brought into very close relation and became practically identical. Is it not true that in the preaching and actions of Jesus the Kingdom of God more or less hit people in the face, so that a choice for or against Jesus was a choice for or against the Kingdom of God? Is it not part of the logic of Jesus's unique claim that he should combine traditions which were largely or even totally (cf Dan 7.13–14) unrelated? To put it another way, why should we attribute less originality to Jesus than to some hypothetical post-Easter prophet, whose name we do not even know?

But who or what does this term Son of man refer to? Initially it is a typical Semitic universal or generalizing term for 'human being'. In this sense it appears ninety-three times in the book of Ezekiel, as the title by which God addresses the prophet. In a further fourteen Old Testament uses it as an elevated term for 'human being' (Ps 8.5; 80.18; Job 25.6 etc.). A difficult problem is presented by the growth of the idea of the heavenly Son of man in Daniel 7.13–14 and apocalyptic, and the meaning of the term here. This heavenly Son of man, who comes on the clouds of heaven, is the representative of God's eschatological Kingdom and of the 'saints of the Most High' (Dan 7.21–22,25), that is, the true Israel which will replace the world kingdoms. In contrast to the fearsome animal figures which represent the previous kingdoms, the human figure is the symbol of the humanity of God's Kingdom of the last times. The Son of man does not acquire individual characteristics until later apocalyptic writings (Similitudes of the Ethiopian Enoch; 4 Ezra). At the time of Jesus, however, this view does not seem to have been very widespread. Certainly there was no definite dogmatic interpretation of references to the Son of man in late Judaism. It was more like a mysterious riddle which Jesus could use simultaneously to express and conceal his claim.

107

In the synoptic gospels three complexes of Son of man sayings can be distinguished. The sayings about the present activity of the Son of man fit into the context of the earthly life of Jesus: the saying about forgiving sins (Mk 2.10), that about the breaking of the Sabbath commandment (Mk 2.28), the comparison of Jesus' situation with that of the foxes and birds (Mt 8.20), the charge that Jesus is a glutton and a drunkard (Mt 11.9), the saying which Jesus calls the 'sign of Jonah (11.30), the comparison of the days of Jesus with the days of Noah because men live with no thought for the future and pay no heed to the call of the Son of man (Lk 17.22,26). All these sayings go very well with Jesus' association and table-fellowship with sinners, his disputes about the Sabbath, his wandering life and his eschatological call to repentance and decision. They connect with the language of the prophet Ezekiel. There the Son of man is filled with the Spirit (Ezek 2.2), he must announce God's word (2.3–4), he lives among a people who will not hear or see (12.2–3); he must prophesy against Jerusalem (4.7), and threaten the end (11.9–11); his word is a riddle and a parable (17.2). In this context, when Jesus describes himself as the Son of man, he is describing himself as the person who typologically shares the fate of human beings, but who is at the same time sent by God, given the Spirit of God, God's eschatological sign and yet rejected by men.

The second group of Son of man sayings talk about the sufferings of the Son of man (Mk 8.31; 9.31; 10.33–34 etc.). The overwhelming majority of exegetes believe that in their present form they date from the post-Easter period, even though in content and basic structure they are directed completely back to the earthly life of Jesus. This view is further confirmed by the fact that already the first group of Son of man sayings talk about the rejection and homelessness of the Son of man. It therefore seems that it was Jesus who first connected the reference to the Son of man with the tradition of the suffering and exalted servant, which was widespread in late Judaism. This could then be used as a starting-point by later, though still very early, Son of man sayings (Mk 14.62), such as the non-synoptic tradition (Acts 7.56), and the Gospel of John in particular has already taken this tradition of the exalted or glorified Son of man a considerable way (3.14; 8.28; 12.23,34; 13.31). The mysterious phrase 'Son of man' allowed Jesus to express the tension which ran through his whole message: The eschatological fulness of time becomes reality in and through a miserable, despised, persecuted and finally executed wandering preacher. The pattern of humiliation and exaltation which was to become so important for later Christology is already present in outline here.

This is the natural place to consider the futuristic and apocalyptic sayings which talk about the Son of man coming at the end of time on the clouds of heaven in great power and majesty (Mk 13.26 par 14.62 par etc). According to many exegetes, these Son of man sayings form the earliest layer of the tradition, but E. Schweizer singles them out as not going back to Jesus. It is extremely probable, however, that Jesus spoke of the Son of man in the third person and threatened that he would appear suddenly in the near future (Mt 24.27,37 par; Lk 18.18; 22.22; Mt 10.23). In this use the Son of man saying is a vehicle of prophetic preaching; it is well-suited to indicating the tension at the centre of Jesus' preaching and the combination of immediate preaching and decision and the imminent coming of the Kingdom of God represented by the Son of man. This is especially true of the saying Mk 8.38, which many exegetes regard as substantially authentic: 'Whoever is ashamed of me and my words . . . of him will the Son of man also be ashamed, when he comes in the glory of his Father . . .' Jesus does not here identify himself with the Son of man, but this does not mean that the Son of man is a saviour-figure greater than Jesus. On the contrary, the important decision has to be made here and now in response to the word of Jesus. The Son of man is hardly more than a symbol for the eschatological, definitive importance of the sayings and work of Jesus and of the decision of faith. It is at the same time a symbol of Jesus' certainty that this is the fulfilment. To claim a personal identity of Jesus with the coming Son of man may not be justified, but there is certainly a functional identity.

The complex and mysterious phrase 'Son of man' indicates that Jesus is the eschatological representative of God and his kingdom, and also the representative of man. The cause of God and men is decided in him and through him. He brings God's grace and God's judgement. The term 'Son of man' is a background against which the main developments of post-Easter Christology can be understood and shown to be legitimate: the Christologies of suffering and of exaltation and the belief in a return, the personal and the universal significance of Jesus.

The full depth of Jesus' claims about himself and the full mystery of his person do not become apparent to us until we turn to the title which assumed the greatest importance in the development of the creeds of the later New Testament period and of the early Church, and which proved to be the most appropriate and most fruitful description of Jesus: 'the Son' or 'the Son of God'.[20]

In discussing the title 'Son' or 'Son of God', we must not start from later dogmatic statements about Jesus as Son of God in a metaphysical sense. This sense is initially completely outside the conceptual possibilities of Jesus or the New Testament in terms either of Old Testament Judaism or of Hellenistic ideas. Pagan mythology contains frequent references to sons of God in a biological or genealogical sense, men born of a divine father and human mother, and in the Hellenistic period famous or extraordinarily talented men (rulers, doctors, philosophers, and so on) were given the title *theos auer.* According to Stoic philosophy all men could be regarded as sons of God because of their participation in the same *Logos*. For the strict monotheism of the Old Testament, the mythological, polytheistic and pantheistic background of such expressions made references to sons of God immediately suspect. When the Old Testament mentioned a son of God, it never referred to descent or any natural connexion, but exclusively to election, mission and the corresponding obedience and service. In this sense Israel is called the son whom God called out of Egypt (Ex 4.22; Hos 11.1; Jer 31.9). As the representative of Israel, the King (Ps 2.7; 89.27–28), and similarly the Messiah (2 Sam 7.14), can be described as the son of God. Later all the pious can be referred to as sons of God (Ps 73.15; Wis 5.5). In all these uses any idea of physical descent is strictly excluded. The status of son of God rests exclusively on adoption; it exists against a background of the Old Testament belief in election and its theocratic hopes.

According to the synoptic Gospels Jesus never describes himself as Son of God. Obviously the term 'Son of God' belongs to the Creeds of the Church. The only point to be discussed is whether Jesus referred to himself as simply 'the Son'. The best way of dealing with this question is to start with a linguistic observation. Jesus always says 'my Father' (Mk 14.36 par.; 11.25 par.) or 'your Father' (Lk 6.36; 12.30,32), or 'your heavenly Father' (Mk 11.25 par; Mt 23.9), but never 'our Father'. The 'Our Father' itself is not an argument against this, because the context is 'When *you* pray, say . . . ' (Lk 11. 2; Mt 6.9). There are strong arguments for attributing the distinction to Jesus himself. The usage is maintained consistently through all the strata of the New Testament, down to the classical Johannine formulation 'my Father and your Father' (Jn 20.17). This exclusive 'my Father' implies a non-transferable, unique relationship between Jesus and God. Whether or not he explicitly claimed the title 'Son' for himself, this way of speaking implies that, while all may be sons of God (cf Mt 5.9,45), he is Son in a special and unique way.

The question whether Jesus himself used the actual title 'Son' centres primarily on Mt 11.27 (=Lk 10.22): 'All things have been delivered to me by my Father; and no one knows the Son except the Father, and no one knows the Father except the Son and anyone to whom the Son chooses to reveal him.' Since the time of the Jena church historian K. von Hase, the phrase 'a bolt from the Johannine sky' has often been used in this context. In fact, however, an example of an influence of the Johannine tradition on the synoptics would be extremely unusual, and is not a likely assumption; more likely is the supposition that the Johannine tradition originates in and is to be explained by this synoptic passage. The real question is whether the saying goes back to Jesus. Against originality, two main arguments are constantly put forward, first, that the mutual knowledge here referred to is a technical term of hellenistic mysticism, and, second, that the use of the term 'Son' alone is a later title of Christ. Since then, however, Jeremias has conclusively demonstrated the Semitic character of this saying. In the Semitic languages, to say that father and son know each other was a common idiom. This means that 'the Son' here is not a title, but embodies a generally valid empirical proposition. The conclusion is that, while the title 'Son' does not go back to Jesus, Jesus did refer to himself as son in a unique way. It is therefore reasonable to assume that Mt 11. 27 is at least a 'reworking of authentic words of Jesus'. The assumption is strengthened by the existence of parallels in other sayings of Jesus (cf Lk 10.23; Mt 5.17; Lk 15.1-7,8-10, 11-32). The mutual knowledge of Father and Son should not be thought of, in the biblical view, as something purely external. It is not a purely intellectual process, but a much broader process of mutual effect, determination, exchange and connexion in love.

A more important question is whether it is possible to elucidate this relationship at all, and to make it more accessible. Can it, for all its uniqueness, be thought of by analogy with our relationship to God? Can we, for example, talk about Jesus' faith?[21] In trying to answer this question, we must first note that Heb 12.2 is the only passage which clearly refers to Jesus' faith, and that there are no literal parallels in the rest of the New Testament. A parallel to the content does, however, occur in the Synoptics in Mk 9.23. Here Jesus is dealing with a plea from the father of an epileptic boy: 'If you can do anything, have pity on us and help us'. Jesus' answer is 'All things are possible to him who believes'. Faith, then, is here a sharing in the almighty power of God and, as such, the power to heal. In this association of ideas only Jesus can be understood as 'he who believes', and to whom — in virtue of that faith — healing is possible. In his absolute obedience Jesus is absolute dependence on and absolute surrender to God. He is nothing in himself, but totally from God and for God. He is totally an empty mould giving form to God's self-communicating love. In this relationship Jesus' attachment to the Father obviously supposes an attachment and a self-giving on the part of the Father to Jesus. The later Son Christology is no more than the interpretation and translation of what is hidden in the filial obedience and submission of Jesus. What Jesus lived before Easter ontically is after Easter expressed ontologically.

There is another dimension to Jesus' hidden claim to be uniquely the Son. The claim does not concern just a 'private' and intimate relationship between Jesus and his father, but also his public mission. Authority has been given to him as Son; all things have been delivered to him so that he can reveal them to others (Mt 11.27). As the Son in a unique and non-transferable sense, he is also the Son for the other sons, the Son whose task is to make the others sons. Being the Son and being sent as the Son are inseparably united. This statement too is illustrated and given added depth by the story of the healing of the epileptic boy. At the end of this story Jesus describes prayer as the condition on which the possibility or impossibility of such a healing depends (Mk 9.29). Mk 11.22-23 similarly describes faith as moving mountains. Jesus' prayer for his disciples does not need to be proved. His intercession is the most obvious element of his own obedience in faith. It reflects both sides, his connexion with the Father and his connexion with us. Jesus believes utterly that God will answer his prayer, and this faith of Jesus's is a participation in the almighty power of God; this praying faith is God's existence for us.[22]

Because Jesus' faith and love are embodied in his prayer, that prayer is our clearest sight of the unity of Jesus' nature and mission. A request is an admission of poverty. Someone who makes a request places himself in the power of another person. In his obedience Jesus is an empty mould for God; in his faith he is a mode of existence of the love of God. Because he is the one who believes totally, he is the person who is totally filled with God's power, he shares in God's almighty power, which consists of love. But by being totally open to God, he is also totally open to us. Being petitioner makes him at the same time Lord. If making a request is the mark of poverty and powerlessness, being able to make a request is proof of a power and potential which must be given by another. Poverty and wealth, power and helplessness, fulness and emptiness, receptivenes and completion are embodied in Jesus. His nature as the Son is inseparable from his mission and his ministry. He is God's existence for others. Nature and mission, essential

110

Christology and functional Christology, cannot be opposed. They cannot evèn be separated; they are mutually dependent. Jesus' function, his existence for others, is simultaneously his essence; conversely, functional Christology implies an essential Christology.

The subject of Jesus' Father-God has been discredited by liberal theology. Adolf von Harnack tried to derive all Jesus' preaching from two elements, God as Father and the infinite value of the human soul, God and the soul, the soul and its God.[23] The result in Harnack is an interiorized and privatized conception of faith, and even a rejection of Christology: 'The Gospel, as Jesus proclaimed it, has to do with the Father only and not with the Son.'[24] As though God could be called Father without any reference to the one who is the Son. However, the problem today has become more difficult rather than less. The problem is how, in a society set on emancipation, and increasingly fatherless society (as Alexander Mitscherlich has described it), the idea of God as Father and of Jesus' sonship as the definitive model of humanity can be made intelligible and relevant. The centre of Jesus' message, the saying about the Kingdom of God and the message of God the Father, brings up the problem of authority and domination, and consequently seems unassimilable. For this reason theologians often prefer to talk about what is for us the more intelligible concept of Jesus' freedom and to make that central. Christian freedom is always a given freedom – given by God. Ernst Käsemann has clearly recognized this connexion and summed it up neatly: 'He brought and lived the freedom of the children of God, who remain children and free only as long as they have the Father as their Lord.'[25] As 'the Son', without qualification, Jesus is the Kingdom of God become a person in the love which communicates itself; as 'the Son', he is the free man par excellence. Our freedom also is determined in him. What that freedom means in specific terms becomes clear as we turn to the rest of Jesus' way – his road to death on the cross. Not until the cross do we realize the most profound meaning of his Sonship.

Notes

[1] G.Bornkamm, art. *'Mysterion'* TDNT, vol. IV, pp. 802-27.

[2] See Origen, 'In Matth. tom. XIV, 7', GCS, vol. 40, p. 289 (on Mt 18.23).

[3] This concept was introduced by Bultmann, *Theologie des Neuen Testaments* (5th ed., Tübingen, 1965) p. 46; ET: *New Testament Theology* (London, 1952), p. 43; see also H.Conzelmann, RGG III, pp. 619-53, esp. 650-1.

[4] See J.Jeremias, *Neutestamentliche Theologie*, vol. I, *Die Verkundigung Jesu* (1971), pp. 116 ff; ET: *New Testament Theology*, Part 1, *The Proclamation of Jesus* (London, 1971), pp. 114 ff.

[5] *Ibid.*, pp. 117; esp., pp. 115-6.

[6] See E.Fuchs, 'Die Frage nach dem historischen Jesus', *Zur Frage nach dem historischen Jesus* (Tübingen, 1960), pp. 143-67.

[7] See K.H.Schelkle, *Jüngerschaft und Apostelamt. Eine biblische Auslegung des priesterlichen Dienstes* (3rd ed., Freiburg 1965), esp. pp. 9-30; M.Hengel, *Nachfolge und Charisma* (Berlin, 1968); J.Ernst, *Anfänge der Christologie* (Stuttgart, 1972), pp. 125 ff.

[8] See H.Schurmann, 'Die vorosterlichen Anfänge der Logientradition', in: *Traditionsgeschichtliche Untersuchungen zu den synoptischen Evangelien* (Düsseldorf, 1968), pp. 83-108.

[9] See J.Obersteiner, H.Gross, W.Koester, 'Messias', LTK, vol. VII, pp. 335-42 (bibliography); W.Grundmann, F.Hesse, M. de Jonge, A.S. van der Woude, art. *'Chrio'*, TWNT, vol. IX, pp. 482-76, esp. pp. 518 ff.; E.Stauffer, 'Messias oder Menschensohn?' *Novum Testamentum* 1 (1956), pp. 81-102; Cullmann, *Christologie, op. cit.*, pp. 111-137; F.Hahn, *Hoheitstitel*, pp. 133-225; W.Kramer, *Christos – Kyrios – Gottessohn, Untersuchungen zu Gebrauch und Bedeutung der christologischen Bezeichnungen bei Paulus und den vorpaulinischen Gemeinden* (Zürich-Stuttgart, 1963), esp. pp. 203-14.

[10]See von Rad, *Theologie des alten Testaments*, vol. 1. op. cit., p. 336; ET: *Old Testament Theology*, vol. 1, pp. 323-24.

[11]See Schweitzer, *Geschichte*, op. cit., pp. 376 ff; ET: *The Quest of the Historical Jesus*, pp. 219-21.

[12]See W.Wrede, *Das Messiasgeheimnis in den Evangelien. Zugleich ein Beitrag zum Verstandnis des Markusevangeliums* (Göttingen, 1901).

[13]Dibelius, *Formgeschichte*, op. cit., p. 232.

[14]Schweitzer, *Geschichte*, op.cit., pp. 376-89; ET: *The Quest of the Historical Jesus*, pp. 222-40.

[15] See the works cited *supra*, p. 71, n. 8.

[16]Schweitzer, *Geschichte*, op. cit., pp. 383, 391.

[17]On this point, see R.Pesch, 'Das Messiasbekenntnis des Petrus (Mk 8, 27-30). Neuverhandlung einer alten Frage', BZ 17 (1973), pp. 178-95; 18 (1974), pp. 20-31.

[18]W.Grundmann, Article *'Chrio'*, TWNT, vol. IX, p. 531; cf F.Hahn, *Hoheitstitel, pp.* 193 ff.

[19]See A.Vögtle, 'Menschensohn', LTK, vol. VII, pp. 297-300 (bibliography); C.Colpe, art. *'Ho Huios tou Anthropou'* TDNT, vol. VIII, pp. 403-81, esp. 433 ff.; E.Sjöberg, *Der verborgene Menschensohn in den Evangelien* (Lund, 1955); H.E.Tödt, *Der Menschensohn in der synoptischen Überlieferung* (Gütersloh, 1959); W.Marxsen, *Anfangsprobleme der Christologie* (Gütersloh, 1960), pp. 20034; E.Schweizer, 'Der Menschensohn. Zur eschatologischen Erwartung Jesu', *Neotestamentica. Deutsche und englische Aufsätze 1951-1963* (Zurich and Stuttgart, 1963), pp. 56-84; P.Vielhauer, 'Gottesreich und Menschensohn in der Verkündigung Jesu', *Aufsätze zum Neuen Testament* (Munich, 1965), pp. 55-91; 'Jesus und der Menschensohn', op. cit., pp. 92-140; O. Cullmann, *Christologie, op. cit.,* pp. 138-98; F.Hahn, *Hoheitstitel*, pp. 13-53.

[20]See R.Schnackenburg, 'Sohn Gottes I', LTK, vol. IX, pp. 851-54 (bibliography); P. Wülfling von Martitz, G. Fohrer, E. Schweizer, E. Lohse, W. Schneemelcher, art. *'Huios'* TDNT, vol. VIII, pp. 334-97, esp. 366 ff.; J.Bieneck, *Sohn Gottes als Christusbezeichnung der Synoptiker* (Zürich, 1951); B.M.F. van Iersel, *Der 'Sohn' in den synoptischen Jesusworten* (Leiden, 1961); T. De Kruijf, *Der Sohn des lebendigen Gottes. Ein Beitrag zur Christologie des Matthäus-evangeliums*, Analecta Biblica, vol. 16 (Rome, 1962); Cullmann, *Christologie, op. cit.,* pp. 276-31; W.Kramer, *op. cit.,* pp. 105-25, 183-93; Hahn, *Hoheitstitel,* pp. 280-333; Jeremias, 'Abba', in: *Neutestamentliche Theologie* I, op. cit., pp. 67-73; ET: 'Abba', in: *New Testament Theology*, vol. 1, pp. 61-68.

[21]On this question, see principally H.Urs von Balthasar, 'Fides Christi', *Sponsa Verbi, op. cit.,* pp. 45-79; G.Ebeling, 'Jesus und Glaube; ET: 'Jesus and Faith' *art. cit.;* W.Thüsing, 'Neutestamentliche Zugangswege zu einer transzendental-dialogischen Christologie', in: K.Rahner and W.Thüsing, *Christologie*, pp. 211-26.

[22]W.Thüsing, *op. cit.*, p. 213.

[23]A. von Harnack, *Das Wesen des Christentums, op. cit.,* pp. 49 ff; ET: *What is Christianity?* (5th ed., London, 1958), pp. 54-9, p. 108.

[24]Harnack, *op. cit.,* p. 108.

[25]E.Käsemann, *Das Problem des historischen Jesus, op. cit.,* p. 212.

V. JESUS' DEATH

V JESUS' DEATH

1. THE HISTORICAL SETTING

The execution of Jesus of Nazareth on a cross is among the most securely established facts of his life. The precise date of the crucifixion is more difficult to establish.[1] All four evangelists agree that it was the Friday of the Jewish Passover week.

There is a dispute over whether the date was the 14th or the 15th Nisan (around March to April). According to the Synoptics, Jesus' last meal seems to have been a Passover meal, in which case he would have died on the Cross on the 15th Nisan. In John the details are different. According to him, Jesus died on the day of preparation for the Passover (Jn 19.14), while the Passover lambs were being slaughtered in the Temple. That would have made it the 14th Nisan. Accordingly, John describes the last meal, not as a Passover meal, but as a farewell meal. Both reports clearly involve certain theological ideas. The Synoptics want to emphasize that the last meal was a Passover meal, whereas John's main concern is to present Jesus as the true Passover lamb (19.36). That makes the historical aspect rather problematic. There is, however, much to be said for the Johannine account. It is unlikely, for example, that the Sanhedrin would have met on the most solemn Jewish feast day. Also, the facts that the disciples (cf Lk 22.38; Mk 14.47) and the arrest party (cf Mk 14.43) are armed, and that Simon of Cyrene is returning from work in the fields (cf Mk 15.21), support the view that Jesus died on the day before the Passover feast, that is 14th Nisan. In that case, astronomical calculations would give us 7th April AD 30 as the probable day of Jesus' death.

Crucifixion was a Roman form of execution. It was used chiefly for slaves, as in the Spartacus revolt. It was forbidden to crucify Roman citizens; they were beheaded. Crucifixion was a particularly cruel and especially degrading punishment. When the Romans used this death penalty for slaves against rebels — freedom fighters — it was regarded as a cruel mockery. Cicero says: 'The idea of the cross should never come near the bodies of Roman citizens; it should never pass through their thoughts, eyes or ears'.[2] Such a shameful death was not even to be talked about among decent people. Jesus, then, was executed as a political rebel. This is attested by the inscription on the Cross, 'The King of the Jews' (Mk 15.26 par).[3] The conclusion is often drawn from this that Jesus was a guerrilla leader of the Zealot type. But the fundamental differences between Jesus and the Zealots make this view quite untenable. Moreover, in the unstable political climate of Palestine of the time, the Romans were suspicious of any sort of mass organization; Roman soldiers were probably incapable of making precise theological distinctions. That would have made it easy for Jesus' opponents to find a pretext for bringing a political charge against him before Pilate. Pilate's record with Rome was already quite poor, which made him an easy target for pressure.

More difficult than why Jesus was condemned by Pilate is the question of what led to the condemnation by the Sanhedrin. In the trial before the Council (Mk 14.53-65 par), two elements seem to have been important, the Messiah issue, which was important to the accusation before Pilate, and Jesus' saying about the destruction of the Temple. The second was designed to secure the conviction of Jesus as a false prophet and blasphemer, for which the penalty was death (cf Lev 24.16; Deut 13.5-6; 18.20; Jer 14.14-15; 28.15-17). The two scenes of mockery support this view.[4] The ridiculing of the offender was intended in each case to parody the crime for which he was condemned.[4] The Roman soldiers dressed Jesus in a purple cloak and a crown of thorns, and mocked him as King of the Jews. Before the Council he was ridiculed as a false prophet. They played a sort of Blind Man's Buff with him: 'Prophesy to us, you Christ! Who is it that struck you?' The condemnation as false prophet and blasphemer had to do with Jesus' behaviour: his breaches of the Sabbath commandment and the Jewish ritual purity regulations; his association with sinners and the ritually impure; and his attack on the Law. All these were a challenge to the fundamentals of Judaism. Since at the time of Jesus the Sanhedrin could not itself carry out a death sentence, a deceitful collaboration took place between the Jewish authorities and the usually hated Roman occupying power. Jesus was caught between millstones of power. Misunderstanding, cowardice, hatred, lies, intrigues and emotions brought him to destruction.

But all that was superficial. The New Testament and Christian tradition see Jesus' death more profoundly. It is insufficient to stress the political misunderstanding and the political aspect of his death, or to regard Jesus as a free man, breaker of the Law and awkward non-conformist eliminated by his opponents. All that doubtless played a part. But for the New Testament Jesus' death is not just the doing of the Jews and Romans, but the saving act of God and Jesus' voluntary self-sacrifice. The important question for us is how Jesus himself understood his death. How did he interpret his failure?

2. THE ESCHATOLOGICAL PERSPECTIVE

Given the state of the sources, the question of how Jesus understood his death presents considerable problems. The source of the sayings (the *logia*)[5] not only omits all trace of a Passion narrative, but contains no references to it. It has no more than a reference to the violent deaths of the prophets, which is applied to Jesus (cf Lk 11.49ff par.); Jesus' disciples are told that they must expect rejection and persecution (Lk 6.22 par). These passages do not, however, attribute any saving efficacy to Jesus' death. The position in the various prophecies of the Passion is very different (see Mk 8.31 par.; 9.31 par.; 10.33-34 par.).[6] All these show Jesus as having foreknowledge of his death and stress the voluntary character of his acceptance of his fate. In addition, they treat Jesus' Passion as a divinely ordained necessity. The almost universal opinion today is that in their present form at least these passages are prophecies after the event. They are post-Easter interpretations of Jesus' death and not authentic sayings. That applies particularly to the third prophecy, which gives very precise details of the actual course of the Passion. If Jesus had foretold his death and Resurrection as clearly as that, the flight of the disciples, their disappointment and their initial refusal to accept the evidence of the Resurrection would have been completely incomprehensible.

This brings us to the actual Passion narratives in the four gospels. They agree to a considerable degree — much more than the rest of the traditional material. The Passion tradition is clearly an old and self-contained element of the New Testament tradition. There can be no doubt that it is close to the historical events, even if many details of the events remain uncertain. More important than questions of historical detail, however, is the fact that the Passion tradition clearly reveals the influence of theological interests. These may be apologetic, dogmatic or devotional, and they show that the Passion narratives were intended not just as narratives, but as preaching. They already interpret the Passion in the light of the Resurrection. The Passion is presented as the sufferings of the Messiah, the sufferings of the Just One, the fulfilment of the Old Testament and therefore the fulfilment of the will of God. The Song of the Suffering Servant (Is 53) and Psalms 22 and 69 had a deep influence on these accounts.

The state of the sources I have described explains the confusion of many exegetes about the death of Jesus. This confusion is almost inevitable if we adopt Wrede's assumption that the earthly life of Jesus was completely un-Messianic, since on that assumption it becomes impossible to explain why Jesus was crucified as 'King of the Jews' or a would-be Messiah. Bultmann even describes the crucifixion of Jesus as no more than a political misunderstanding. He believes that 'the greatest difficulty . . . is the fact that we cannot know how Jesus saw his death.'[7] In Bultmann's view we cannot even rule out the possibility that Jesus broke down at the end.[8] Willi Marxsen similarly believes that the historian 'can say with a high degree of confidence that Jesus did not see his death as a saving event'.[9] If he had, Marxsen believes that his activity, which was directed at the present and implied that the Eschaton was already arriving, would become unintelligible. Similar doubts and opinions can be found among 'modernist' Catholic theologians of the early years of this century. The 'modernists' believed that Jesus himself had no sense of his death as a saving event, and that idea was an invention of Paul's. In this view, Jesus was overpowered by his enemies and let himself be led to death, nobly submitting to it as a martyr for his cause. This view that the saving character of Jesus' death was a doctrine which began with Paul was rejected by Pius X in the *Syllabus of Errors*.[10] Hence the consternation when Catholic theologians such as H. Kessler and A. Vögtle more or less adopted Marxsen's idea.[11] The most detailed criticism of these views is that of H. Schürmann.[12]

The state of the sources makes it very difficult to say how Jesus saw his own death. Attempts to escape the difficulties have tried to show that the Old Testament and the Judaism of Jesus' time possessed theologoumena which enabled Jesus to give his death a soteriological interpretation. Even though the idea of a suffering Messiah cannot be attested, the motions of the sufferings of the just man and of the expiatory power of such sufferings (2 Macc 7.18,37ff; 4 Macc 1.11; 6.29; 9.23-4; 17.22) were widespread.[13]

These observations are no doubt correct and important, but they do not answer the question. The real question is not whether Jesus could have thought of his death as a redemptive death, but whether he did in fact think of it as a redemptive death. It is this question of fact, given the source data, which creates the new problem.

The most notable contribution to the solution of these problems came from Schweitzer.[14] He argued that the coming of the Kingdom of God and the trials of the eschatological or last times, the coming of the Messiah and the messianic age of suffering, cannot be separated. The proclamation of suffering belongs to the preaching of the approach of the Kingdom because it is a reminder of the eschatological tribulation.[15] Accordingly from the very beginning, as the Our Father shows, Jesus had talked about the danger of temptation (Mt 6. 13; Lk 11.4), by which he referred to the trials of the end-time, which he had probably also foretold to his followers from the beginning (Mt 10.34ff). Jesus certainly saw the trials of suffering and persecution as part of the lowly and hidden character of the Kingdom of God, and as such they passed into the mainstream of his preaching. There is therefore a more or less straight line from Jesus' eschatological message of the *basileia*, the Kingdom, to the mystery of his Passion.

This interpretation fits the factual details of Jesus' life very well. We must assume that Jesus had to and did take into account a violent death. Anyone who acted as he did had to be prepared for extreme consequences. Early on, he faced the charge of blasphemy (Mk 2.7), alliance with the devil or magic (Mt 12.24 par.), and the accusation of infringing the law of the Sabbath (Mk 2.23-24; Lk 13. 14-15). His enemies watched him to find grounds for arraigning him (Mk 3.2), and it is clear that they tried to trap him with trick-questions (Mk 12.13ff, 18ff, 28ff). Obviously Jesus had to contend with the deadly hostility and the real threat of death which came from the Pharisees, from the very beginning of his mission. In this the Pharisees combined with their traditional enemies the Herodians, and later with the Romans. With good reason, Jesus demanded complete adherence, a break with family obligations, from his disciples (Mt 8.21-22; Lk 9.59-60). Opting for Jesus does not mean peace, but a break with the *status quo* (Mt 10.34; Lk 12.51). Here again, the idea of the trial in the last times, the *peirasmos*, is in the background.

The fate of the Baptist (Mk 6.14-29; 9.13) must also have kept Jesus in mind of the possibility of his own violent death. Perhaps John's execution in particular convinced him that he too had to suffer the fate of the prophets. Lk 13.32-33, 'in the strict sense a piece of biographical material',[16] shows that he had taken over this widespread tradition of late Judaism: 'Go and tell that fox, "Behold, I cast out demons and perform cures today and tomorrow, and on the third day I finish my course. Nevertheless I must go on my way today and tomorrow and the day following; for it cannot be that a prophet should perish away from Jerusalem."' (cf Mt 23.34-39). The parable of struggle about the wicked wine-growers belongs in this context (Mk 12.1-12).

116

Its message is: 'Just as the secret murder of the son by the tenants will result in the certain intervention of the vineyard owner, the murder of Jesus, God's eschatological representative, which will be deliberate, will bring into action God's judgment on the guilty leaders of the people'.[17] Jesus sees his own fate prefigured in that of the prophets. Just as they were persecuted and rejected in Jerusalem, for him too the decisive moment will come in Jerusalem. Jesus sees it as the ultimate, eschatological crisis, the moment of decision about grace and judgment.

Jesus can in no sense be said to have gone unsuspecting to Jerusalem, but it is uncertain whether he went there with the firm intention of confronting his people with his message and forcing them to make a last-minute decision (cf Lk 19.11; 24.21; Acts 1.6). It is unlikely that he wanted to force the decision and the coming of the Kingdom, as Schweitzer assumed. That would contradict his trust in the Father to whom he left the future completely. It is nevertheless clear that his followers made messianic proclamations in Jerusalem (Mk 11.7ff par.) which caused a considerable stir, perhaps even a popular disturbance. It is certain that there was a clash in the Temple (Mk 11. 15ff par.), but it is hardly likely that his supporters would have tried a revolutionary action such as the occupation of the Temple hill. We should probably see the cleansing of the Temple as a prophetic symbolic action, rooted in Old Testament expectations (Is 56.7; Jer 7. 11), and symbolizing the dawn of the eschatological age, the end of the old Temple and the start of a new one. Jesus adopted those messianic hopes. He prophesied the destruction of the old Temple and the building of a new one; that is shown in the saying, very probably genuine, in Mk 13.2, which says that no stone will be left upon another. This context seems to have involved the question of Jesus' authority (Mk 11. 27-28), and certainly the Temple incident provoked the Jewish authorities. It was the first step to the trial of Jesus, and was one of the main factors in his condemnation by the Sanhedrin (cf Mk 14.58; 15.29).

Summary. The conflict between Jesus and his opponents took place in an eschatological context. Jesus was preaching the end of the old age and the coming of the new, and the arguments over his identity were connected with the conflict between the old and the new age. Ultimately, Jesus wanted and accepted that conflict.

The eschatological perspective is very evident in the passages dealing with the Last Supper (Mk 14.17-25 par.; 1 Cor 11.23-25).[18] In their present form these passages are definitely not authentic accounts; they show very clear signs of liturgical stylization. Whether they are nothing but community tradition, liturgical aetiology, or also preserve historically reliable recollections, need not be decided here. What is certain is that they contain at least one saying which did not become part of the later liturgy and must therefore be regarded as a genuine saying of the Lord. That is Jesus' declaration 'Truly, I say to you, I shall not drink again of the fruit of the vine until that day when I drink it new in the kingdom of God' (Mk 14.25; cf Lk 22.16,18).[19] That saying indicates that the last meal with the disciples, whatever else it is, is a symbolic eschatological action by which Jesus gives his followers, in the present, a share in the eschatological blessings. At the last meal Jesus is looking forward, not just to his approaching death, but also to the Kingdom of God which will come along with it. His death is connected with the coming of the *basileia*. This eschatological interpretation of his death agrees with the overall implication of his eschatological message, according to which God's lordship comes in lowliness and obscurity. Even when facing death — indeed, then particularly — Jesus maintained the eschatological character of his preaching and activity.

A final piece of evidence for this view is the saying with which, in the accounts of Mark and Matthew, Jesus died, 'My God, my God, why hast thou forsaken me?' (Mk 15.34; Mt 27.46).[20] This saying was felt as a problem from the beginning. Luke already found it intolerable; he makes Jesus die with the words, 'Father, into thy hands I commend my spirit' (23.46). In John, Jesus dies with a cry of victory, 'It is finished' (19.30). Even before the biblical tradition had become fixed, therefore, it was felt to be scandalous that Jesus should die abandoned by God. The same unease shows in the subsequent history of exegesis. Exegetes can, of course, point to the fact that the cry, 'My God, why hast thou forsaken me?', is a quotation from a psalm (Ps 22) which has influenced the whole Passion narrative. According to the practice of the time, saying the opening verse of a psalm implied the whole psalm. And this psalm is a lament which turns into a song of thanksgiving. The religious man's suffering is experienced as abandonment by God; but in his suffering and in the agony of death the religious man finds that God has been Lord all along, and that he saves him and brings him into a new life. The psalm uses the language of apocalyptic to put this experience into the form of a typical, paradigmatic fate. Being saved from death now becomes the way in which the eschatological kingdom of God intervenes. Consequently Jesus' words, 'My God, my God, why hast thou forsaken me?' are not a cry of despair, but a prayer confident of an answer: and one which hopes for the coming of God's kingdom.

We cannot be quite sure if Jesus recited Psalm 22 aloud as he died; perhaps that is a very early interpretation of Jesus' death in the light of the Resurrection. However, even if that were an interpretation which regarded Jesus' death as the fulfilment of the apocalyptic tribulations and as the coming of the Kingdom of God, it would still be a completely faithful reflection of Jesus' intention throughout. Jesus' faith did not give way, but he experienced the darkness and distress of death more deeply than any other man or woman. When he cried out to God in death, he called not just on the God of the Old Testament, but on the God he called Father in an exclusive sense, the God with whom he felt uniquely linked.[21] In other words, he experienced God as the one who withdraws in his very closeness, who is totally other. Jesus experienced the unfathomable mystery of God and his will, but he endured this darkness in faith. This extremity of emptiness enabled him to become the vessel of God's fulness. His death became the source of life. It became the other side of the coming of the Kingdom of God — its coming in love.

Summary: Jesus' message of the coming of the Kingdom of God as the coming of the new age includes an expectation of the eschatological trial. His message calls for a total break with the present age, and the ultimate implication of this is the acceptance of death. In this sense, Jesus' death on the cross is not just the ultimate consequence of his courageous activity, but the resumé and sum of his message. Jesus' death on the cross is the final spelling out of the only thing he was interested in, the coming of God's eschatological rule. This death is the form in which the Kingdom of God exists under the conditions of this age, the Kingdom of God in human power-lessness, wealth in poverty, love in desolation, abundance in emptiness, and life in death.

3. THE SOTERIOLOGICAL IMPLICATIONS

In very early layers of the post-Easter tradition Jesus' death was already interpreted as a saving and expiatory death 'for us' and 'for many'.[22] It was elucidated in terms of the fourth Servant Song: 'He had no form or comeliness . . . he was despised and rejected by men; a man of sorrows . . . Surely he has borne our griefs and carried our sorrows . . . He was wounded for our transgressions, he was bruised for our iniquities; upon him was the chastise-ment that made us whole, and with his stripes we are healed . . . When he makes himself an offering for sin, he shall see his offspring, he shall prolong his days . . . because he poured out his soul to death, and was numbered with the transgressors; yet he bore the sin of many, and made intercession for the transgressors' (Is 53.1-12). This song of the suffering servant of God is used in the very early creed in 1 Cor 15.3-5, and in the early tradition of the Last Supper (1 Cor 11.24; Mk 14.24 par.) to interpret the death of Jesus as a representative expiatory death for the salvation of men. Subsequently this interpretation became fundamental to the Christian understanding of the Redemption in general and the Eucharist in particular.

Historical criticism challenged this interpretation by claiming to show that it did not go back to Jesus himself. It is certainly true that it is impossible to provide anything like proof that Jesus himself used the words 'for many' at the Last Supper as an interpretation of his death. There is also debate about the historical authenticity of the saying in Mk 10.45, where Jesus' sacrifice of his life is called 'a ransom *(lutron)* for many'; these words do not occur in the Lucan parallel (cf Lk 22.27). On the other hand, if the inter-pretation of Jesus' death as an expiatory surrender to God for men could not be supported at all by reference to the life and death of Jesus himself, the core of the Christian faith would come dangerously close to mythology and false ideology. In that case it would be as if God had used the later preaching to go over Jesus' head and give his death a significance of which Jesus had no idea, and one which — if, as some scholars believe, he broke down at the end — he in fact excluded. This would be completely contrary to the way in which Jesus' preaching says God acts in and with men.

A number of attempts have been made to show that Jesus himself attributed a soteriological effect to his death, though attempts to go behind individual sayings of Jesus at this point are very unsafe. They can only succeed if a convergence can be shown to exist between individual sayings and Jesus' general intention *(ipsissima intentio)*. However, this can be shown, in two ways. The first starts from the premiss that Jesus thought of his death in relation to his message of the coming of the Kingdom of God. But the Kingdom of God is the essence of salvation. Therefore the eschatological interpretation of Jesus' death implies a soteriological interpretation. Hence we can talk of Jesus' hidden soteriology, analogous to his hidden Christology.

The second approach starts from the observation that the kingdom of God received in Jesus a personal embodiment in the form of service. Jesus was among his disciples as one who serves (Lk 22.27). This service of Jesus to his friends should not be regarded as just kindness. Certainly Jesus' association with the sinners, outcasts and misfits of his time brought them a degree of human liberation, but it went further: Jesus' healing of human alienation went to its deepest roots. The real liberation Jesus brought consisted in the remission of guilt towards God. The new community he brought and established was community with God. This redemptive service won him from the very beginning the hostility of his opponents (Mk 2.1-12; Lk 15), who regarded it as blasphemy and condemned him to death for it. Following Jesus means following him in this service: 'If anyone would be first, he must be last of all and servant of all' (Mk 9.35 par.). Service, love which includes one's enemies, in short, living for others, is the new way of living which Jesus inaugurated and made possible. A life like this involves being prepared for anything, leaving everything (Mk 10.28 par.), even risking your life (Mk 8.34-35 par.). Against this background, the idea that his sacrifice of his life was a service for his fellows, just as all his activity had been, must have forced itself on Jesus. The late Jewish theologoumena about the representative and expiatory death of the just man pointed in the same direction. The fact that Jesus did not directly claim the title servant of God any more than those of Messiah and Son of God does not show that he did not know himself to be the servant of God who served and suffered for many. His whole life had that character, and there is no evidence against, but much in favour of the claim that he maintained this view even in death; in other words, that he saw his death as a representative and saving service to many. In this way, in his life and in his death, Jesus is the man for others. Existing for others is his very essence. It is that which makes him the personified love of God for men.

This background gives historical plausibility to a number of disputed sayings. It enables us to show, for example, that the second of the three announcements of the Passion definitely has a historical core. That is the saying, 'The Son of man will be delivered into the hands of men' (Mk 9.31 par).[23] The ransom saying in Mk 10.45 acquires a basis in the life of Jesus when considered in this overall context, all the more so since the relevant Lucan parallel, which does not contain the saying, shows hellenistic influence and must be later. Finally, in this perspective, which pays attention to Jesus' intention in general, the Last Supper sayings about his laying down his life for many (Mk 14.24) must be allowed greater probability than is often assumed, in basic content and subject-matter, if not literally. Reasoned probability is as far as historical research can go. However, such detailed questions of historical authenticity are not so important for theology provided no reasonable doubt remains about the substance. In this case, the substance of the later soteriological formulas is firmly grounded in the life of the earthly Jesus.

There is still one important objection to be considered.[24] Does not the assumption that Jesus had an indirect knowledge all along of the saving effect of his death, but said nothing about it, lead to an intolerable contradiction with his proclamation of the Kingdom of God? This proclamation implies that salvation or damnation are decided here and now in relation to the preaching and actions of Jesus. How can this be reconciled with the belief that it is only through the death of Jesus that God brings about the salvation of men? Doesn't that retrospectively devalue all Jesus' previous activity and make it no more than preliminary? This objection overlooks the fact that the rejection of Jesus' message by Israel as a whole created a new situation. Even Jesus' immediate disciples misunderstood him at the end, and he was forced to make his last journey in lonely anonymity. He was on his own. He made it, like all his others, in obedience to his Father and for the service of others. That obedience and service became the only point at which the promised coming of the Kingdom of God could become reality. It became reality in a way which made all previous models useless. Finally, in the ultimate loneliness and complete darkness of blind obedience, all Jesus could do was to leave to the Father the manner of its coming. Jesus' obedient death is therefore the distillation, the essence, and the final transcendent culmination of his whole activity. That does not mean that his redemptive work is restricted to his death, but that his death gives it final clarity and definitiveness.

Jesus' death also made something else obvious and definite: the hidden character of his message and claim. The helplessness, poverty and insignificance with which the Kingdom of God appeared in his person and activity came to a final, even scandalous culmination in his death. Jesus' life ended in a final uncertainty. The story of Jesus, and its end, remain a question to which only God can give the answer. Unless Jesus' work failed, this answer can only say that a new age dawned in his death. That is what is meant by the belief that Jesus was raised from the dead.

Notes

[1] Cf J. Blinzler, *Der Prozess Jesu;* P. Winter, *On the Trial of Jesus* (Berlin, 1961); J. Jeremias, *Abendmahlsworte, op. cit.,* pp. 31-5 (bibliography).

[2] Cicero, *Pro Rabirio,* V,)16; cf idem. *In Verrem actio secunda,* book V, LXIV,)165, LXVI, 169.

[3] For references, see *supra,* p. 71, n. 8.

[4] See J. Jeremias, *Neutestamentliche Theologie* I, *op. cit.,* pp. 82 ff; ET: *New Testament Theology,* 1, pp. 77-8; *Abendmahlsworte, op. cit.,* pp. 72 ff.

[5] See H. Kessler, 'Die theologische Bedeutung des Todes Jesu', pp. 236 ff.

[6] See G. Strecker, 'Die Leidens – und Auferstehungsvoraussagen im Markusevangelium' (Mk 8, 31; 9, 31; 10, 32-34)' ZTK 64 (1967), pp. 16-39; Kessler, *op. cit.,* pp. 248 ff.

[7] R. Bultmann, *Das Verhältnis der urchristlichen Christusbotschaft zum historischen Jesus,* Sitzungsberichte der Heidelberger Akademie der Wissenschaften, Philos.-hist. Klasse, Jahrgang 1960, 3. Abhandlung (Heidelberg, 1960), p. 11.

[8] *Ibid.,* p. 12.

[9] W. Marxsen, 'Erwägungen zum Problem des verkündigten Kreuzes', in: *Der Exeget als Theologe. Vorträge zum Neuen Testament* (Gütersloh, 1968), pp. 160-70, esp. 165.

[10] See DS 3438.

[11] See H. Kessler, 'Die theologische Bedeutung des Todes Jesu', in: *Erlösung als Befreiung* (Düsseldorf, 1962); A. Vögtle, 'Jesus von Nazareth', in: R. Kottje and B. Moelle (ed.), *Ökumenische Kirchengeschichte I (Alte Kirche und Ostkirche)* (Mainz and Munich, 1970), pp. 3-24.

[12] H. Schürmann, 'Wie hat Jesus seinen Tod verstanden? Eine methodologische Besinnung', in: P. Hoffmann (ed.), *Orientierung an Jesus,* pp. 325-63.

[13] See E. Lohse, *Märtyrer und Gottesknechte. Untersuchungen zur urchristlichen Verkündigung vom Sühnentod Jesu Christi* (Göttingen, 1955), pp. 9-110; E. Schweizer, *Erniedrigung und Erhöhung bei Jesus und seinen Nachfolgern* (2nd ed., Zürich, 1962), pp. 53 ff; Kessler, *op. cit.,* pp. 253 ff.

[14] See A. Schweitzer, *Das Messianitäts- und Leidensgeheimnis, op. cit.,* pp.81-98; ET: *The Mystery of the Kingdom of God.* The problems raised by this hypothesis will be discussed shortly.

[15] See H. Seesemann, Article *'Peira',* TDNT, vol. VI, p. 30.

[16] R. Bultmann, *Geschichte der synoptischen Tradition, op. cit.,* p. 35; ET: *The History of the Synoptic Tradition, op. cit.,* p. 35.

[17] M. Hengel, 'Das Gleichnis von den Weingärtnern Mc 12, 1-12 im Lichte der Zenonpapyri und der rabbinischen Gleichnisse', ZNW 59 (1968), pp. 1-39, esp. 38.

[18] See H. Schürmann, *Der Paschamahlbericht Lk 22, (7-14) 15-18* (Münster, 1953); *Der Einsetzungsbericht Lk 22, 19-20* (Münster, 1955); G. Bornkamm, *Jesus von Nazareth, op. cit.,* pp. 147-9; ET: *Jesus of Nazareth, op. cit.,* pp. 160-2; 'Herrenmahl und Kirche bei Paulus', *Studien zu Antike und Urchristentum. Gesammelte Aufsätze II* (Munich, 1970), pp. 138-76; Jeremias, *Abendmahlsworte, op. cit.;* P. Neuenzeit, *Das Herrenmahl, Studien zur paulinischen Eucharistieauffassung* (Munich, 1960); E. Käsemann, 'Anliegen und Eigenart der paulinischen Abendmahlslehre', in: *Exegetische Versuche und Besinnungen,* vol. I, pp. 11-34.

[19] See G. Bornkamm, *Jesus von Nazareth, op. cit.,* pp. 147 ff; ET: *Jesus of Nazareth, op. cit.,* pp. 160-1; H.E. Tödt, *Der Menschensohn in der synoptischen Überlieferung,* pp. 193, 279; F. Hahn, 'Die alttestamentlichen Motive in der urchristlichen Abendmahlüberlieferung', EvTh 27 (1967), pp. 337-74, esp. 340, 346.

[20] See H. Gese, 'Psalm 22 und das Neue Testament. Der älteste Bericht vom Todes Jesu und die Entstehung des Herrenmahles', ZTK 65 (1968), pp. 1-22.

[21] Moltmann's interpretation (*Der gekreuzigte Gott, op. cit.,* pp. 138 ff; ET: *The Crucified God,* London, 1974, pp. 145-53) is too speculative.

[22] See W. Schrage, 'Das Verständnis des Todes Jesu Christi im Neuen Testament', in: E. Bizer *et al., Das Kreuz Jesu Christi als Grund des Heils* (Gütersloh, 1967), pp. 49-89;

Kessler, 'Die theologische Bedeutung des Todes Jesu', pp. 265 ff.

[23] See J. Jeremias, *Neutestamentliche Theologie* I, op. cit., pp. 264 ff; ET: *New Testament Theology*, Part 1, *op. cit.*, pp. 281-6.

[24] See W. Marxsen, 'Erwägungen zum Problem des verkündigten Kreuzes', *op. cit.*, pp. 164-5; A. Vögtle, 'Jesus von Nazareth', *op. cit.*, pp. 20-1.

VI. THE BASIS OF BELIEF IN JESUS' RESURRECTION

B. CHRIST, RISEN AND TRANSCENDENT

VI. THE BASIS OF BELIEF IN JESUS' RESURRECTION

1. THE FINDINGS OF TRADITION

The violence and scandal of Jesus' death on the cross seemed the end of everything.[1] Even Jesus' disciples apparently saw his death as the end of their hopes. They returned, disappointed and resigned, to their families. Jesus' message that the Kingdom of God was at hand seemed to be discredited by his end. There were theologoumena in the Judaism of the time which could be used to explain Jesus' death in theological terms; but Jesus had related his 'cause' so closely to his own person that this 'cause', the coming of the Kingdom of God, could not simply continue after his death. The ideas and ideals of Jesus could not be fostered and passed on, as those of Socrates had been after his death. The message stood and fell with his person. After Jesus' death, therefore, it was not possible to fix instead on Jesus' 'cause' and hand on his message of freedom in a sort of Jesus Movement.

In spite of that, there was continuity after Good Friday; indeed in some senses it was then that movement really began. The meeting of the scattered group of disciples took place, meetings of the communities and churches were formed; a world-wide mission was undertaken, first to the Jews, then to the pagans. The powerful historical dynamism of this revival can only be made comprehensible, even in purely historical terms, by positing a sort of 'initial ignition'. Religious, psychological, political and social elements in the situation, as it was at the time, can be cited in explanation. Yet, seen from the point of view of historical circumstances, Jesus' 'cause' had very slender chances of surviving. Jesus' end on the cross was not only his private failure but a public catastrophe for his 'mission', and its religious discrediting. The renewal must therefore be seen as strong enough not only to 'explain' the unnatural dynamism of early Christianity, but to 'come to terms with' that problem of the cross.

The answer given by the New Testament to the question of the Church's foundation and belief is quite unambiguous. The testimony of all the biblical books is that soon after his death Jesus' disciples proclaimed that God had raised him from the dead; that he who had been crucified had proved to be living; and that he had sent them, his disciples, to proclaim that message to the world. In making this extraordinary announcement all the New Testament writings speak with a single voice; 'Whether then it was I or they, so we preach and so you believe' (1 Cor 5.11); 'This Jesus God raised up, and of that we are all witnesses' (Acts 2.32). This unanimous evidence of the whole New Testament forms the basis and the core of the New Testament message: 'If Christ has not been raised, then our preaching is in vain and your faith is in vain' (1 Cor 15.14; cf. 17.19).

Such clear and unambiguous language was evidently not easy for the disciples to accept at first. The gospels and Acts of the apostles report their initial disbelief and stubbornness (Mk 16.14), their despair (Mt 28.17), their scoffing (Lk 24.11; cf 24.24), their resignation (Lk 24.21), their fear and dismay (Lk 24.37; cf. Jn 20.24-29). Yet this sober, critical, reserved attitude, far removed from extravagant enthusiasm of any sort, speaks for rather than against the disciples and their witness. That witness carries conviction most strongly, because of the fact that all the witnesses were ready to die for their message. The fact that they were prepared to bear witness with their lives and not just with their words makes it impossible simply to push the biblical message to one side or dismiss it as a fanaticism not to be taken seriously.

As soon as one examines the evidence of Jesus' Resurrection in detail, one comes up against a variety of difficult problems. Firstly the problem of the tradition of the Resurrection message itself. On looking into this more deeply, one discovers that in contrast to the Passion tradition, where all four evangelists give a relatively unified account and follow the same order of events, in spite of a few differences of detail, the accounts of Easter and the witnesses show substantial differences. The biblical evidence is divided between two different strands of tradition, within which there are yet further considerable differences: there is the Easter kerygma and there are the Easter stories.

The Easter kerygma is revealed in firm and brief, kerygmatic and liturgical formulations of belief. We can often see these credal statements as apart from their context, as originally independent entities; they are often considerably older than the corresponding New Testament writings among which they are found today. So we are faced here not with non-binding accounts, merely the narratives of individual disciples, but with binding public formulations of the beliefs of the first Christian communities.

Characteristic of these is the very old acclamation which is probably derived from the liturgy: 'The Lord has risen indeed and has appeared to Simon!' (Lk 24.34). The most famous and important formula is found in Cor 15.3-5: 'Christ died for our sins in accordance with the Scriptures, he was buried, he was raised on the third day in accordance with the Scriptures and he appeared to Cephas, then to the twelve'. This formula was inserted by Paul as a tradition which he had already been given. We have here therefore an ancient text, perhaps in use by the end of 30 AD in the oldest missionary communities, probably in Antioch. This text brings us chronologically near to the traditional events surrounding Jesus' death and Resurrection. Since the text itself is in verse form, it is moreover a solemn text and of binding force. Similar statements, which draw together and sum up beliefs are found in Acts 10, 40f and 1 Tim 3.16; witnesses are no longer directly cited here, but instead revelations and manifestations in general.

In addition there is a series of credal formulations and hymns, which do not mention appearances, but give direct testimony of the Resurrection of Jesus. Here it is worth noting in particular the two-verse confession of faith in Romans 1.3f and the hymn to Christ in Phil 2.6-11, which are both pre-Pauline. In addition there is the old catechetical formula in Rom 10.9: 'If you confess with your lips that Jesus is Lord and believe in your heart that God raised him from the dead, you will be saved'. Many statements of belief in the Resurrection are found scattered in the early chapters of Acts, for example 2.23: 'This Jesus God raised up, and of that we are all witnesses' (cf 3.15: 5.31f. among others). Other texts are Romans 10.5-8; Eph 4.7-12; 1 Pet 3.18-22; 4.6.

A distinction should be made between this Easter kerygma and the Easter stories found at the end of the four gospels (Mk 16.1-8 *passim*). With the Easter stories belong the accounts at the end of the gospels of Luke and John about the meal taken by the risen Christ with his disciples and about proof by touching the risen Lord (Lk 24.13-43; Jn 20.19-29; 21). These accounts too contain traditions about the post-Resurrection appearances. They are clearly different in kind from the kerygmatic formulas, in that the narrative is more expansive in style. The appearances in the kerygmatic tradition, in which Peter occupies a central role, and the appearances in the Easter stories, where different names, including women's, play an important part, do not harmonize. What is more important is that in the Easter stories there are accounts of the finding of the empty grave which are missing from the other tradition. Whereas the traditions regarding the appearances originally point towards Galilee, the stories of the tomb belong of course to Jerusalem.

The evangelists' Easter stories, particularly the stories about the tomb, present serious difficulties. The basic question is: are we dealing with historical accounts, or at least accounts with an historical core, or are we dealing with legends, which express beliefs in the form of narratives? Are the Easter stories, and in particular the stories of the tomb, a product of Easter faith or its historical origin?

Opinions on this point differ widely. The generally accepted view is undoubtedly that the Easter belief stems from the discovery of the empty tomb and that the angel's (or angels') announcement and even the appearances of the risen Lord himself follow from that discovery. This interpretation has been defended again recently by Von Campenhausen[2] in particular, using historico-critical methods. The opposite view maintains that the Easter stories are secondary in importance to the Easter kerygma, their purpose is apologetic, and they are intended to demonstrate the reality and corporeality of the Resurrection in contrast to attempts at spiritualistic interpretations. We find in them a very powerful and therefore theologically doubtful form of the Easter belief. Here Jesus' Resurrection is already a provable fact and a this-worldly phenomenon.

126

A precise analysis of the grave stories shows: 1. There are substantial discrepancies between the four evangelists' accounts. All four report the women's experiences at Jesus' tomb on Easter morning. But Mark (16.1) and Luke (24.10) mention three women (although not the same ones), whereas Matthew (28.1) says two and John (20.1) only one (although 20.2 runs: 'we do not know. . .'). Different reasons are given, too, for going to the tomb. Mark and Luke say the intention is to anoint the body, Matthew to see the tomb. According to Mark (16.8), the women told no one afterwards, according to Matthew (28.8) they ran to tell the disciples. Matthew (28.2-5) and Mark (16.5) mention the angel who appeared to the women, Luke (24.3f) speak of two angels, as does John (20.11ff), on Mary Magdalen's second visit. According to John (20.13ff) the angel does not give the women the news of the Resurrection, unlike the Synoptics. These and other differences which cannot be harmonized show that the events of Easter morning can no longer be reconstructed; indeed that a purely historical account is not what matters in the Easter stories.

2. The oldest account, on which all the others depend, is in Mark 16.1-8. This means that Matthew and Luke only concur, in so far as they also harmonize with Mark; clearly, then the Mark text serves as a basis for both. Since all the other accounts are clearly dependent on Mark as the oldest text, an analysis of this pericope is essential. Such an analysis reveals that in its present form at any rate, it is in no way an historical account.[3] The introduction begins with a definite improbability. The wish to anoint a dead body, which has already been put in its shroud in the tomb, three days later, is not given any explanation, such as being a custom of the time, and is unintelligible in the climatic conditions of Palestine. The fact that the women do not realize until they are already on the way that they would need help to roll back the stone and enter the tomb betrays a degree of thoughtlessness which is not easy to explain. We must assume therefore that we are faced not with historical details but with stylistic devices intended to attract the attention and raise excitement in the minds of those listening. Everything is clearly constructed to lead very skilfully to the climax of the angel's words: 'He is risen, he is not here; see the place where they laid him' (16.6). It is remarkable, however, that although the women are given the task of telling his disciples that Jesus is going before them into Galilee and that they will see him there, they are silent after the final remark and say nothing to anyone of their experience. Clearly we see here not a temporary silence, but a lasting silence, a typical motif in Mark, and one of several clear indications that Mark was the editor of this account.

3. If Mark's emendments are ignored, what remains is a very old pre-Marcan tradition. The great age of this tradition is attested in particular by the fact that the account in the later tradition, right up to the aprocryphal Petrine gospel, is increasingly filled out with legendary features. In contrast, the reserve which characterizes the tradition as expressed in Mk 16.1-8 is proof of its great age. Only the kerygma of the angel is legendary in the sense in which the term is used in form criticism. The important point here is not primarily the emptiness of the tomb; it is rather the proclaiming of the Resurrection, and the reference to the tomb is intended as the symbol of this faith in the Resurrection. In conclusion: this ancient tradition is not an historical account of the discovery of the empty tomb, but evidence of faith. In terms of form criticism, this tradition can be most easily described as cultic; that is, it deals with a narrative intended as the basis for a cultic ceremony.[4] We know from other sources that in Jewish society at that time it was normal to honour the tombs of distinguished men. So the primitive Christian community in Jerusalem may well have honoured Jesus' tomb and have assembled yearly at or in the empty tomb on the anniversary of the Resurrection for a cultic ceremony, during which the joyful message of the Resurrection would be proclaimed and the empty tomb used as a symbol.[5]

4. The classification of Mk 16.1-8 as cultic does not in itself imply any judgment about the historicity or, indeed, non-historicity of a fundamental event. In this case there are even some arguments which can be advanced in favour of the view that remembered historical facts have been re-worked and altered in this account. The most important

argument for an historical core is that any such ancient tradition, stemming as it did from Jerusalem itself, would not have lasted there a single day, if the emptiness of the tomb had not been a positive fact for all those concerned. It is, however, striking that in all the Jewish polemic against the Christian message of the Resurrection this obvious argument is nowhere found.

Hundreds of other hypotheses can, of course, be advanced, if one so wishes. But Campenhausen points out with some justice: 'Anyone who wishes to take into account possible substitution, confusion or other accident, may naturally allow his imagination full play – anything is possible and nothing provable here. But this has then no longer anything to do with critical research. If one examines what there is to examine, one cannot avoid accepting as fact the news of the empty tomb itself and of its early discovery. There is a great deal that is convincing and definite to be said for it and little to be said against it; it is, therefore, in all probability, historical'.[6] It is, of course, impossible from an historical view-point to go any further than the statement that it is definitely a very ancient tradition, which must very probably be described as historical; but then it is impossible to go further than this in the case of other traditions too.

To establish that there is an historical core to the empty tomb stories is not the same as providing proof of the Resurrection as a fact. Historically it can only be put forward as probable that the tomb was found empty; how it became empty cannot be established historically. Of itself, the empty tomb is an ambiguous phenomenon. Different interpretations of it exist even in the New Testament (cp Mt 28.11-15; Jn 20.15). It only becomes clear and unambiguous through the proclamation, which has its source in the appearances of the risen Christ. For the faithful the empty tomb is not a proof but a sign.

Originally, therefore, we have two separate traditions. Both strands of tradition seem to be very old. But they probably existed initially quite separately from one another. Mark must have been the first to combine them. In his version the angel directs the women to go to the disciples and to Peter in particular and promises the appearances of the risen Christ in Galilee: 'He is going before you into Galilee; there you will see him as he told you' (16.7). This initially relatively loose juxtaposition becomes increasingly close later on. Luke transposes the appearances to Jerusalem (24.36-49). In John's account the juxtaposition is even closer, for according to him the risen Christ appears to Mary Magdalen straight-away at the tomb (20.14-17). John gives accounts too of appearances that Jesus made to the apostles in Jerusalem (20.19-23; 24-9) and also in Galilee, in the following chapter (21.1-23). Here both strands of tradition have finally been bound into one.

The tomb-stories have left their mark most clearly on traditional Easter piety and credal statements about the Resurrection. When we speak of Jesus' Resurrection, we think almost involuntarily of pictures such as that by Matthias Grünewald, which shows Christ going forth from the tomb transfigured. But from even a first glance at the evidence of tradition within the New Testament, it is clear to us that this interpretation is not an automatic one. For the early Church it was the conviction of the witnesses of the post-Resurrection appearances which played a central role and not the stories of the tomb. Even if the stories of the tomb are probably very old, they were not connected with the tradition of the appearances, which originates in Galilee, until much later. In view of the facts of tradition we must first of all start from the early Easter creeds and traditions of the appearances and try to classify the stories of the tomb from them. We must in fact adopt an opposite course to that of traditional Easter piety and its beliefs.

There are, however, many obstacles in the way of any such attempt. I have already mentioned the irreconcilable divergences between the kerygmatic tradition and the Easter stories. But the two traditions are not unified within themselves. In 1 Cor 15, beside the tradition which mentions Peter and the Twelve (15.5), a second tradition is cited which refers to James and all the apostles (15.7); moreover there is a reference to an appearance before five hundred of the brethren, which is mentioned nowhere else (15.6). The Easter stories are even less unified, as has already been established. The number and names of the women, the number of their visits to the grave, the number of the angels, all change. There are several inconsistencies and additional glosses between the individual accounts. No harmonization is possible.

In spite of these irreconcilable divergences all traditions agree on one thing: Jesus appeared to certain disciples after his death; he proved himself living and was proclaimed to have risen from the dead. That is the centre, the core, where all the traditions meet. But it is clearly a moving centre, a core that cannot be simply ascertained or apprehended.[7] The various statements are, as it were, always on the move to try to put this central point into words. The actual centre, the Resurrection itself, is, however, never directly reported or even described. No New Testament witness claims to have seen the Resurrection itself. This border-line is only crossed in the later apocryphal gospels. The canonical writings of the New Testament are aware of the impossibility of such direct comment on the Resurrection as a concrete fact.

Even when looked at from a purely linguistic viewpoint, there is no question of the New Testament tradition of Jesus' rising from the dead being drawn from neutral factual statements, but rather of statements of faith and the testimonies of believers.[8] In these texts it is not just what is said that is important, but that it is said and how it is said. Here the content and form of the profession of faith cannot easily be separated. The reality of the Resurrection is inseparable from its testimony. This means that in considering the Resurrection, we are not considering an unique and finished, identifiable fact of the past, but a present reality which influences Christians today. Historical facts, the empty grave in particular, can serve as indicators and signs for faith, but they cannot provide proof of the Resurrection. Far more important than such 'facts', however, is the existential proof of credibility which the witnesses of the Resurrection gave in their life and in their death for their faith.

2. HERMENEUTICAL ESSENTIALS

The Resurrection witnesses talk about an event which transcends the sphere of what is historically verifiable; to that extent they pose an exegetical as well as an historical problem. The answer to the question of how theologically responsible discussion is possible depends upon fundamental hermeneutical decisions (which have to be taken beforehand) whether and to what extent a metahistorical dimension is recognized and how it is co-ordinated with what is historically verifiable.

In traditional theology, hermeneutical discussion of the Resurrection testimonies was greatly neglected. It was, in general, regarded as sufficient simply to quote the testimony of faith.[9] Since it was never questioned fundamentally, it was never the subject of fundamental reflection, as was the case with the problem of the Incarnation. Hence the doctrine of the Resurrection was ousted from the central fundamental position accorded it in the New Testament. In contrast with the Incarnation and the Passion, the Resurrection never played a formative part in Christology; it served more or less as a miraculous affirmation of faith in the Godhead of Christ and the redeeming power of the sacrifice of the cross. This situation only altered fundamentally with the advent of modern critical theology. At the same time the historical and exegetical factors were determined by ideological, philosophical or hermeneutical assumptions, as they arose.

People today will consider something historically true and real, if it is demonstrated to be historically credible and at least basically capable of objective verification: *Verum quod factum.* More precisely, historical phenomena are understood in context and by analogy with other events. Where this understanding of factual reality is absolute, there is no place for the reality of the Resurrection, which cannot be explained by reference to context or by analogy with the rest of reality. Hence many different hypotheses were advanced to explain the content and origins of the Easter belief 'intelligibly'.

The essentials of the whole modern discussion were anticipated in the *Wolfenbüttel Fragments,* or selections from the writings of Hermann Samuel Reimarus, published by Lessing in 1774-80. The two fragments, entitled 'The Resurrection story' and 'The purpose of Jesus and his disciples',[10] contain arguments which are still advanced today, in particular the argument that the Easter stories in the gospels present an impenetrable web of contradictions which cannot be knit together into a unified account of events. Reimarus therefore considers them as pure fiction and the invention of believers; for him they are a deception practised by the disciples. The hopes of Jesus' disciples were completely dashed by the arrest and crucifixion of their master. So they emptied the tomb and invented the appearances and messages of the risen Lord.

The deception hypothesis was later abandoned; it was too rough and ready. In its place came other explanations; the removal of the body hypothesis, the substitution hypothesis, the trance hypothesis, the evolution hypothesis and the well-known vision hypothesis. The only hypotheses to retain any importance today are the evolution and vision hypotheses. The evolution hypothesis assumes that the Resurrection faith is a

130

'fabrication' made up of religious ideas and expectations current at the time. In support of this view the Old Testament promises and hopes are cited, as also the Greek myths and mysteries about the death and resurrection of gods and the neo-Judaic apocalyptic with its ideas of resurrection and ecstasy. The most widespread and still influential hypothesis is that of the vision, first put forward by D. F. Strauss.[12] It attributes the Easter belief not to 'objective' appearances, but to subjective visions (hallucinations) experienced by the disciples, which spawned a whole 'epidemic of visions of Christ', each set off by the other.

Individual attempts at explanation have therefore altered greatly in modern times. Common to them all, however, is a tendency to view the problem of the Resurrection as a problem of fact in the narrow sense. The Church's apologetic made the mistake of accepting this way of looking at the problem as valid without further criticism. Instead of correcting the over-narrow statement of the problem, it only gave a different answer to the problem as it was put. The apologetic was certainly able to show that all the hypotheses put forward, which claimed to explain the Easter faith, could not in fact explain it and that they were not decisive either historically and exegetically nor psychologically, nor in any other way. From a positive point of view, the attempt was made to prove the Resurrection was historical fact. That is, insistence was laid upon the fact of the empty tomb. But this had the effect of avoiding discussion of Jesus' Resurrection as a side-issue or fringe problem. Yet the Easter faith is not first and foremost faith in the empty tomb but faith in the risen and living Lord.

That had the effect of putting the whole problem theologically in a false perspective. Whereas in the Scriptures Easter is presented as the central mystery of faith, it became more and more an external symbol of authenticity and an external proof of faith. This is a complete reversal of the proper way of looking at Easter. Easter is not a fact to be cited as evidence for believers; Easter is itself an object of faith. The Resurrection itself is not historically verifiable, but only the faith in it of the first witnesses and the fact, among others, of the empty tomb. Even supposing that we could demonstrate the fact of the empty tomb, that would be very far from providing any proof of the Resurrection. The fact of the empty tomb is ambiguous. Even in Scripture it is a phenomenon which is interpreted in various ways, and we find even here the hypotheses of theft or removal of the body (Mt 27.64; 28.1ff; John 20.13 ff). The empty tomb is simply a sign on the way to faith and a sign for someone who already believes.

A change was only brought about by the advent of dialectical theology and its emphasis on the eschatological character which informs and directs Christianity. For Karl Barth,[13] however, eschatology is far from being the whole story; for him the resurrection of the dead is rather a paraphrase for the word of God and his Kingdom. It is not to be considered in the same way as an historical fact. It is exclusively the act of God, for which there is no analogy, which happens in space and time and to that extent cannot be idealized, symbolized or allegorized. The empty tomb, therefore, although only a sign and a secondary factor, is an essentially indispensable factor, and anyone wishing to disregard it runs the risk of Docetism.

In spite of the considerable theological advances made, Barth's conception is nonetheless lacking in hermeneutical reflection. It owes a great deal to Rudolf Bultmann, who, in spite of criticism on minor points, agrees with Barth to the extent that for him too Jesus' rising from the dead is in no way an objective fact. In order to make discussion of it comprehensible, however, Bultmann was able to continue the humanistic method of understanding developed by Schleiermacher and Dilthey in contradistinction to the scientific method of explanation. Explaining is a matter of a subject-object relationship; where it is, however, a question of a subject-subject relationship and the interpretation of the words and acts of the historical person, that is, a question of the interpretation of religious conviction and religious testimony, nothing can be ascertained objectively or proven, but can only be understood from subjective impact and sympathy. In Schleiermacher's thought there is a development from the dogma dealing with the 'objective' content of Revelation to an interpretation of subjective religious experience and faith. This hermeneutical method was taken a substantial stage further in Heidegger's existentialist philosophy, which was adopted by Bultmann in particular and used in his re-interpretation of the Resurrection evidence in the New Testament. He was not concerned with explaining the 'fact' of the Resurrection, but with understanding the phenomenon of faith in the Resurrection in its significance *pro me*. Therefore Bultmann's central thesis is: 'Faith in the Resurrection is nothing other than faith in the cross as an act of salvation': that is, faith that the cross is an eschatological event. This is possible on the basis of proclamation. Therefore Bultmann can say too: 'The Easter faith is faith in the Church as bearer of the kerygma. It is equally the faith that Jesus Christ is present in the kerygma'.[15]

Karl Barth encapsulated Bultmann's conception as: Jesus is risen in the kerygma. To this Bultmann replied: 'I accept this formula. It is completely correct, given only that it is correctly understood. It presupposes that the kerygma itself is an eschatological event; and it means that Jesus is truly present in the kerygma, that it is *his* word which people hear in the kerygma. . . To believe in Christ present in the kerygma is the essence of the Easter faith'.[16] If this central thesis is accepted, then all the problems about historical fact disappear. The only comprehensible historical event is the Easter faith of the first disciples. The question then is: how did that Easter faith come about? How did the Easter kerygma originate? According to Bultmann, the origins of the Easter faith for the historian are reduced to visionary events. For the believer, on the other hand, 'the historical event of the origin of the Easter faith means . . . the self-manifestation of the Risen One, the act of God, in which the salvation of the Cross is fulfilled'.[17] The emergence of the Easter faith is itself an eschatological event and as such a subject of faith. For Bultmann the Easter faith is not simply a subjective conviction of the saving importance of the cross. It is rather that, in believing, 'something' happens to the disciples and to believers. It is a question of an act of God, which can be legitimized only as such and not historically.

This position is not devoid of ambiguities. It leaves the impression that Easter, for Bultmann, is something that happens not to Jesus, but to the disciples. Easter and the emergence of the Easter faith coalesce. Easter is then no longer a phenomenon which comes before faith and in which the believer believes, but the phenomenon of faith itself. A further danger arises from this position. If the Easter faith is in Christ, present in the kerygma of the Church and acting in us, then Christology is not only absorbed into soteriology but even turns abruptly into ecclesiology. Bultmann can even speak of the Easter faith as belief 'in the Church as bearer of the kerygma'.[18] At this point there is criticism not only from Catholic theology but from Barth, Käsemann, and others. The critics say that Christ's precedence and pre-eminence before and above our faith is no longer maintained. It must be added that Bultmann himself is aware that there is a contradiction with Scripture in his theology of the Resurrection, particularly with the important evidence of 1 Cor 15. As an historian, Bultmann has admitted frankly enough that Paul's line of argument, with its emphasis on quite definite historical witnesses, points in quite a different direction, but he considers he can describe Paul's arguments as fatalistic.[19]

Bultmann's initiative has been taken up and developed in various ways. In addition to the views of Ebeling,[20] the arguments of Marxsen are the most important.[21] Like Bultmann, he takes as his starting-point the difference between the historical and the theological. Only what can be tested as historical, counts as historical. 'Faith cannot set down historical facts'.[22] Where faith gains over and above the purely historical is on the plane of significance. These basic theses already decide the question: the Resurrection of Jesus cannot be described as an historical event. 'Historically it can only be established. . . that after Jesus' death people maintained an occurrence took place which they described as seeing Jesus'.[23] A distinction is made between the occurrence and the interpretation of that occurrence. The seeing leads by way of a process of deduction to the interpretation: Jesus is risen.[24] The statement 'Jesus is risen' is therefore not an historical statement, but an interpretation of what was seen. Such an interpretation should not, however, be objectivized and historicized; it is simply a statement of considered opinion.[25]

Besides this retrospective interpretation of what was seen, Marxsen believes he can discover an older forward-looking interpretation, which is orientated not personally but functionally: that is, the mission to carry on Jesus' work. According to Marxsen, therefore, the Resurrection means that Jesus' work continues; in the kerygma the experience of the coming of the Kingdom of God recurs again and again. The kerygma of the Church now takes Jesus' place; and that is where Jesus' offer is found today. 'Where this really affects me, then I know: He is living'.[26] The difference between Bultmann and Marxsen lies above all in the fact that for Bultmann the Resurrection expresses the eschatological importance of the cross, while Marxsen refuses this reduction of everything to the cross and has as his focal point the earthly Jesus. For Marxsen Easter is no longer the central fact of Christian faith, but only the precondition for Jesus' work to continue; yet it is not basically a new beginning.[27]

A more profound scrutiny might well be undertaken of the exegetical problems inherent in Marxsen's position, particularly the weaknesses in his interpretation of the accounts of the post-Resurrection appearances. Since I am mainly concerned here with the hermeneutical requirements, it must suffice to point out that there is a misconception in the concept of an 'occurrence', in the sense in which Marxsen uses it. A 'occurrence' is never a dull event, which can only be interpreted subsequently one way or the other; it is rather an intentional bringing-about, that has a meaning which is understood as such from the beginning, in one way or another. Even if such an understanding does not have to be a conscious one, the experience and its expression in language can never fundamentally be separated. In fact the New Testament texts always speak of a quite definite sight, the sight of the Risen One, of the Lord. If this designation of Jesus as the object of the seeing is allowed to stand unabbreviated, then the statement of his Resurrection has to be accepted as a logical conclusion. The question, therefore, round which everything revolves, is whether the accounts of the appearances only represent legitimizing formulas so that the work of Jesus can be continued, or whether they express the experience of a new reality and therefore possess a substance of their own. The question at issue is really whether Marxsen has assessed correctly the value of the position of Easter *vis-à-vis* the earthly Jesus.

The question posed above has been studied in particular by R. Pesch.[29] He continues (without acknowledgment) work done by F. C. Baur and also works from the evolution hypothesis, in the new form in which it was put by Martin Buber. Pesch advances the thesis, already put forward by A. von Harnack and more recently by U. Wilckens,[30] that the manifestation accounts and formulas are legitimizing formulas. Pesch goes further than Marxsen in trying to dispense with the 'occurrence' of seeing Jesus and to find the foundation for the Resurrection faith in the eschatological claim of Jesus, which was interpreted after his death using the neo-Judaic concepts of ecstasy and resurrection. The Resurrection belief is here the expression of the permanent validity of Jesus' eschatological claim; the foundation for the belief is not the appearances but Jesus himself. Since Jesus is the eschatological experience of the love of God in person, it would be possible to speak of Jesus' mediation through Jesus himself (W. Breuning). Setting aside the question of whether Pesch is interpreting the New Testament manifestation accounts and the later Judaic 'parallels' correctly (and most experts do not think so), we are left with the basic problem of whether belief in a unique divine act (which the Resurrection is seen to be in Scripture) can be sufficiently explained as the result simply of considered thought or whether it does not require a non-deducible, new insight given by God, which the authors of the New Testament tried to express using the concept of the post-Resurrection appearances. Would not an understanding achieved by a simple process of deduction devalue the breach made by the cross and the relative new beginning of Easter? This basic question, which Pesch's position reveals, confronts us with the task of elucidating the relationship between the historical and theological statement of a problem and thus avoiding a biassed kerygma theology as well as historicism or a regression into liberal theology.

A new phase in the discussion of Barth and Bultmann was introduced by Wolfhart Pannenberg,[31] in particular, with his interpretation of revelation as history. Pannenberg is concerned to examine the importance of the historical statement of a problem within theology. If, for instance, faith in the Resurrection supersedes the Resurrection itself, then such a faith can scarcely be distinguished any more from a subjective certainty. Therefore Pannenberg tries to find support for such faith in the historical Jesus. But, in contrast to Marxsen, even Jesus' eschatological claim to authority, which Pannenberg understands proleptically, would remain an empty assertion if it were not confirmed by God. God's raising of Jesus from the dead is this proof and endorsement of Jesus. For him everything now depends upon proving the historical reality of the Resurrection. Pannenberg rejects decisively Barth's view that the historical question is completely inapplicable to the Resurrection. For him there is no just argument for maintaining that the Resurrection really took place if it is not an historical fact. He thus lays upon historical research a massive burden of proof and gives the fact of the empty tomb considerable theological weight once again.

This change of emphasis and the resultant excessive demands made on historical research have been criticized many times. What is often overlooked by Pannenberg's critics is that he can, of course, only prove the historicity of the Resurrection by considering the findings of tradition 'in the light of the eschatological hope of a resurrection of the dead'.[32] Pannenberg thus places the historical statement of the problem in a wider hermeneutical perspective and basically takes the mutual interdependence of facts and interpretation into consideration. He envisages a solution which lies beyond the extremes of verifiably historical fact and of disintegration into a significance merely for the believer. The intention is one which must fundamentally meet with approval, even if Pannenberg does in fact strain the historical method and perhaps gives the fact of the empty tomb an importance which cannot be attributed to it from the evidence in the New Testament.

Catholic theology today usually tries to find a solution to this problem by using the category of the sign. The historical events in themselves are either insignificant or ambiguous; they become revealing and unequivocal in a wider context of relevance. Conversely the relevant words are empty and hollow, if they do not interpret real events and are not ratified by them. For this reason it is more appropriate to talk not of historical proof but of signs. The empty tomb is in this sense a sign, which should exclude any Docetism, however conditioned. Thus the comments of the second Vatican Council on revelation in general are particularly relevant to the Resurrection: 'This plan of revelation is realized by words and deeds having an inner unity: the deeds wrought by God in the history of salvation manifest and confirm the teaching and realities signified by the words, while the words proclaim the deeds and clarify the mystery contained in them'.[33]

After this basic clarification of the relationship between the hermeneutical and historical statements of the problem there remains the question of the appropriate hermeneutical limits to the problem. It goes without saying that such anthropological considerations are dismissed out of hand as irrelevant by Karl Barth's dialectical theology, because from the human viewpoint there is no continuity from death to life, and any and every continuity and identity have their sole basis in God's faithfulness to his creation. Yet precisely this idea of the bond of faithfulness between God and his creation makes it impossible to regard the Resurrection as a pure *creatio ex nihilo*. In his faithfulness God takes up the hopes which he has himself implanted in his creatures. So it is possible to put in a plea for the justice of an anthropological and hermeneutical statement of the problem within the theological interpretation of Barth himself, and to interpret the anthropological structures as the grammar which God makes use of in a non-deducibly new way. Revelation as revelation is not possible for man in other than human terms and concepts.

Essentially, four different attempts at an anthropological approach to the Resurrection faith should be mentioned. Karl Rahner[34] and, following him, Ladislaus Boros[35] and H. Ebert[36] all start from a phenomenology of human freedom, which tends essentially towards the absolute and the definitive and therefore finds fulfilment in eternity. Eternal life is God's final definitive act of freedom for man. J. Ratzinger[37] makes similar points using a phenomenology of love, which is stronger than death. According to Gabriel Marcel, to love another human being is to say: you will not die.[38] In a different way, Pannenberg[39] tries to start from the phenomenology of hope. According to him, it is in the nature of man to go on hoping beyong death and this, man's eternal condition, is the meaning of the image and symbol of the resurrection of the dead. Finally Jürgen Moltmann[40] adds the hope for justice, trying like U. Horkheimer to make Pannenberg's conception more concrete in meaning. Human sympathy is only ensured when finally the murderer does not triumph over the Victim. Bultmann sees the concept of a general resurrection of the dead in neo-Judaic apocalyptic as having followed logically from thinking through to its conclusion the idea of God's invincibly victorious justice. The whole problem of the Resurrection moves therefore into the context of the theodicy problem; it fits too in the anthropological problem of the divinity of God, his justice and faithfulness in the world's history of suffering.

All these attempts arrive by different phenomenological routes at the same conclusion: the question of man's purpose in life cannot be answered from within his own history but only eschatologically. Implicitly, therefore, in all the fundamental processes of his life, man is driven by the problem of life and its ultimate purpose. The answer will not be found until the end of history. For the moment all man can do is to listen to and look at history and try to find signs in which that end is portrayed or even anticipated. Those signs will always be ambigious within history; they will only become clear in the light of faith's perception of that end of history, just as conversely that perception must constantly make sure of its own validity in the light of history. Only if the problem is seen in this comprehensive perspective can the testimonies of the early Church and of the later church tradition be understood meaningfully.

3. THEOLOGICAL BASIS

The first Resurrection witnesses rely on their evidence on the appearances of the Risen Lord. Even the old formula of belief in 1 Cor 15.3-5 mentions an appearance to Peter and afterwards to the Twelve. Elsewhere, too, Peter plays a prominent role in the Easter testimonies (Lk 24.34; Mk 16.7; Jn 21. 15-19). Peter is clearly the primary witness of the Resurrection. Therefore a *primatus fidei* is due to him, by reason of which he is *centrum unitatis* of the Church. It is striking, of course, that parallel to Peter and the Twelve, James and the other apostles are named two verses later. This has led, according to von Harnack, to the conjecture that 1 Cor 15.3-7 reflects the relationships in the leadership in the Jerusalem community.[41] Originally the Twelve, with Peter as their spokesman, formed the authoritative nucleus, whereas James took over the leadership later. From this the conclusion is drawn that the naming of the appearances of the Risen Lord has the function of legitimizing certain authoritative figures in the Church. We are dealing with legitimizing formulas. There is certainly much that is right and important in the idea that the appearances establish the official position of the apostles and always contain the motif of a mission. We do not find the truth and reality of Easter other than in the witness borne by the apostles. Faith in Christ is the truth of the testimony, the basic law of which is expressed vividly in Rom 10.14f, 17: 'And how are they to believe in him of whom they have never heard? And how are they to hear without a preacher? And how can men preach unless they are sent? . . . So faith comes from what is heard'.

The question is, of course, whether the theme of the mission should be made independent, whether the Easter appearances should be interpreted purely functionally, and whether that functional interpretation should be balanced against a personal one — one concerning the person of Christ? To answer this question it is necessary to examine the use of language in the New Testament more closely. The decisive term is the same in 1 Cor 15.3-8 as in Lk 24.34: *opthe* (cf also Acts 9.17; 13.31; 26.16). This can be translated in three ways: (1) passive: he was seen; the activity is then on the part of the disciples; (2) passive: as a paraphrase of God's action: he was shown, he was revealed; the activity is then on the part of God; (3) middle: he showed himself; he appeared; the activity then is on the part of Christ himself.

Only the second and third meanings need to be considered; the concept is a fixed concept even in the Old Testament to describe theophanies (cf Gen 12.7; 17.1; 18.1; 26.2; and elsewhere). The appearances of the Risen Lord are described according to the model for theophanies; according to one understanding of the New Testament, we are dealing with the processes of revelation in which we come to know God himself. Therefore the New Testament can also state that God made the Risen Lord manifest (Acts 10.40). An appearance understood in this sense is of its nature not immediate and is determined by the 'dialectic of the idea'.[42] God reveals himself as the hidden God (cf Jn 45.15). God's revelation is not enlightenment, but the revelation of his hiddenness and mysteriousness.

This conclusion leaves a fairly wide scope for interpretation. It is taken furthest by Marxsen. He speaks of an occurrence of the vision. Citing Gal 1.15f. and 1 Cor 9.1 in support, he maintains that it was not a vision of the Risen One which was claimed, but a vision of Jesus as the Lord, the Son. We should therefore not start from the appearances of the Risen Lord but from an occurrence of the vision, which is interpreted with the help of the Resurrection. 'The Resurrection of Jesus' is therefore an interpretation of the occurrence of the vision. There are, however, not only grave hermeneutical objections to this thesis, but historical and exegetical ones too. It can, for instance, be proved exegetically that the passage Gal 1.15f is concerned not with a vision, but with a revelation of the Risen Lord; 1 Cor 9.1, however, deals with a vision of Jesus as the Lord. Accordingly the formula does not occur alone anywhere, but always with the formula *egerthe* or *egegertai* — he was raised from the dead. The word *opthe* should not be taken out of context and isolated, in order to make it the starting-point for a theory. We must therefore begin from this point: The disciples have seen the Risen Lord. What does that mean?

There is a dispute between K. H. Rengstorf[43] and W. Michaelis[44] over the meaning of the evidence of the appearances. Rengstorf starts from the fact that God himself is the active subject; in spite of this he wants to record the moment of perception visually. His interpretation therefore runs: God made Christ accessible to human perception through sight. Michaelis, on the other hand, concludes from the fact that it is a matter of solidly established revelation terminology, that the question of the *how* of this revelation is considerably neutralized or subordinated to theological evaluation. He does not emphasize sensory perception, since what is at issue is not the becoming visible but the being revealed. K. Lehmann[45] is right to stress that the question cannot be solved at the level of these two alternatives. It can be advanced against Rengstorf's thesis that the New Testament is careful to keep any suggestion of the visionary away from the Easter appearances; there is never any mention of 'apparitions', of day-dreams or dreams at night, of ecstatic raptures or anything similar. This caution is striking and significant. For the same reason the classification of subjective vision is inadequate, as much as that of objective vision advanced by H. Grass[46] in particular. On the other hand it can be argued against Michaelis that it is not a matter of the disciples being overwhelmed by an anonymous numinous transcendence. It is a matter of a revelation, entirely predetermined, the Revelation of Jesus the Crucified as the Risen and Transcendent Lord. It is a matter clearly of an entirely personal process which, according to Phil 3.12, consists of Christ's making a person his own.

A deeper interpretation of this can be drawn from a reading of Gal 1.12, 16. Here Paul speaks in apocalyptic terms of the *apokalypsis Iesou Christou*. In the case of the appearances we are dealing with eschatological events, more precisely with the presentiment of the final eschatological revelation which belongs to God alone. That is the reason for the statement in Gal 1.15f that God 'was pleased to reveal his Son in me'. It is stated fully in 2 Cor 4.6: 'For it is the God who said, "Let light shine out of darkness", who has shone in our hearts to give the light of the knowledge of the glory of God in the face of Christ'. It is God then who reveals and what he reveals is his own glory. But he reveals his glory in the countenance of Jesus Christ. He who has been crucified is 'seen' in the *doxa*, the glory of God; that is, the glory of God is seen as the glorification of the Crucified One. What flashes upon the witnesses is the glory of God, his divinity, which shows itself in his identification with the crucified Christ and his awakening from death to life.

138

An analysis of the appearances reported in the gospels leads to a similar conclusion. The Risen Lord is encountered in greeting and blessing, in salutation, conversation and instruction, in comfort, directives and tasks, in the founding of a new community. The disciples react initially with confusion, fear, non-recognition, doubt, disbelief; the Risen Lord has first to 'overwhelm' them. After this overwhelming in faith comes the moment of mission and authorization. Both are perhaps described most magnificently in Mt 28.16-20. Something of the divine *exousia* shines out of this passage, something of the unapproachable grandeur and the non-identifiable nature of Christ's manifestation. He is known only in the act of faith and adoration. In other accounts he appears to them while going away (Lk 24.31; Jn 20.11f). He is not to be conjured up in his appearances; he manifests himself in his departure; he comes as one who is going. He withdraws into the divine dimension.

An interpretation along these lines meets with difficulties in various other texts which mention touching the Risen Lord and sharing a meal with him (cf Lk 24.38ff; Jn 20.26f). At first glance these seem to be intolerably drastic statements which very nearly touch the limits of the theologically possible and run the risk of founding a 'powerful' Easter faith. Clearly there is a dual purpose behind these texts: firstly, it is intended to prove the identity of the Risen with the Crucified Lord; the Risen Lord is recognized by the marks of his wounds. Secondly, there is an apologetic reason; a biassed spiritualism has to be avoided and the corporeality of the Resurrection must be emphasized. John noticed, however, the misleading nature of his stylistic device; so he finishes his account with the resounding maxim: 'Blessed are those who have not seen and yet believe' (20.29). This final comment puts everything into the right light, in which these texts can be interpreted according to the purpose of their message: the foundation of the Easter faith.

Summary. (1) In the appearances we are not dealing with objectively tangible events. The observer from a neutral distance will find no point of contact. We have before us a total state of being possessed by Jesus, a state of impact and absorption, the awakening of faith. In the appearances Jesus finally achieves validity and recognition in the belief of his disciples. It is, however, a mistake to interpret what happened as meaning that faith was made easy for the first witnesses of faith by a miraculous event, as if extravagant miracles had, so to speak, 'knocked them over' and forced them to their knees. This would lead to the grotesque conclusion that those who first preached faith did not believe themselves, since they were dispensed from faith by having seen. So it needs to be made clear that this was a *believing* seeing.[48] To express it better: it was an experience in faith. But although they were an experience in faith, the 'appearances' were not simply the expression of a belief. There were actual encounters with Christ present in the spirit. Faith did not establish the reality of the Resurrection, but the reality of the Resurrected Christ obtruding in spirit upon the disciples' established faith. For this reason it is essential to distinguish between the emergence of the Easter faith and the basis of that faith, the Resurrection of Jesus himself.

2. The encounter with the Risen Lord is described in the New Testament as meeting God and knowing God. The disciples became aware of the reality of the Kingdom of God which had finally come in Jesus Christ through his death, the shining of God's glory on the countenance of their crucified Lord. The appearances are about the eschatological self-revelation of God. This is the real basis of the Easter faith and of all faith, if faith means to have God alone as the basis and purpose of life, to honour God alone. The basis of such a faith can never be isolated facts or proofs, but only the faithfulness and truth of God himself impressing themselves on man. In this sense it can be said that in these appearances the basis for faith stemmed from Jesus of Nazareth, as the witness of faith.

3. The Easter experience of faith of the first disciples shows the basic structures of faith, as it constitutes the experience of the Christian in general. In this way, however, it is distinguished substantially from our faith which we think of as imparted through the experiences of the early witnesses and their tradition. We stand with our faith on the foundation of the apostolic testimony. The beginning is never merely the first point of a series of further moments in time; the beginning contains what follows and it is the never-repealed law which governs everything else. The beginning transcends and makes immanent the moments which result from it; its structure is different from theirs qualitatively and not just quantitatively and can therefore never really be called back even cognitively.[49] These general reflections on the nature of the beginning, when applied to our problem, mean that it is not possible for us to have a proper conception of a faith not mediated to us by tradition and that we can therefore only understand the Easter appearances by analogy, as the beginning of this faith. We will have to hold fast to the fact that what is at issue here is a personal encounter with Christ. The decisive question is not what objectively took place, but whether we are ready, as the first disciples were, to give ourselves to be absorbed by Jesus Christ.

If the Easter faith and thus faith in Christ rests upon the testimony of the apostles, then the only means of access to it that we have is through the apostolic witness which is handed down in the Church as the community of believers. Only in and through this witness is the Risen Christ, through his Spirit, a present actual reality in history, for historical reality is never independent of the fact that it is known in history. In this sense, in fact only in this sense, can it be said: Jesus is risen in the kerygma. He is a permanent presence in history through the witness of the apostolic Church.

Notes

[1]Cf essentially K.H. Rengstorf, *Die Auferstehung Jesu. Form, Art und Sinn der urchristlichen Osterbotschaft* (2nd ed., Witten, 1954); H. Grass, *Ostergeschehen und Oster-*

berichte (3rd ed., Göttingen, 1964); W. Marxsen, *Die Auferstehung Jesu als historisches und als theologisches Problem* (4th ed., Gütersloh, 1966); J. Kremer, *Das älteste Zeugnis von der Auferstehung Jesu. Eine Bibeltheologische Studie zur Aussage und Bedeutung von 1 Cor 15,1-11* (Stuttgarter Bibelstudien 17) (2nd ed., Stuttgart, 1967); P. Seidensticker, *Die Aufererstehung Jesus in der Botschaft der Evangelisten. Ein traditionsgeschichtlicher Versuch zum Problem der Sicherung der Osterbotschaft in der apostolischen Zeit* (Stuttgarter Bibelstudien 26) (Stuttgart, 1967); W. Marxsen, U. Wilckens, G.Delling, H.-G. Geyer, *Die Bedeutung der Auferstehungsbotschaft für den Glauben an Jesus Christus* (Gütersloh, 1967); ET: *The Significance of the Message of the Resurrection for Faith in Jesus Christ* (London and Naperville, Ill., 1968); K. Lehmann, *Auferweckt am dritten Tag nach der Schrift. Früheste Christologie, Bekenntnisbildung und Schriftauslegung im Lichte von 1 Cor 15.3-5* (Quaestiones Disputatae, QD, vol. 38) (Freiburg, 1968); H. Schlier, *Über die Auferstehung Jesu Christi* (Einsiedeln, 1968); W.Marxsen, *Die Auferstehung Jesu von Nazareth* (Gütersloh, 1968); ET: *The Resurrection of Jesus of Nazareth* (London, 1970); W.Pannenberg, 'Dogmatische Erwägungen zur Aufererstehung Jesu', in: KuD 14 (1968), pp. 105-118; *idem, Grundzüge, op. cit.,* pp. 47-112; F.Mussner, *Die Auferstehung Jesu* (Munich, 1969); A.Kolping, *Wunder und Auferstehung Jesu Christi* (Bergen-Enkheim, 1969); H. Urs von Balthasar, 'Mysterium Paschale', in: MS III/2, pp. 133-319, esp. pp. 256 ff; G.Kegel, *Auferstehung Jesu – Aufererstehung der Toten. Eine traditionsgeschichtliche Untersuchung zum Neuen Testament* (Gütersloh, 1970); H.Ludochowski, *Auferstehung – Mythos oder Vollendung des Lebens?* (Aschaffenburg, 1970); U.Wilckens, *Auferstehung. Das biblische Auferstehungszeugnis historisch untersucht und erklärt* (Stuttgart-Berlin, 1970); B.Klappert (ed.), *Diskussion um Kreuz und Auferstehung* (4th ed., Wuppertal, 1971); *idem, Die Auferweckung des Gekreuzigten. Der Ansatz der Christologie Karl Barths im Zusammenhang der Christologie der Gegenwart* (Neukirchen, 1971, esp., pp. 1-82 (and bibliography); A.Geense, *Auferstehung und Offenbarung. Über den Ort der Frage nach der Auferstehung Jesu Christi in der heutigen deutschen evangelischen Theologie* (Göttingen, 1971); X.Léon-Dufour, *Résurrection de Jésus et message pascal* (Paris, 1972); A.Gesché, 'Die Auferstehung Jesus in der dogmatischen Theologie', in: J.Pfammatter, F.Furger (eds.), *Theologische Berichte* II (Zürich, 1973), pp. 275-324 (and bibliography); E.Fuchs, W.Künneth, *Die Auferstehung Jesu Christi von den Toten. Dokumentation eines Streitgesprächs*, ed. C.Möller (Neukirchen, 1973); R.Pesch, 'Zur Entstehung des Glaubens an die Auferstehung Jesu. Ein Vorschlag zur Diskussion', in: TQ 153 (1973), pp. 201-28; H.Küng, 'Zur Entstehung des Auferstehungsglaubens. Versuch einer systematischen Klärung', in: TQ 154 (1974), pp. 103-17.

[2] Cf H. von Campenhausen, *Der Ablauf der Osterereignisse und das leere Grab* (2nd ed., Heidelberg, 1958).

[3] On what follows, cf M.Brändle, 'Die synoptischen Grabeserzählungen', in: *Orientierung* 31 (1967), pp. 179-84.

[4] Thus, primarily, L.Schenke, *Auferstehungsverkündigung und leeres Grab. Eine traditionsgeschichtliche Untersuchung von Mk 16. 1-8* (Stuttgarter Bibelstudient 33) (Stuttgart, 1968).

[5] Cf J.Jeremias, *Die Heiligengräber in Jesu Umwelt. Eine Untersuchung zur Volksreligion der Zeit Jesu* (Göttingen, 1958).

[6] H. von Campenhausen, *Ablauf der Osterereignisse, op.cit.*, p. 42.

[7] Thus, essentially, H. Urs von Balthasar, 'Mysterium Paschale', *art. cit.*, pp. 288 ff.

[8] See on this point A.Gesché, 'Auferstehung Jesu', *art. cit.*, pp. 301 ff.

[9] Cf see the survey on pp. 000 of the present work.

[10] See the two fragments in: G.E. Lessing, W XII, pp. 397-428, and XIII, pp. 221 to 327.

[11] Cf M. Buber, 'Zwei Glaubensweisen', in: W I, pp. 724-6. U. Wilckens has recently offered an interpretation with the same emphasis in *Auferstehung, op. cit.*

[12] D.F. Strauss, *Das Leben Jesu, rev. ed., vol. 2*, pp. 655 ff; ET: *The Life of Jesus Critically Examined* (new ed. London, 1973), pp. 700 ff.

[13] K. Barth, *Die Auferstehung der Toten. Eine akademische Vorlesung über 1 Kor 15*

(Munich, 1924); *idem, Die kirchliche Dogmatik* III/2 (Zollikon-Zürich, 1948) pp. 529-47; *idem,* op. cit., IV/1 (Zollikon-Zurich, 1953), pp. 311-94; ET: *Church Dogmatics,* vol. 3/2: *The Doctrine of Creation;* vol. 4/1 (London & Edinburgh, 1936-62): *The Doctrine of Reconciliation.*

[14] R. Bultmann, 'Neues Testament und Mythologie', in: *Kerygma und Mythos* I, p. 46; ET: 'New Testament and Mythology' in: *Kerygma and Myth* (London, 1953), p. 103.

[15] *Idem, Das Verhältnis der urchristlichen Christusbotschaft zum historischen Jesus, op. cit.,* p. 27; ET: p. 15.

[16] *Ibid.*

[17] *Idem,* 'Neues Testament und Mythologie', *art. cit.,* p. 47; ET: p. 104.

[18] *Idem, Das Verhaltnis der urchristclichen Christusbotschaft zum historischen Jesus, op. cit.,* p. 27; ET: p. 15.

[19] *Idem,* 'Neues Testament und Mythologie', *art. cit,* p. 45; ET: 102. also, *idem,* 'Karl Barth, "Die Auferstehung der Toten", in: GuV L, pp. 54 ff.

[20] Cf G.Ebeling, *Das Wesen des christlichen Glaubens* (3rd ed., paperback, Munich-Hamburg, 1967), pp. 53-66.

[21] Cf W.Marxsen, *Die Auferstehung Jesu als historisches und theologisches Problem, op. cit.,* and *idem, Die Auferstehung Jesu von Nazareth;* ET: *The Resurrection of Jesus of Nazareth, op. cit.;* the following references are to the first of these two works.

[22] *Op. cit. supra,* p. 10.

[23] *Ibid.,* p. 20, cf. p. 16.

[24] *Ibid.,* pp. 14, 22, 27.

[25] *Ibid.,* pp. 15, 34.

[26] *Ibid.,* p. 35.

[27] Cf W.Marxsen, *Anfangsprobleme der Christologie, op. cit.,* pp. 20 ff; ET; pp. 30 ff.

[28] See especially the critical comments of K.Lehmann, *Auferweckt am dritten Tag, op. cit.,* pp. 340 ff, and H.Schlier *Uber die Aufererstehung Jesu,* op. cit., pp. 40 ff.

[29] Cf R.Pesch, *Zur Entstehung des Glaubens an die Auferstehung Jesu, op. cit.,* and in TQ 153 (1973) the contributions to the debate by W.Kasper 'Der Glaube an die Auferstehung Jesu vor dem Forum historischer Kritik', *art. cit,* pp. 229-41; K.H.Schelke, 'Schöpfung des Glaubens?', *art. cit,* pp. 242 ff; P.Stuhlmacher, 'Kritischer müssten mir die Historisch-Kritischen sein!', *art. cit.,* pp. 244-51; M.Hengel, 'Ist der Osterglaube noch zu retten?' *art. cit.,* pp. 252-69; and R.Pesch, 'Stellungnahme zu den Diskussionsbeiträgen', *art. cit.,* pp. 270-83. See also: K.Küng, 'Zur Entstehung des Osterglaubens', *art. cit.,* and recently: W.Breuning, 'Aktive Proexistenz — Die Vermittlung Jesu durch Jesus selbst', in: TThZ 83 (1974), pp. 193-213.

[30] Cf U.Wilckens, 'Der Ursprung der Uberlieferung der Erscheinungen des Auferstandenen, Zur traditionsgeschtlichen Analyse von 1 Cor 15. 1-11, in: W.Joest, W.Pannenberg (eds.), *Dogma und Denkstrukturen* (Göttingen, 1963), pp. 59-95; *idem, Auferstehung, op. cit.,* esp., p. 147.

[31] Cf W.Pannenberg, *Grundzüge, op. cit.,* pp. 47-112; *idem, Dogmatische Erwägungen zur Auferstehung Jesu, op. cit.;* see also the preparatory essays in: *idem,* 'Dogmatische Thesen zur Lehre von der Offenbarung', in: *idem* (ed.), *Offenbarung als Geschichte* (4th ed., Göttingen, 1970); *idem.* 'Die Offenbarung Gottes in Jesus von Nazareth' in: *Theologie als Geschichte = Neuland in der Theologie. Ein Gespräch zwischen amerikanischen und europäischen Theologen,* ed. J.M.Robinson and J.B.Cobb, Vol 3 (Zürich-Stuttgart, 1967), pp.135-69.

[32] *Ibid.,* p. 95.

[33] Vatican II, Dogmatic Constitution *Dei Verbum.*

[34] Cf K.Rahner, *Zur Theologie des Todes* (QD, vol. 2) (Freiburg, 1958); ET: *On the Theology of Death* (London, 1960); idem, 'Dogmatische Fragen zur Osterfrömmigkeit', in: *Schriften* IV, *op. cit.,* pp. 157-72; ET: *Theological Investigations,* vol. 4 (London, 1966); *idem,* 'Das Leben der Toten', in: *op. cit.,* IV, pp. 429-37; *idem,* 'Christologie', *op. cit.,* pp. 38-40.

[35] Cf L.Boros, *Mysterium Mortis, Der Mensch in der letzten Entscheidung* (Olten, 1962); ET: *Moment of Truth: Mysterium Mortis* (London, 1963).

[36] Cf H.Ebert, 'Die Krise des Osterglaubens. Zur Diskussion über die Auferstehung Jesu', in: *Hochland* 60 (1967-8), pp. 305-31.

[37] Cf J.Ratzinger, *Einführung in das Christentum. Vorlesungen über das apostolische Glaubensbekenntnis* (2nd ed., Munich, 1968), pp. 249-57; ET: *Introduction to Christianity* (London, 1969), pp. 205-51.

[38] G.Marcel, *Le mystère de l'etre*, 2 vols. (Paris, 1951); ET: *The Mystery of Being*, 2 vols (London-Chicago, 1950-1).

[39] Cf W.Pannenberg, *Was ist der Mensch? Die Anthropologie der Gegenwart im Lichte der Theologie* (2nd ed., Göttingen, 1964), pp. 31-40; *idem, Grundzüge, op. cit.*, pp. 79-85.

[40] Cf J.Moltmann, 'Gott und Auferstehung. Auferstehungsglaube im Forum der Theodizeefrage', in: *Perspektiven der Theologie* (Munich-Mainz, 1968), pp. 36-56; *idem, Der gekreuzigte Gott op. cit.*, pp. 161-6; ET: *The Crucified God* (London, 1974), pp. 130 ff.

[41] Cf A. von Harnack, *Die Verklärungsgeschichte, der Bericht des Paulus 1 Kor 15.3 ff und die beiden Christusvisionen des Petrus* (Berlin, 1922).

[42] Thus, primarily, H.Schlier, *Über die Auferstehung Jesu Christi, op. cit.*, p. 21, and K.Lehmann, 'Die Erscheinungen des Herrn. Thesen zur hermeneutisch-theologischen Struktur der Ostererzählungen', in: *Wort Gottes in der Zeit. Festschrift fur K.H. Schelke*, eds H. Feld and J. Nolte (Düsseldorf, 1973), p. 367.

[43] Cf K.H. Rengstorf, *Die Auferstehung Jesu, op. cit.*, pp. 93-100.

[44] Cf W.Michaelis, *Die Erscheinungen des Auferstandenen* (Basle, 1944); *idem*, art. 'orao', in: TW V, pp. 357-60.

[45] Cf K. Lehmann, 'Die Erscheinungen des Herrn', *art. cit.*, pp. 370 ff.

[46] Cf H. Grass, *Ostergeschehen, op. cit.*, pp. 233-249.

[47] Cf H. Schlier, *Über die Auferstehung Jesu Christi, op. cit.*, pp. 33 ff.

[48] Cf G. Ebeling, *Das Wesen des christlichen Glaubens, op. cit.*, pp. 64 ff.

[49] Cf A. Darlapp, art, 'Anfang', in: LTK I, pp. 525-9.

VII. THE CONTENT OF FAITH IN JESUS' RESURRECTION

VII. THE CONTENT OF FAITH IN JESUS' RESURRECTION

1. JESUS' RESURRECTION AS AN ESCHATOLOGICAL ACT OF DIVINE POWER

Scripture uses two terms[1] in particular to describe Jesus' Resurrection: the transitive *egeirein,* to awaken from the dead, in the active and passive sense, and the transitive and intransitive *anastanai,* to arise or to make arise. In both cases it is a question of a metaphorical figure of speech, of a comparison with being woken up; that is, an awakening from sleep. It is important to be aware of the graphic character of the language of the Resurrection; for us, who are still on this side of the boundary of death, the reality to be expressed eludes direct conception or formulation; we cannot help speaking in images and similes. The traditional usage of both concepts is found in both the Greek world and Judaism. They mean either the awakening of the dead which returns them to earthly life, or the general eschatological resurrection of the dead which neo-Judaism expected. When, therefore, the Resurrection of Jesus is referred to in the New Testament it is intended to convey that with Jesus the eschatological events have begun to take place. Jesus is the first to rise from the dead (Acts 26.23; 1 Cor 15-20f; Col 1.18). Jesus' Resurrection is therefore given a place in the eschatological perspective of hope and is characterized as an eschatological event. Accordingly, his rising from the dead does not mean a return into the old life. He does not return to decay or corruption (Acts 13.34): 'For we know that Christ being raised from the dead will never die again; death no longer has dominion over him. . . the life he lives he lives to God' (Rom 6.9f). The Resurrection is not a resumption of the old life, but the beginning of the new creation (cf 1 Cor 15.42ff).

The neo-Judaic hope in the general resurrection of the dead at the end of time is neither a subsequent addition nor a superfluous insertion in the faith of the Old Testament. The origin of this hope is faith in Yahweh as Lord of Life and death, who holds all in his hand, to whom everything belongs and in whom there can be complete confidence, even beyond death itself. 'The Lord kills and brings to life; he brings down to Sheol and raises up' (1 Sam 2.6; cf Det 32.39). Hence Job can say from the depths of his affliction: 'For I know that my Redeemer lives, and at last he will stand upon the earth; and after my skin has been thus destroyed, then from my flesh I shall see God' (Job 19.25f) Accordingly the Jewish 'Shemon Israel' can define God as 'God who makes the dead live'. Paul often echoes this expression (Rom 4.17; 2 Cor 1.9). The Resurrection is so much God's work and so characteristic of him that it can be used as a sign by which God is recognized.

The New Testament seldom speaks actively of Jesus' Resurrection in this sense (1 Thess 4.14; Lk 24.7; Jn 20.9), but for the most part passively in veiled descriptions of God's way of acting with the resurrected Jesus (Mk 16.6 passim; Lk 24.34; Jn 21.14; Rom 4.25; 6.4, 9; 7.4; 8.38: 1 Cor 15.4 , 12f, 16f, 20; 2 Tim 2.8). In many passages Jesus' Resurrection is attributed directly to God (cf 1.Cor 6.14; Rom 10.9; 1 Cor 15.15 *et al*). This is especially the case in the antithetical formulations of Acts: '(You) killed the Author of life, whom God raised from the dead' (3.15; cf 2.23f; 5.30 *et al*). The raising of Jesus from the dead is therefore an act of divine power, an act of 'the working of his great might' (Eph 1.19f; cf Col 2.12), of his glory (Rom 6.4) and his Spirit (Rom 8.11; 1 Pet 3.18). The formula, God 'that raised from the dead Jesus our Lord' (Rom 4.24, 8.11; 2 Cor 4.14; Gal 1.1; Eph 1.20; Col 2.12) thus becomes immediately a New Testament predicate of God and a name of honour. Jesus' Resurrection is not only God's decisive eschatological act, but his eschatological revelation of himself; here it is finally and unsurpassably revealed, who God is: he whose power embraces life and death, existence and non-existence, who is creative love and faithfulness, the power of the new life, on which there is complete reliance even in the collapse of all human potentialities. The Resurrection of Jesus is the revelation and realization of the Kingdom of God proclaimed by Jesus. In raising Jesus from the dead God proved his faithfulness in love and thus finally identified himself with Jesus and his work.

Faith in Jesus Christ's Resurrection thus has its roots in the most fundamental confession of faith, faith in the creative potential and in the faithfulness of God. Finally it has its roots in faith in God's divinity. Conversely, it is equally true that God's divinity only shows itself conclusively in Jesus' Resurrection. The decision for or against Easter faith is not taken on the grounds of some miraculous event or other but on whether one is ready to see reality from God's viewpoint and to rely totally upon that God in living and in dying. In making such a decision, therefore, what has to be considered is whether one feels one can live from one's own potentialities or whether one dares to live from what absolutely cannot be controlled, from God. Easter faith has confidence in God's possession of a potential far beyond existing reality, far beyond death, and dares to bet on that God 'with whom all things are possible' in life and in death. Hence the faith of Easter is an attack on that enclosed view of the world which sets itself absolute limits and leaves no space for the non-deducible new creative potentialities of God. The Resurrection faith is no single corrective for such a view of life; conformity with the laws of nature is not, as it were, promptly abrogated. It is rather that any such philosophy of life is put in question. The problem is that of making a basic decision about the direction and meaning of existence. If faith in the Resurrection is seen in this light, then faith as a whole is placed in question with it. A Christian faith which was not also a faith in the Resurrection, would be of wood not iron. With the faith in the Resurrection stands and falls the Christian concept of God. The Easter faith is therefore not a supplement to belief in God and in Jesus Christ, it is the entirety and essence of that belief.

2. JESUS' RESURRECTION AS EXALTATION

The Resurrection of Jesus is the final endorsement of Jesus' person and message. It means not only the finality of his message and his work, but the finality of his person. What does that imply? Merely that in the person and actions of Jesus the final model of man is set before us? Is the message of the Resurrection then the legitimation of a human pattern of behaviour, which is determined by radical freedom for God and for men? The legitimation of a freedom characterized by faith and love? Or does it say over and above that, as the traditional profession of faith declares, that Jesus did not remain dead, but lives? But then we are faced immediately with all kinds of difficult problems about the historicity and corporeality of the Risen Christ, about the condition of the Transfigured Christ.

To examine the Christological dimension of the Resurrection, I shall start with an analysis of the old confessional formula 1 Cor 15.3-5. This confession of faith consists of two verses, parallel in form, each two lines long:
'Christ died for our sins in accordance with the Scripture,
that he was buried,
that he was raised on the third day in accordance with the Scriptures,
and that he appeared to Cephas, and then to the Twelve'.
On the basis of the parallel structure of the two verses, it is possible to interpret the second verse by analogy with the first. In the first verse an historical statement is made first of all ('Christ died'), then a soteriological meaning is adduced for this historical event ('for our sins'), a meaning which is interpreted as the fulfilment of the Old Testament promises ('in accordance with the Scriptures'); the second line ('that he was buried') serves as corroboration, for, according to Jewish understanding, burial is the final signing and sealing of death. If one carries this schema over to the second verse, then it becomes clear that the statement of the Resurrection must be a matter of an historical event too, the soteriological sense of which is expressed with the aid of the theologoumenon of the third day, for which 'scriptural proof' is once again given; the appearances to Peter and the Twelve serve as corroboration of this story of salvation.

To what extent is a more soteriological than historical significance to be attributed to the statement 'on the third day'.[2] It should be borne in mind that behind the words there was originally an historical date, either the discovery of the empty tomb or the first appearance on the third day. That the historical nature of the statement is nonetheless secondary is clearly shown by the fact that the phrase 'on the third day' is replaced elsewhere by 'after three days' and 'after the third day'. More important is the fact that there is a rabbinical theologoumenon, in which Yahweh promises the Israelites, or the just respectively, not to leave them in need any longer than three days. This theologoumenon has a place in Hos 6.2: 'After two days he will revive us; on the third day he will raise us up, that we may live before him'. The legend which tells how Jonah lived for three days and three nights in a fish's belly (Jon 2.1) might also be cited. The expression 'the third day' means then that Yahweh had intervened with Jesus' Resurrection to set free the Just One; the Resurrection of Jesus is an act of salvation, in

146

which the Scriptures are fulfilled. It is the decisive turn in the history of salvation, the final proof of God's faithfulness, justice and love.

If the third day is therefore to be understood primarily not as a calendar or chronological date but as the expression of the profound meaning for our salvation of Jesus' Resurrection, that does not mean that the Resurrection should be allowed to dissolve into mere symbolic significance. The theologoumenon of the third day is used precisely in order to express the importance of the real event for salvation and to emphasize that God intervened effectively in a real historical situation for which there was no other solution. The theologoumenon of the third day is therefore concerned with the historicity of salvation, with salvation-history. It brings us to the decisive question of the historicity of the Resurrection itself. The answer to this question depends of course to a very great extent on what one means by historicity. It was pointed out at the beginning that it is not a matter of an historically verifiable fact in the sense of a generally objectively and neutrally examinable fact. The reason for this observation has meanwhile become clear: the Resurrection of Jesus is the unique and incomparable Act of God, which as such does not represent a fact among other facts. Nonetheless — and this is what emerges from the juxtaposition of the first and second verses of 1 Cor 15.3-5 — this act of God does not take place in a 'higher history' far away beyond the history of men, but right beside the Crucified and Buried One. The Resurrection finds its historical term in Jesus of Nazareth, crucified and buried, which prevents its being regarded as purely an event of faith. The basis for the continuity and identity between the Crucified and Risen Jesus can, nonetheless, only be found in God's faithfulness to his bond and as a creator. This lifts the Resurrection of Jesus out of the context of analogy with other events and indicates that a new era has dawned in history.

The more profound theological dimensions of this event are expressed in Scripture chiefly by the words 'exalted' and 'exaltation'.[3] In the pre-Pauline hymn to Christ in the letter to the Philippians[4] (2.9) the term 'exaltation' is used instead of 'resurrection'; this vision is echoed in many passages in the New Testament (Lk 24.26; Eph 4.8ff; 1 Tim 3.16; Heb 12.2; 2 Pet 1.11; Acts 5.6). In other places the exaltation is the direct consequence of the Resurrection and mentioned directly with the latter, as for instance in the old two-tier-Christology of Rom 1.3f. (cf also Acts 5.30f; 1 Thess 1.10; Eph 1.20; 1 Pet 1.21; 3.22 et al). The Risen Christ lives his life to God (Rom 6.9f). Therefore in Mt 28.16ff the Risen Christ appears exalted in the only report of a post-Resurrection appearance in this gospel — and shows his divine authority. But it is in John's gospel that the association is closest and most significant of cross, Resurrection, Exaltation and sending of the Spirit. 'Exaltation' is an expression with two meanings in the Fourth Gospel. It describes the exaltation on the cross as well as the exaltation to the Father (Jn 3.14; 8.28; 12.32), the glorification (7; 39; 12.16 et al). Obedience on the cross as the innermost core of Jesus' being (4.34; 5.30) and as Jesus' entrusting of himself to the Father is both a departure to his Father (13.1) and an entry into eternal glory (17.5, 23f). Therefore the Risen Christ appears to Mary Magdalen as on the way to his Father, as ascending to his Father (20.17). Raised in exaltation to his Father in the sole event of the cross, he possesses all power and can draw everything to himself (12.32). Therefore on Easter evening the Risen Christ grants the disciples the gift of the Holy Spirit, through whom he permits them to share in his power (20.22). Here we have the theology of Easter in all its magnificence: the dying Jesus gives himself in obedience to the will of his Father; the Father accepts that obedience, so that Jesus' self-offering fulfils its purpose, is accepted by God and signifies his exaltation. Good Friday, Easter, Ascension and Pentecost form a single indivisible mystery, the one pasch of the Lord, the one transition of Jesus through death to life, by which he opened up new life for us too in the Holy Spirit.

The unity which almost all the New Testament writings show between the Resurrection and Exaltation seems to disintegrate in the case of Luke, who 'inserts' a period of forty days between Resurrection and Ascension. Moreover Luke seems, in contrast to the rest of the New Testament, to describe the Ascension as Jesus' outwardly visible disappearance (Acts 1.9f). These statements have very much left their mark on average religious ideas. It has admittedly to be taken into account that Luke's forty days are not intended as an exact historical period of time, but as a round figure. Forty is in fact a sacred number (the Israelites' journey through the wilderness; Jesus' sojourn in the wilderness). Forty is the one number available to denote a fairly long period of time. What is at issue is a holy period of a considerable length and especially marked out as significant. It is the time during which the Lord appeared to the disciples.

In keeping with the above is Luke's 'report' of the Ascension in the midst of a post-Resurrection appearance. For this reason Acts 1.3 also explicitly mentions a vision. Here, too, as in the story of the tomb, an angel is ready to interpret. These parallels prove that Luke's Ascension story is an Easter story. Elsewhere in Luke there is mention of Christ's appearing from heaven (Acts 10.40; 13.30); according to Luke, Jesus already entered into his glory after the Resurrection (Lk 24.26; cf 23.42f). In his account of the Ascension, Luke depicts it vividly, using the symbol of the cloud. The cloud which bears Jesus away from the sight of the astonished disciples is not a meteorological phenomenon, but a theological symbol. Even in the Old Testament the cloud is God's vehicle and the sign of his all-powerful presence. Therefore in our account the cloud means nothing more than that Jesus is taken up into the sphere of divine glory and divine life and that he is with his people in a new way sent from God. So the Ascension story emerges as a − final − Easter story. The forty days perform the function for Luke of connecting the time of Jesus with the time of the Church; here the two epochs overlap; we are faced here then with the idea of continuity between Jesus and the Church, which Luke can only express in this way. The Ascension is the last Easter story and at the same time the beginning of the Church.

At first, we find the idea of exaltation strange today. But that was not the case in neo-Judaism. E. Schweizer has demonstrated the important role of the idea of the suffering and exalted figure of a just man.[7] Elijah, Enoch and other just men were taken up into heaven, to be kept there like Baruch as witnesses for the last judgment; similarly, the return of Elijah on the last day

148

was awaited (Mt 11.14; 16.14; 17.10). In neo-Judaism exaltation (or ecstasy) was the only category available to express the fact that a human being on earth would still play a part in the eschatological events. Exaltation was therefore a current category, which was used in an attempt to express a person's eschatological importance.

This is why the earliest statements on the exaltation of Jesus are also in an explicitly eschatological context; Jesus is exalted for a certain (brief) time, so that he can then appear from heaven as the eschatological Messiah and as such come again (1 Thess 1.10; Acts 3.20f).[8] It then has to be stated: eschatological fate is decided by this Jesus of Nazareth, who was crucified and now lives with God; anyone who confesses him now, will be saved at the Judgment. Anyone who confesses his faith in Jesus Christ, whose future is obscure, can hope and trust from now on. 'Who is to condemn? Is it Jesus Christ, who died, yes, who was raised from the dead, who is at the right hand of God, who indeed intercedes for us? Who shall separate us from the Love of Christ? Shall tribulation, or distress, or persecution, or famine, or nakedness, or peril, or sword?' (Rom 8.34f).

Here a second aspect of the idea of exaltation becomes clear and is subsequently worked out more and more thoroughly. If the actual confession of Jesus Christ is so decisive, then his position as ruler cannot be purely future, it must be present as well. Now there develops from what was the originally — it would seem — only future position as ruler, his position as ruler here in the present. That is not a fundamental break, for the older idea too had its place in the actual confession of Jesus Christ, which is only re-affirmed at the coming again. Even if the emphasis shifts somewhat, the eschatological aspect is not simply given up (cp. 2 Tim 4.1; 18; 1 Cor 15.24ff). The present position of power is unfolded in the light of texts from the Psalms in particular; in this Psalm 110.1 plays a special part: 'Sit at my right hand, till I make your enemies your footstool' (cf Mk 14.16 *passim*; 16.19, Acts 2.23; Eph 1.20; Heb 1.3, 13; 8.1; 10.12f). Exaltation means therefore heavenly enthronement and installation in divine dignity and authority. When exalted, Jesus shares in divine power (Rom 1.3f; 1 Cor 5.4; 2 Cor 12.9; Phil 3.10; Eph 1.20f; 1 Pet 3.22) and divine glory (*doxa*) (Phil 3.21; 2 Cor 4.4; 1 Pet 1.21). From this 'position of power' he intercedes with the Father for us (Rom 8.34) and protects us on the day of God's Judgment (Rom 5.9). According to John's gospel the Risen Christ enters into eternal love with the Father (17.23). In short: Resurrection and Exaltation mean: Jesus lives wholly and for ever in God (Rom 6.9f). Raising up to the right hand of God does not therefore imply being spirited away to another-worldly empyrean, but Jesus' being with God, his being in the dimension of God, of his power and glory. It does not mean distance from the world, but a new way of being with us; Jesus is now with us from God and in God's way; expressed in imagery: he is with God as our advocate: *semper interpellans pro nobis* (Heb 7.25).[9]

To summarize, it is possible to characterize Jesus' Resurrection as the inner unity of an historical and an eschatological and theological event. The Resurrection of Jesus has an historical dimension in that it happens to Jesus of Nazareth who was crucified. The Resurrection of Jesus means that the cross, which in human terms means the end, failure and disgrace, means simultaneously God's act of power and therefore a new beginning and a reason for hope. Resurrection means that the obedience of Jesus really is accepted where he wants it to reach: with God; and that God accepts it, in taking Jesus to himself. The Resurrection is the fulfilled and fulfilling end of the death on the cross. It is therefore not a separate event after the life and suffering of Jesus, but what is happening at the most profound level in the death of Christ: the act and suffering of a human being's bodily surrender to God and the merciful loving acceptance of this devotion by God. The Resurrection is as it were the profound divine dimension of the Cross, since God finally reaches man and man finally reaches God.[10] In this paradoxical unity of cross and Resurrection God's love and power enter human existence wholly and irrevocably unto death and conversely man gives himself up in obedience to the will of the Father. Each is one side of a process. Cross and Resurrection together form the one *Pascha Domini*.

With this interpretation of the rising from the dead the question arises once again of the corporeal nature of the Resurrection. Basically, if the historicity of the Resurrection is taken seriously, then the corporeality follows from that: as an actual historical man, Jesus of Nazareth is inconceivable without his body. If one is to avoid a Christological Docetism, there is no way round the corporeality of the Resurrection. The question can only be then the way to think of that post-Resurrection corporeality. It is clear that this question throws up serious problems and can present religious difficulties. Little progress, however, is made on the lines of scholastic speculations on the material identity of the earthly and glorified body or the characteristics or composition of the Resurrection body. The basic question is what is meant in Scripture by body and corporeality.

Body (*soma*) is in Scripture not only an important but a very difficult concept. According to Scripture the body is so vital to man, that a being without a body after death is unthinkable (1 Cor 15.35ff; 2 Cor 5.1ff). For the Hebrew the body is not the tomb of the soul as it is for the Greek (*soma-sema*) and certainly not the principle of evil from which man's true self has to set itself free, as it was for the Gnostics. The body is God's creation and it always describes the whole of man and not just a part. But this whole person is not conceived as a figure enclosed in itself, as in classical Greece, nor as a fleshly substance, as in materialism, nor as person and personality, as in idealism. The body is the whole man in his relationship to God and his fellow man. It is man's place of meeting with God and his fellow man. The body is the possibility and the reality of communication.

The relationship to God and one's fellow men can be variously qualified. The body is the place in which man stands at times in a certain relationship of mastery; it is the place where man is either at the mercy of sin, selfishness, envy, ambition and so on, or where he stands in Christ's service. For the man who acknowledges Jesus Christ, the body is the place where he must put obedience to the test and carry it out. It is the place of concrete obedience. So, says Paul, we should serve God with our body (Rom 12.1f); we should glorify God with our body (1 Cor 6.20). Therefore the body belongs to the Lord and the Lord to the body (1 Cor 6.13). According to the master-slave relationship in which we find ourselves, the body is either superficial or pneumatic. A pneumatic body, which Paul talks of in the Resurrection chapter 1 Cor 15, is not a body constructed from some artificial miraculous spiritual substance. The *soma pneumatikon* is far more a body characterized by the *pneuma*, a body entirely directed by the spirit of God. The *pneuma* here is therefore not the stuff, the substance, of which this body is made, but the dimension, in which the body is: it is in the divine dimension.

Thus we can finally say what the pneumatic body of the Resurrected is: the totality of the person (not just the soul) that is finally in the dimension of God, that has entered entirely into the Kingdom of God. Corporeality of the Resurrection means then: The whole person of the Lord is finally with God. The Resurrection corporeality means something else too, however: that the Risen Lord is still in contact with the world and with us and indeed as the one who is now with God; he is therefore with us in a divine way and that means in a totally new way. Therefore Paul can say that the body of the Lord is the body for us *(to soma to huper humon)* (1 Cor 11.24). Jesus' permanent and yet new way of being for us and with us is most clearly expressed in the Eucharist, where Christ gives himself to us and communicates with us. Corporeality of the Resurrection means then nothing other than that Jesus is permanently with God with all his person and comes from God and is with us in a new way.

This biblical view of the body can be verified anthropologically.[12] According to modern anthropology it is not simply to be equated with physicality and materiality. Corporeality means rather the total involvement of man in the world; it implies that a man is so part of the world and the world so part of the man that in his body the man can call a piece of the world his own, indeed that he is himself a piece of the world. Through and in his body man stands in relationship to the world's reality in its entirety. The body is, as it were, the 'between' which joins man and the world. This bodily *in-the-world-ness* of man and this *in-man-ness* of the world is so essential and constituent for both, that man would not exist without this real being-in-the-world and conversely the world as such would not exist without this reference to man. It is therefore not the case that man would first be man (that is, spirit, self, and so on) and then would have a reference to the world. Man as man is first himself through his relation to the world: that is, through his body. An existence released from his body is therefore impossible for man.

The short anthropological considerations may help to elucidate the biblical findings. The corporeality of the Resurrection means that Jesus Christ while entering God's dimension through his Resurrection and Exaltation is at the same time completely in the world in a new divine way and is by us and with us 'to the close of the age' (Mt 28.20). Through Jesus' Resurrection and Exaltation a 'piece of the world' finally reached God and was finally accepted by God.

The newness which has come into our sphere through Jesus' arrival with God and through his new coming to us, is traditionally called 'heaven', borrowing from the language of myth. Heaven means originally the upper place, the floor which is above the earth (the empyrean). Usually this heaven is imagined as empty space into which Jesus was taken up and into which the saints will move in solemn procession at the end of time. These are more or less mythological ideas: theologically, heaven is the dimension which arises when the creature finally arrives with God. To go to heaven means to come to God; to be in heaven, means to be with God. Heaven is an eschatological phenomenon; it does not simply *exist*; it comes into being, more precisely, at the moment when the first created being is eschatologically and finally taken up by God. Heaven takes shape therefore in the Resurrection and Exaltation of Christ. Jesus is not actually taken up into heaven, but in being finally accepted with God, heaven starts to exist. Heaven is the pneumatic resurrected body of Christ.

Against the background of what has been said above, a few points emerge on the matter of judging scholastic speculations about the characteristics and constitution of the Resurrection body. All the attributes, incapability of suffering (*impassibilitas*) and imperishability (*immortalitas*), finesse (*subtilitas*) and dexterity (*agilitas*): that is, intellectual formation and complete control and mastery over the body through the spirit, the overcoming of all alienation in man, and finally clearness (*claritas*), transfiguration by the glory of God; all these could be understood basically as the effect of the final validation of the whole man in the glory of God – in spite of all the problems of such speculations individually. The question of the material identity of the transfigured resurrection body with the earthly body presents more of a problem. Most theologians hold the identity not only of the corporeality but even of the material physicality. Yet if we can disregard for a moment the question of what this material identity might mean in face of constant metabolism and disregard too the consequences for basically insoluble problems arising throughout (as, for instance, at what age the dead rise again), we are still faced with the real question whether Paul in 1 Cor 15.35-44 does not in fact stress the discontinuity between earthly and glorified body and dismiss the whole question finally as pointless: 'But some one will ask, "How are the dead raised? With what kind of body do they come?" You foolish man! What you saw does not come to life unless it dies. .. So it is with the resurrection of the dead. What is sown is perishable, what is raised is imperishable. It is sown in dishonour, it is raised in glory. It is sown in weakness, it is raised in power, it is sown in physical body, it is raised a spiritual body'. But the body is spiritual, that is man in his human and worldly connexions, when this connexion with the world is completely penetrated by the love of God. Concrete statements can scarcely be made about the *how* of such a pneumatic body. In any case, in Scripture such questions are completely unimportant in comparison with the statements about the significance for salvation of the corporeality of the Resurrection.

The whole of reality arrives at its apex in God with the body of Christ. Heaven projects into time. It is only logical that the Church as the place where Christ is present in faith, hope and love, should be called the body of Christ. When Paul says our home is in heaven (Phil 3.20) and that we are taken up with Christ in heaven (Eph 2.6; cf Col 1.5; 3:3), that heaven is first of all there where men are 'in Christ' in faith and love as well as in hope and patience and commit themselves with their world to the finality which has come with Christ. In this way the whole of reality is taken up into the new historical dynamic, which finds its fulfilment when God has become 'all in all' (1 Cor 15.18).

The importance which Jesus Christ has for our salvation by reason of his Resurrection and Exaltation is expressed by Scripture in the confession of Jesus as the *Kyrios*. Beside the creed 'Jesus is the Christ', it is the creed 'Jesus is the *Kyrios*' which plays a decisive role in the early Church (Rom 10.9, 1 Cor 12.3; Phil 2.11). This title is intended to express the position of power in heaven of the Risen and Exalted Christ.

The origins of this title have been and still are much debated. In the ancient mystery cults it played a large part as a description of the divinities current at the time; it is also found in the Roman cult of the emperors. Religious historians (especially W. Bousset) as well as Bultmann and his school in more recent times, derive this title therefore from the hellenistic world. This theory meets however, the great difficulty that we find the title *Kyrios* in Aramaic form in the cultic invocation of the Palestinian communities 'Maranatha' (1 Cor 16.22; Acts 22.20; Did 10.10, 6). This fact also indicates that this Aramaic invocation is found even later in texts that are otherwise in Greek, that it was in very early usage and so was handed down to the hellenistic communities as a holy tradition. Therefore Foerster,[14] Cullman, Schweizer and the majority of Catholic writers are right to declare that the title is Palestinian in origin.

The significance of the meaning is far more important than the origin of the quotation. The Maranatha can be interpreted in different ways. It can mean 'Our Lord is come' (he is there, present) or 'Our Lord, come'. In the first case we have a credal statement, in the second case we have an invocation asking for the *parousia* to come quickly. Paul uses the word *Kyrios* unequivocally to describe the present resurrected Lord. There are two aspects included in this idea: Jesus is risen, he is with God; but through his Spirit he is also present in the Church (2 Cor 3.17), especially in word and sacrament. For Paul, therefore, Jesus is not primarily the teacher and the model, but the Lord who is present in the word and in the eucharistic celebration and who takes both the apostle and every ordinary Christian into his service. 'None of us lives to himself, and none of us dies to himself. If we live, we live to the Lord, and if we die, we die to the Lord; so then, whether we live or whether we die, we are the Lord's'. (Rom 14.7f).

Indirectly, by allusion, in Paul (1 Cor 8.6) and fully worked out in the deutero-Pauline writings (Eph 1.10f; Col 1.15-20; Heb 1:2f) and in John (1.1-10), this Kingdom of Christ is extended to the whole cosmos and taken back to the beginning of creation. The whole universe is subject to Christ. He is, as it were, the viceroy of the Kingdom of God; in him and through him God's Kingdom is set up. This cosmological and protological explanation of the confession of Christ is an appropriate conclusion from the eschatological character of Jesus' life, death and Resurrection. If the end and fulfilment of history dawns and the purpose is achieved in him, in whom everything finds its fulfilment, if with him salvation has come, then it is because from the beginning of time everything has been made dependent on Christ. The affirmation of Jesus' life and work by the Father is at the same time the affirmation of all reality; it is the salvation of the world.

3. JESUS' RESURRECTION AS A REDEMPTIVE EVENT

The Resurrection of the Crucified One and his establishment in a position of divine authority and power is not an isolated event for the New Testament, but the beginning and anticipation of the general resurrection of the dead. Jesus is the 'first fruits of those who have fallen asleep' (1 Cor 15. 20; Col 1.18; Acts 26. 23; cf 3. 15; Rev 1. 17 f). More precisely, Paul does not derive his understanding of the general resurrection from the Resurrection of Jesus, but on the contrary understands Jesus' Resurrection in terms of hope in the resurrection of the dead: 'But if there is no resurrection of the dead, then Christ has not been raised' (1 Cor 15. 13; cf 16).

The Resurrection of Jesus exists, therefore, in a universal perspective. It is more than a unique, completed event. It is an event which is open to the future; one indeed which opens the world to the future. It implies the eschatological fulfilment of man in his wholeness; it implies a new humanity and a new world. It is the prefiguration and the foreglimpse of that towards which the whole creation looks, sighing and groaning in eager longing: the revelation of the freedom of the children of God (cf Rom 8. 19 ff), and the reign of freedom that is to come.

The indispensability of the eschatalogico-apocalyptic horizon of the Easter faith and consequently of Christian belief and of theology as a whole has been admirably demonstrated by Käsemann.[15] Pannenberg[16] has shown that what we are concerned with here is an essential human dimension; not one, however, that is wholly inaccessible to us now, but one that is based in the infinite destiny of man and in the hope that orientation to everlastingness gives us now. Moltmann in his theology of hope has reached systematic conclusions from that basis about our understanding of the world and man, and our conception of God. To be sure, we must not overlook the fact that apocalyptic does not acknowledge the resurrection of any man before the general resurrection. To that extent, the news of Jesus' Resurrection signifies an adjustment of the apocalyptic world-view: an adjustment which means in fact that the New Testament concept is not one of any particular future for the world, but has to do with the future of Jesus Christ. What it has in mind is the universal extension of what was ultimately apparent in Jesus as a person

154

and in his destiny. Kreck[18] is right to stress how true it is that eschatology not only determines Christology, but is also subject to Christology.

Jesus Christ himself is our future and our hope. In the New Testament the God of hope (Rom 15. 13) is not one of abstract features alone. He has real human characteristics: the human countenance and human form of the Man who gave himself for us.

The Christological glosses on, and realization of, the apocalyptic projects of late Judaism are essential for a correct understanding of what is distinctively Christian. By that I do not mean only that the future of all reality has already begun with Jesus and is decisively determined by him, but far more: that the person and activity of Jesus are that future; that through his Resurrection he became the world's salvation: 'put to death for our trespasses and raised for our justification' (Rom 4. 25). That is to say: Jesus' Resurrection means more than the final acceptance and confirmation of Jesus and his reception into community of life and love of God. In the Resurrection and Exaltation of Jesus, God also accepted Jesus' existence for others and finally established peace and reconciliation with the world. In and through Jesus, God's love is now finally addressed to all men.

This fundamental point is first and foremost a critical corrective not only of the abstract utopias of modern times, but of attempts to derive a Christian ideology of history from hope based on Jesus' Resurrection. Attempts of that kind are possible in another, indeed a contrary, direction. Like the early Christian enthusiasts, we can so stress the existence in Christ that has already begun, that we render neutral the continuing reality of the old world. That particular emphasis can lead to distance or even flight from the world; it can also lead to moral anarchism. On the other hand we could also try to draw a progressive, evolutionary or revolutionary ideology of history from Easter. Both conceptions forget the Christological basis of the Christian notion of the world process, and its necessary unity of cross and Resurrection. A Christological basis means that the Easter hope sets a Christian on the way of the cross, which is none other than the way of actual, bodily obedience in everyday life (cf Rom 12. 1).

We must not confuse Christian hope with contempt for the world. Instead we must see Christian hope as based in God's creative and covenantal fidelity. Then Christian hope is loyal to the earth. As hope in eternal life, it not only respects life but turns lovingly towards all that is living and alive. A man who hopes becomes an active emblem of hope in life. On the other hand, that hope should not be confounded triumphalistically in some universal historico-theological principle of progress. Christian hope states indeed that in the end God will be 'all in all' (1 Cor 15. 28). Yet ultimately this all-in-all God does not appear in a purposive process of historical development. Such an evolution is grounded rather in faith in the love of God: a love which has made its appearance eschatologically and finally in the death and Resurrection of Jesus; a love to which henceforth all that is future belongs, and belongs underivably. Hope of that kind permits of no historical speculation, but certainly invites historical practice. The belief that love persists for ever (1 Cor 13.8) means that only that which is done out of love will endure for ever and is lastingly inscribed in the condition and growth of reality.[19] Certainly we may say of that love which espouses reality, that its victorious Easter power is shown in its endurance and persistence through trials and stresses: 'We are afflicted in every way, but not crushed; perplexed, but not driven to despair; persecuted, but not forsaken; struck down, but not destroyed; always carrying in the body the death of Jesus, so that the life of Jesus may also be manifested in our bodies' (2 Cor 4. 8-10).

The love and loyalty of God became eschatologically and ultimately clear and effective in the cross and Resurrection of Jesus. That love and that loyalty are the eschatological reality pure and simple which determines the present and to which the future as a whole belongs. This new existence 'in Christ' means for a Christian that he is dead and buried with Christ in order to rise again with him (Rom 6. 4 f). Since the hope and reality of the future resurrection even now determine the present, the deutero-Pauline writings are able to describe the Resurrection as an already present reality (cf Eph 2. 6; Col 3. 10 ff).

The new existence in Jesus Christ is not however some mysterious potion which quasi-magically transforms man and mankind. The eschatological reality granted in Jesus changes the objective situation of all men, and makes it possible for all men to enter that new reality by faith and baptism. Insofar as Jesus Christ belongs objectively and ontologically to the situation of every man, the Resurrection is a power or an 'existential' which precedes our decision and qualifies and requires it.[20] Whenever a man gives himself through faith and baptism to that reality, he is a new creation in Jesus Christ (2 Cor 5. 17; Gal 6, 15); then it is true to say that 'It is no longer I who live, but Christ who lives in me' (Gal 2. 20).

Scripturally, the new being in Christ can be described in a number of ways: life, justice, redemption, peace, forgiveness, and so forth. None of these terms is dispensable. In our present situation, however, the new existence in Christ is most readily comprised in the notion of Christian freedom. Christian freedom is the actualization for us of what Resurrection means in history.

Freedom[21] is an ambiguous word much used and much misused. Paul already sees himself as having to define Christian freedom in the face of its misuse and misunderstanding. 'All things are lawful for me' would seem to have been a saying of the Corinthian enthusiasts (cf 1 Cor 6. 12; 10. 23). Paul takes up the catchphrase but corrects it in two respects. He reminds the Corinthians that this freedom originates in Jesus Christ. Christian freedom is not acquired simply; and is not simply acquired. It is a freedom which Christ alone vouchsafed us; a freedom which is granted us (cf Gal 5, 1-13); a freedom bound up with Christ, so that the man made free through it belongs really to Christ, as Christ belongs to God (cf 1 Cor 3. 21-3; 6. 13-20). The freedom grounded in Christ and determined by Christ is freedom for one's fellow man; freedom which takes care, and does not destroy, but builds up.

Therefore we say: ' "All things are lawful for me", but not all things are helpful' (1 Cor 6. 12; 10. 23). The yardstick of Christian freedom is the selfless love of God which appeared in Jesus Christ and which takes effect in Christians.

Christian freedom can be described in three practical respects. Firstly it is freedom from sin. In a universal human sense, freedom is primarily freedom from external and internal pressures. Such 'powers' which enslave men are not as far as Scripture is concerned the body, or the matter and things of this world, as they were for the Platonists. These things of the world are made by God and he makes them as good things. They deprive us of freedom only when they take on an anti-creative power of their own and become ultimates, idols which no longer serve man but are served by him. This can happen in any all-consuming care for life, future, money and possessions, and in blind pursuit of pleasure and enjoyment. Those are false ways of taking care for one's life. They are a choice of life in transient flesh instead of in God who makes the dead live. Scripture calls that kind of decision against God sin. That before all else makes man unfree. Therefore Christian freedom is first and foremost freedom from sin (cf Rom 6. 18-23; Jn 8. 31-6). It is positive: freedom for God in Jesus Christ (Rom 6. 11).

Secondly Christian freedom is freedom from death. The wages of sin is death (Rom 6.23; cf 5. 12-21). Sin runs after life, but chooses what is transient and impotent. In doing so it misses real life and plunges into death. Death consequently is no externally decreed divine punishment for sin, but its inward result (Rom 8. 13; Gal 6. 8). Condemnation to death is the essence of enslavement. Death is not only the last moment of life but the power and the fate which threatens all life. It is announced in numberless trials, pains, sufferings and sorrows. Death itself is the final intensity of the imprisonment and futurelessness of our life. Therefore Christian freedom must be freedom from death (cf Rom 6. 5-9; 1 Cor 15. 20-22). That does not mean that suffering and dying lose their actuality for a Christian. But it does mean that anyone whose life is in Christ is no longer basically directed towards what perishes in death.

Death has lost its sting. The right attitude to death is not fear but hope, which can accept even suffering and death, because nothing in the world, neither life nor death, can separate us from the love which has appeared in Jesus Christ (Rom 8. 31-9). It is precisely in human weakness that the power of the Resurrection takes effect (2 Cor 7. 10; 12. 7-9). This freedom from death has a positive meaning: it implies the predominance of a freedom in life to which we can commit ourselves without any fear or anxiety.

This Christian freedom risks everything. It is also freedom from the law (Rom 7. 6). Paul knows that the law is sacred, just and good in itself (Rom 7. 12); but in practice it requires revolt and thereby becomes an occasion of sin (Rom 7. 8). On the other hand, fulfilment of the law can be an occasion of self-glorification instead of divine glorification (Rom 2. 23). The law that set out the will of God in practical terms can also restrict that will to certain instances, and thus reduce or hide its absoluteness under legalities. The very law which God devised as a help to sinners can become an occasion of disobedience and illegality and therefore enslavement. Freedom from the law then, is clearly the opposite of arbitrariness and license. True self-will is not free but quite unfree, because it means slavery to one's own ego and the whim of the moment. He is really free who is free from himself and his interests, in order to be disposable wholly for God and others. Positive freedom from the law is love (Gal 5. 13). Love is the fulfilment of the law (Rom 13. 10). It fulfils the requirements of the law from within. But love is the reality which proved victorious in the Resurrection of Jesus. It offers freedom to anyone who surrenders himself to it in faith.

Jesus' new redemptive presence among his disciples not only establishes hope and freedom, but gathers a new body of disciples round the Lord who is present in a new way. The appearances of the Resurrected One continue the eschatological apostolate of the earthly Jesus in a new way. After Easter therefore the Church was established as the community of the people of God of the new Covenant.

It is not possible here to discuss in detail the difficult problem of the foundation of the Church. Only a few essential indications are possible.[22] The findings of the New Testament sources are best represented by the idea (also put forward by the second Vatican Council) of an extended establishment of the Church; one that took place in stages, and which extends to the entire activity of Jesus, earthly as well as exalted.[23] In the apostolate of the earthly Jesus, among his disciples, at his meals, and especially the last meal before his death, and so forth, there are pre-paschal *vestigia ecclesiae,* which could be used as 'foundation stones' in the new post-Easter situation. The new community needed no express word of establishment. It was established with the Easter appearances and the mandate to preach and baptize grounded in those appearances (Mt 28. 19). That means that the Church is in fact the apostolic Church, which must contain commissioned witnesses of the Gospel (cf. Rom 10. 14 ff). The word of reconciliation and the service of reconciliation were first established in the work of reconciliation (2 Cor 5. 19); Like the apostolic proclamation which grounded the Church, the eucharistic community is directly established with the Easter appearances. The Resurrected resumes the eucharistic community with his disciples that was interrupted by his death. He is now with and among his own in a new way — in the sign of the meal. Hence many of the Easter appearances take place in the context of meals (Lk 24. 30 f; 36-43; Jn 21. 9-14). The Eucharist, in addition to the Word, is the genuine place of encounter with the Risen Lord. In that sense, we may say not only that Jesus was 'raised into the kerygma', but that he 'rose again in the liturgy'.

Once the disciples had broken their community with Jesus by denial and flight, the new assurance of the eucharistic community also became a sign of forgiveness. The Resurrection also establishes the forgiveness of sins and the assurance of the eschatological Shalom. John most clearly brought this out by explaining the new band of disciples as the place where forgiveness of sins is possible: 'If you forgive the sins of any, they are forgiven; if you retain the sins of any, they are retained' (20.23). Accordingly, reacceptance into the company of the disciples is also a sign of reacceptance into communion with God. Essentially, that is what later became the 'sacramentality' of penance. The Eucharist and the sacrament of penance do not derive primarily from an isolated act of foundation by Jesus. They are established with the Resurrection and the appearances of the Resurrected One. They are a symbolic expression of the new redemptive presence of Jesus in and among his own

The new gathering into a community provoked by Easter, and the profession of that community are therefore part of the eschatological event. The Church itself is an eschatological phenomenon insofar as in all historical precedence it shares in the eschatological and ultimate nature of the new history opened up with the Resurrection. That means in fact that the Church is indestructible, or indefectible. Church will always be. But the Church is only the Church of Jesus Christ as long as it persists in faith in Jesus Christ the Crucified and Resurrected. It is characteristic of the eschatological nature of the Church that it can never fundamentally depart from the truth of Christ.[25] The saving truth of God is permanently granted to the world by Jesus Christ in and through the Church. Christ is lastingly present in history in the Church's proclamation of faith and doctrine, in its liturgy and in its sacraments and in its whole life.

Notes

[1] On the terminology, see E.Fascher, *'Anastasis − Resurrectio −* Auferstehung. Eine programmatische Studie zum Thema "Sprache und Offenbarung", in: ZNW 40 (1941), pp. 166-229; K.H.Rengstorf, *Die Auferstehung Jesu, op. cit.,* pp. 22 ff; J.Kremer, *Das älteste Zeugnis, op. cit.,* pp. 40-7; A.Oepke, art. *'anistēmi'* in: TW I, pp. 368-72; *idem,* art, *'egeiro',* in TW II, pp. 334-6.

[2] See the exhaustive commentary in K.Lehmann, *Auferweckt am dritten Tag, op. cit.,* (bibliography); *idem,* art, *'Triduum mortis',* in: LTK X, p. 339.

[3] See here G.Bertram, art *'hypsos', inter alia,* in: TW VIII, pp. 600-19; *idem,* art. 'Erhöhung', in: RAC VI, pp. 22-43; E.Schweizer, *Erniedrigung und Erhöhung bei Jesus und seinen Nachfolgern* (2nd ed., Zürich, 1962); F.Hahn, *Hoheitstitel, op. cit.,* esp. pp. 112-32; 189-93; 251-68; 290-2; 348-50.

[4] See primarily E.Käsemann, 'Kritische Analyse von Phil 2. 5-11', in: *idem, Exegetische Versuche und Besinnungen* I, *op. cit.,* pp. 51-95; G.Bornkamm, 'Zum Verständnis des Christus-Hymnus Phil 2. 6-11', in: *idem, Studien zu Antike und Christentum. Gesammelte Aufsätze,* vol. 2 (Munich, 1963), pp. 177-87; J.Gnilka, *Der Philipperbrief* (Freiburg, 1968), pp. 131-47 (bibliography), pp. 111 ff.

[5] See, in more detail, W.Thüsing, *Die Erhöhung und Verherrlichung Jesu im Johannesevangelium* (2nd ed., Münster, 1970); R.Schnackenburg, *Das Johannesevangelium* II (Freiburg, 1971), pp. 498-512 (excursus).

[6] Cf G.Lohfink, *Die Himmelfahrt Jesu. Untersuchungen zu den Himmelfahrts − und Erhöhungstexten bei Lukas* (Munich, 1971); *idem., Die Himmelfahrt Jesu − Erfindung oder Erfahrung?* (Stuttgart, 1971).

[7] Cf E.Schweizer, *Erniedrigung und Erhöhung, op. cit.,* esp. pp. 21-33.

[8] Cf F.Hahn, *Hoheitstitel, op. cit.,* pp. 126-32, and see also the critical viewpoint of

159

W.Thüsing, *Erhöhungsvorstellung und Parusieerwartung in der ältesten nachösterlichen Christologie* (Stuttgarter Bibelstudien 42) (Stuttgart, 1969).

[9] Cf J.Ratzinger's comments in art. 'Himmelfahrt Christi', II. Systematisch', in: LTK V, pp. 360-2.

[10] Cf K.Rahner, *On the Theology of Death, op. cit.;* idem, 'Dogmatische Fragen zur Osterfrömmigkeit', *art. cit.; idem,* 'Christologie', *art. cit., pp. 44-7.*

[11] Cf on the following, E.Schweizer, F.Baumgärtel, art. *'soma',* in: TW VII, pp. 1024-91.

[12] For literature, see III, ch. II/1, of this book.

[13] See on this, J.Ratzinger, art. 'Himmel, III. Systematisch', in: LTK V, pp. 355-8; idem., art. 'Himmelfahrt', *art. cit.*

[14] See on this, G.Quell, W.Foerster, art, *'kyrios',* in: TW III, pp. 1038-98, esp. 1078 ff; O.Cullmann, *Christologie, op. cit.,* pp. 200-44; F.Hahn, *Hoheitstitel, op. cit.,* pp. 67-132; I.Hermann, *Kyrios und Pneuma. Studien zur Christologie der paulinischen Hauptbriefe* (Munich, 1961); W.Kramer, *Christos – Kyrios – Gottessohn, op. cit.,* esp. pp. 61 ff; E.Schweizer, *Erniedrigung und Erhöhung,* pp. 77-86; *idem, Jesus Christus im vielfältigen Zeugnis des Neuen Testaments* (8th ed., paperback, Munich-Hamburg, 1968), pp. 145 ff, 172 ff; ET: *Jesus* (London, 1971).

[15] See in this regard E.Käsemann, 'Zum Thema der urchristlichen Apokalyptik', in: *idem, Exegetische Versuche und Besinnungen II, op. cit.,* pp. 105-31.

[16] W.Pannenberg, *Grundzüge, op. cit.,* pp. 78 ff.

[17] Cf J.Moltmann, *Theologie der Hoffnung. Untersuchungen zur Begründung und zu den Konsequenzen einer christlichen Eschatologie* (7th ed., Munich, 1968); ET: *Theology of Hope* (London, 1967); idem, 'Gott und Auferstehung', *art. cit.;* idem, *Der gekreuzigte Gott, op. cit.,* ET: *The Crucified God, op. cit.*

[18] See in this regard W.Kreck, *Die Zukunft des Gekommenen. Grundprobleme der Eschatologie* (Munich, 1961), pp. 82 ff.

[19] Cf Vatican II, Pastoral Constitution *Gaudium et Spes.*

[20] See in more detail III, ch, II/1.

[21] See on this topic, H.Schlier, art. *'deutheros' et. al.,* in: TW II, pp. 484-500; *idem,* 'Über des vollkommene Gesetz der Freiheit', in: *idem, Die Zeit der Kirche. Exegetische Aufsätze und Vorträge* I (4th ed., Freiburg, 1966), pp. 193-206; *idem,* 'Zur Freiheit gerufen. Das paulinische Freiheitsverständnis', in: *idem, Das Ende der Zeit. Exegetische Aufsätze und Vorträge* III (Freiburg, 1971), pp. 216-33; E.Käsemann, *Der Ruf der Freiheit* (5th ed., Tübingen, 1972); D.Nestle, art. 'Freiheit', in: RAC VIII, pp. 269-306; H.Küng, *Die Kirche* (Freiburg, 1967), pp. 181-195; ET: *The Church* (London, 1968), pp. 150-3, 155-8.

[22] On this problem see H.Küng, *The Church, op. cit.,* pp. 54-79; A.Vögtle, 'Der einzelne und die Gemeinschaft in der Stufenfolge der Christusoffenbarung', in: *Sentire ecclesiam. Das Bewusstsein von der Kirche als gestaltende Kraft der Frömmigkeit,* eds, J.Daniélou and H.Vorgrimler (Freiburg, 1961), pp. 50-91.

[23] Thus in Vatican II, Dogmatic Constitution *Lumen Gentium,* 2-5.

[24] Cf the study by G.Koch, *Die Auferstehung Jesu Christi* (Tübingen, 1959); and further M.Kehl, 'Eucharistie und Auferstehung. Zur Deutung der Ostererscheinungen beim Mahl', in: GuL 43 (1970), pp. 90-125.

[25] This is not the place to enter into the discussion about the infallibility of the Church. See my contribution 'Zur Diskussion um das Problem der Unfehlbarkeit', in: StdZ 188 (1971), pp. 363-76, reprinted in H.Küng (ed.) *Fehlbar?* (Zürich, 1973), pp. 74-89.

160

III THE MYSTERY OF JESUS

I. JESUS CHRIST – SON OF GOD

I. JESUS CHRIST – SON OF GOD

1. SON OF GOD IN LOWLINESS

The decisive question for Christianity has always been 'Who do you think Christ is? Who is he?' Answers to this question are very varied, not only in later history but even in the New Testament. Jesus has many names in the New Testament. He is called Christ, Prophet, Son of man, Servant of God, High Priest, Saviour, Lord *(Kyrios)*, Son of God. Evidently no single title is adequate to indicate who Jesus is. Jesus is the man who fits no formula.

In order to express this unique meaning one title, as distinct from all others, increasingly came to prevail in the New Testament; apparently it proved to be the most appropriate and most fruitful: Jesus, the Son of God.[1] Paul can sum up his whole message in the formula: 'The gospel of God concerning his Son' (Rom 1.3,9; cf 2 Cor 1.19; Gal 1.16). From then onwards the confession of Jesus' divine sonship has been regarded as the distinguishing mark of Christianity. It is true that other religions also speak of sons of the gods and of incarnations. Christianity can take up the question of salvation which is involved here. But it links with its confession of Jesus' divine sonship an eschatological claim that in Jesus of Nazareth God revealed and communicated himself once and for all, uniquely, unmistakably, definitively and unsurpassably. The confession of Jesus Christ as Son of God is therefore a brief formula which gives expression to what is essential and specific to Christian faith as a whole. Christian faith stands or falls with the confession of Jesus as Son of God.

Although the confession of Jesus Christ as Son of God represents the core of the Christian tradition, there are many Christians today who have difficulties with this statement. The most familiar and most fundamental objection to this profession of faith is that it seems to present us with a remnant of an unenlightened mythological way of thinking. It was of course easier than it is for us today for mythological thinking and feeling to take the step from the human to the divine. The divine was – so to speak – the dimension in depth of all reality, filling everything with a numinous radiance. Everywhere, in any encounter and in any happening, it could suddenly make its presence felt. At that time therefore geniuses beyond the normal human scale (rulers of states, philosophers) were venerated as divine and as sons of God. Such a mingling of divine and human was absolutely alien to strict biblical monotheism. Even in the Old Testament, therefore, there could be no talk of a son or of sons of God without a far-reaching demythologization of that title. It may be easier to understand the title today if we first briefly trace the history of this new interpretation.

Although the Old Testament uses the title of Son for the people of Israel (cf., among other texts, Exod 4.22-3; Hos 11.1), for the king as representative of the people (cf., among other texts, Ps 2.7; 2 Sam 7.14) or – as in late Judaism – for any devout and righteous Israelite (cf., among other texts, Ecclus 4.10), this usage is not based either on the background of mythological-polytheistic thinking or on the pantheistic background of Stoic philosophy, according to which all men in virtue of their common nature have the one God as Father and are therefore called sons of God. The title Son or Son of God in the Old Testament must be understood against the background of election-faith and the theocratic ideas based on it. Consequently divine sonship is not founded on physical descent, but is the result of God's free, gracious choice. The person so chosen as Son of God receives a special mission within salvation history, binding him to obedience and service. The title of Son of God therefore is understood, not as natural-substantial, but functionally and personally.

The New Testament must be understood first of all in the light of the tradition of the Old Testament. Nevertheless it produces once more an important new interpretation of the title 'Son' or 'Son of God'. As we have shown, Jesus himself never explicitly adopted either the title of Messiah or that of Son of God. He did however claim to speak and act in place of God and to be in a unique and untransferable communion with "his Father." This claim represents something unique in the history of religion which could not be adequately expressed by either the Jewish-theocratic or the hellenistic-essential understanding of Son of God. When therefore the community after Easter answered Jesus' pre-Easter claim and its confirmation by the Resurrection with the confession of Jesus as Son of God, it did not produce a sort of subsequent apotheosis or award him a dignity going beyond his own claim. On the contrary, these titles as understood at the time still fell short of Jesus' claim. The early Church therefore had to find once again a fresh interpretation of these titles. This it did, not in an abstract, speculative way, but in an historical, concrete way. The early Church did not interpret Jesus' person and fate solely with the aid of the title of 'Son' or 'Son of God'; it interpreted afresh the meaning of those predicates also on the basis of Jesus' life, death and Resurrection. The concrete history and fate of Jesus thus became the explanation of the nature and action of God. Jesus' history and fate were understood as the history of the event of God himself. John described this state of affairs in Jesus' words: 'He who has seen me has seen the Father' (Jn 14.9). In this sense it is possible to speak of a Christology 'from below' in the New Testament.

The concrete, historical interpretation of the Son of God predicate means that Jesus' divine sonship is understood, not as supra-historical essence, but as reality which becomes effective in and through the history and fate of Jesus.[2] It is this way of thinking which explains why in the oldest strata of the New Testament there is no mention of the fact that Jesus is Son of God from the very beginning, but that he is 'designated Son of God in power by his resurrection from the dead' (Rom 1.4). In the synoptic gospels we already reach a further stage of Christological reflection: at his baptism in the Jordan Jesus is accepted (Mk 1.11) or proclaimed (Mt 3.17) as Son of God.

164

Accordingly, Mark can put at the head of his entire gospel the title: 'The Gospel of Jesus Christ, the Son of God' (1.1). For Mark the marvellous works of Jesus in particular are the 'secret epiphany' of his divine sonship. At a third stage of development Luke sees Jesus' divine sonship as substantiated by his miraculous begetting through the power of the Holy Spirit (1.35).

This gradual pushing back of the Son of God predicate even then was very diversely interpreted. Some early Judaeo-Christian communities, known as Ebionites, spoke of Jesus being adopted as Son of God in the first place in virtue of his moral endurance. But this implies a failure to see that Jesus' Resurrection and Exaltation do in fact confirm his pre-Easter claim. It is impossible therefore to say that Jesus became Son of God only through the Resurrection. Nor do the baptism pericopes say anything about such a coming to be, since they are more interested in Jesus' function and position as Son than in his being Son of God by nature. Second century Adoptionism therefore anachronistically imposed on the early tradition later formulations of the problems and alternatives which simply did not exist there.[3]

Despite these fundamental misunderstandings, a great deal in this approach is right. The scriptural eschatological-historical understanding of reality does not involve any supra-historical concept of essence; being is here understood, not as an essence, but as actuality, that is, as being active. The statement, 'being is coming to to be', is of course not the same as asserting that being consists in becoming. It is in history that what a 'thing' *is*, is proved and realized. In this sense Jesus' Resurrection is the confirmation, revelation, putting into force, realization and completion of what Jesus before Easter claimed to be and *was*. His history and his fate are the history (not the coming to be) of his being, its ripening and self-interpretation.[4] Thus it also becomes clear that the full meaning of Jesus' pre-Easter claim and manifestation, his dignity as Son of God, dawned on the disciples only at the end and after the completion of his way: that is, after Easter.

The new interpretation of the title of Son and Son of God emerging in stages in the New Testament is usually described as a transition from a more or less functional to a mainly essential and metaphysical Christology. This is true, at least to the extent that the older strata of the New Testament do not yet show any interest in ontological statements in the later sense. In the older two-stage Christology it is a question of the appointment of Jesus as Son of God 'in power' (Rom 1.4). Here we have a theocratic-functional understanding. The statement, 'Thou art my beloved Son', at Jesus' baptism (Mk 1.11) also belongs to this messianic-theocratic tradition: it is in fact a quotation made up from Ps 2.7 and Is 42.1. But the Transfiguration pericope already speaks of a transformation of the figure of Jesus *(metamorphothe)* (Mk 1.2), which implies an ontological understanding of the Son of God title. With the conception by the Holy Spirit it is wholly and entirely a question, not only of a function, but of the being of Jesus; nevertheless there is a mention of the throne of David and of ruling over the house of Jacob (Lk 1.32f.). Christology of being ('ontic' or 'ontological Christology') and Christology of mission exist side by side. Even though their unity was not an object of reflection in the earlier tradition, they cannot be played off against each other.

The intrinsic unity of ontological and mission theology becomes thematic, particularly in the fourth gospel. There is no doubt that this gospel speaks of a divine sonship of Jesus as ontologically understood. The unity of Father and Son is clearly stated (10.30); it is realized as a unity of both mutual knowledge (10.15) and common operation (5.17, 19, 20). But the messianic understanding of the Son of God title is also to be found here (1.34; 10.36; 11.27). The ontological statements are not understood in themselves and for their own sake, but are intended to bring out the soteriological interest. Jesus shares in the life of God in order to transmit this life to us (5.25f.). The ontological statements therefore provide an intrinsic substantiation of the soteriological statements. Conversely, Jesus' obedience in carrying out his mission is the form of existence of his ontological divine sonship. Not only is the unity between Father and Son mentioned, but the subordination of the Son to the Father: 'The Father is greater than I' (14.28). Thus the Son submits himself completely in obedience to the will of the Father (8.29; 14.31). This obedience is the very nature of the Son: 'My food is to do the will of him who sent me' (4.34).

Hence, even in John's gospel the unity of nature between Father and Son is not yet really conceived as metaphysical, but is understood as a unity of willing and knowing. The Son is the person who submits himself unreservedly in obedience to God. Thus he is wholly and entirely transparent for God; his obedience is the form in which God is substantially present. Obedience effected and brought about by God himself is the historical mode of existence and manifestation of the divine Sonship. In his obedience Jesus is the setting forth of God's nature.

What is known as functional Christology is essentially a Christology in its realization. It not only gives expression to an external function of Jesus, but sees his function (that is his all-consuming service and his obedience in regard to his mission) as the expression and realization of his being, or of God's being in him and with him. This functional Christology is itself a form of ontic Christology. 'Being' however is understood here not as mere existence but as reality, not as substance but as personal relation. Jesus' being is realized as proceeding from the Father to men. Thus it is precisely functional Christology which gives expression to God's nature as self-giving love.

The concrete, historical interpretation of Jesus' divine Sonship appears most clearly in Paul's theology of the cross. The cross together with the Resurrection is symbol and ideograph of God's action; it is God's eschatological-definitive self-utterance. It is also in the light of the cross that the Son of God predicate acquires its decisive interpretation. Christology 'from below' is therefore possible only as a theology of the cross.

This thesis can be proved exegetically in a variety of ways.[5] For the first Christians, coming to terms with the crucifixion really amounted to a matter

166

of life and death. At a very early stage therefore they tried to proclaim the scandalous cross as God's will and God's deed, as the embodiment of God's power and wisdom (1 Cor 1.24). At first they did so by way of Scriptural proof. The confession in 1 Cor 15.3-5 already says that Christ was crucified 'in accordance with the scriptures' (cf Mk 14.21,49). This is not a reference simply to an isolated saying in the Old Testament. For the saying in Mk 9.12f. and Lk 24.26f. that the Messiah must suffer greatly is nowhere recorded. What is meant here is Scripture as a whole. Essentially it is a question of a postulate of the Easter faith. Only later do we find explicit references to Is 53. Above all, the passion history is now recorded in the language of the Psalter (especially Ps 22) and an attempt is made to draw out an explicit scriptural proof (Mk 8.31; 9.12; 14.21). What has to be said is that the cross is not an absurdity, but God's decree and will. The cross is the recapitulation of God's speech and action in the Old Testament.

If the cross is God's will, then it is not an historical accident or chance but a necessity willed by God. The New Testament texts therefore speak of a 'must' *dei*, according to which everything happens (cf Mk 8.31). Obviously it is not a question either of an historical or of a natural necessity, but of a necessity fixed by God which is beyond rational explanation. This 'must' is derived from an apocalyptic manner of speaking. The cross therefore is at the heart of God's plans and at the centre of world history. It has been set up from the very beginning. John's Revelation speaks of the lamb slaughtered from the beginning of the world (Rev 13.8; cf 1 Pet 1.20). On the cross it is finally revealed who God is and what the world is. It is the revelation of the eternal mystery of God.

There is another New Testament tradition which represents the same interest with the aid of formularies relating to Christ's self-offering.[6] Its great antiquity is evident from the fact that it is found already in the Last Supper tradition: 'This is my body which is given for you' (1 Cor 11.24; Lk 22.19). In the older New Testament tradition it is God himself who authorizes this self-offering. It is he who gives up the Son of man into the hands of men (Mk 9.31 par; Mk 10.33 par; 14.21 par; Lk 24.7). Similar expressions are found in the Pauline writings. Romans 4.25 (itself a pre-Pauline text) sounds almost like a profession of faith: 'who was put to death for our trespasses and raised for our justification'. The passive here is a periphrasis for the name of God. It is the same with Romans 8.32; 'but he gave him up for us all'. The death of Jesus therefore is only superficially man's work; at the deepest level it is God's eschatological saving deed. For it is a question of the self-offering not of just any man, but of the Son of man (Mk 9.31). It is therefore an eschatological event. In it God acted decisively and definitively.

Both the 'scripture proofs' and the self-offering formularies are meant essentially to bring out only one thing: although superficially men are the agents and the guilty ones at the crucifixion, although it is possible to see even the demons at work there (cf 1 Cor 2.8), in the last resort the cross is God's work. This of course is a supremely paradoxical, even apparently almost absurd statement, and it contradicts all our familiar ideas of God. It is generally supposed that God reveals himself in power, strength and glory. But here he is seen as the very opposite of what is regarded as great, noble, fine and reputable: in utter powerlessness, shame, unsightliness and futility. The cross then can be interpreted only as the self-emptying *(kenosis)* of God.

According to the Christ-hymn in Philippians he who was in the form of God empties himself and assumes the form of a servant; he who is free becomes voluntarily obedient (Phil 2.6-8). God evidently exercises such supreme power and freedom that he can as it were renounce everything without 'losing face'. So it is precisely in powerlessness that God's power is effective, in servitude his mastery, in death life. What the world considers strong and wise is reduced to absurdity. What is otherwise folly, weakness and scandal is here the embodiment of God's power and wisdom. This logic of the cross does not involve a static paradoxicality: contradictories are not simply asserted simultaneously. What we find are dynamic 'breakthrough formulations'[7]: 'though rich, for your sake he become poor, so that by his poverty you might become rich' (2 Cor 8.9; cf Gal 4.5; 2.19; 3.13f; 2 Cor 5.21; Rom 7.4; 8.3f). It is a question therefore, not merely of a new interpretation of God in the light of his action in Jesus Christ, but at the same time of a change in our reality. By taking on our misery, God breaks through the network of fate and makes us free. The revaluation, the crisis and the revolution of the image of God lead to the crisis, change and the redemption of the world.

If Scripture itself did not give clear hints of the direction our thought should take, it would presumably be impossible for theology to attempt from its own resources to grasp conceptually this revolutionary new way of looking at God and his action. For Scripture, the paradox of the cross is the revelation of the love of God surpassing all understanding: 'God so loved the world that he gave his only Son' (Jn 3.16; cf Gal 1.4; 2.20; 2 Cor 5.14f). The cross then is the radicalizing of the message of the kingdom; the message of the world-transforming love of God for the poor and outcast. It is love which endures and reconciles the paradoxicality without minimizing it, for it is the peculiarity of love to establish unity in the midst of diversity. Love means unity and fellowship with the other person, who is affirmed in his otherness, and thus unity and reconciliation in persistent duality.

The Christian interpretation of the understanding of God in the light of Jesus' cross and Resurrection leads to a crisis, even a revolution, in the way of seeing God. God reveals his power in powerlessness; his all-power is also suffering; his time-transcending eternity is not rigid unchangeability, but movement, life, love, imparting itself to what differs from it. God's transcendence therefore is also his immanence; God's being God, his freedom in love. We encounter God, not in abstraction from all that is concrete and particular, but quite concretely in the history and fate of Jesus of Nazareth. Scripture has itself drawn the conclusion from all this and designates Jesus Christ, not only as Son of God, but as God.

Only in comparatively few and late passages of the New Testament is Jesus explicitly described as God. In the main Pauline letters the predication of divinity of Jesus Christ is found in not more than two passages and there is considerable disagreement about their interpretation (Rom 9.5; 2 Cor 1.2). It is certainly impossible to build an entire Christology on these texts. Christology must therefore take its starting point in the source and at the centre of the New Testament faith in Christ, in the Easter confession of Jesus as *Kyrios*. This title was used already in the Septuagint as the Greek translation of the Old Testament name of God, *Adonai*. The application of the *Kyrios* title to the risen Christ goes back to the ancient liturgical invocation, 'Maranatha' (1 Cor 16.22; Rev 22.20; *Didache* 10.6). In the pre-Pauline Christ-humn in Philippians the *Kyrios* title occurs likewise within a doxology: the whole cosmos prostrates itself before the risen Christ and by this prostration confesses his divine dignity: 'Jesus Christ is *Kyrios*' (2.11). The *Kyrios* predicate is found mostly in connexion with invocations; in 1 Corinthians 1.2, Christians are more or less defined as those who invoke the name of the Lord Jesus Christ. In John's gospel too both the *Kyrios* and the God predicate are part of a confession and expression of worship: 'My Lord and my God' (20.28). Later the Roman governor, Pliny, reports to his emperor, Trajan, that the Christians sing their hymns *Christo quasi Deo.*[8]

The confession of Jesus as God is rooted therefore, not in abstract speculations, but in faith in the exaltation of the risen Christ. The 'living situation' of this confession is the liturgical doxology. It declares that God has definitively and unreservedly expressed and communicated himself in the history of Jesus.

Against this background in the school of Paul and in the Johannine writings an explicit confession of Christ as God is reached. Colossians 2.9 explicitly states: 'In Christ the whole fulness of deity dwells bodily.' The statement of Titus 2.13 can be translated in two ways. Either 'awaiting the appearing of the glory of our great God and of our Saviour Jesus Christ' or 'awaiting the appearing of the glory of our great God and Saviour Jesus Christ.' Since 'God-Saviour' is a stock formula, the second translation could well be the more probable. If this is so, then Jesus here receives the title of the 'great God' (cf. 2 Pet 1.1, 11; 2.20; 3.2, 18). The letter to the Hebrews says that Christ 'reflects the glory of God and bears the very stamp of his nature' (1.3). The verses of the Psalms, 45. 6-7 and 102. 25-27, in which God is addressed are linked with this and applied to Christ: 'Thy throne, O God, is for ever and ever. . . therefore God, thy God, has anointed thee with the oil of gladness beyond thy comrades,' and 'Thou, Lord didst found the earth in the beginning, and the heavens are the work of thy hands . . . thou art the same, and thy years will never end' (1.8ff).

The clearest statements, which are also of the greatest weight for later developments, are found in the Johannine writings. The prologue of the fourth gospel[9] itself makes three basic statements. Verse 1a begins: 'In the beginning was the *Logos*'. Who this *Logos* is, is not stated; but there can be no doubt that for John the *Logos* is the one of whom it is said in verse 14 that he became flesh. It is said then of the historical person of Jesus Christ that he existed already at the beginning. This formula 'in the beginning' recalls Genesis 1.1: 'In the beginning God created . . .' As distinct from Genesis however there is nothing in John about God creating the *Logos* in the beginning, as if the latter were the first and noblest of God's creatures. The *Logos* is already at the beginning: that is, he exists absolutely, timelessly-eternally. The timeless present is used in 8.58 to say the same thing: 'Before Abraham was, I am.' There can be no doubt therefore that in John's gospel the pre-existence statement is meant to be an ontic statement.

The statement in verse 1b continues the process of concretization: 'The *Logos* was with God.' This 'being with God' is described in 17.5 as fellowship in glory, 17.24 as unity in love, 5.26 as being filled with the life of God, so that according to 17.10 Father and Son have everything in common and 10.30 can state forthrightly: 'I and the Father are one'. This unity however is a 'being with God', that is, a unity in duality, a personal communion. This is vividly expressed in 1.18 which speaks of the Logos as the one 'who is in the bosom of the Father' and therefore can make him known. It is through this pre-existent 'being with God' therefore that the authority and dignity of the incarnate Logos are to be justified. Since he participates in the glory, love and life of the Father, he can impart glory, love and life to us. For that reason the Logos is the life and light of men (1.4). Since in him the origin of all being becomes manifest, so too the origin and goal of our existence become manifest. Here too the ontic statement serves as a salvation statement and may not be regarded as an independent speculation for its own sake.

The climax comes in the statement in verse 1c: 'and the *Logos* was God.' 'God', without article, is predicate here and not subject. It is therefore not identical with *ho theos* mentioned earlier. Nevertheless it has to be said that the *Logos* has the character of divinity. Despite the distinction between God and *Logos,* both are united by the one divine nature. At this point it becomes clear that *theos* is not merely the designation of a function, but an ontological statement, even though this ontological statement is orientated to a salvation statement. The functional statement therefore is the object of the ontological statement. The function however is founded also in the nature; the ontological statement therefore is not merely a encodement of the functional statement. The ontological statement without the salvation statement would be an abstract speculation; the salvation statement without the ontological statement would be without force and groundless. Jesus Christ then in his nature and being is the *Logos* of God in person, in whom the question about life, light and truth is definitively answered.

The gospel reaches its climax in a disputation which obviously reflects Jewish-Christian controversies in the Johannine community. The Jews ask about the messiahship of Jesus (10.24); Jesus goes beyond this question by declaring: 'I and the Father are one' (30). Thereupon they accuse him: 'You, being a man, make yourself God' (33), and they want to stone him for blasphemy. John has Jesus justify the possibility of divine sonship by quoting Psalm 82.6: 'I said, you are gods' (34). Jesus continues: 'If he called them Gods to whom the word of God came (and scripture cannot be broken), do you say of him whom the Father consecrated and sent into the world, "You are blaspheming," because I said, 'I am the Son of God'? (35f). The Jews refuse to believe and demand the death sentence from Pilate: 'By the law he ought to die, because he has made himself the Son of God' (19.7). John on the other hand closes his gospel with Thomas's confession: 'My Lord and my God' (20.28) and says that the whole purpose of his gospel is to lead men to believe 'that Jesus is the Christ, the Son of God' (20.31). Similarly the first letter of John ends with the statement: 'He is the true God and eternal life' (5.20).

The biblical statements about Jesus as true God then are clear and unambiguous. But how can this confession be reconciled with biblical monotheism? The New Testament is aware of this problem even if it does not raise any speculative considerations about it. But it prepares the way for them by maintaining simultaneously alongside the divinity of Jesus, alongside his unity with God, his distinction from the Father. If Jesus' obedience is the concrete realization of his being God, then it is *a priori* impossible ever to blur the distinction between him and the Father. Jesus therefore retorts to a man who kneels before him: 'No one is good but God alone' (Mk 10.18). Likewise the New Testament always uses the designation *ho theos* consistently only of the Father, never of the Son or the Spirit; the Son is always described without article only as *theos*[10]. He is only image (Rom 8.29; 2 Cor 4.4; Col 1.15) and revelation (1 Jn 1.1f), manifestation (epiphany) (1 Tim 3.16; 2 Tim 1.9f; Tit 3.4) of the Father.

The New Testament usually describes the relationship of Father, Son and Spirit in terms of a hierarchic-functional scheme[11]: 'All are yours; and you are Christ's; and Christ is God's' (1 Cor 3.22f); 'but I want you to understand that the head of every man is Christ, the head of a woman is her husband, and the head of Christ is God' (1 Cor 11.3); it is Christ's task to submit everything to God and at the end to hand over the Kingdom to him (1 Cor 15.28). Even in the fourth gospel we read: 'The Father is greater than I' (14.28). Correspondingly, the New Testament and primitive Christian doxology are addressed, not to 'Father, Son and Holy Spirit', but to the Father through the Son in the Holy Spirit. Our way in the Holy Spirit through Christ to the Father corresponds therefore to the movement from the Father through Christ in the Holy Spirit to us.

The New Testament however does not stop at these triadic formulas orientated to salvation history. Even at a comparatively early stage, it can show the operation of the Father, Christ and the Spirit as completely parallel, alongside one another (cf 1 Cor 12.4-6). This approach seems to have been expressed concisely in liturgical formularies at a comparatively early date: 'The grace of the Lord Jesus Christ and the love of God and the fellowship of the Holy Spirit be with you all' (2 Cor 13.14; cf 1 Pet 1.1f). Towards the very

171

end of the New Testament development, what is known as the baptismal precept of Matthew's gospel sums up the theological and practical development of the early Church in Trinitarian form: 'Go therefore and make disciples of all nations, baptizing them in the name of the Father and of the Son and of the Holy Spirit' (28.19). We apparently find the Trinitarian scheme wherever there is an attempt to interpret systematically the abundance and wealth of Christian experience by confessing in concise form that the one God encounters us once and for all concretely in the history and fate of Jesus and is permanently present in the Holy Spirit[12].

The Trinitarian confession is not an unrealistic speculation, but is meaningful in that it recalls what happened for us once and for all in Jesus Christ, considers its ground and nature, and expresses the consequences for the understanding of God. The Trinitarian confession therefore is 'the' brief formula of the Christian faith and the essential statement of the Christian understanding of God. It determines the meaning of the term 'God' through the history of revelation and bases this history on God's nature. In this sense we must say with Karl Rahner that the inner divine (immanent) trinity is the trinity of the history of salvation and vice-versa.[13]. In substance the trinitarian confession means that God in Jesus Christ has proved himself to be self-communicating love and that as such he is permanently present among us in the Holy Spirit.

2. SON OF GOD FROM ETERNITY

If God has wholly and definitively communicated himself through Jesus Christ in the Holy Spirit and thus defined himself as the 'Father of our Lord Jesus Christ', then Jesus belongs to the eternal nature of God. The confession of the eschatological character of the Christ-event by its very nature was bound therefore to lead to the question of the protological nature and of the pre-existence of Jesus.[14] Contrary however to a view sometimes maintained, 'these pre-existence statements are not merely the ultimate conclusion of a gradual process of extending backwards the divine sonship of Jesus from the Resurrection by way of his baptism and conception to his pre-existence. If they were understood in that way, they would merely lengthen time and history backwards and stretch them to infinity. Such a highly dubious conception of eternity is not really to be found in the New Testament. That is clear from the simple fact that the statements about Christ's descent do not occur only at the end of the New Testament tradition process as the product of such a backward projection, but at a comparatively early stage; in practice at the same time as the formation of the Christology of exaltation. As will be shown, it is not a question of extending time into eternity, but of founding salvation history in God's eternity.

The pre-Pauline Christ-hymn of Philippians 2.6-11-15 already speaks of Jesus Christ who was in the form of existence *(morphe)* of God, took on the form of existence *(morphe)* of a servant, and whom God *therefore (dio)* raised up as *Kyrios* over all powers. Ernst Käsemann has brought out afresh the meaning of the term *morphe*; it describes 'the sphere in which someone exists and which determines him like a force-field'. Yet even if this amounts to an ontological statement, there is no interest in speculation as such on the pre-existent state of things. It is a question of a happening, of a drama; 'Christology comes into view here within the framework of soteriology.' For it is man's nature to be in bondage under cosmic powers, Since Christ comes – so to speak – from outside or from above and is therefore subject to these powers out of free obedience, he dissolves the fatal connexion and as the new cosmocrator takes the place of *Ananke* or 'necessity'. Redemption is here understood as liberation, as liberation which however is founded in the obedience of Jesus and is gained in obedience to him. The pre-existence theme does not arise from a speculative interest, but serves as a basis for the soteriological concern.

How 'obvious' descendence-Christology must have been even at a very early stage, is clear also from the fact that Paul already uses formularies to express the idea. Such mission formularies, probably already available,[16] are found in Gal 4.4: 'When the time had fully come, God sent forth his Son' and Rom 8.3: 'God sent his own Son in the likeness of flesh.' Again pre-existence is not explicitly mentioned as such, but presupposed in the interest of a soteriological statement. At the same time it is not a question of the Incarnation as such, as in the later tradition, but of coming under the law and into the flesh which is in the power of sin, in order to liberate us from this power and impart the Spirit of sonship: the Spirit who justifies us in saying to God 'Abba! Father' (Gal 4.6; Rom 8.15). In John's gospel these themes are extensively developed. Here Jesus says repeatedly of himself that he was sent by the Father (5.23, 37; 6.38f, 44; 7.28f, 33 etc.), that he came from heaven (3.13; 6.38; 51) or 'from above' (8.23), and that he came from the Father (8.42; 16.27f). We have already spoken of the pre-existence statements in the prologue of John's gospel. What is the object of these statements, which we find so unfamiliar?

The pre-existence and mission theme is meant to express the fact that Jesus' person and fate do not have their source within the context of events in this world, but that God himself acts in a way that is beyond any mundane explanation. This freedom, inexplicable in terms of the present world, breaks through the interconnections of fate and liberates us for the freedom of the sons of God. The statements about the pre-existence of the one Son of God provide the reasons for our sonship and our salvation.

As soon as we try to find a more precise interpretation of the pre-existence statements in the New Testament we are faced by a variety of problems. First of all there is the problem arising from the study of comparative religion. The question is whether the New Testament, when it speaks of the pre-existence and descent of the Son of God, has adopted extrabiblical mythological ideas which today can and must be demythologized. Certainly the ideas of pre-existence and Incarnation have not dropped out of heaven.

The New Testament picks up patterns already existing in these ideas. Thus, since the school of comparative religion — especially R. Reitzenstein — tried to reconstruct a Primal Man-Saviour myth from the Gnostic sources known at the time, the question has arisen as to whether the statements about Jesus' divine Sonship in particular, which until then had been regarded as specifically Christian, are an expression of the universal religious syncretism of the time. The Primal Man-Saviour myth speaks of the descent or fall of primal man into matter; in order to redeem him a Saviour figure descends, reminds men of their heavenly origin, thus bringing them the true Gnosis through which they are redeemed, since they can now follow the Saviour on his way upwards.

Rudolf Bultmann and his school have tried to make the conclusions of the study of comparative religion fruitful for the interpretation of the New Testament. They thought they could prove a dependence of the New Testament pre-existence and Incarnation statements on these Gnostic ideas. The programme of demythologizing the New Testament pre-existence statements seemed thus to be authorized by the study of comparative religion.

Meanwhile, however, particularly as a result of the studies of C. Colpe, [17] we have learned to judge the source material with much more discrimination. The Gnostic Saviour myth cannot be presupposed as a coherent factor: it developed only under Christian influence. Moreover Gnosticism was not interested in the Incarnation of the Saviour, but in man's becoming redeemer and being redeemed through the knowledge of the origin of his being. The Saviour myth is so to speak a mere illustrative model, a means of ascertaining the true nature of man. Gnosticism therefore is concerned with the interpretation of the *universal* fate of man, alienated in his nature and in need of redemption. For the New Testament on the other hand it is a question of the interpretation of the unique and *particular* fate of Jesus Christ. For the New Testament Christ is not the prototype of man in need of salvation, either in the Gnostic sense of *salvator salvatus* or as *salvator salvandus*.

When we consider the fundamental differences between Gnosticism and Christianity, we have to say that the Gnostic ideas can at best serve as secondary means of expression of the New Testament message. Today therefore the immediate source of the New Testament pre-existence statements is again sought mainly in the field of the Old Testament Judaism. Here — as distinct from Gnosticism — we find an historical way of thinking. According to the ideas of Old Testament Judaism, people and events important for salvation history exist in an ideal or — especially according to apocalyptic ideas — real way even before the creation of the world in the plan or in the world of God. According to apocalyptic ideas, that holds particularly of the figure of the Son of man (Dan 7.13f). Rabbinic theology likewise taught a pre-existence of the Messiah (understood as an idea) and also of the Torah (= Wisdom), of the Throne of Glory and other factors. [18]

The parallels are clearest in Old Testament speculation on wisdom. [19] Wisdom personified is understood as emanation, reflection and image of God (Wisdom 7.25); she is present, giving counsel, at the creation of the world (8.4; 9.9) and can be called 'author of all things' (7.12); God sends her (9.10, 17); he has her dwelling in Israel (Ecclus 24.8ff). For this reason it is generally thought today that the ideas of the pre-existence of Jesus were conveyed to the New Testament through Judaism's speculation on wisdom.

These conclusions from the study of comparative religion do not of course offer any solution of the essential theological problem. On the contrary, they only underline its urgency. For 'the history of ideas is not a chemistry of concepts that have been arbitrarily stirred together and are then neatly separated again by the modern historian. In order for an "influence" of alien concepts to be absorbed, a situation must have previously emerged within which these concepts could be greeted as an aid for the expression of a problem already present'.[20] The 'living situation' of these ideas in the New Testament is the eschatological character of the Christ-event.

What the pre-existence statements of the New Testament really do is to express in a new and more profound way the eschatological character of the person and work of Jesus of Nazareth. Since in Jesus Christ God himself has definitively, unreservedly and unsurpassably revealed and communicated himself, Jesus is part of the definition of God's eternal nature. It follows therefore from the eschatological character of the Christ-event that Jesus is Son of God from eternity and God from eternity is the 'Father of our Lord Jesus Christ'. The history and fate of Jesus are thus rooted in the nature of God: God's nature proves to be an event. Thus the New Testament pre-existence statements lead to a new, comprehensive interpretation of the term God.

To think of God and history together is not as difficult for the Bible as it is for Western philosophy under Greek influence. In Greek metaphysics from the pre-Socratics to Plato and Aristotle and on to neo-Platonism, immutability, freedom from suffering and passion *(apatheia)* were always regarded as the supreme attributes of the divine.[21] The God of the Old Testament on the other hand is known as God of the way and of guidance, as God of history. When Yahweh therefore reveals himself in Exodus 3.14 as 'he who is', this is not to be understood in the sense of the philosophical conception of being, as a reference to God's aseity, but as an effective assurance and promise that God is the one who 'is there' effectively in the changing situations of the history of his people. The fact that Yahweh is a God of history of course does not mean, even for the Old Testament, that he is a God who comes to be. On the contrary, the Old Testament is clearly distinguished from myth by the fact that it contains no sort of theogony or divine genealogy. God in the Old Testament has no beginning and as a living God he is not subject to death. God's eternity is something taken for granted in the Old Testament: it does not mean however immobility, unchangeability and timelessness; it means mastery over time, proving its identity, not in unrelated, abstract self-identity, but in actual, historical fidelity.[22] God's becoming man and thus becoming history in Jesus Christ is the surpassing fulfilment of this historical fidelity to his promise that he *is* the one who is present and the one existing with us.

When early Christianity moved out of the Jewish sphere and came into contact with the (popular) philosophical thinking of the hellenistic world, there was bound to be conflict.[23] The prelude to this conflict came in the controversies of the second to the third century with what was known as Monarchianism (one source [*arche*] doctrine), a collective term for all endeavours in the second to the third century to link the divinity of Christ with Jewish or philosophical monotheism. Monarchianism tried to see Jesus Christ either as endowed with an impersonal divine power *(dynamis)* (the dynamic Monarchianism of Theodotus of Byzantium and Paul of Samosata) or as a special mode of appearance *(modus)* of the Father (modalistic Monarchianism of Noetus, Praxeas and Sabellius). Tertullian gave the latter system the nickname of Patripassianism, because its teaching in effect makes the Father suffer under the mask *(prosopon)* of the Son. The great controversy however started only in the fourth century in the dispute with Arius (born about 260 in Libya), an Alexandrian priest and a disciple of Lucian of Antioch (a latter-day Origen).

Arius' teaching must be understood against the background of middle Platonism. That was characterized by a markedly negative theology: God is ineffable, unbegotten, did not come to be, is without origin, unchangeable. For Arius therefore the basic problem was the adjustment of this unoriginated and indivisible being to the world of coming-to-be and multiplicity. To solve this problem he made use of the *Logos,* a *deuteros theos,* the first and noblest creature and at the same time the mediator of creation. Consequently, he is created in time out of nothing, changeable and fallible: he was assumed as Son of God purely because of his moral probation. With Arius it is evident that the God of the philosophers has supplanted the living God of history. The soteriologically defined Logos doctrine of Scripture has been turned into cosmological speculation and moral theory. His theology represents a crucial hellenization of Christianity.

Athanasius, the deacon and later Bishop of Alexandria, in particular, took up the debate with Arius. He was the intellectual driving force at the first general council of Nicaea. It is significant that the Fathers of Nicaea did not get involved in the speculations of Arius, but wanted solely to protect the teaching of Scripture and tradition. For this reason they fell back on the creed of the Church of Caesarea (DS 40), which consisted essentially in biblical formularies, and – prompted by Arius' heresy – added interpretative phrases.

The crucial statement of the Nicene Creed runs: 'We believe . . . in one Lord Jesus Christ, the Son of God, born as only-begotten of the Father, that is, from the being of the Father, God from God, light from light, true God from true God, begotten and not made, one in being *(homoousios)* with the Father, through whom all things came to be, those in heaven and those on earth, who for us men and for our salvation came down, became flesh and became man . . .' (DS 125).

Two things are notable about this formulary: (1) It is not an expression of abstract theory, but a liturgical profession of faith ('we believe'). This profession is orientated to salvation history and has its origin in biblical and ecclesiastical tradition. The new dogma therefore is to be understood as an aid to faith and as interpretation of tradition. The Church bases its faith, not on private speculation, but on the common and public tradition: this tradition however it understands, not as a dead letter, but as living tradition which it unfolds in the process of coping with new questions. (2) The 'new' ontological statements are meant, not to make void the salvation statements, but to help to safeguard them. The real object of the ontological statements interpreting tradition on the true divinity of Jesus is to say that the Son belongs not to the side of creatures, but on the side of God; consequently he is not created but begotten and of the same being *(homoousios)* as the Father. This term *homoousios,* drawn from the emanation theory of Valentinian Gnosticism, was therefore not intended at Nicaea in the philosophic-technical sense: the Greek concept of essence was not to be superimposed on the biblical idea of God. The term was meant solely to make clear that the Son is by nature divine and is on the same plane of being as the Father, so that anyone who encounters him, encounters the Father himself.

What lay behind this was not primarily a speculative interest, but first and foremost a soteriological concern which Athanasius continually inculcated: if Christ is not true God, then we are not redeemed, for only the immortal God can redeem us in our subjection to death and give us a share in his fulness of life. The doctrine of the true divinity of Jesus Christ must therefore be understood within the scope of the early Church's soteriology as a whole and its idea of redemption as deification of man. Man, created in the image of God, can attain his true and proper being only by participation (*methexis*) in the life of God: that is, through becoming like God (*homoiosis theou*). But since the image of God is corrupted by sin, God must become man so that we may be deified and again reach a knowledge of the invisible God. This physical (= ontic) theory of salvation has nothing to do with a physic-biological, still less a magical conception of salvation, as is frequently maintained. What is in fact behind it is the ancient Greek idea of *paideia:* the formation and education of man through imitation and participation in the figure of the divine archetype, seen in the image.[24]

Like every later council, Nicaea was not merely the end, but also a new beginning of the debate. The period after Nicaea is one of the darkest and most confused in the history of the Church. The essential reason for the new controversies lay in the vagueness of the term *homoousios* in the Nicene profession of faith. Many thought that the distinction between Father and Son had not been safeguarded and therefore sensed in this term a concealed Modalism. They would have been satisfied with the change of a single letter and the use of the term *homoousios* instead of *homoiousios*. But this term again was suspect as implying a mitigated Arianism (Semi-Arianism). The great Cappadocians (Basil, Gregory of Nazianzen, Gregory of Nyssa) were the first to suggest a way out of this dilemma with the aid of the distinction between the one nature (*ousia*) and the three hypostases (*hypostasis*). The distinction did not occur in this form in the philosophy of the time. It represents a genuine achievement of theology in coping intellectually with the data of the Christian faith. At that time of course 'hypostasis' was not yet understood as person, but referred to individuality, the concrete realization of the universal nature.[25] However unsatisfactory this definition may be for us today, it means nothing less than that the universal nature was no longer regarded as the supreme reality and that Greek ontological thinking was giving way to thinking in terms of persons. In any case, the way was now free for the next council to count as ecumenical, the first council of Constantinople (381).

This second general council did not produce any new Christological dogma. What it did was to confirm the Creed of Nicaea and thus to re-acknowledge the principle of tradition. But it stood clearly for a living tradition, as is evident from the fact that it did not hesitate to alter the Creed at the point at which it had proved to be misleading and – in the light of the progress of theology in the meantime – inadequate. The Nicene formula, 'born from the being of the Father', was dropped (DS 150). Instead of this, the Christology of Nicaea was supplemented in a positive sense with a corresponding pneumatology against heresies which questioned the true divinity of the Holy Spirit (*Pneumatomachi*) and was thus also brought up to the latest stage of the Church's awareness of faith and to the current state of theology.

The Nicene-Constantinopolitan Creed is still today the official liturgical profession of faith of the Church; and until the present day it is also the binding force uniting all great Churches of East and West. The question of bringing the Church up-to-date in living continuity with its tradition, and that of the unity of the divided Churches, are settled quite substantially by this Creed, which is ecumenical in the proper sense of the term. The discussion about all this has been carried on under the headings of hellenizing or dehellenizing Christianity. For the Liberal Protestant historiography of dogma, especially as represented by Adolf von Harnack, dogma was 'in its conception and development a work of the Greek spirit on the soil of the Gospel'. Gospel and dogma are not related to each other simply as a given theme and its necessary exposition: between these two a new factor has appeared, the cosmic wisdom of Greek philosophy.[26] Harnack therefore wanted to return behind the development of Christological doctrine to the simple and straightforward faith of Jesus in the Father. In the meantime, the headings 'hellenizing' and 'de-hellenizing' have also found their way into Catholic theology, frequently as slogans.[27]

The above shows that we must be much more discriminating in our judgment of Harnack. In principle, in virtue of its eschatologic-universal claim, Christianity simply could not avoid entering into discussion with the Greek philosophy of *logos* and being, which also asserted a universal claim: it was a question, not of a self-surrender, but of a self-assertion on the part of Christianity.[28] Essentially it was a question of the *aggiornamento* of the day, of the hermeneutically necessary attempt to express the Christian message in the language of the time and in the light of the way in which the questions were then raised. Seeberg therefore rightly observed: 'It is not "hellenizing", Romanizing or Germanizing as such which corrupt Christianity. These forms in themselves merely show that the Christian religion had been independently thought out and appropriated in the epochs in question and that it had become an element in the intellectual formation and culture of the peoples. The danger of this process however consists in the fact that the peoples or the age concerned, in order to make Christianity intelligible, might not merely formally translate it but weaken it and reduce it materially to another plane of religion. The history of dogma must note the former as a fact which is inseparable from a powerful historical development; the latter, on the other hand, it must critically scrutinize.'[29]

If however we consider the Creed of Nicea and Constantinople from this fundamental standpoint, we shall observe how surprisingly exact the early Church was in keeping to the dividing line between legitimate and illegitimate hellenizing. Arianism was an illegitimate hellenizing, which dissolved Christianity into cosmology and ethics. As against this, Nicea represented a de-hellenizing: for dogma, Christ is not a world-principle but a salvation-principle. The distinction made at Constantinople between *ousia,* and *hypostasis* in principle even meant breaking through Greek ontological thinking towards a personal way of thinking. Not nature, but person was now the final and supreme reality.

It is understandable that the theology of the early Church did not succeed in grasping at once in all its consequences the basic decision made in Nicaea and Constantinople. That would have required a complete remoulding of all the categories of ancient metaphysics. In fact the corrections of ancient thought remained for the time being more or less restricted to particular points. So it came about that, as a result of the *homoousios* of Nicaea, metaphysical ontological thinking found its way into theology and finally largely supplanted scriptural thinking in terms of eschatology and salvation-history. Christianity thus lost much of its historical dynamism and perspective on the future. Here lies the very considerable grain of truth in the thesis of the de-eschatologizing of Christianity as the precondition and consequence of its hellenizing. The immediate result was that the traditional image of God, contrary to the intention of Nicaea and Constantinople, remained deeply marked by the Greek idea of God's unchangeability, freedom from suffering and passion (*apatheia*). For God to *become* man and above all to suffer and die, thus became the great problem.

In the early tradition, especially in Ignatius of Antioch, the idea of abasement is at first simply repeated: 'The timeless, the invisible, who was made visible for our sake; impalpable, beyond suffering, who for our sake was subject to suffering.'[30] The same statement is found substantially in Irenaeus: the impalpable, incomprehensible and invisible makes himself visible, comprehensible and palpable to men in Christ; the immeasurable Father became measurable in Christ; the Son is the measure of the Father, because the latter has become comprehensible in him.[31] These paradoxes become particularly acute in Tertullian's 'On the Flesh of Christ': 'The Son of God was crucified: just because it is something shameful, I am not ashamed. And the Son of God died: it is completely credible, because it is absurd. He was also buried and rose again: it is certain because it is impossible . . . Thus the sum-total of both substances displayed man and God: the one born, the other not born; the one corporeal, the other spiritual; the one weak, the other powerful and strong; the one dying, the other living.'[32] This is the context of the famous formula: *credo quia absurdum est* ('I believe because it is absurd').

The acuteness of such paradoxical formularies cannot however obscure the fact that the Fathers have thus transformed the *Kenosis*-Christology into what had originally been the alien categories of the philosophical doctrine of God. They were faced with the question of how the infinite, invisible, immortal, could become finite, visible, mortal. As soon as this question was raised reflexively, the problem was bound to occur of how the finite could be *capable* of the infinite. Does that not mean introducing a development and a coming-to-be in God? Rejecting that, Origen at an early stage expressed the common conviction: 'Made man, he remained what he was.'[33] And Augustine says in the same sense: 'So he emptied himself: accepting the form of a servant, not losing the form of God; the form of a servant came in, the form of God did not depart.'[34]

Even theologians like Origen's disciple, Gregory Thaumaturgus, in the East or Hilary in the West, who see the limitations of these statements, cannot safeguard the depth of suffering. They argue that incapacity for suffering would imply a limitation and lack of freedom in God and therefore God must be able to suffer; but God suffers voluntarily, suffering is not imposed on him by fate; he remains therefore his own master in suffering. Suffering then is his strength, his triumph. The suffering of Christ was accompanied by a sense of joy. But the question arises as to whether this explanation safeguards the depth of suffering. This image corresponds less the the Jesus of Gethesmane than to Plato's suffering yet just man, who is happy even when he is tortured and when his eyes are gouged out.[35]

Luther's *theologia crucis* first breaks through the whole system of metaphysical theology. He tries consistently to see, not the cross in the light of a philosophical concept of God, but God in the light of the cross. That is expressed programmatically in the theses of the Heidelberg disputation of 1518: 'No one is worthy of the name of theologian who perceives the invisible things of God as understood through the things that are made, but only one who understands the visible and concealed things of God as perceived through the suffering and the cross.'[36] The hidden mystery of God is not one beyond this world, we are not interested in speculating about a God outside our world; for Luther, the hidden God is the God hidden in the suffering and the cross. We should not try to penetrate the mysteries of God's majesty, but should be content with the God on the cross. We cannot find God except in Christ; anyone who tries to find him outside Christ will find the devil.

From this starting point Luther manages a complete reconstruction of Christology. He does in fact accept the Christology of the early Church, but he gives it a new emphasis. He is not concerned with the question of the mutual compatibility of the concept of God and the concept of man. It is only in the light of Christ that we know what God and man are. Hence all statements about the majesty of the divine nature are transferred to the human: above all, the humanity of Christ shares in the ubiquity of the Godhead. But on the other hand the Godhead shares in the lowliness of the humanity, in the latter's suffering and dying.

At this point, however, unsolved problems emerge for Luther. For, if the humanity shares in God's attributes of majesty, how can the genuine humanity of Jesus be maintained? If on the other hand the Godhead enteres into suffering, how is the God-forsakenness of Jesus on the cross to be understood? Thus Luther's theology of the cross gets into difficulties with the historical picture of Jesus given to us in Scripture. Scripture faces us afresh with the task of a radically christological rethinking of God's being; but it shows us also the dilemma in which theology is thereby involved.

The survey of tradition shows that the Nicene-Constantinopolitan confession of Jesus Christ as true God is not by any means obsolete. This creed in fact presents theology with a task which has not been completed up to the present time. The idea and concept of God and his unchangeability need to be submitted to a new, basic Christological interpretation in order to make effective once more the biblical understanding of the God of history.

Piet Schoonenberg has recently made a creditable, even though unsuccessful, attempt in this direction.[37] He starts out from the principle which has guided my own reflections up to now: 'Our whole thinking moves from reality towards God and can never move in the opposite direction . . . In no respect do we conclude from the Trinity to Christ and to the Spirit given to us, but always the other way round'. For Schoonenberg this means that 'the content of the divine pre-existence of Christ can be determined only in the light of his earthly and glorified life'.[38] From this correct starting-point however, he concludes that we can neither affirm nor deny that God, considered apart from his self-communication in salvation-history, is Trinitarian. According to Schoonenberg, an inference from the revelation of the Trinity in salvation history to the inner-divine Trinity would be possible only 'if the relationship between God's unchangeability and his free self-determination were open to our understanding. Since this is not the case, the question remains unanswered and unanswerable and thus drops out of theology as meaningless'. But it seems that this abstention cannot be maintained in practice, as Schoonenberg himself shows later when he says: 'The distinction between Father, Son and Spirit, therefore, must be described as personal in terms of the economy of salvation; but as an inner-divine distinction at most as modal'.[39] Contrary to his original reserve, Schoonenberg describes the Modalist doctrine of the Trinity as true in so far as it refers to the inner-divine being in itself. This is in glaring contrast to the principles set up by himself.

If we look for the reasons for these self-contradictory theses, we find that they are essentially rooted in an *a priori* philosophical assumption. The theologian however must not start out from such a 'critique of pure reason', but from the New Testament evidence, according to which God has revealed to us his innermost nature and mystery in an eschatological-definitive way in Jesus Christ. This means that, for faith, there is no dark mystery of God 'behind' his revelation. God in fact reveals himself in Jesus Christ unreservedly and definitively as the one who he is: 'God is love' (1 Jn 4:8,16). Theologically considered, his mystery is this unfathomable and inexplicable love and not the abstract philosophical problem of how unchangeability and free self-determination are related to each other. If then God reveals himself in Jesus Christ eschatologically and definitively as love communicating itself, God's self-communication between the Father and the Son is the eternal nature of God himself. If we are to make this truth of Scripture and tradition intellectually effective, we must probe more deeply than Schoonenberg has done.

Today we must try to do something like what the early Church councils did for their time. With the aid of modern conceptual tools, we must critically examine and discuss the Gospel of Jesus Christ as Son of God. We are only at the beginning of this task. It is particularly difficult as a result of the fact that modern thought at first led to the disintegration and denial of the truth as understood in the Bible and in the early Church. It would however be wrong to assume that the history of modern thought is merely a history of the destruction of the Christology of the Bible and the early Church and not also a permanent process of critical clarification and 'sublation' (eliminating but also preserving). The modern principle of subjectivity, the process by which man becomes aware of his freedom as autonomy and makes it the starting point, measure and medium of his whole understanding of reality, is indisputably within the context of the history of Christianity; and in that history Christology and Trinitarian doctrine in particular had a substantial share in the breakthrough to perception of the absolute priority of the person and his freedom before all other values and goods, however exalted. Modern thought has taken up these Christian themes, which up to a point were still superimposed in antiquity and the Middle Ages, and — although partially in a one-sided and secular way — developed them.

As soon as God too was conceived against the background of subjectivity, he could no longer be understood as supreme, most perfect and unchangeable being. Thus, prepared both by medieval Scotism and Nominalism and by thinkers like Meister Eckhart and Nicholas of Cusa, the concept of God was desubstantialized. In this respect, two ways were conceivable, which — as W. Schulz has shown[40] — have constantly replaced each other in the course of modern times. Either God was conceived as the ultimate, transcendental condition of the possibility of freedom, which can maintain its absolute claim only in the medium of absolute freedom in a world that is relative; or he was conceived as being of all beings — that is, in the last resort, as supersubstantial — so that all reality is ultimately only a moment in the infinite. The first possibility tends to functionalize the idea of God and perhaps to raise the question whether the doctrine of the Trinity has any practical importance for man. Kant thought that it had no practical consequences. The second possibility amounts to a renewal of Modalism; the three divine persons are understood as self-interpretations of the one divine being in the world and in history. In both cases Jesus Christ can be regarded only as a symbol, cypher, image, mode of appearance, either of man or of the divine.

It was a stroke of genius on Hegel's part to have reconciled these two modern ways of thinking. For him the absolute is not substance, but subject, which exists however only by emptying itself to what is other than itself. 'The true is the whole. But the whole is only Essence completing itself through its development. It must be said of the absolute that it is essentially result, that only at the end is it what it truly is'.[41] In Hegel this historical knowledge of God is imparted wholly Christologically. It reaches its climax at the point where Hegel gives an interpretation of the cross and attempts to conceive the death of God. He quotes the Lutheran hymn, 'O great distress, God himself is dead', and describes this event as 'a monstrous, dreadful spectacle which brings before the mind the deepest chasm of severance'.[42] Yet it is precisely this severance which for Hegel makes the event of the cross the external representation of the history of absolute Spirit. For it is part of the nature of the absolute Spirit to reveal and manifest itself: that is, to be represented in the other and for others and itself to become objective. It is essential therefore to the nature of absolute Spirit to set up in itself the distinction from itself, to be identical with itself in the distinction from itself.[43]

For Hegel this is a philosophical interpretation of the biblical saying: God is love. For it is characteristic of love to find itself in the other, in emptying itself: 'Love is a distinguishing of two who, absolutely speaking, are not distinct'.[44] In this self-emptying, death is the highest point of finiteness, the supreme negation and thus the best intuition of the love of God. But in the distinction love means also reconciliation and unification. Thus the death of God means simultaneously the cancellation of emptying, the death of death, the negation of negation and the reality of reconciliation. The saying about the death of God has therefore a double meaning: it has a meaning for God; it shows God as a living God, as love. But it has a meaning also for death and for man; it shows that negation is in God himself and that the human is thus assumed into the divine idea. In God there is scope for man, his suffering and death; God is not the oppression of man, but freedom of love for man.

In this exposition Hegel has attempted to think of God wholly in the light of Jesus Christ. But has he really succeeded? Has he not turned the scandal of the cross into a speculative good Friday? He says himself that God is not a mystery for speculative reason. The cross becomes speculatively transparent, dialectically transfigured and reconciled. It is only the representation and intuition of what happens and has eternally happened in the absolute spirit in itself. It is not an underivable historical event of love, but the expression of a principle of love; not a free historical happening, but a necessary fate. Goethe's saying is relevant here: 'There the cross stands, thickly wreathed in roses. Who put the roses on the cross?'[45] But is the death of God taken seriously if it is understood as necessary? Surely that approach also misses the whole depth of human suffering? is not man, his suffering and death, then a necessary moment in the process of the absolute spirit and is not the freedom of God and man thereby cancelled?

Not without reason, post-Hegelian theology insisted on the underivability of reality (Schelling), of existence (Kierkegaard), and of the inflexibility of material conditions (Marx). In the light of the Christian tradition we shall have to say first of all that there are not only finite and infinite, nature and history, but freedom and unfreedom, God's love and man's guilt and sin, to be reconciled, Where however the problem of reconciliation affects not only God and man in the abstract, but is set within the concrete situation, reconciliation can be effected only in a completely underivable event of freedom which cannot be made speculatively intelligible.

Criticism of Hegel should not overlook the fact (and the same could be shown to be true of Fichte and Shelling) that his philosophy provides the theologian with conceptual tools which are more useful than the metaphysically characterized tradition for doing justice to the Christ-event and for thinking of God, not in abstract philosophical terms, but as the God and Father of Jesus Christ. God's being God must then be conceived as freedom in love which is aware of itself in lavishing itself. But God can prove himself to be that self-communicating love in the history of Jesus Christ only if he *is* this love in himself: if, that is, he *is* in himself the identity and difference between free appeal open to free response and free response open to free acceptance in love. The inner-divine Trinity is – so to speak – the transcendental condition of the possibility of God's self-communication in salvation history in Jesus Christ through the Holy Spirit. It is nothing other than the consistent exposition of the proposition 'God is love' (1 Jn 4.8,16).

Although it is impossible in this context to go into the doctrine of the inner-divine Trinity in detail, what the categories of idealist philosophy can achieve may perhaps be shown in connection with a question often discussed at the present time. The question raised in Protestant theology especially by Karl Barth and in Catholic theology by Karl Rahner is whether and how far the modern concept of person, differing as it does from the ancient-medieval concept of *hypostasis-subsistentia,* can be used in trinitarian doctrine: that is, whether we can speak of three divine 'persons'. Instead of that Barth wants to speak of three modes of being,[46] Rahner of three distinct modes of subsistence.[47] It is well-known that Fichte in the 'atheism conflict' claimed that the term 'person' meant being opposite to other reality, implying finiteness: hence it would not be applicable to God. Hegel took up these problems and showed that to be a person it is essential to abandon isolation and particularity, to enlarge oneself towards universality, and, by giving up abstract personality and by becoming absorbed in what is other than oneself to acquire concrete personality. The person therefore is a reconciliation of universality and particularity and thus the realization of the essence of love. For 'love is a distinguishing of two who are nevertheless not distinct for each other.' Love is 'distinction and the cancelling of distinction'.[48]

All that amounts to a paraphrase of the traditional definition of the divine persons as subsistent relations and also the best justification for describing them as persons. If on the other hand we abandon the term 'person' and speak instead of modes of being or subsistence in Trinitarian doctrine, the 'benefit' of the latter is lost. Instead of concrete freedom in love, an abstract concept of being is made ultimate and supreme, although the whole point of Trinitarian doctrine is to say that reality as a whole is profoundly personal or interpersonal in its structure.

If God *is* the Free in love, this means that his love can never be exhausted as between Father, Son and Spirit, but that in the excess of his love for the Son he always has scope for what is other than himself: scope for the world and for man. In the Son God from eternity in freedom knows the sons; in the Son from eternity he is a God of men and for men. Here lies the profound meaning of the idea of the pre-existence of the Son. Far from being a purely speculative idea, it means that God as the God of Jesus Christ is a God of men who exists as eternally devoted to man.

This idea naturally loses its force if the scholastic theory is accepted, that in principle any one of the three divine persons might have become man.[49] Any such suggestion of arbitrariness (even if subsequently 'qualified' by appropriate arguments of convenience) dissolves the intrinsic connection between immanent and economic Trinity, turning the former into an essentially useless speculation and the latter into an optional and arbitrary action of God. Barth however seems to go to the opposite extreme with his thesis that 'originally God's election of man is a predestination not merely of man but himself'.[50] At the same time we must completely agree with Barth that there is no dark mystery behind God's concrete decision for salvation and that this decision does not take the form of an abstract, rigid decree. God's mystery and decision for salvation mean that in Jesus Christ he is the God of men, but is so in fact in the freedom of his love. But this freedom in love seems to be questioned if we say that in the election of grace God determines himself and is God by that very fact. Hans Urs von Balthasar rightly sees at work in this thesis an idealist form of thought and the method of the principle posing and presupposing itself, the freedom of grace not defined as excess and overflow of love, but as founded on necessity.[51]

If God is the Free in love, there is in God not only scope for the world and man, God *in* his eternity has also time for man. God's eternity is then not rigid, abstract and absolute self-identity, it is God's identity in becoming different: God's eternity is then proved by his fidelity in history. Eternity is to be defined, not simply negatively as timelessness, but positively as mastery over time. If God therefore becomes, he becomes, not in a human, but in a divine way. It is not history which imparts identity to God, he is not a God who comes to be, who would first have to grasp and realize himself in time. On the contrary, it is God who gives history its identity, who endows it with coherence and meaning. Here again lies the deeper significance of the idea of pre-existence. It does not imply any projection of time backwards into eternity: it intimates that God in his Son from eternity and in freedom is a God of history and has time for man.

3. THE SON OF GOD AS THE FULNESS OF TIME

Jesus Christ is not only the final self-definition of God, but the final definition of the world and man. Since the eschatological fulness of time has been attained in him, the meaning of reality as a whole comes to light in him. Here lies the meaning of the statements about Christ's mediatorship of creation which for us today can be understood at first sight only with difficulty.[52]

Statements about Christ's mediatorship of creation are found already in comparatively early writings of the New Testament. In 1 Cor 8.6 we read: 'There is one Lord, through whom are all things and through whom we exist.' For Paul this is not an extravagant speculation, but the ground of Christian freedom: for the question raised in this chapter is whether a Christian could eat meat bought in the ordinary way, but – as was customary at the time – consecrated to idols. Paul justifies Christian freedom by pointing out that there is only one God, from whom everything originates, and one Lord, through whom everything is. Christ's dominion therefore is universal: it is the ground however, not of bondage, but of freedom – a freedom which must be tempered anyway by love of one's brother (8.7 ff.). This universality of the rule of Christ is also brought out in 1 Cor 10.4 where Paul, recalling Jewish speculations, says that the water-yielding rock, which accompanied the people of Israel in the journey through the desert, 'was Christ.' Similarly, 1 Pet 1.11 speaks of the Spirit of Christ already at work in the prophets. The pre-existence of Christ therefore proves once more to be a soteriological statement; that is, a statement about Christ's universal significance for salvation.

The statements about the mediatorship of creation are most extensively developed in Colossians 1.15-17:

He is the image of the invisible God,
the first-born of all creation;
for in him all things were created,
in heaven and on earth,
visible and invisible,
whether thrones or dominions or principalities or authorities—
all things were created through him and for him.
He is before all things,
and in him all things hold together.

To this first strophe on the universal mediatorship of creation corresponds a second (1.18-20) on Christ's universal mediatorship of salvation, according to which everything has been reconciled in him and a universal peace (Shalom) established. Again the idea of creation is used to serve and justify the soteriological interest. On the other hand the universal significance of Christian salvation has consequences for the Christian's behaviour in the world, since it liberates him from the worship of earthly agencies, from the spell of paganism and the legalism of Judaism, to which the Colossians were obviously in danger of falling back. This universal Christology justifies both Christian freedom and Christian responsibility for the world.

The rest of the New Testament texts relating to a universal Christology can only be briefly mentioned here. Hebrews 1.3: 'He reflects the glory of God and bears the very stamp of his nature, upholding the universe by his word of power'. The recapitulation therefore runs: 'Jesus Christ is the same yesterday and today and forever' (13.8). Also according to Revelation 1.17 Christ is 'the first and the last.' The pre-existence statements of John's prologue, already discussed, say likewise that everything came to be through the *Logos* and that he was therefore the light and life of men from the very beginning (1.3f). Only in Jesus Christ does it become clear what truth, light, life, for which men strive, really are. For it is he who is light, life and truth (Jn 8.12; 14.6 and frequently elsewhere).

The statements about the mediatorship of Jesus Christ in creation are therefore intended to serve and justify those about redemption. They are meant to bring out the eschatological-definitive and universal character of the person and work of Jesus Christ as the fulness of time (Gal 4.4) and to underline Christian freedom and responsibility in the world.

The statements about Jesus' mediatorship of creation have the same roots in the history of religion as the pre-existence statements: the Old Testament speculation on wisdom.[53] This was an eminently suitable way of expressing the eschatological universal character of the Christ-event. With the aid of the sapiential tradition, which it had largely in common with other peoples (especially Egypt), the Old Testament already attempted to explain the universality of Yahweh's action in salvation history in and with Israel and so to link together creation and salvation history.[54] The New Testament developed a wisdom-christology at a very early stage in the logia source, known as Q.[55] It is found in the threats against 'this generation' which does not know the wisdom of God (Mt 23.34-36, 37-39; Lk 11.49-51; 13.34f; cf Mt 11.16-19; 12.41; Lk 7.31-35; 11.31). The logia source itself therefore, from which some at the present time try to reconstruct a Rabbi Jesus in order to play him off against what they call the Christ-speculation of the Church, is the very basis of such 'speculations'.

The theme of the wisdom of God as the folly of the cross, resisted and contradicted by the wisdom of this world, is found again in 1 Cor 1 and 2.[56] Even the theology of the cross therefore cannot be played off against a sapiential Christology within a universal horizon: but it is an important corrective, so that God's wisdom in Jesus Christ and the wisdom of the world are not confused and the cross of Christ is not 'made void' (1 Cor 1.17). Wisdom Christology is developed extensively in the deuteropauline letters. Eph 3.10 speaks of the manifold wisdom of God, which is active everywhere and assumes a variety of forms. According to God's eternal plan it appeared in Christ, in whom all treasures of wisdom and knowledge are hidden (Col 2.3), and is proclaimed by the Church (Col 1.26f). This wisdom-Christology evidently forms a parallel to the *Logos*-Christology of John's prologue.

The eschatologically founded universality of salvation in Jesus Christ is most comprehensively expounded with the aid of the term *mysterion*[57]. In Scripture 'mystery' means, not primarily a conceptual mystery, but – corresponding to apocalyptic linguistic usage – God's eternal decree of salvation, unfathomable for man, which will be made manifest at the end of the world. This is the sense in which Mk 4.11f speaks of the mystery of the kingdom of God and thus implicitly refers to Jesus himself.

This Christological concentration and concretization of the mystery of God is most exhaustively discussed in Eph 1. In Christ·God formed the eternal decree of his will to bring about the fulness of time (1.9f); for in Christ he predestined us in love and grace to sonship (1.5). In him we are so to speak predefined; to him we are all committed. *In* Christ the mystery not known to former times (Rom 16.25f), hidden from eternity in God, the creator of the universe (Eph 3.9), has been made manifest. This revelation of the mystery is concretely realized by the proclamation of the Church (Eph 3.6,8ff). Since the mystery of the gospel (Eph 6.19) is entrusted to it, the Church consisting of Jews and Gentiles, in which Christ is among us, can also be described as the content of the mystery (Eph 3.6; Col 1.26).

The Church here is set within the broadest perspectives of salvation history and world history and it is the point at which the meaning of history and of reality as a whole comes to light: it is the public manifestation of the mystery of all reality. In the unity of peoples realized in the Church the goal of God's mystery in Jesus Christ is portrayed even now: the restoration of broken unity, the recapitulation and pacification of the universe (Eph 1.10). This universal rule of Christ is however again transcended: for its own part it promotes the praise and glorification of God (1.6, 12, 14). The definition which brings all reality under the rule of Christ is not bondage, but sonship in the acknowledgement of the one Father (cf. also Rom 8.29f). The dialectic of dominion and bondage as law of history is thus cancelled in favour of sonship, and the attainment of full age consists in the glorification of God, the Creator and Redeemer of the universe.

If Jesus Christ is wisdom in person and the recapitulation and goal of all reality, then reality as a whole and each individual reality acquires from him and for him its definitive place and its definitive meaning. But then too that which is centre, ground and goal of the existence of Jesus – his sonship, his being for God and for men – must intrinsically determine all reality in a hidden and yet effective way.

Such a universal Christology means first of all that creation and redemption, nature and grace, Christianity and world, may not be placed alongside one another or opposed to one another in a dualistic sense. Christianity, grace and redemption are not merely additional luxuries, not a superstructure or a kind of second storey above 'natural' reality; on the other hand for faith 'natural' reality is neither an indifferent nor simply a wicked world. The fact is that Christ is hidden and yet everywhere working effectively and everywhere seeking to prevail. We are to serve him in ordinary life in the world and already many a one has met him there without knowing him. Christianity therefore can only be a Christianity open to the world: it betrays its innermost being if it withdraws in a sectarian spirit to the ghetto.

In the history of theology projects for such a universal Christology can be seen to belong to one of three great epoch-making systems.[58] In antiquity and the Middle Ages a cosmic Christology was worked out. 'Cosmos' for the Greeks was a term used not only in physics but also in metaphysics. 'Cosmos' therefore meant, not merely the universe, but the embodiment of all reality, the order governing the whole. The unity and beauty of the world are found in the one, all-pervading Logos. Everywhere and in everything fragments and traces of the *Logos* are found *(logos spermatikos)*. As early as the second century the apologists took up this theory and gave it a christological interpretation. According to them the Logos revealed himself corporeally in his fulness in Jesus Christ, while only grains of truth are found in the pagan religions and philosophies. This cosmic Christology presupposed a sacral view of the world which betrayed its intrinsic ambiguity in the Enlightenment: if Christianity is understood as incarnate reason, this must lead to a 'reasonable' interpretation of Christianity. The modern emphasis on subjectivity led to the elimination of the magical features of this world-picture: the divine, unconditioned and absolute, was not experienced in man's reason, freedom and conscience. Thus there came into existence a Christology in terms of anthropology. Christ was understood as the answer to man's uncertainty, as the fulfilment of that on which man's existence is always intent in its quest for wholeness. Within Catholic theology, Karl Rahner in particular has produced a project for such an anthropological approach to Christology.[59]

At the 'end of modern times' (Romano Guardini) however man is increasingly aware of himself not only as lord of reality, but also as helplessly delivered up to the historical powers of technology, science, politics and the rest, which he has himself produced. Reality as a whole is now no longer understood cosmically or anthropocentrically, but as a process of exchange and a mediation event between world and man: that is, as history.[60] In German idealism in Schelling and Hegel, in Baader and in Russia in Soloviev, the great speculations began in the philosophy of history, Christology and sophiology, in which Christ was portrayed as basic law and goal of historical development. In this respect in the Catholic theology of the last decades the work of Teilhard de Chardin in particular has played a considerable part.[61] He thought it was possible to show an uninterrupted process from cosmogenesis by way of noo-(anthropo-)genesis to Christogenesis. For him Christ was the Omega Point of cosmic and historical evolution which, he maintains as against Marxism, does not end up in a collective consciousness but in a personally structured megasynthesis in which Christ is 'a special radiant centre at the heart of a system', the heart of the world. On the Protestant side, in the light of quite different assumptions, Wolfhart Pannenberg and Jürgen Moltmann have attempted such an 'integration' in terms of a theology of history and thus at the same time emphasized the aspect of the mission and world responsibility of the Christian.

Undoubtedly these are all splendid and ingenious projects of a Christocentric total view of reality. Nevertheless, their intrinsic danger must not be overlooked, which consists in transforming the uniqueness of Jesus Christ into something universal and ending with a Christianity which is found anonymously everywhere in mankind, paying for its universality by the loss of its concreteness and uniqueness of meaning. For that reason the relationship between Christianity and world, nature and grace, creation and redemption, must be discriminatingly defined. On the one hand light falls from Jesus Christ on reality as a whole; it is only in his light that the meaning of reality can finally be determined (analogy of faith). But if this Christological interpretation is not to be imposed in a purely external way on reality and thus become an ideology, it must correspond to the nature of reality: reality itself therefore must be Christologically shaped, so that light falls on Christ also from reality (analogy of being). With these two analogies we are dealing so to speak with an ellipse with two focal points. The tension between the two must not be unilaterally relaxed.

The temptation to adopt a one-sided solution comes from different sides. First of all integralism[62] is under the constant temptation of wanting to standardize reality in a quasi-totalitarian manner in the light of Christ and thus of forgetting that Christ establishes his universality, not by servile oppression, but by filial freedom in love. Respect for freedom however implies respect and tolerance even for the freedom which has made a wrong choice. As opposed to the temptation of integralism there is that of secularism. The latter sees Jesus Christ as the evolution of the world become aware of itself, as symbol and cypher of an authentic human existence. Christianity here is essentially all that is humanly noble and good; the difference between Christianity and the world becomes blurred. Christ is only the clarification (revelation) of what is anonymously Christian. If we think only in terms of this system of revelation and epiphany, we shall overlook the historical character of the Christ-event, which not only reveals the meaning of reality, but realizes it in such a way that only in the encounter with Jesus Christ is the definitive meaning of man decided.

This differentiated historical unity of creation and redemption is the great theme of the outline of salvation history by Irenaeus of Lyons, the father of Catholic dogmatics. Since man is created in the image of God, he is oriented to assimilation by grace to the archetype. When man through sin withdrew from this orientation to fellowship with God, God did not abandon him. In Jesus Christ God recapitulated and renewed everything. He became, that is, 'what we are, in order to perfect us to be what he is'[63]. By becoming man, he showed us the true image of man; as reflection of the invisible Father, he could also assimilate us again to our archetype.[64] Thus the Son of God made man is the surpassing fulfilment of history. 'He brought all newness by bringing himself.'[65]

This theme of surpassing fulfilment was expressed by high medieval theology in the formula: 'Grace does not destroy, but presupposes and perfects nature'.[66] This axiom has often been misunderstood, as if it meant that grace presupposed a human nature as developed and perfect as possible, practically a robust human vitality. At the same time it was forgotten that God in Jesus Christ assumed and redeemed precisely the moribund, weak and foolish. It was also forgotten that man's nature in the concrete is always a nature determined historically and therefore by freedom: a nature which in the concrete is in a state either of sin or of salvation, but never neutral, as pure nature — so to speak — in the forecourt of Christianity.

Originally therefore this axiom was meant not as a concrete, material ontic statement, but as a formal, ontological structural formula implying that grace is not a factor existing on its own, but represents a gift of God to a creature already presupposed (*suppositum*): a creature which for its own part is fit to be endowed with grace by God and reaches its perfection only as thus endowed. A distinction therefore must be made between the 'natural' constitution of man (*perfectio formae*) and the completion of man (*perfectio finis*).[67] In other words: man finds the completion of his nature by transcending it in view of God and his grace. This transcendence belonging to the nature of human freedom finds its supreme realization in the Pasch, that is, in the passing of Christ from death into life with the Father.

In the death and resurrection of Christ, therefore, that which constitutes man's deepest nature reaches its unique and supreme realization: love surpassing itself and emptying itself. Jesus himself universalizes this basic law: 'Whoever would save his life will lose it; and whoever loses his life for my sake and the gospel's will save it' (Mk 8.35). 'Unless a grain of wheat falls into the earth and dies, it remains alone; but if it dies, it bears much fruit. He who loves his life loses it, and he who hates his life in this world will keep it for eternal life' (Jn 12.24f). These sayings now acquire what amounts to ontological relevance: all that is, is only in transition to something else; every particularity has its truth only by being assumed into a whole. The living reality must go out of itself in order to preserve itself. The 'I' must empty itself at a 'thou' in order to gain itself and the other. But fellowship, society and mankind, can find and retain their unity only within a common reality encompassing and overlapping their members: a mediation which itself can only be personal. Unity among men is possible therefore only in self-transcendence leading to a common acknowledgment of God. To express it in a more general way: whatever exists finds its identity not through an absolute, aloof being-in-itself, but — concretely — only through a relationship and self-transcendence to what is other than itself. So love, which constitutes the innermost centre of Jesus' existence, is the bond that holds all things together and gives meaning to everything.

This Christological interpretation of reality is obviously in sharp contrast to that way of thinking which is dominant today and determines the life of society, particularly in the West, which takes the self-interest of the individual as its starting point. But more especially today it is faced with an outline of universal history which is supremely relevant to world politics, declaring that conflict is the means of attaining the goal of history, the kingdom of freedom. For Karl Marx history as a whole is a history of class-struggles;[68] the basic law of history is the dialectic of dominion and servitude, of alienation and liberation (emancipation). Christianity is no less realistic in its view of man's alienation: it sees man as alienated through the power of sin, which also exercises an influence and finds objective expression in unjust and inhuman social and economic conditions. This alienation is so deep-rooted that man cannot liberate himself by his own power either as an individual or as a group or class. What is necessary is a radically new beginning and this Christ brought in his love for God and man. In Christianity therefore it is a question, not of emancipated freedom, but of liberated freedom, freedom set free. The Christian model is not the relationship of master and servant, but that of father and son, the son being released and set free by the father for his own existence. But when sonship is seen as the essence of the Christian understanding of man, it is not conflict but love which becomes the mover of history.

Love of course means also absolute determination and unconditional commitment to justice for all. Since it unconditionally accepts and affirms the other *as* other, it also gives him what is his due; it is therefore the soul and the surpassing fulfilment of justice, the power to adapt the demands of justice to changing historical situations and at the same time if need be to renounce legitimately-acquired legal titles. In that way love becomes the mover of history. A universal Christology is credible only if it is not merely a theory but presses for implementation in practice. From the confession of Jesus Christ as Son of God there emerges a new view of man, destined to sonship, to freedom, which is realized in love. This new image of man Jesus Christ himself exemplified in his own life and made possible for us in a unique way.

If in concluding we ask, 'Why did God become man?', we must answer with the Apostles' Creed: 'for us and for our salvation'. The Incarnation of God is the recapitulation and surpassing fulfilment of history, the fulness of time; through it the world reaches its wholeness and salvation.

This answer throws a new light on the classic controversy between Thomists and Scotists on the motive of the Incarnation of God.[69] The question is whether God would have become man even if there had been no sin: whether, that is, the primary purpose of the Incarnation was redemption from sin or the recapitulation of the universe in Christ. If we analyze this scholastic controversy more closely, it can be reduced in point of fact to an abstract question on the sequence of the divine decrees: 'Did God decide on on the Incarnation in view of his foreknowledge of sin or did he permit sin on the presupposition of the Incarnation?'[70] For us this question is simply unanswerable. We must give up any attempt at a theology of possibles, based on what God might have done. We can agree that the Thomists are right to start out only from the revelation of God in Jesus Christ and that, according to revelation, God redeemed the world in its sin by recapitulating it anew in Jesus Christ. We can then perceive in the reality what is possible to God: Jesus Christ as the reality of revelation is also its possibility from eternity. In him God is love in which he assumes and reconciles what is other than himself and thus liberates it for himself: that is, for love. The death of God on the cross and the Resurrection as the negation of this negation can thus be understood as the climax of God's self-revelation for the salvation of the world. They are that 'than which nothing greater can come to be'.[71]

Notes

[1] On the literature see above p.112, n. 20.

[2] On the biblical understanding of reality, cf T. Boman, *Das hebräische Denken im Vergleich mit dem griechischen* (Göttingen, 1968[5]), pp. 35 ff; C. Tresmontant, *Essai sur la pensée hebraique* (Paris, 1953); idem, *Etudes de métaphysique biblique* (Paris, 1955); W. Kasper, *Dogma unter dem Wort Gottes* (Mainz, 1965), pp.58-109. The biblical understanding of reality properly needs an ontological interpretation, but it is impossible to provide this here. It would be the basis for an historical understanding of reality which sees being as process, without however reducing everything to a relativizing coming-to-be. The starting point of such reflections would have to be a rethinking of the Aristotelian-scholastic modes of being, actuality (*actus*) and potency (*potentia*). In this respect potency should not be understood as the mere possibility of being, but as ability to be (Nicholas of Cusa: *possest*).

[3] Cf. W Marcus, *Der Subordinationismus als historiologisches Phänomenon. Ein Beitrag zu unserer Kenntnis von der Entstehung der altchristlichen 'Theologie' und Kultur unter besonderer Berücksichtigung der Begriffe OIKONOMIA und THEOLOGIA* (Munich,1963).

[4] W. Künneth in his *Theologie der Auferstehung* (4th ed., Munich, 1961, pp. 114ff) gives a highly individual interpretation, distinguishing between Jesus' divinity and his sonship. He claims that Jesus was always Son of God, but acquired his divinity (*kyriotes*) only through the Resurrection. Pannenberg rightly rejects this view in his Christology (*Grundzüge*, pp. 133ff; ET: *Jesus-God and Man*, London, 1968, pp. 135ff), and insists that Jesus is Son of God 'retroactively' from his resurrection. So too D. Wiederkehr, 'Entwurf einer systematischen Christologie' in *Mysterium Salutis*, Vol III/1, pp. 518-30. This legal terminology is not entirely appropriate to express the ontological state of affairs — rightly stressed by Pannenberg — that the Resurrection was the final and definitive realization of what Jesus had been from the beginning. Cf. also B. Welte, 'Zur Christologie von Chalkedon' in the same author's *Auf der Spur des Ewigen* (Freiburg, 1965), pp. 452-8.

[5] On what follows, cf K.H. Schelke, *Die Passion Jesu in der Verkündigung des Neuen Testaments;* U. Wilckens, *Weisheit und Torheit. Eine exegetisch-religionsgeschichtliche Untersuchung zu 1 Kor 1 und 2* (Tübingen, 1959); W. Schrage, *Das Verständnis des Todes Jesu Christi im Neuen Testament, loc. cit.;* H. Urs von Balthasar, *Mysterium Paschale, loc. cit.*

[6] Cf W. Popkes, *Christus Traditus. Eine Untersuchung zum Begriff der Dahingabe im Neuen Testament* (Zürich-Stuttgart, 1967).

[7] E. Stauffer, 'Vom logos tou staurou und seiner Logik' in ThStK 103 (1931), pp.179-88.

[8] Plinius, *Liber X. Ad Traianum imperatorem cum eiusdem responsis*, xcvi, 7, in Pliny,

Letters and Panegyricus (ed., B.Radice), vol II (London, 1969), p.288. The liturgical prostration as the 'living situation' of early Christian Christology has been emphasized very effectively recently by G. Lohfink, 'Gab es im Gottesdienst der neutestamentlichen Gemeinden ein Anbetung Christi?' in BZ NF 18 (1974), pp. 161-79.

[9] Cf R. Bultmann, *Das Evangelium des Johannes* (11th ed., Göttingen, 1950, pp. 1-57; ET: *The Gospel of John*, (Oxford, 1971), pp. 13-83; R. Schnackenburg, *Johannesevangelium*, I, pp. 208-57; ET: *The Gospel according to St John*, vol. I (London 1968, pp. 221-81); O. Cullmann, *Christologie*, pp. 253-75; ET: *The Christology of the New Testament* (2nd ed., 1963), pp. 249-69.

[10] Cf H. Kleinknecht, G. Quell, E. Stauffer, K.G. Kuhn, art. *'theos'* in TW III, pp.65-123; K. Rahner, 'Theos im Neuen Testament' in *Schriften* I, pp. 91-167; ET: 'Theos in the New Testament' in *Theological Investigations*, vol. I (London, 1961), pp. 79-148.

[11] W. Thüsing, *Per Christum in Deum. Drei Studien zum Verhältnis von Christocentrik und Theocentrik in den paulinischen Hauptbriefen* (Münster, 1965).

[12] Cf F.J.Schierse, 'Die neutestamentliche Trinitätsoffenbarung' in *Mysterium Salutis* II,pp. 85-131, particularly p. 128.

[13] Cf K.Rahner, 'Der dreifaltige Gott als transzendenter Urgrund der Heilsgeschichte' in *Mysterium Salutis* II, especially 327ff; ET: *The Trinity* (London, 1970), pp. 21ff; H. de Lavalette, art. 'Dreifaltigkeit' in LTK III, 543-8.

[14] Cf W. Pannenberg, *Grundzüge*, pp. 155ff, 169ff; ET: *Jesus – God and Man* (London, 1968), pp. 156ff, 169ff.

[15] See above p. 159, n. 4; quotations from Käsemann, *op.cit.*, pp.68,71.

[16] Cf W. Kramer, *Christos-Kyrios-Gottessohn*, pp. 108-112.

[17] CF C. Colpe, *Die religiongeschichtliche Schule. Darstellung und Kritik ihres Bildes vom gnostischen Erlösermythus* (Göttingen, 1961).

[18] Cf the detailed treatment of H.L Strack, P. Billerbeck, *Kommentar zum Neuen Testament aus Talmud und Midrasch* (5th ed., Munich, 1969), I, p. 974; II, pp 353-7.

[19] Cf E. Schweizer, 'Zur Herkunft der Präexistenz-vorstellungen bei Paulus' in the same author's *Neotestamentica*, pp. 105-9; U. Wickens, G. Fohrer, art. *'sophia'* in TW VII, pp. 456-529; R. Schnackenburg, *Johannesevangelium*, I, 290ff (Excursus); ET:*The Gospel according to St John*, vol, I (London, 1968), pp. 494ff.

[20] W. Pannenberg, *Grundzüge*, p. 153, ET: *Jesus – God and Man* (London, 1968), p.153.

[21] A recent summary treatment is that of W. Maas, *Unveränderlichkeit Gottes. Zum Verhältnis von griechisch-philosophischer und christlicher Gotteslehre (Paderborner Theologische Studien* 1) (Munich, 1974).

[22] Cf T. Boman, *Das hebräische Denken*, pp.35ff; C.H. Ratschow, 'Anmerkungen zur theologischen Auffassung des Zeitproblems' in ZThK 51 (1954), pp. 360-87; H.Sasse, art. aion in TW I, pp. 197-209; G. Delling, *Das Zeitverständnis des Neuen Testaments* (Gütersloh, 1940). Cf on this topic also the new interpretations of K. Barth, E. Brunner, E. Jüngel, J. Moltmann, W. Kasper, H. Küng, H. Mühlen, K. Rahner and J. Ratzinger.

[23] On the following, cf the presentations in A. von Harnack, *Lehrbuch der Dogmengeschichte*, vol. I ('Die Entstehung des kirchlichen Dogmas') (5th ed., Tübingen, 1931; ET: *History of Dogma*, vol. I, 2nd ed. (London-Edinburgh, 1897), Division I ('The Genesis of Ecclesiastical Dogma'), pp. 141-317; F. Loofs, *Leitfaden zum Stadium der Dogmengeschichte* (6th ed., Tübingen, 1959, especially pp. 1-263; R. Seeberg, *Lehrbuch der Dogmengeschichte*, vol. I ('Die Anfänge des Dogmas im nachapostolischen und altkatholischen Zeitalter') (3rd ed., Leipzig-Erlangen, 1920; M. Werner, *Die Entstehung des christlichen Dogmas* (Berne-Leipzig, 1941); A. Adam, *Lehrbuch der Dogmengeschichte*, vol. 1 ('Die Zeit der alten Kirche') (Gütersloh, 1965); W. Köhler, *Dogmengeschichte als Geschichte des christlichen Selbstbewusstseins*, vol. 1 ('Von den Anfängen bis zur Reformation') (3rd ed., Zürich, 1951); A. Grillmeier/H. Bacht, *Das Konzil von Chalkedon, Geschichte und Gegenwart*, vol. I ('Der Glaube von Chalkedon') (4th ed., Würzburg, 1973); A. Gilg, *Weg und Bedeutung der altkirchlichen Christologie* (Munich, 1955); G.L. Prestige, *God in Patristic Thought* (London, 1964); P.T. Camelot, *Ephesus und Chalcedon* (Mainz, 1963); L.Ortiz-Urbina, *Nizäa und Konstantinopel*

(Mainz, 1964); A. Grillmeier, *Christ in Christian Tradition. From the Apostolic Age to Chalcedon* (London, 1965); J. Liebaert, 'Christologie. Von der Apostolischen Zeit bis zum Konzil von Chalcedon (451)', with a biblical-Christological introduction by P. Lamarche (*HDG* III/1a) (Freiburg, 1965); F. Ricken, 'Das Homoousios von Nikaia als Krisis des altchristlichen Platonismus' in *Zur Frühgeschichte der Christologie* (QD Vol 51), ed., B. Welte (Freiburg, 1970), pp.74-99; P.Smulders, 'Dogmengeschichtliche und lehramtliche Entfaltung der Christologie' in *Mysterium Salutis*, III/1, pp.389-475.

[24]Cf. G. Greshake, *Gnade als konkrete Freiheit. Eine Untersuchung zur Gnadenlehre des Pelagius* (Mainz, 1972); *idem*, 'Der Wandel der Erlösungsvorstellungen in der Theologiegeschichte' in: *Erlösung und Emanzipation (QD*, Vol. 61), ed., L. Scheffcyk (Freiburg, 1973), pp. 69-101.

[25]On the meaning of the ancient term *hypostasis*/person cf. Chapter III/1 pp. 230-274.

[26]A. von Harnack, *Lehrbuch der Dogmengeschichte*, vol, I, p.20; ET: *History of Dogma*, vol. I, 2nd ed., 1897, p. 17.

[27]For a survey of the history and state of the problem see A. Grillmeier, 'Hellenisierung-Judaisierung des Christentums als Deuteprinzipien der Geschichte des kirchlichen Dogmas' in *Scholastik* 33 (1958), pp. 321-55, 528-58; the same author, 'Die altkirchliche Christologie und die moderne Hermeneutik' in J. Pfammatter — F. Furger, eds., *Theologische Berichte* I (Zürich, 1972) pp. 69-169; P. Stockmeier, art. 'Hellenismus und Christentum' in SM II, pp. 665-76; *idem, Glaube und Religion in der frühen Kirche* (Freiburg, 1972); W. Pannenberg, *Grundzüge*, pp. 296ff; ET: *Jesus — God and Man*, (London, 1968), pp. 287ff.

[28]Cf. W. Kamlah, *Christentum und Geschichtlichkeit. Untersuchungen zur Entstehung des Christentums und zu Augustins 'Bürgschaft Gottes'* (2nd ed., Stuttgart, 1951).

[29]R. Seeberg, *Lehrbuch der Dogmengeschichte*, I, p. 3.

[30]Ignatius of Antioch, *Letter to Polycarp* III, 2 (J.B. Lightfoot, ed., *The Apostolic Fathers*, II, pp. 343f); *idem, Letter to the Ephesians* VII, 2 (Lightfoot, pp. 47f).

[31]Irenaeus, *Adversus haereses* IV, 20, 4 (ed., W.W. Harvey, II, 216).

[32]Tertullian, *De carne Christi* V (PL 2, 760-762).

[33]Origen, *De principiis, praef.* IV (GCS 22.10).

[34]Augustine, *Sermo* 183, IV, 5 (PL 38, 990).

[35]On the problem itself, cf W. Elert, *Der Ausgang der altkirchlichen Christologie. Eine Untersuchung über Theodor von Pahran und seine Zeit als Einführung in die alte Dogmengeschichte*, eds, W. Maurer and E. Bergsträsser (Berlin, 1957); H. Küng, *Menschwerdung Gottes. Eine Einführung in Hegels theologisches Denken als Prolegomena zu einer künftigen Christologie* (Freiburg 1970); H. Urs von Balthasar, *Mysterium Paschale*, loc. cit.

[36]M. Luther, *Disputatio Heidelbergae habita, These* 19f, in WA I, 354; cf W. von Loewenich, *Luthers Theologia crucis*, (4th ed., Munich, 1954).

[37]P.Schoonenberg, *Hij is een God van Mensen* ('s-Hertogenbosch, 1969); ET: *The Christ* (London, 1970); *idem*, 'Trinität — der vollendete Bund. Thesen zur Lehre vom dreipersönlichen Gott,' in *Orientierung* 37 (1973), pp. 115-7. On the latter, cf K.Reinhardt, 'Die menschliche Transzendenz Jesu Christi. Zu Schoonenbergs Versuch einer nicht-chalkedonischen Christologie' in TThZ 80 (1971), pp. 273-89; A. Schilson, W. Kasper, *Christologie im Präsens*, pp. 115-22.

[38]P. Schoonenberg, *Trinität*, loc. cit.

[39]*Art.cit.*, p.116.

[40]Cf W. Schulz, *Der Gott der neuzeitlichen Metaphysik*, 3rd ed., 1957; H. Krings, E. Simons, art.'Gott' in: *Handbuch philosophischer Grundbegriffe* II (Munich, 1973), pp. 613-41.

[41]G.W.F. Hegel, *Phänomenologie des Geistes (Phenomenology of Mind)* (ed. J. Hoffmeister), p. 21.

[42]The same author, *Vorlesungen über die Philosophie der Religion* II/2 (ed. Lasson), p. 158.

194

[43] *Op.cit.*, pp. 53ff.

[44] *Op.cit.*, p. 75.

[45] J.W. von Goethe, 'Die Geheimnisse. Ein Fragment' quoted in J. Moltmann, *Der gekreuzigte Gott*, p. 37; ET: *The Crucified God* (London, 1974), p. 35.

[46] K. Barth, *Die Kirchliche Dogmatik* I/1 (Zollikon-Zürich, 1947), pp. 373ff; ET: *Church Dogmatics*, I/1, Edinburgh, 1963 (reprint), p. 400; H. Berkhof, *Theologie des Heiligen Geistes* (Neukirchen-Vluyn, 1968), pp.'128ff.

[47] K. Rahner, 'Der dreifaltige Gott als transzendenter Urgrund der Heilsgeschichte' in *Mysterium Salutis* II, 364ff, 385ff; ET: *The Trinity* (London, 1970), pp. 73ff, 103ff.

[48] G.W.F. Hegel, *Vorlesungen über die Philosophie der Religion*, II/2 (ed. Lasson), p. 75.

[49] Thomas Aquinas, *Summa Theologiae* III, q.3 a.5.

[50] K. Barth, *Die Kirchliche Dogmatik* II/2 (3rd ed., Zollikon-Zürich, 1948, 1; cf. 101ff, ET: *Church Dogmatics*, II/2 (Edinburgh, 1957), p.3.

[51] H. Urs von Balthasar, *Karl Barth*, pp. 186ff.

[52] Cf. K. Pflegler, *Die verwegenen Christozentriker* (Freiburg, 1964) H. Urs von Balthasar, *Karl Barth*, pp. 336ff; H. Küng, art. 'Christozentrik' in LTK II, 1169-1174; *idem, Rechtfertigung. Die Lehre Karl Barths und eine katholische Besinnung* (Einsiedeln, 1957), pp. 127ff, 138ff, 277ff; ET: *Justification. The Doctrine of Karl Barth and a Catholic Reflection* (London, 1964), pp. 118ff, 129ff, 272ff; W. Pannenberg, *Grundzüge* pp. 169ff; ET: *Jesus- God and Man* (London, 1968, pp. 168ff); H. Riedlinger, 'Die kosmische Königsherrschaft Christi' in *Concilium 2* (1966), *pp. 53-62; ET:* 'How Universal is Christ's Kingship' in *Concilium* January 1966, pp. 56-65; O. Rousseau, 'Die Idee des Königtums Christi in the same issue of *Concilium*, pp. 63-69, ET: 'The idea of the Kingship of Christ', pp. 67-74.

[53] Cf above p. 193, n. 19.

[54] Cf. G. von Rad, *Weisheit in Israel* (Neukirchen Vluyn, 1970); ET: *Wisdom in Israel* (London, 1972).

[55] Cf U. Wilckens/G. Fohrer, art *sophia* in TW VII, pp 515-519.

[56] On this cf *loc.cit.*, pp. 519-523; H. Schlier, 'Kerygma und Sophia. Zur neutestamentlichen Grundlegung des Dogmas', *idem, Die Zeit der Kirche*, pp. 206-32; U. Wilckens, *Weisheit und Torheit*.

[57] Cf. G. Bornkamm, art. *mysterion* in TW IV, 809-834, especially 823ff; H. Schlier, *Der Brief an die Epheser. Ein Kommentar* (6th ed., Düsseldorf, 1968), especially pp. 60ff, 153ff; J. Gnilka, *Der Epheserbrief* (Freiburg, 1971), especially pp. 76ff.

[58] Cf. the surveys in H. Urs von Balthasar, *Glaubhaft ist nur Liebe;* J. Moltmann, 'Gottesoffenbarung und Wahrheitsfrage', *idem, Perspektiven der Theologie*, pp.13-35, and frequently in Part I, especially pp. 16ff.

[59] Cf above Part I, Chapter III/3.

[60] On this see above, Part I. Chapter III/4.

[61] Cf. above, p. 24, n. 9.

[62] Cf. O. von Nell-Breuning, art. 'Integralismus' in LTK V, 717f.

[63] Irenaeus, *Adversus haereses* V, *praef.* (ed. W.W. Harvey, II, 314).

[64] Cf. *op.cit.*, V, 16, 2 (Harvey, II, P. 268).

[65] *Op. cit.*, IV, 34,1 (Harvey II, p.269).

[66] On the history of this axiom, cf J. Beumer, 'Gratia supponit naturam. Zur Geschichte eines theologischen Prinzips' in Gr 20 (1939), pp 381-406, 535-52; B. Stoeckle, *Gratia supponit naturam. Geschichte und Analyse eines theologischen Axioms* (Rome, 1962) (bibliography). On the objective meaning, cf E. Przywara, 'Der Grundsatz "Gratia non destruit, sed supponit et perficit naturam". Eine ideengeschichtliche Interpretation' in *Scholastik*, 17 (1942), pp 178-86; J. Alfaro, 'Gratia supponit naturam' in LTK IV, 1169-1171 (bibliography); J. Ratzinger, 'Gratia praesupponit naturam' in the same author's *Dogma und Verkündigung* (Munich-Freiburg, 1973), pp 161-181.

[67] See in particular H. Volk, 'Gnade und Person' in the same author's *Gott alles in allem*, especially pp. 119ff.

[68] Cf K. Marx - F. Engels, *Manifest der Kommunistischen Partei* in W II *(study edition)*

(Darmstadt, 1971), pp. 8-17; ET: *The Communist Manifesto* (Penguin ed., 1967; p. 79.
[69] *Cf.* on this R. Haubst, *Vom Sinn der Menschwerdung. 'Cur deus homo'* (Munich, 1969), and the summary of the history of theology in H. Urs von Balthasar, *Karl Barth*, pp. 336-44.
[70] M. Schmaus, *Katholische Dogmatik*, II/2 (6th ed., Munich, 1963), p. 70.
[71] F. W. J. Schelling, *Die Philosophie der Offenbarung*, Part II, in W VI (ed. M. Schröter), pp. 561 and 566.

II. JESUS CHRIST – SON OF MAN

1. JESUS CHRIST TRUE MAN AND THE ACTUALITY OF OUR SALVATION

The New Testament takes for granted the fact that Jesus Christ was a real human being. It is stated as something quite obvious that Jesus was born of a human mother; that he grew up; that he knew hunger, thirst, weariness, joy, sorrow, love, anger, toil, pains, God-forsakenness and, finally, death. In the New Testament the reality of the corporeal existence of Jesus is seen as an undisputed fact, and therefore (apart from some late writings) it is not discussed but merely assumed. The New Testament writings anyway are hardly interested in the details of his human existence. We learn practically nothing of the appearance and person of Jesus or of his 'spiritual life'. The New Testament is concerned neither with the bare facts of the life of Jesus nor with the concrete details of the circumstances of his life, but with the meaning of that human existence for salvation. Its whole interest lies in declaring that in him and through him God spoke and acted in an eschatological-definitive and historically surpassing way in order to reconcile the world to himself (2 Cor 5.18). This concrete human being, Jesus of Nazareth, therefore is the point at which the eschatological salvation also of each and every human being is decided: 'Everyone who acknowledges me before men, the Son of man also will acknowledge before the angels of God; but he who denies me before men will be denied before the angels of God' (Lk 12.8f; cg. Mk 8.38). This actuality of the event of salvation and of the decision for salvation constitutes the scandal of Christian reality: 'And blessed is he who takes no offence at me' (Mt. 11.6).

The Easter kerygma takes up this theme with the basic statement of identity: the Risen is the Crucified and the Crucified is the Risen. Thus the significance of the concrete person Jesus of Nazareth for salvation is retained also for the post-Easter situation. At the same time the scandalous character of the events is stressed by the fact that the cross, the sign of shame and of death, becomes the sign of glory and of life. What is folly for the Gentiles and scandal for the Jews becomes for the believer the sign of God's power and wisdom (cf 1 Cor 1.18). Paul turns this theology of the cross against the early Christian enthusiasts, who imagine that they are already wholly filled with the Spirit of God, forgetting that their lives are still governed by the concrete cross of Christ and must be lived in the shadow of that cross in concrete, corporeal obedience in the ordinary routine of the world.

The gospels make this theme their programme and choose the narration of the story of Jesus as the form of their proclamation. The fourth gospel expressly states the dominant idea of that story: 'and the Word became flesh (*sarx*) and dwelt among us' (1.14).[1] 'Flesh'[2] in Scripture designates man from the standpoint of his wretchedness, frailty, weakness and ordinariness. It is meant to bring out the fact that God's Word has entered completely into our human existence, even down to its ordinary, daily routine, its futility, frustration and emptiness. It is however, nowhere simply stated, 'God became man', but 'he became *this* man, Jesus of Nazareth'. The restriction to this single human being implies at the same time a judgment on all others, in whom the Word did not become flesh.

The incarnation statement of the fourth gospel therefore involves a certain de-mythologizing and de-sacralizing of man and a relativising of what people otherwise regard as great, significant and reputable. In this sense the statement about the Word becoming flesh is a critical truth from which it is impossible to deduce a triumphalist Incarnation theology. For this statement must certainly not be taken to mean that God's Word has made human existence generally a sign and sacrament of salvation, still less entered into the structure of our concrete world, its power and its wealth, endorsing and even transfiguring them. It has in fact an exclusive-critical sense: in this one man God is permanently in our midst.

This concreteness of the promise of salvation and of the decision required for salvation is the reason for the real scandal of the Christian reality and no proclamation or theology can conceal or minimize it: for it is this scandal alone which provides the assurance that God has entered into our human existence in a concrete way.

The scandal of this actualness has to be imprinted on Christianity in its entirety. That is why there is a concrete Church with concrete, binding statements and concrete, binding signs of salvation. Even if we are aware of their historicity and need not conceal the sinfulness of the Church, we cannot simply exchange these statements and signs for others with the dubious excuse that such 'externals' are not essential. But neither may the Church deny the scandal of the Christian reality by itself seeking to be a triumphalist Church of glory, blessing and displaying worldly power and worldly wealth. Through the Church too the word of God must enter completely into the flesh of the world, down to the very roots of the human reality. Anyone who recognizes this will no longer play off the theology of the incarnation and the theology of the cross against one another.

What was an obvious assumption in the Scriptural documents soon became a problem of life and death for the Church. When the Church crossed the frontiers of Judaism and advanced into the very different intellectual world of Hellenism, it became involved in what was perhaps the most serious crisis it had ever had to sustain and which was far more dangerous than the external persecution of the first centuries. This intellectual movement, which threatened the very substance of the Christian faith, is generally known as Gnosticism.[3]

There is considerable debate among scholars about the origin and nature of Gnosticism. Today however there is a general movement away from the views of the early Fathers that Gnosticism was primarily an internal phenomenon of the Church, a reinterpretation of the faith with the aid of Hellenistic conceptual forms. Even before

Christianity, Gnosticism was a widespread syncretistic religious movement. We know moreover through the discoveries at Qumran that it had established itself not only on Hellenistic soil, but also on the soil of Judaism. Only in a secondary way did Gnosticism also take Christian elements in a reinterpreted form into its 'system' and presumably in this way first arrived at the Primal Man-Saviour myth.

According to Gnosticism, redemption comes about through knowledge. Man is released from the enigmas of human existence by reflecting on his heavenly destiny and mentally getting away from the clutches of the material world. That is why Gnosticism is characterized by a sharp dualism: an opposition between light and darkness, good and evil, mind and matter, God and world. It is not concerned with redemption of the body and of matter, but with redemption from the body and from matter. This leads either to contempt for the body, marriage and procreation, or to unrestrained libertinism. Evidently it is a question here of a basic possibility of mastering human existence in answering the question of the whence and whither of man and the world, in particular of the origin and the conquest of evil.

At a very early stage Gnostic trends appeared within the Church. The Gnostics described themselves as 'spirituals' and claimed to be Christians of a higher grade, considering themselves above the 'fleshly' understanding of congregational Christianity. In the light of their dualistic presuppositions Christ could not have assumed a real body. They spoke therefore of an apparent body and were given the name of Docetists (*dokema* = vision, illusion).[4] Some ascribed to Jesus an apparent body without any reality (Marcion, Basilides), others taught that he had a pneumatic, astral body (Appelles, Valentine). The Gnostic temptation was not limited to the first centuries, but accompanied the Church and theology throughout their whole history. The whole of the Middle Ages is marked by a Gnostic undercurrent (the Albigenses in particular). Gnostic features are found in some of the starting-points of idealistic thinking where man is seen merely as mind and, therefore, the figure of Christ and the redemption are spiritualized on the pretext of interiorizing, spiritualizing and deepening Christianity. This trend need not always go so far as to make Christ a pure myth or give him significance merely as an idea or cypher. But all that is concrete and historical is dismissed as external, inessential or even as a hindrance. The objectifying and materializing of faith is resisted, but frequently with the result that it is de-historicized and spiritualized. Even in theology there is a 'jargon of "authentic being" (*Eigentlichkeit*)' (Theodor W. Adorno). It is not without reason that Ernst Käsemann has accused kerygmatic theology of kerygmatic Docetism.

It would be wrong however, to see the temptation to Docetism merely in theology and to overlook its much more dangerous subliminal influence on faith and the life of the Church. In the history of Christian piety the figure of Jesus had often been so idealized and divinized that the average churchgoer tended to see him as a God walking on the earth, hidden behind the façade and costume of a human figure but with his divinity continually 'blazing out', while features which are part of the 'banality' of the human were suppressed. In principle we can scarcely say that the doctrine of the true humanity of Jesus and its meaning for salvation have been clearly marked in the consciousness of the average Christian. What is found there often amounts to a largely mythological and Docetist view of Jesus Christ.

The controversy with Gnosticism was and is a life-and-death struggle for the Church. It is uncertain whether Paul already had to deal with Gnosticism in his conflict with his Corinthian opponents (2 Cor 10-13) and with the 'strong' in Corinth (1 Cor 8-10), with their striving for wisdom (1.17-2.5), their over-emphasis on glossolalia (12-14) and denial of the Resurrection (15)[5] or — which is more likely — with enthusiasts. On the other hand, at Colossae, Judaistic-Gnostic trends clearly appeared,[6] demanding abstinence from certain foods and drinks and the observation of certain cults (2.16ff; cf. 1 Tim 4.3ff and elsewhere) and thus failing to appreciate the universal salvation mediatorship of Jesus (1.15ff), in whom God dwells corporeally (*somatikos*) in his whole fulness (2.9). The emphasis on the corporality of salvation serves here to justify Christian freedom, which of course means anything but absence of restraint: for the very fact that Christ is all in all means that we must be renewed in him in the image of the Creator (3.10f) and do everything in the name of Jesus, giving thanks to the Father (3.17). All fields of human life now provide concrete scope for service and obedience.

This controversy is quite clearly carried on in the first and second letters of John and now expressly in Christological terms.[7] Just as the fourth gospel begins with the confession of the incarnation of the Logos, so John's first letter opens with the sentence: 'That which was from the beginning, which we have heard, which we have seen with our eyes and touched with our hands, concerning the word of life . . . that we proclaim also to you' (1.1,3). Even at this stage this late apostolic writing pronounces an anathema on all who deny the incarnation: 'By this you know the Spirit of God: every spirit which confesses that Jesus Christ has come in the flesh is of God, and every spirit which does not confess Jesus is not of God. This is the spirit of antichrist . . . (4.2f; cf. 4.15; 5.5f). It is equally clearly stated in John's second letter: 'Many deceivers have gone out into the world, men who will not acknowledge the coming of Jesus Christ in the flesh; such a one is the deceiver and the antichrist . . .' (v.7).

With the incarnation therefore it is a question of the dividing-line, not only between Christianity and non-Christianity, but between Christianity and anti-Christianity. The confession of the coming of God in the flesh is the essential criterion by which the Christian reality is distinguished. This confession means that life, light and love have appeared concretely in our world (1 Jn 1.2; 4.9) and that in faith and love we can overcome the world of death, of lying and hatred (5.4).

The creeds of the early Church counter the errors of Docetism in a very simple, but very profound way, by professing faith in God's creation and listing the most important facts of the life of Jesus: birth, suffering and death. It is only in the Middle Ages that we find explicit condemnations of Gnosticism. The Second Council of Lyons (1274) confesses the true and complete humanity of Christ and declares that it was not merely apparent (DS 852). Similarly the Council of Florence in the Decree for the Jacobites (1441) attacks the Manichees, who held that there was merely an apparent body, and the Valentinians, who wanted to admit only a heavenly body (DS 1340f).

The errors of Gnosticism and Manichaeism were not however rejected as a result of official doctrinal statements so much as intellectually overcome by theology and their profoundly anti-Christian character laid bare. For Gnosticism is less a heresy than an un-Christian and anti-Christian doctrine. Ignatius of Antioch made this clear at an early stage. His line of argument is wholly soteriological. Any denial of Jesus' humanity means denying the reality of our salvation: for if he had only an apparent body, then he only apparently suffered and we are only apparently saved (Smyrn 2), but then the Eucharist too is only an appearance (Smyrn 6). In the last resort it is pointless to suffer in the body and endure persecution for Jesus (Smyrn 4.2). Everything then becomes illusory. That is why Ignatius quite bluntly described Christ as a 'flesh-bearer' (*sarkophoros*) (Smyrn 5; cf. Trall 10).

These arguments were taken up and more fully developed especially by Irenaeus of Lyons. It was Irenaeus who first stated the basic principle which is constantly repeated in subsequent tradition: '. . . because of his infinite love he became what we are, in order to perfect us to be what he is.'[8] In Irenaeus this idea is connected with his theory of recapitulation (*anakephalaiosis*), according to which Christ represents the recapitulation and the culmination of the whole history of mankind. In his body and in his human life he repeats all phases of mankind's development, beginning from its child-hood stage, and leads it to full age and fulness: that is, to God. He is the recapitulation and head of creation precisely in his corporeality. As opposed to Gnosticism, Irenaeus makes the unity of creation and redemption the basic principle of his theology – and of any Catholic theology. The Church too made the same basic theological decision when it set up the canon of Scripture from the Old *and* New Testament against Marcion, who wanted to separate the Creator-God of the Old Testament from the Saviour-God of the New Testament and consequently to curtail the biblical writings. *The unity of creation and redemption is therefore 'the' basic hermeneutical principle for the interpretation of Scripture.*

In view of the basic significance of the humanity of Jesus Christ for our salvation it is necessary to ask more precisely, against the background of modern anthropology, what the coming of God in the flesh means. We start out from the question of what is to be understood by the body of man and attempt in the light of this first of all to get at what is meant by 'flesh' (*sarx*), in order then to be better able to understand how far the coming of Jesus in the flesh can mean salvation for us.

Modern anthropology[9] has liberated itself from Greek dualism and from the Cartesian division of man into *res cogitans* (soul) and *res extensa* (body). Body and soul are not simply two factors existing alongside or in each other, but form an indivisible whole. Man is wholly body and he is wholly soul and both are at all times the whole man. Our mental life also, our thinking and our free will, is and remains not only externally linked to a bodily substratum – as, for instance, for certain brain functions – but has inwardly a profoundly corporeal character: the body enters even into the most sublime achievements of the human mind. This becomes clearest in the phenomenon of human speech. But laughing and crying are also expressions of the whole man; human gesture is an expression of thought, it pins down and underlines the thought. Man expresses himself in playing, singing and dancing. Man is said not only to take nourishment, but to take part in a meal; he has not only a head, but a face. Man is himself only in the expression, he 'exists' in it. Man therefore not only has a body, he *is* this body. In it the whole man discloses and reveals himself. The body is expression, symbol, excarnation, essential medium of man. In the body the whole man is 'there', that is why the body can be preactically understood as man's 'being there' and his presence.

There is a second experience. We know that man can also hide himself behind his countenance, that he can put on a mask and play an alien rôle; he can use words, not only to reveal himself, but also to conceal his thoughts and intentions. Man's corporality means that he can dissociate himself from himself, that he can hold himself back and refuse to give himself. At the same time man learns that he cannot even establish the harmony which really ought to exist between soul and body; he disappears in his body. For the body as a given fact is never wholly expression. That is why it offers a certain resistance to the mind. The body then is not only a symbol and expression of man, but his seclusion and withdrawal.

This viewpoint is confirmed by a further observation. Man's body is not only the expression of the human soul, but likewise the field in which the world exercises its influence on man. Through the body we are implanted into the material world: we not only belong to this world, but we are also delivered up to it even to the extent that we may perish by its external violence. Through the body we are present to things and they are present to us. The body is a part of the world that belongs to us in such a way that we are this part; but it is also a part of the world through which we belong to the world and no longer completely to ourselves. The body is 'between' man and the world. The environment determines us through the body, not only externally and accidentally, but inwardly in what we are. The fact of being situated in the world is an essential characteristic of our existence.

Through his body however, man is not only implanted in his environment, but involved with his contemporaries. Through our body we are in a blood fellowship with our family, our nation, our race and ultimately with all mankind. But our involvement with our contemporaries goes deeper: this constitutes not only our corporal existence, but to a decisive degree our personal identity. Our freedom is concretely possible only insofar as the others grant us a space for freedom and respect it. Actual freedom therefore, as Hegel showed, is based on mutual affirmation and acceptance in love. Hence concrete freedom is ultimately possible only within a joint system of freedom where everyone has through everyone else his concrete scope for living and freedom. Within this scheme the individual again becomes aware of himself only in encounter with others who are significant (Peter Berger). Thus we are defined in our existence by what the others are; our existence is essentially co-existence.

If I recapitulate all that I have said, the conclusion emerges that man in his corporeality is a deeply equivocal phenomenon. The body can be the expression and realization of man's nature; but it can also be the point at which man is exposed. The body can be both sign of salvation and happiness and sign of disaster, disintegration and inner conflict. Man's corporeality shows the whole ambiguity of what man is in the last resort: a being who can find his realization only corporeally and in the world, but who can also miss his destiny in this realization and himself perish. For the term 'man' or 'human' is particularly dubious: intermingled in it are the ideas of high and low, noble and common, banal and extraordinary. 'Today the expression "that is human" excuses everything. People get divorced: that is human. People drink: that is human. They cheat in an examination or in a competition: that is human. They ruin their youth in vice: that is human. They are jealous: that is human. They embezzle: that is human. There is not a vice which has not been excused with the aid of this formula. So the term "human" is used to describe the most infirm and inferior aspect of man. Sometimes it becomes a synonym even for "bestial". What an odd use of language! For the human is the very thing that distinguishes us from the animal. "Human" means intelligence, heart, will, conscience, holiness. That is human.'[10]

In this tension – not indeed metaphysical, but factual – between soul and body, man and man, man and world, the question of salvation arises. For salvation means the integrity of human existence in and with the world. But in these tensions man experiences his disintegration and thus his disastrous situation. Here he experiences his factual lack of freedom, deterioration and self-alienation. The equivocal situation is given an unequivocal interpretation in Scripture and the Church's tradition. For Scripture and tradition the basic relationship and basic tension are seen not as between soul and body, man and world, spirit and matter, individual and society, man and mankind, but as between God and man, God and world, Creator and creature. These relationships and tensions among men and within the world can be integrated only if man in his wholeness rises towards God; for God alone as Creator encompasses all these dimensions and brings them together as the oneness which unites them all. But when the fellowship of God and man breaks down, it must lead also to disintegration in man, both between men and between the world and man.

Scripture described that situation of distance from God and the resulting self-alienation as sin (*hamartia*).[11] But sin is not merely a particular, responsible act on man's part, opposed to the will of God. Sin in Scripture is experienced as encompassing situation and as power which every man accepts in virtue of his ontological and not merely ethical or practical solidarity with all others and then ratifies by his own act. This shared sinfulness therefore is not merely something external to man, not merely a bad example, evil influence, seductive atmosphere: it characterizes each man inwardly in what he *is* in the sight of others and of himself. This concept of shared sinfulness as a factual existential of man is really the objective expression of what is meant by the misleading and unfortunate term 'original sin'.[12]

Original sin means that the universal situation determining everyone inwardly is in fact opposed to the original saving will of God, who created everything in view of Christ and wills to fulfil all in him. It means that the salvation which God had intended for man as man is not actually mediated through his origin, so that there is in fact an opposition between his orientation to Christ and his determination through the universal shared sinfulness.

Here lies the deepest reason for the disruption in man and in the world. The alienation from God and from the saving will he formed in Christ leads to the alienation of man from himself: to the inner conflict between mind and body, knowing and willing, to man's crisis of identity which affects even the somatic sphere in suffering, sickness and liability to death. In addition there is alienation between men: hatred, lying, strife, injustice, oppressive conditions of dependence and incapacity for contact, understanding, conversation. Finally there is alienation between man and his world: irrational dependence on anonymous natural and social forces and consequently lack of freedom even to the point of perishing through those forces. In a word: instead of love as the meaning of existence we have selfishness, isolating and asserting itself, the result being incoherent, impenetrable futility.

This experience of the disintegration and disruption of reality in itself and the experience of the incurable tension between the persistent hope of salvation and the actual disastrous situation have led constantly to systems of metaphysical dualism. But in this way the tension is relaxed only by relieving man's freedom of the burden and placing an intolerable burden on God. The wrong in the world is then attributed to God and he is turned into a devil. Tradition clearly recognized this danger and — for the sake of man's freedom and God's — based the sinful situation (original sin) on a free historical act (primordial sin) in which we are jointly involved and to which we assent by our own decision. Despite all the well-known difficulties which arise at this point, anyone who rejects the theory must see for himself how he is to avoid either dualistic Manichaeism or harmonizing idealism. If someone for the sake of freedom wants to sail between Scylla and Charybdis, if he does not want either to define metaphysically the power of sin or to minimize it and if he wants to be able to justify his solution intellectually, he must see that the traditional doctrine of original sin — not in its misleading terminology, but in the sense in which it is really meant — is one of the greatest achievements in the history of theology and one of the most important contributions of Christianity to the history of ideas.

What has been said represents an attempt to link up with the ideas of present-day anthropology and to clarify the biblical term 'flesh'. I have described the situation in which our redemption takes place and thus simultaneously prepared the way for an understanding of redemption. It can now be seen how much the reality of our salvation and redemption depends on the coming of Jesus Christ into this concrete situation. In what follows therefore we shall show that the only possible redemption is one that is concrete and historical.

If my analyses hitherto have been correct, liberation from the present state of alienation is possible only as a result of an underivable new beginning within history. Our joint confinement under sin involves the impossibility of any individual or group within history overcoming the disaster. Every lost opportunity is really wasted and cannot simply be called back. How much our past pins us down and burdens our future is confirmed by experience. Moreover, every sin produces consequences which the sinner cannot estimate or arrest and thus becomes the cause of further sin, since it conditions the action of others negatively from the outset. Instead therefore of seeking their self-development and making it possible together, individuals mutually destroy the conditions of their freedom and throw one another back on their own resources. The attitude of love is corrupted by selfish motives or even openly replaced by the principle of self-assertion. When however someone makes a good start or risks a new approach, he is likely to fail because of the defensiveness or mistrust of others, to get lost in the impenetrability of the problems or to break down in face of the objective structures of injustice. Thus there is an almost 'natural' momentum belonging to the history of sin: it becomes increasingly enclosed within a vicious circle. If nevertheless there is to be any salvation, it will require a new beginning, someone who will enter into this situation and break through it.

Against this background, it is understandable that Jesus Christ is proclaimed in Scripture as the New Adam (Rom 5.12-21). In fact, by entering into the world in person as the Son of God he changes the situation of everyone. Every man's living space acquires a new dimension and the man himself had become new. Every man is now defined by the fact that Jesus Christ is his brother, neighbour, comrade, fellow citizen, fellow man. Jesus Christ is now a part of man's ontological definition. But since God himself comes with Christ, each man enters into a personal relationship through Christ with God. With Christ's coming a new *kairos*, a new opportunity of salvation, is opened to the whole world and to all men. With him the situation of all has become new, because in the one humanity the existence of each and every one is determined by the existence of all. It is precisely in the body of Christ that salvation is personally exemplified and offered to us.

Through the Incarnation of God in Jesus Christ the disastrous situation in which all men are caught up and by which they are determined in their innermost being is changed. It has broken through at one point and this new beginning from now on determines anew the situation of all men. In the light of this, redemption can be understood as liberation.

The definition of redemption as liberation is completely in accordance with biblical usage. In the original sense of the term, 'redemption'[13] means more or less release, rescue, liberate, drag out or lead out. Often very concrete situations of distress are mentioned: sickness, mortal peril, captivity, calumny, persecution and oppression. The work of redemption begins with the leading of Abraham out of the land of his ancestors (Gen. 12.1f). The decisive act of redemption is the liberation of Israel from bondage in Egypt (Exod 6.6; 13.3ff and frequently). At the time of the prophets it becomes the model of eschatological redemption (Ps 78.12f; Jer 23.7f; 43.16f). In the Old Testament in particular we find two roots of the word. The term *goal* relates to family law. The *goel* is the next of kin who is responsible for redeeming for the family estate the life and property of the family which has lost its freedom. Applied to God, this title brings out the whole depth of the idea of election and covenant (cf. especially Is 41.14; 43.14; 44.24 and frequently). It is in the book of Job that God is most movingly described as redeemer: 'For I know that my Redeemer lives, and at last he will stand upon the earth' (19.25). Here Yahweh is acknowledged as guardian even beyond death of those without rights.

With the second term, *pidin*, the important thing is not blood-relationship or the person of the redeemer, but simply the payment of a ransom. Since in this case there is no 'ransomer' who is under a legal obligation, the term *pidin* is appropriate to bring out the meaning of redemption as pure act of grace. The gracious character of redemption is also expressed by the fact that Yahweh never pays a ransom: what he does is to act by his own power, as when he releases Israel from bondage in Egypt (Deut 7.8; 9.26 and elsewhere). The reference to sin however is almost completely lacking in the idea of redemption. Redemption is almost synonymous with rescue from captivity, later from distress, affliction and death. And still later the term retained the sense of hope of redemption from alien rule (cf. Lk 1.71). Its content now became that of eschatological expectation.

The New Testament was able to take it up in this sense. The most important text in this connexion is the saying about ransom in Mark 10.45 (= Mt 20.28): 'For the Son of man came not to be served but to serve, and to give his life as a ransom for many.' The saying can scarcely be traced back to Jesus. It contains many enigmas: there is no mention of the recipient of the ransom, nor are we told from what the many are ransomed; neither are we told why a ransom has to be paid at all, why God does not set men free without ransom. The saying is not however a part of dogmatic teaching on reconciliation; it becomes intelligible only in the light of the story of Jesus' death.

In the New Testatment letters the term 'redemption' occurs in set phrases (1 Tim 2.6; Tit 2.14; 1 Pet 1.18f). Paul stresses particularly redemption in Christ (Rom 3.24; cf Col 1.13f; Eph 1.7): Christ has been made our redemption by God (1 Cor 1.30). Jesus Christ then is redemption in person; redemption cannot be separated from his person and his fate. It is not something separable from Jesus and the cross. In primitive Christianity the term 'redemption' thus acquired a specific content which cannot be traced outside it. This content cannot be determined and concretized from outside. Tradition has constantly made this mistake and today there is a danger of making it again in a different way: it could be by imperceptibly assimilating the Christian view of freedom to an abstract-liberalistic attitude or − on the other hand − by drawing up a 'theology of liberation' and at the same time − as occasionally happens − more or less imperceptibly making a Marxist-inspired situation-analysis the basis of theological statements. But the meaning of Christian redemption as liberation can be clarified only by asking about the nature of Christian freedom: and that can be defined only in the light of the freedom of Jesus Christ, which reached its perfection on the cross.

If we define redemption as the freedom brought by Jesus Christ and as the freedom which is Jesus Christ himself, then we are really paraphrasing what text-book theology describes as objective redemption.

Objective redemption as distinct from subjective means salvation as existing prior to the subjective act by which we appropriate it. And salvation in fact exists in such a way that it qualifies us even before our decision and alone makes this decision possible. This basic transformation however must not be understood as if the world were changed by Jesus Christ in some kind of miraculous way and as if salvation and redemption were imposed above our heads without personal decision and without faith. For it is the new situation created by Christ which alone gives us freedom to make the decision. It removes the encumbrances of the former situation and creates a new, real opportunity. Man is no longer without an alternative. The corporeality of salvation therefore is not an argument against the personal character and freedom of the decision for salvation, but in fact makes this decision possible and provokes it.

There is another misunderstanding which must be rejected. Redemption is obviously not available as objects are; objective redemption consequently may not be understood as a kind of container or treasury of grace, from which individuals are assigned their subjective grace. Availability here too exists between persons. As original sin is conveyed through the old humanity, so redemption is conveyed through the new humanity, through those who believe in Jesus Christ and who as believers are touched by him, through the Church, which is represented symbolically by Mary under the cross (cf Jn 19.15-27).

The sense of salvation as thus mediated and of this concrete character of grace has been largely lost in the Church's tradition as a result of the controversy with Pelagianism.[14] As against a one-sided ethical understanding of grace as good example, Augustine in particular stressed the inward and spiritual nature of grace and its ontological character. Yet within the framework of a personally and intersubjectively orientated ontology the two need not be in opposition. Today, however, in the light not only of the history of ideas but of pastoral considerations, it seems to be time to see grace as concrete freedom and thus not only to revalue 'external grace' — which was undervalued in Scholasticism — but to attach a relatively higher theological value to the renewal of the Church and its congregations. The reality of redemption through Jesus Christ is conveyed and made present through concrete encounter, conversations, living communion with human beings who are touched by Jesus Christ.

More important than the question of mediation is the question of the content of redemption. It is in answering this question that doctrine of the true humanity of Jesus Christ again acquires importance for salvation. For Jesus Christ in his living personality is salvation. This means that redemption in a Christian sense must not be understood as purely inward, personal and existential; nor may it be interpreted in a purely supernatural sense as if it in no way affected the natural order. Salvation means the salvation of the one and entire human being: it is a question of the new man who is liberated from the alienations of his former existence to a new freedom, not *from* the body and *from* the world, but *in* the body and *in* the world.

The maxim 'Save your soul' and the description of the pastoral ministry of the Church as 'cure of souls' are therefore at least one-sided and can easily lead to flight in face of man's concrete needs, requirements and concerns. Pastoral ministry means care for man in his wholeness, care for the integrity and identity of human existence. Jesus Christ is salvation in his living personality, but as crucified and risen. He establishes the identity and integrity of human existence in conditions of alienation and disintegration. The way to this identity and integrity of human existence runs therefore by way of the cross and Resurrection. The solid reality and concreteness of salvation means that there is no longer any situation from which salvation and hope are excluded in principle, any state totally godless and remote from God, and which cannot become a situation open to salvation, in so far as it is grasped as such in faith. Thus, through the coming of Jesus Christ, a way and a new freedom are opened to us: a way which does not lead back simply to the restoration of man in his original state, but leads forward to a new human existence.

2. JESUS CHRIST WHOLLY HUMAN AND THE HUMAN CHARACTER OF SALVATION

Just as Scripture takes for granted the true humanity of Jesus of Nazareth, so it assumes as obvious that Jesus is wholly man. It is true that the Bible nowhere says that Jesus of Nazareth had a human mind-soul: this became a problem only in the later history of dogma. But the Bible does assume it, for otherwise it could not ascribe to Jesus mental acts and attitudes like joy and sorrow, compassion and anger, love and affection. Jesus encounters us in the gospels as someone who asks questions and is surprised, who has friends and is deeply affected by the rejection with which he is confronted. The gospels however never discuss Jesus' mental life and it is scarcely possible from the scant evidence of Scripture to write a psychology of Jesus. The numerous attempts made in this direction have either turned out to be very one-sided or have soon had to face the unusual and unique figure of a Man who eludes any psychological scrutiny.[15]

If we want to take up the discussion on the full humanity of Jesus as understood in Scripture, we cannot begin with a psychology of Jesus. The starting-point must be what Scripture says about Jesus' obedience. In Luke's gospel the first words uttered by Jesus are: 'Did you not know that I must be in my Father's house?' (2.49). Luke too gives as his last words before his death: 'Father, into thy hands I commit my spirit' (23.46). All the evangelists show Jesus, before all great decisions in his life, spending the night in prayer alone on the mountain. The gospels describe his grappling with his Father's will in the garden of Gethsemane in a particularly impressive way: 'Abba, Father, all things are possible to thee; remove this cup from me; yet not what I will, but what thou wilt' (Mk 14.36 par).

Paul uses the theme of obedience to describe the whole way of Jesus: 'he humbled himself and became obedient unto death, even death on a cross' (Phil 2.8). In this way be becomes the antitype to the disobedience of the first Adam (Rom 5.19). This theme is taken up again in the letter to the Hebrews: 'For we have not a high priest who is unable to sympathize with our weaknesses, but one who in every respect has been tempted as we are, yet without sin' (4.15). 'In the days of his flesh, he offered up prayers and supplications, with loud cries and tears, to him who was able to save him from death, and he was heard for his godly fear. Although he was a Son, he learned obedience through what he suffered; and being made perfect he became the source of eternal salvation to all who obey him' (5.7-9). Thus he is 'the pioneer and perfecter of our faith' (12.2).

According to John's gospel, Jesus Christ lives entirely to do the will of his Father and to accomplish his mission. His food is to do the will of him who sent him (4.34). Of himself he can do nothing; what the Father does, he does also (5.19); he seeks neither his own will (5.30) nor his own honour (8.50). His whole existence consists in obedience to his mission. He can therefore say: 'I and the Father are one' (10.30; cf 17.10f). This means more than a simple unity of wills. Mutual knowledge (10.15; 17.25) means also a mutual existence in one another (14.10f; 10.38; 17.21). The one existence in love reaches its completion at the time of the passion. It is love for the Father (14.31) and therein response to the Father's love (3.16; 3.35; 5.20; 10.17; 15.9, etc.). But Jesus' surrender of his life takes place, not merely through external violence, but in complete freedom: 'No one takes it from me, but I lay it down of my own accord. I have power to lay it down, and I have power to take it again' (10.18). Like Paul, John depicts Jesus' self-surrender as determined by the motive of love. Christ's self-sacrifice thus becomes a paradigm for Christian brotherly love: 'Greater love has no man than this, that a man lay down his life for his friends' (Jn 15.13). For John's revelation Jesus' love is God's love (1 Jn 3.16). Jesus' self-sacrifice is not a supreme example of human possibilities. It not only surpasses the self-sacrifice of a devout person, but is qualitatively different, since it possesses an eschatological quality: it is the self-sacrifice of Christ, the only and beloved Son.

The statements on Jesus' obedience assume that Jesus was endowed with reason and free will; they assume the existence of what the metaphysical tradition called the mind-soul. If then the later history of dogma and theology defended the mind-soul of Jesus and thus his full and uncurtailed human existence, it was because there was a soteriological problem behind the metaphysical.

The question of the full humanity of Jesus in body and soul is involved in that of the voluntariness of his obedience and thus of the human character of salvation. It is concerned with the fact that God, even in his own cause, does not act by passing over or going beyond man, but always through man and by means of his freedom. Jesus therefore is not a mere means of salvation in God's hands, but the personal mediator of salvation.

This question first became acute as a result of the anti-Docetist defensive action of the Fathers of the Church. The Incarnation of the *Logos* had to be especially emphasized. Set formulas were soon developed and used in an attempt to pin down the mystery of the persons of Christ. Among them were *pneuma-sarx, Logos-sarx*. These are found especially in the works of the Apostolic Fathers.[16]

These formulas were meant to establish the fact that the *Logos* really entered into flesh. At the same time the Fathers took it for granted that Christ had an intellectual soul. Ignatius of Antioch calls Christ *teleios anthropos.*[17] Clement[18] and Irenaeus[19] agree in stating that Christ 'offered his flesh for our flesh, his soul for our soul'. Tertullian[20] and Origen[21] too declare that Christ had a human soul. The *pneuma-sarx* and *Logos-sarx* Christology however became misleading as soon as the originally biblical meaning of *sarx* ceased to be that understood in hellenistic areas. In the Bible 'flesh' means the whole man as bodily constituted. In Greek on the other hand it was very easy to understand by 'flesh' the body as distinct from the soul or mind. Hence it was very easy to make the mistake of thinking that the *Logos* had assumed only human flesh or a human body and not a human soul.

The West largely avoided this misunderstanding, since Tertullian at an early stage replaced the ancient *pneuma-sarx* and *Logos-sarx* system by the two natures system.[22] In the East it took longer to clarify the terminology. Arius developed an extreme *Logos-sarx* Christology. According to him the *Logos* in Jesus takes the place of the human soul. The criticism of Arius by the Fathers, especially Athanasius, scarcely touches this point, but is almost exclusively concerned with the denial of the true divinity of Jesus. This confusion found expression particularly in the work of Apollinaris of Laodicea, a friend of Athanasius.[23] In contrast to Arius, he firmly maintained the divinity of Jesus Christ and — like Athanasius — wanted to bring out the close connexion between divinity and humanity. He thought however that he could maintain that unity only by making the humanity of Christ incomplete and letting the *Logos* take the place of the human soul. In his last writings however Apollinaris admitted that the *Logos* had not only assumed human flesh but also a human soul. For this reason he tried now to solve the problem of unity with the aid of the Platonic trichotomy, distinguishing between flesh (*sarx*), sensual soul (*psyche*) and mind-soul (*nous* or *pneuma*). Apollinaris now taught that the *Logos* had indeed assumed a sensual soul (*psyche*), but not a mind-soul (*pneuma*).

Apollinaris produced two arguments. The first was philosophical: two complete substances could not form a unity; therefore the humanity of Christ could not be a complete substance. The second argument was theological: if the *Logos* possessed a human soul, his sinlessness would not be assured and thus our redemption would be imperilled; for the sake of Jesus' impeccability, the *Logos* must be the actual moving principle (*hegemonikon*) in Jesus. Apollinaris therefore defended a consistent Christology 'from above': redemption comes about solely through the *Logos* who uses the human *sarx* merely as an instrument. The one mediator Jesus Christ, who is wholly on the side of God and wholly on the side of men, now becomes as Jesus a mere means in God's hands. As a friend of Athanasius, Apollinaris was also held in the highest esteem. Many of his writings circulated under a false name and anonymously exercised a great influence. This influence can be seen in the work of Cyril of Alexandria in particular, and through him in the whole Alexandrian school of theology. Cyril was one of the few Fathers who became known to the Middle Ages. He had a considerable influence, particularly on Aquinas.

Another factor became important for the development of Christology. The Germanic tribes first came to know Christianity in the form of Arianism. When they later came across the Church at large, a typically anti-Arian Christology developed: a Christology that is, which so emphasized the true divinity of Jesus Christ that the true humanity was lost to sight and Jesus himself was often distorted into a purely divine figure; Jesus Christ was seen as a God walking on earth. Jungmann has illustrated this transformation with the aid of liturgical prayer formularies. While prayer had formerly been addressed to 'Jesus Christ our Lord', it was now formulated as to 'Jesus Christ our God.'[24]

As the significance of Jesus' humanity in mediating salvation was forgotten, the intercessory salvation-mediatorship of the saints — especially Mary — became more prominent. The consequences appeared also in ecclesiology where the one-sided emphasis on the divinity of Christ meant that excessive importance was attached to the authority of the Church's ministry. The more it was forgotten that Christ is our brother, the more the fraternal dimension in the Church was ignored and the authoritative factor was stressed exclusively. These consequences were naturally most obvious in the Christology generally prevailing in the minds of ordinary Christians. Here Apollinarism has persisted even to the present time as a subliminal heresy, not as a theological slip but as a temptation to devout but ignorant Christians who are very surprised when they are told that Christ was a man like us. In connexion with the Redemption they think only of Jesus' physical pains and scarcely of his personal obedience and his complete surrender to the Father. In this respect there has evidently been a failure on the part of catechetical and homiletic instruction[25] has evidently failed in this regard.

Apollinarism is essentially a hellenization of the Christian faith. In this theory God and man form a symbiosis in Jesus Christ. The man is curtailed; God becomes a part of the world and a principle within the world. The basic idea of biblical Christology — that the coming of the reign of God in the person of Jesus Christ means both the freedom and the salvation of man — is thus misunderstood and turned into its opposite: God and man mutually delimit one another and in effect are mutually exclusive. Apollinarism anticipates though in the language of ancient philosophy, the problems of modern atheistic humanism.

Apollinarism was rejected in antiquity by various synods: by the Synod of Alexandria under the presidency of Athanasius (362), the Council of Constantinople (381) and the Roman Synod under Pope Damasus (382) (DS 159). The Council of Chalcedon (451) expressly added to the Creed of Nicaea — according to which Jesus Christ is one in being with the Father — an *homoousios hemin* (one in being with us men) and stated: 'perfect in divinity and perfect in humanity, truly God and truly man, consisting of a rational soul and a body (*ek psyches logikes kai somatos*), one in being with the Father according to the divinity and one in being with us also according to the humanity, like us in all things except sin (cf. Heb 4.15)' (DS 301). This statement was repeated by the *Quicumque* Creed (DS 76) and by the Second Council of Constantinople (553) (DS 425). The Council of Vienne (1311/1312) against Peter Olivi interpreted the Church's teaching in terms of Scholastic Aristotelianism and stressed the fact that the mind-soul is the sole substantial form of the man Jesus (DS 900).

The reasoning of the Fathers was for the most part soteriologically orientated. Only sporadically however is the view expressed that Jesus' atoning obedience presupposes an intellectual soul with free will.[26] In properly theological terms the Fathers opposed Apollinaris with the aid of a principle originally derived from Gnosticism but which Irenaeus had already turned against that system.[27] The principle was that like could only come about through like. Irenaeus therefore concluded that the redemption of the body could only come about through the body of Jesus Christ. Later the further conclusion was drawn that the redemption of the soul could come about only through the soul of Jesus Christ. Origen then formulated the principle: 'the whole man would not have been saved if HE had not assumed the whole man.'[28] In the struggle against Apollinaris, Gregory of Nazianzen provided the classic formulation of this principle, which was afterwards found in the same or in a similar form in the works of many of the Fathers: 'What is not assumed is not healed; what is united with God is also saved.[29] In Latin this important axiom runs: *Quod non est assumptum, non est sanatum.*[30] If then the *Logos* in Jesus Christ did not assume a real human mind-soul, he cannot have redeemed us in our human intellectual nature.

A more philosophico-metaphysical argument was adopted in addition to the soteriological arguments. It is used against Apollinaris' first objection that two complete substances cannot in turn form a higher unity. Against this, the Fathers – especially Origen[31] and Augustine[32] and subsequently Aquinas[33] – tried to show that Apollinaris' basic mistake lay in his conception of man's nature as a self-contained reality. Under this assumption, the union of God with a whole and complete man is obviously inconceivable. But if we start out from the fact that the human mind as such has an openness transcending everything finite, then it is not only capable of union with God, but is even the sole possible presupposition for the Incarnation of God. Since the mind alone is really open for God, a union of God with an unanimated body is in the last resort impossible. If God wills to be corporeally present in the world he cannot achieve this except by becoming a complete man, endowed with human freedom. Human freedom is the condition set by God himself for the Incarnation. This led to the famous formula: 'The Word assumed the body by the intermediary of the soul' (*verbum assumpsit corpus mediante anima.*)[34]

Apollinaris' problem is far from being settled even today. It is a basic theme of modern criticism of religion and of modern atheistic humanism that God and man are mutually exclusive. For Feuerbach, Marx, Nietzsche, Sartre, Bloch and Camus the acknowledgment of God renders human freedom impossible. For Sartre, atheism is practically a postulate of freedom.[35] Recently of course the intrinsic dialectic of this emancipatory understanding of freedom has been increasingly recognized. It is acknowledged that the modern history of freedom and revolution is in danger of degenerating into a new history of violence and oppression; that industrialization and technicalization are releasing a mechanism of conformity and infantilism on something approaching a planetary scale; that the management and technology which man invented in order to rule the world are becoming a scarcely penetrable network in which man is increasingly entangled. Man's own creations have got beyond his control and are now developing their own momentum. A secondary system of nature and fate has emerged.[36]

In this situation where the old models break down, the doctrine of the full humanity of Jesus acquires a new significance. What faces us here is not only a new model for understanding human freedom, but a new beginning in the history of freedom: the freedom of God as the reason and condition for the freedom of man, but the freedom of man as willed by God and the condition appointed for God's operation in the world. In Jesus Christ therefore it is definitely revealed, not only who God is for man, but also who man is for God. In Jesus Christ the definitive nature of God and man becomes apparent to us.

The question of the unity of divine and human freedom together with the simultaneous permanent distinction between the two will occupy us at greater length in the next chapter, when I reach the subject of Jesus Christ as mediator between God and men. In this connexion it is first of all purely a question of the model, and the possibility of a new human existence which is bestowed on us through him. Four basic features of such a human existence as determined by Jesus Christ emerge:

1. Human existence is existence in receptivity, existence owed and therefore existence in thanksgiving. Man cannot of himself get away from the essential structures of his existence. Of himself he is a torso, a fragment. In his freedom he is hunger and thirst for the unconditional, definitive and absolute. The attempt however to achieve this own fulfilment is too great a strain for him. Man can receive the fulfilment of his existence only as a gift. Grace and salvation therefore are the gift of human existence. This existence in receptivity liberates us from the intolerable burden of having to play God, and to be God ourselves. Grace means that we can be men and accept ourselves and others as men, since we ourselves are infinitely accepted as men. In this perspective, the supreme possibility and supreme realization of human existence is the Eucharist. At the same time the Eucharist is not understood merely as a sacramental celebration. The sacramental celebration of the Eucharist is the supreme concentration of what represents the basic attitude and essential character of human existence.

2. Human freedom is freedom liberated and set free. Human freedom is conditioned freedom; furthermore, it is to a large extent misspent and wasted freedom. As long as man is conditioned or even dominated by finite values and finite goods — however great — he is not truly free. Only the bond with the infinite and absolute freedom of God as the ultimate ground and meaning of man makes the latter free *from* all intramundane claims to absoluteness and thus also free *for* engagement in the world. It is therefore the bond with

God which helps man to learn to walk upright (Ernst Bloch) and, with head held high, to face all authorities in this world. God does not oppress man, but sets his creative forces free. Indebted human existence is realized in play and celebration. Only where man is not merely *homo faber*, worker, but also *homo ludens*, man at play, can he be described as genuinely human and as a free man who rises above life's immediate needs. Jesus' exhortation, not to be anxious and concerned for our life, but first to seek the kingdom of God and his justice (cf Mt 6.25-33), reveals an essential basic feature of a redeemed human existence.

3. Human freedom is perfected in obedience. As existence in receptivity, man is wholly and entirely response — response personified. He exists in the act of listening. This reception is at one and the same time supreme activity, commitment to accept demands, making oneself available, and being ready to serve. In the light of Christ human freedom does not mean despotism. Despotism is not freedom, but unfreedom: it is dependent on the whim and mood of the moment. But neither is a person free because he has as much as possible — himself, the others, and world — under his control and dominion. This unilaterally liberating understanding of freedom soon changes dialectically into its opposite. Christian freedom consists not in control, but in being available. Availability is unreserved openness and constant readiness: disposability for the call and demand which confronts the person. That person is truly free who is also free of himself so that he can be free for others. Such freedom presupposes one's own unpretentiousness; unpretentiousness in the material sense, but also a mental unpretentiousness: refaining from self-assertion, from seeking to establish oneself and one's own claims. Non-violence and powerlessness, modesty and straightforwardness, ability to criticize and ability to hear are forms of expression of humanity as Jesus lived and taught them. Later these new opportunities of a Christian humanism were recapitulated more or less systematically in the three evangelical counsels. But in effect one counsel is in question: the one opportunity of human existence which the Gospel opens up to us: human existence as availability for love.

4. Faith is itself the quintessence of man's salvation. Traditional theology regarded faith as the subjective appropriation of objectively given redemption: in this sense it is merely the condition of salvation, not the reality itself of salvation. Yet the reality of salvation as it came in Jesus Christ consists solely in the fact that in him God has entered into the human complex of fate and disaster, and in doing so has opened up a new beginning and offered an alternative. That did not happen without man being involved; but in and through the obedience of Jesus who laid himself open completely to the coming of the reign of God, and became a completely vacant and empty receptacle for God's living presence. Jesus' obedience, his availability for God and for others, is the actual way in which salvation exists in history. The new opportunity of human existence revealed by Jesus (that is, human existence in receptivity and in obedience) is also the opportunity and reality of salvation

In effect, this is a paraphrase of the biblical meaning of the term 'faith'. In the Bible, faith does not mean merely accepting something as true, but neither is it merely trust. The Old Testament designated what we call 'believing' mostly with the word *aman*: its basic meaning is 'being firm, secure, reliable.' We come across the word today in the form of the liturgical response 'Amen'. Believing means saying 'Amen' to God, holding fast to him, and taking him as our ground. Believing means allowing God to be wholly God, and that means recognizing him as the sole ground and meaning of life.

Faith is existence in receptivity and in obedience. To be able and to be permitted to believe is grace and salvation, since man finds in faith foothold and ground, meaning and goal, content and fulfilment, and is thus redeemed from the instability, aimlessness, meaninglessness and emptiness of his existence. In faith he can and may accept himself, since he is himself accepted by God. In faith we are accepted as sons of God and are destined to share in the nature and form of the one Son of God (Rom 8.29).

3. JESUS CHRIST THE MAN FOR OTHERS AND SOLIDARITY IN SALVATION

Neither for Scripture nor for the ancient East as a whole does man ever stand before God as an isolated individual. Both sin and salvation are seen clearly in their social dimension. This awareness is sustained by the idea of an all-encompassing sacral system. The individual is deeply involved in the community by reason of a common origin and a common destiny. His evil deed is always a burden on the whole people. A sinner was regarded as a common danger in a very direct and realistic sense. Therefore the worshipping community had to dissociate itself from him solemnly and demonstratively, and to break off solidarity with the wrongdoer. That was done by excommunication and cursing. Only by that kind of atonement could the people be reconciled with God. Atonement however was also possible through vicarious actions. The best-known atonement ritual was the transmission of the sins of the people by imposing hands on a goat and driving it into the desert thus burdened with the sins of all (Lev 16.20ff).[37]

A much deeper understanding of such vicarious action is found in the prophetical proclamation. Cultic reconciliation without inward conversion is described as vain and is adversely criticized. Charitable activity and patient endurance of suffering and death come to the fore as opportunities for atonement. At the time of the Maccabees the idea develops of the vicariously atoning significance of the suffering and death of a righteous man. The unjust suffering and martyrdom of the just one are satisfaction not only for his own sins, but for the sins of the others: it breaks through the network of disaster to become the sign of God's mercy.[38]

The unique climax of this theology of vicarious suffering in the Old Testament is the fourth song of the servant of God: 'He has born our sicknesses and carried our pains . . . He was wounded for our transgressions, he was bruised for our iniquities; upon him was the chastisement that made us whole, and with his stripes we are healed . . . The Lord has laid on him the iniquity of us all . . . When he makes himself an offering for sin, he shall see his offspring, he shall prolong his days; the will of the Lord shall prosper in his hand . . .' (Is 52.13-53.12). To be sure, the identity of this servant of God is disputed. Apparently there is no historical figure, neither an individual nor Israel as a whole, which fits this character. The figure becomes a pointer to someone who is to come. Judaism however never ventured to apply the statements about suffering to the expected Messiah. Only the cross made it possible to understand the Old Testament in that way.

In any case, it is disputed whether Jesus saw himself as the servant of God of Deutero-Isaiah — as, for instance, Joachin Jeremias assumes — or whether the statements about his vicarious suffering and death merely represent post-Easter proclamation. But it is possible, with Eduard Schweizer,[40] to detect an implicit idea of representation in Jesus' own approach. Jesus called for discipleship. And it is part of discipleship that he goes on ahead of us, prepares a way for us and takes us with him on this way. Discipleship means that he does something 'for us'. The call to discipleship implies the idea of representation.

The post-Easter proclamation correctly grasped the centre and meaning of Jesus' life and work when it made the 'for us' (*huper hemon*) and 'for the many' (*huper pollon*) the main theme of his history and fate and defined him as the man for others.[41] Jesus is the fellow man purely and simply.

The *huper* formulas[42] are found even in the very early strata of tradition. Even in the pre-Pauline creed of 1 Cor 15.3-5 it is said that 'Christ died for our sins'. And in the Last Supper tradition — likewise pre-Pauline — we find: 'This is my body which is given for you' (1 Cor 11.24; cf Lk 22.19); 'This is my blood of the covenant, which is poured out for many' (Mk 14.24 par). There is also the important statement by Jesus that the Son of man did not come to be served, but to serve, and to give his life 'as a ransom for many' (Mk 10.45). In these contexts *huper* has a triple meaning: (1) for our sake; (2) for our good, for our benefit; (3) in our place. All three meanings are implied and intended at one and the same time when it is a question of expressing Jesus' solidarity with us as the very centre of fhis human existence.

Paul develops and deepens this theology of representation. According to him a real exchange comes about in Christ, a reversal of standpoints in our favour: 'Though he was rich, yet for your sake he became poor, so that by his poverty you might become rich' (2 Cor 8.9). 'Who, though he was in the form of God, took the form of a servant' (Phil 2.6f). It is by his own choice therefore that Christ becomes identified with us: by identifying himself with man and taking our place, he changes the situation, our poverty is transformed into riches. This exchange Paul calls reconciliation (*katallage*). The Greek word contains the adjective *allos* (other). Reconciliation therefore means

216

becoming other. In this sense Paul says (2 Cor 5.18ff) that God has reconciled the world to himself. 'For our sake he made him to be sin who knew no sin, so that in him we might become the righteousness of God' (5.21). 'Christ died for all, that those who live might live no longer for themselves but for him who for their sake died and was raised' (5.15). Reconciliation by representation also implies a mission to vicarious existence for others. God's act of reconciliation in Christ has the effect of making us jointly determined by God's newly creating love and therefore destined for one another. This solidarity is the reality of the new creation.

The idea of the solidarity of Jesus with us is explained at length in the Letter to the Hebrews: 'Therefore he had to be made like his brethren in every respect, so that he might become merciful . . . For because he himself has suffered and been tempted, he is able to help those who are tempted' (2.17f; cf 2.14). 'We have not a high priest who is unable to sympathize (*sympathein*) with our weaknesses, but one who in every respect has been tempted as we are' (4.15). 'Who for the joy that was set before him endured the cross, despising the shame' (12.2).

The Synoptics express the same idea extremely vividly and graphically by giving an account of the hidden life at Nazareth and of the poverty of Jesus who did not know where to lay his head (cf Mt 8.20). They describe Jesus therefore as poor among the poor, as homeless, who for that reason has pity and compassion for men in their needs (Mk 6.34). They proclaim Jesus as the one who has wholly become our brother. These themes of course inspired many saints, and, in our times, people like Charles Péguy, Simone Weil and Charles de Foucauld.[43]

If we sum up all these statements of Scripture, it is possible to bring out as an essential, basic feature of Jesus' human figure, the fact that he does not find his nature in being hypostasis, self-subsistence, which the Greeks — for instance — regarded as the highest perfection; instead, it is his nature to exist for others; it is self-surrender, self-abandonment; he is the one who steps aside, who stands up for others, and identifies with others.

According to Scripture Jesus Christ is the man for other men. His nature is devotion and love. In this love for men he is the concrete form of existence of the rule of God's love for us. His fellowship with men is therefore the form of appearance (epiphany) of his divine sonship. His transcendence to his fellow man is the expression of his transcendence to God. As in relation to God he is wholly existence in receptivity (obedience), so in relation to us he is wholly existence in devotion and representation. In this dual transcendence he is mediator between God and men.

Jesus' unique yet universal position in history is founded in representation as the decisive centre of his existence. For it is through his representation that he has a universal significance as one and unique. Something occurred through him once and for all: the reconciliation of the world. This universal significance Scripture expresses by incorporating Jesus, not only into the history of his people from the time of Abraham and David, but into the history of mankind as a whole from Adam onwards (cf the two genealogies). Paul expresses it in a lapidary formula: 'born of woman, born under the law' (Gal 4.4). By his birth Christ enters into the continuity of our human race; he thus enters into mankind's history of disaster, under the curse expressed by the law. Hence, according to Philippians, Jesus does not assume human nature in the abstract, but the form of a servant, *morphe doulou*; he submits voluntarily to the powers of fate which enslave man. In that too he becomes our brother.

Jesus takes on himself our guilt-entangled history, but, through his voluntary obedience and his vicarious service, gives it a new quality and establishes a new beginning. The history of disobedience, of hatred and lying is brought to a halt in his obedience and service. Even more: in his suffering and dying on the cross, where his obedience and service reach their supreme perfection, these powers of injustice wear themselves out on him and rush to their death; since he does not respond to them, he swallows them up − so to speak − in his death. His death is the death of death, the death of injustice and lying. Jesus Christ then is not only a member of mankind, but the beginning of a new humanity. Hence Christ, according to Rom 5.12-21 and 1 Cor 15.45-47, is the new Adam, through whose obedience the disobedience of the first Adam is expiated. According to Jn 10 he is the shepherd who gathers his flock by surrendering his life for them. According to Heb 2.9-11, Jesus tasted death for everyone, in order thus to become through his suffering author of salvation, and as Son to be the ground of the sonship of the many and to make all men his brothers.

The idea of representation offers us a total view of the biblical conception of history.[44] Adam represents the totality of mankind. In him the blessing or curse of all is decided. After his fall, God chooses Israel; the election holds indirectly for all nations: in Abraham all the nations of the world are to be blessed (Gen 12.3). But even Israel as a whole does not fulfil this task, its place is taken by a holy remnant (Is 1.9; 10.21). This remnant again is reduced finally to one man: in Isaiah the servant of God who vicariously atones for the many (53.4ff), in Daniel the Son of man as representative of the people of the saints of God (7.13ff). The New Testament names this One, who has fulfilled the mission of the suffering servant of God and that of the Son of man and who thus stands for the salvation of the whole people and of all men: Jesus Christ. So the course of the history of salvation up to Christ takes the form − as indicated − of a progressive reduction: mankind − people of Israel − remnant of Israel − the One, Jesus Christ. Up to then the tendency is from plurality to unity. But after this point has been reached, the movement opens out again from unity to plurality. Jesus Christ is the first-born of many brothers (Rom 8.29; cf Col 1.15, 18; Rev 1.5), he establishes the new people of God and he is the beginning of the new humanity. Thus he recapitulates the whole previous development and at the same time opens up a new history. He is at once end, goal and recapitulation and also the beginning of a new future.

This twofold movement is most clearly described in the outline of salvation history given by Paul in Galatians 3.6-4.7. Paul starts out from the promise given to Abraham for his descendants and thence for all nations. This promise is fulfilled in Jesus as the One (3.16). By faith in him all men become descendants of Abraham (3.26). In him all have become one (3.28) and all are thus made sons and heirs (4.4-7). The new opportunity opened up by Christ also establishes reconciliation and unity among men. If all are 'one' in Christ, then it no longer counts to be Jew or Greek, slave or free, man or woman (Gal 3.28; Col 3.11). In Christ the primeval rift in mankind is healed again, and the hostility between Jews and Gentiles is removed. He has reconciled both 'in one body, in his person bringing the hostility to an end'. He is our peace (Eph 2.13ff). Through him and in his person God has established the universal Shalom promised already in the Old Testament, the reconciliation of all nations. *Shalom (peace) is therefore the embodiment of that salvation which was promised in the Old Testament and which, according to the New Testament, has come through Christ.*[45]

The creed of Nicaea took up the biblical *huper*-formulas with the statement: *qui propter nos homines et propter nostram salutem descendit de caelis* (DS 125). That provides the heading for the whole life and work of Christ: 'for us men and for our salvation.'

The early Church had to defend the solidarity of Jesus Christ with the whole human race, especially against Valentinian Gnosticism and with reference to some Apollinarists who asserted that Christ possessed a heavenly (pneumatic) body, not derived from the totality of the human race, but directly created by God. The Apostles' Creed stated that he was 'born of the Virgin Mary' in order to oppose these views by firmly maintaining Jesus' racial unity with the rest of mankind.

The same idea is found in the Athanasian Creed: 'He is God as born before time from the substance of the Father, and he is man as born in time from the substance of his mother' (DS 76). Similarly, the Council of Chalcedon declared: '. . . from the Virgin Mary, Mother of God, according to the humanity' (DS 301). The Valentinian heresy was again expressly condemned at the Council of Florence in the Decree for the Jacobites (DS 1341). The article of faith on the birth of Jesus from Mary the virgin therefore is not a 'Gnostic discovery', but an anti-Gnostic statement which is intended to bring out Jesus' racial unity with us.[46]

The idea of representation was made into a theme of theological tradition, especially from the standpoint of 'satisfaction'. The satisfaction theory was elaborated explicitly for the first time by Anselm of Canterbury in his work, *Cur Deus Homo.*[47] Anselm starts out from the order of the universe. This intelligible universal order is disturbed by sin, with the result that man is abandoned to futility. This disturbance must be offset, and that means making satisfaction. If God were to compensate for the disturbance out of sheer mercy, that would be contrary to justice. The principle must be: either satisfaction or penalty.[48] God then must demand compensation, satisfaction, from man. But that demand breaks down when it comes to man. For sin is directed against the infinite God and therefore is itself infinite. Anselm clarifies this sequence of thought mainly with the notion of God's honour. Man was created for obedience, for service, and for devotion to God. By sin he has evaded that goal. But the offence is measured by the greatness of the person offended. God's honour is infinite and so also therefore is man's guilt. An infinite satisfaction is necessary, but finite man cannot render it.

We must conclude that man is obliged to restitution, but only God can make it. Only one person can produce the satisfaction which restores the order of the universe and the honour of God: someone who is both God and man, the God-man. This answers the question, *Cur Deus Homo?*, 'Why did God become man?' But it still does not answer the question of why God had to go so far as to the cross in order to redeem us. Anselm therefore starts out again from the fact that Jesus' life of obedience is not sufficient for redemption since man simply as creature is already bound to obedience. Satisfaction can be made only by doing something which Jesus as man is not otherwise bound to do. That is his death, for as sinless he is not subject to the fate of death. Since Jesus himself had no need of that satisfaction, God can credit it as merit to all others. The deficit in the account of all the others is compensated by the surplus available in Christ. Through his voluntary death, therefore, Jesus has again 'adjusted' the disturbed order of the universe and has made satisfaction for all.

Anselm's satisfaction theory created a precedent. But Aquinas corrected and qualified it.[49] In particular, he turned into a pure suitability what Anselm intended as a proof that God *had* to act in that way. The freedom of God's love is better safeguarded in that way. In this Thomistic form, Anselm's satisfaction theory became the common property of the theology of the schools.[50] Although it represents one of the classical theologoumena, it was never made into a dogma.

Anselm's satisfaction theory can be understood only against the background of the Germanic and early medieval feudal system.[51] The letter consists in the mutual bond of loyalty between feudal lord and vassal. The vassal receives fief and protection from the lord and thus a share in public power; the lord receives from the vassal the pledge of allegiance and service. Acknowledgment of the lord's honour is therefore the basis of order, peace, freedom and law. That honour is not the lord's personal honour, but his social status by which he is the guarantor of the public peace. Infringement of that honour means lawlessness, discord, unfreedom, and chaos. The demand for the restoration of that honour therefore does not mean personal satisfaction for the lord, but the restoration of the order of the whole. Anselm accordingly distinguishes between God's honour 'as it affects himself' and God's honour 'as far as it concerns the creature'.[52] From the first standpoint nothing can be added to it and nothing taken away. But if man no longer acknowledges God, the order of justice in the world is destroyed.

The infringement of God's honour is not a question of God, but of man, of the order and beauty of the world. It is not God's personal honour which has to be restored, but the disfigured and out-of-joint world, which is in order only as long as it upholds the honour of God. It is not a question of restoring the honour of a jealous God; nor that of an abstract legal system and of accounts that have to be balanced. In the acknowledgement and restoration of God's honour we are concerned with freedom, peace, order and the fulfilment of the meaning of the world. But, since God freely created man and since he wants to be freely acknowledged by his creature, he simply cannot secure this restoration out of pure love – so to speak – without involving man. By binding himself to the order of justice, God safeguards the honour due to man, respects man's freedom, and keeps faith with his creation. God's self-binding to the order of justice is the expression of his fidelity as Creator.

If we consider Anselm's satisfaction theory in this perspective, it accords completely with biblical thought and imagery. According to Scripture, God's righteousness[53] in the covenant opens up a living-space for man where he can be not only the recipient of divine goodness but God's free partner. By acknowledging God as Lord, man is granted life; God's rule is the ground of man's freedom. The disobedience of sin on the other hand produces disorder, discord and death. Because Jesus Christ in free obedience takes on himself that death caused by sin and thus acknowledges God as God also in his righteousness, the New Covenant is established and peace and freedom again become possible in the world. By taking our place Jesus Christ does not replace our action – representation is not substitution[54] – but makes it possible, by liberating us for discipleship in the obedience of faith and for the service of love.

In modern times Anselm's theory has come to be less understood and increasingly rejected. Behind this attitude is the disintegration of the medieval 'order' and the rise of modern individualism. Even the nominalists, already imbued with this individualistic mentality, could only use the legal concept of 'imputation' to answer the question how the merits of Jesus Christ could benefit us. They said that God simply imputes his merits to us. The concept of forensic imputation became the standard, particularly for Protestant orthodoxy. With the rise of the Enlightenment such transference of guilt and merit began to seem inconceivable and even immoral. Hugo Grotius' attempt to find a middle way was disastrous. He said that God wanted to punish his innocent son as an example.[55] In this form the satisfaction theory is quite intolerable. Liberal theology criticized mainly what it regarded as the idea of juridical equivalence in Anselm's theory; Adolf von Harnack and Albert Ritschl opted all the more for Abelard's theory of redemption which, they thought, was more ethical in character.[56] It would however be an over-simplification to assume that the Enlightenment and Liberalism had *merely* rejected a misunderstood and distorted theory of satisfaction. Their individualistic image of man in principle allowed no understanding of the idea of representation.

The idea of solidarity in salvation and disaster was thus lost. Not only in the Enlightenment and Liberalism, but in the ordinary piety of the Churches, an individualistic view of salvation, the notion of redemption as a private affair, became increasingly widespread. 'Save your soul' was the slogan used for missions to the people. But how can you save your own soul and not save the soul and even the body of the other person?

Where the representation idea is alive, as in the Sacred Heart devotion or in Marian piety, and especially in the movements which began with Lourdes and Fatima, and where vicarious prayer and sacrifice still play a part, the great biblical and patristic idea is present in a devotionally depreciated form. But is this development of one of the most important basic Christian ideas the form appropriate to the present situation? Perhaps — in view of the increasing growth of the unity of mankind and of the increasing awareness of solidarity — we ought to reflect again on the profundity of the Christian idea of representation. It seems that we now have the opportunity of stating and realizing afresh a basic Christian truth. For the future of faith much will depend on whether the biblical idea of representation and the modern idea of solidarity are successfully combined.

The idea of representation seems strange to the modern way of thinking mainly because the starting-point of modern thought is the autonomy of the person. This means that man is self-contained, self-controlled; he is responsible for himself and no one can deprive him of his responsibility. Hegel criticized the abstractness of the standpoint and opposed it with the notion of a concrete freedom.[57] Marx's criticism was even more effective: 'Man' as such is an abstract being; in actual life, 'man' exists only as a complex of social relationships.[58] At the end of the modern era then, we have a metacriticism of modern criticism. Whereas the modern age at first criticized all existing institutions in the name of freedom, we are now reflecting again on the conditions of freedom. We ask: How is freedom possible in real life? At the same time we have come to realize that the other and the others represent not only a limitation of freedom, but its condition. The realization of freedom presupposes a joint order of freedom.

This thesis can be justified in a variety of ways. Everyday experience confirms the fact that human existence can develop in a human way only in an atmosphere of acceptance, in love and trust.[59] Human language especially shows that human subjectivity exists only in intersubjectivity, in men's existence with one another, as orientated to one another and for one another. This I—Thou relationship cannot however be played off against objective relationships as between things. Actual freedom depends on economic, legal and political conditions; it is possible only when others respect our sphere of freedom. The freedom of the individual therefore presupposes an order of freedom. The freedom of the individual is the freedom of all; and the freedom of all of course presupposes that the freedom of each individual is respected. Each one helps to sustain the freedom of the other, and conversely each is sustained by all the others. Representation is an essential element of real-life freedom. Representation understood in this way is not substitution. The substitute renders the person replaced superflous, whereas the representative gives him scope, keeps his place open and vacates the place again. Representation therefore takes nothing away from the other: on the contrary it alone makes possible the other's freedom. Solidarity means giving the individual his own scope. It even means protecting and defending him. But it also implies that the individual is expected to commit himself in the same way for the others. The solidarity of all and the responsibility of each individual are mutually inclusive. As long as unfreedom, injustice and discord prevail anywhere in the world, our freedom too is insecure and incomplete. Freedom is really possible only in solidarity, in being free for others.

The foregoing can be made more actual with an example: the phenomenon of death, for it is in a man's death before all else that something happens vicariously for others. We know (not least as a result of Heidegger's analyses)[60] that death does not merely represent the last moment in man's life, but even casts its shadow in advance: in the constant menace of death, in sickness and in daily leave-takings. Death qualifies the whole life of man as finite, limited, transitory life. It is in the light of the phenomenon of death therefore that man first truly becomes aware of himself. There he experiences himself as a mortal man, as existence for death. Death has an hermeneutical function for man. But no one experiences his own death. It confronts us always as someone else's death: the death of parents, of a friend, of wife or husband, sister or brother, and so on. But in the death of others we encounter something of ourselves, and we become aware of our own fate, our own having to die. That is why another's death can move us so deeply and affect us existentially. In the other's death we become aware of what our life is: existence as given, outside our control. In the other's death our life is given us anew. In death something happens vicariously for others. No one dies only for himself, but always for others too.

Up to now my analyses have been abstract. They have been concerned with solidarity and representation as man's basic structure. But in real life the joint involvement of all men is the basis of a universal complex of disaster. This situation of disaster consists in the fact that in practice men do not accept one another as men and do not grant one another living space, but cut themselves off from and use one another as means to secure their own existence. Order is imposed, not by human solidarity, but by selfishness and self-interest. When human beings use each other like that as means, as commodities, as man-power and numbers, then anonymous factors like money, power, personal or national prestige become ultimate values to which man is subordinated as a means, and on which in the last resort he is dependent. Since the time of Hegel and Marx particularly this reversal of the relationship between person and thing has been described by what was originally an economic-legal term: 'alienation'.[61] This concept expresses the fact that men become strangers to one another under conditions which, as anonymous objective factors, themselves gain power over men. Joint involvement helps decide a situation in which we have always been 'sold' to 'powers' and authorities', so that we no longer belong to ourselves (cf Rom 7.15-24).

Against this background, the article of faith about the expiatory character of, and the significance for salvation of Jesus' vicarious death becomes more intelligible. It is not a mythological statement which has become absolutely unrealizable for us today. It is an article of faith which can find support in anthropological and sociological data, even though it cannot be deduced from them. Anthropological considerations cannot provide more than aids to understanding. They do however hint at the direction in which we must transcend them. Firstly, human personality involves something absolute and represents a value in itself, in virtue of which man can never be a means, but always an end.[62] The unconditional acceptance of man as man breaks down however at man's finiteness. Absolute solidarity among men is possible only in God, only as realization of and participation in God's unconditional love for every human being. Secondly, assuming our present solidarity in disaster, which no individual can evade, this absolute solidarity in God's love is possible only if an underivably new beginning is set up in history. Theological mediation for its own part must also be an historical mediation. Only when God becomes man and as such is absolutely the man for others, is the ground prepared for the opportunity of a new existence and a new solidarity among men, and for peace and reconciliation in the world. Mediation among men is possible only through the one mediator between God and men (cf 1 Tim 2.5).

The necessity of a theo-logical foundation of solidarity among men becomes particularly clear if we do not merely look hopefully for a future realm of freedom, justice and peace, but remember the past generations and incorporate them into our solidarity. Without solidarity with the dead and with their mute suffering, any solidarity among men and any faith in redemption would not only be incomplete but would remain abstract. In the last resort, it would be hollow. If the sufferers of the past remained unconsoled and the wrong done to them were unatoned, the murderer would triumph at the end over his victim. Then the right of the stronger would finally count in history and history would be purely a history of the victors. A solidarity restricted to the present and the future would be a further wrong done to the victims of the past. In the end they would be the waste-products of history. Yet no man can call back the dead and make good the sufferings of the past. That is possible only for God, who is Lord over life and death. He can see that justice is done even to the dead, if he himself enters into the realm of death, identifying with the dead, in order in that way — since in fact death cannot hold him — to burst through the bonds of death and break its power. In this connexion the meaning of *descensus ad inferos* (or *inferna*), 'descent into the realm of death' in the Creed becomes intelligible in theological terms.[63] This theme, attested by Scripture (especially 1 Pet 3.18ff), the Apostles' Creed (DS 16; 27ff; 76 etc.) and the Church's dogma (DS 801; 852; 1077), is not an obsolete *mythologem*, although it makes use of secondary sources of mythical imagery. It is a question of an essential element of faith in the salutary significance of the death and Resurrection of Jesus Christ. That does not mean that we are dealing here with a new salvation-event properly so called, added to death and Resurrection. The real meaning is that Jesus *in* his death and *through* his Resurrection *truly* enters into solidarity with the dead and thus establishes *true* solidarity among men even beyond death. It is a question of finally rendering death powerless through life in God and of the universal and final victory of God's justice in history.

Finally, this Christian understanding of representation and solidarity must be distinguished from two other attempts, at present very effective and influential, to establish solidarity and peace among men. The Christian idea of representation and the idea based on this of a universal solidarity are distinct from that system of exchange which Hegel and Marx analyze as identified with bourgeois society and the capitalist system.[64] The *admirabile commercium* of the Christian doctrine of redemption is here deprived, not only of its theological, but of its personal character and reduced to a problem of distribution of goods; men are subjected to the objective pressures of material things. In Marxism there is a political counterpart to this technological concept. The fundamental principle is that there must be a 'restoration of the human world, of relationships.'[65] Hence the recognition of man does not come about indirectly through a mediator.[66] Emancipation from religion is seen as the condition of all other emancipations. But the decisive question must be: How is such emancipation possible? The individual evidently cannot bring about this emancipation, for he is subject to the universal conditions of unfreedom. A basic new beginning is therefore necessary. But the group, class, society or the nation as a whole, is equally incapable of bringing about emancipation, for such action can lead only to a new oppression of the individual. For solidarity presupposes reciprocity. 'One for all' means something only if 'all for one' also counts, if — that is — the absolute value and dignity of each individual in society is safeguarded. Society then cannot establish man's dignity but only recognize it and provide for its concrete realization. Unconditional recognition and acceptance of every human being is in effect possible only through God. Only when the love of God for man becomes an event in history, can a new beginning be made in history. Only through the historical solidarity of God in the God-man, Jesus Christ, can solidarity be established among men.

The solidarity of God with men manifested and realized in Jesus Christ establishes a new solidarity among men. The Christian idea of representation then assigns to Christians and to the Churches the world as the place of their service and binds them to co-operate in a new order of peace in freedom sustained by the idea of solidarity. Then Christian love, realizing the love of God and thus accepting every man unconditionally, also becomes an absolute commitment to justice for everyone.

Anselm's question, 'Why did God become man?', arises again. We can give an answer similar to that of Anselm. The order of the universe (peace and reconciliation among men) is possible only if God himself becomes man, the man for others, and so establishes the beginning of a new human solidarity. Obviously that does not mean that the Incarnation is logically necessary in the sense that it could be deduced from first principles. The situation is precisely the opposite. Principles like those of peace, freedom and justice are worked out from the very beginning with reference to Christ as the grammar in which and through which God's love is to be directly and underivably expressed and realized. Christian faith is always thrown back on Jesus Christ, the mediator between God and men, and therefore of men and one another.

Notes

[1] For this reason the thesis that there is a danger of Docetism in the fourth gospel seems scarcely credible. It was maintained by F.C. Bauer and has recently been renewed by E. Käsemann in *Jesu letzter Wille nach Johannes 17* (Tübingen, 1966), esp. pp.51f. Cf. R. Schnackenburg, *Johannesevangelium*, I. pp.234f; E.T.: *The Gospel according to St John* Vol.I. (London, 1968), pp.267-8.

[2] E. Schweizer, F. Baumgartl, R. Meyer, art. *'sarx'* in: TW VII, pp. 98-151.

[3] Cf F. Colpe, E. Haenchen, G. Kreschmer, art. 'Gnosis' in: RGG II, pp. 1648-1661 (bibliography); R. Haardt, art. 'Gnosis' in SM II, pp.476-86 (bibliography); W. Bauer, *Rechtgläubigkeit und Ketzerei im ältesten Christentum* (Tübingen, 1934); W. Bousset, *Hauptprobleme der Gnosis* (Göttingen, 1973); R. Bultmann, art. *'ginosko'* in TW I, pp. 688-719; idem, *Das Urchristentum im Rahmen der antiken Religionen* 2nd ed., (Zurich, 1954); ET: *Primitive Christianity in its Contemporary Setting* (London, 1960), C. Colpe, *Die religionsgeschichtliche Schule. Darstellung und Kritik ihres Bildes vom gnostischen Erlösermythus* (Göttingen, 1961); R. Haardt, *Die Gnosis, Wesen und Zeugnisse* (Salzburg, 1967), E. Haenchen, 'Gab es eine urchristlische Gnosis' in, idem, *Gott und Mensch* (Tübingen, 1965), pp.265-98; H. Jonas, *Gnosis und spätantiker Geist*, Vol.I, *Die mythologische Gnosis. Mit einer Einleitung zur Geschichte und Methodologie der Forschung* 3rd ed., Göttingen, 1964); Vol.II/1, *Von der Mythologie zur mystischen Philosophie* (Göttingen, 1954); G. Quispel, *Gnosis als Weltreligion* (Zürich, 1951); H. Raschke, *Das Christusmysterium. Wiedergeburt des Christentums aus dem Geist der Gnosis* (Bremen, 1954); R. Reitzenstein, *Die hellenistischen Mysterienreligionen. Nach*

ihren Grundgedanken und Wirkungen (Darmstadt,1956); *idem, Das iranische Erlösungs-mysterium* (Bonn, 1971); L. Schottroff, *Der Glaube*ⁿde *und die feindliche Welt. Beobachtungen zum gnostischen Dualismus und seine Bedeutung für Paulus und das Johannesevangelium* (Neukirchen, 1970); R. McLachlan Wilson, *Gnosis and the New Testament* (Oxford, 1968).

[4]Cf A. Grillmeier, art. 'Doketismus' in LTK III, pp.470f; R. Schnackenburg, *Johannesbriefe* 2nd ed., (Freiburg, 1963), pp.15-20, 24f.

[5]See especially W. Schmithals, *Die Gnosis in Korinth, Eine Untersuchung zu den Korintherbriefen* (3rd ed., Göttingen, 1969); ET: *Gnosticism in Corinth* (Nashville, 1971).

[6]Cf G. Bornkamm, 'Die Häresie des Kolosserbriefes' in: ThLZ 73 (1948), 11-20.

[7]R. Schnackenburg rightly doubts whether this was already a question of Docetism in the later sense. Cf R. Schnackenburg, *Johannesbriefe*, pp. 20ff.

[8]Irenaeus, *Adversus haereses* V,*praef.* (ed., W.W. Harvey II, 314).

[9]Cf F.P. Fiorenza, J.B. Metz, 'Der Mensch als Einheit von Leib und Seele', in: MS II, pp.584-636; J.B. Metz, art. 'Leiblichkeit' in: HThG II, pp.30-37; W. Maier, *Das Problem der Leiblichkeit bei Jean-Paul Sartre und Maurice Merleau-Ponty* (Tübingen, 1964); W. Pannenberg, *Was ist der Mensch? Die Anthropologie der Gegenwart im Lichte der Theologie* (Göttingen, 1964); K. Rahner, A. Görres, *Der Leib und das Heil* (Mainz, 1967); K. Rahner, 'Die ewige Bedeutung der Menschheit Jesu für unser Gottes-verhältnis' in *Schriften* III, pp.47-60; ET: 'The eternal significance of the humanity of Jesus for our relationship with God' in: *Theological Investigations*, vol.III, 1967, pp.35-46; G.Siewerth, *Der Mensch und sein Leib* (Einsiedeln, 1953); M. Theunissen, *Der Andere, Studien zur Sozialontologie der Gegenwart* (Berlin, 1965); W. Welte, 'Die Leiblichkeit des Menschen als Hinweis auf das christliche Heil'; *idem, Auf der Spur des Ewigen,* pp.83-112.

[10]Cardinal J.G. Saliège, quoted in J. Ratzinger, 'Gratia praesupponit naturam' *loc. cit.,* pp.178f.

[11]G. Quell, G. Bertram, G. Stählin, W. Grundmann, art., *'hamartano'* in TW I, 267-320.

[12]It is impossible to comment in detail here on the many-sided discussion on original sin. Cf U. Baumann. *Erbsünde? Ihr traditionelles Verständnis in der Krise heutiger Theologie* (Freiburg, 1970); J. Gross, *Geschichte des Erbsündendogmas. Ein Beitrag zur Geschichte des Problems vom Ursprung des Übels,* 4 vols (Munich, Basle, 1960-1972); H. Rondet, *Problèmes pour la réflexion chrétienne. Le péché originel, l'enfer et autres études* (Paris, 1946); P. Schoonenberg, *De Macht der Zonde* ('s-Hertogenbosch, 1962); ET: *Man and Sin* (London, 1965); the same author, 'Der Mensch in der Sünde' in MS II, pp.845-941 (bibliography); K.H. Weger, 'Theologie der Erbsünde', with an excursus by Karl Rahner, 'Erbsünde und Monogenismus', (QD Vol.44) (Freiburg, 1970); H. Haag, 'Biblische Schöpfungslehre und kirchliche Erbsündenlehre' (*Stuttgarter Bibelstudien* 10) (Stuttgart, 1966); M. Flick, Z. Alszeghy, *Il peccato originale* (Brescia, 1972); Z. Alszeghy, M. Flick, 'Il peccato originale in prospettiva evaluzionistica' in: Gr 47 (1966), pp.202-25; A. Vanneste, 'Le Décret du Concile de Trente sur le péché originel' in: NRTh 87 (1965), pp.688-726; *idem,* La Préhistoire du Décret du Concile de Trente sur le péché originel' in: NRTh 86 (1964), pp.355-69, 490-510; 'La Theologie du péché originel' in: *Rev. du Clergé Afric.,* Sept. 1967, pp.492-513; L. Scheffczyk, art. 'Erbschuld' in: HThG I, pp293-303.

[13]Cf J. Gewiess, F. Lakner, A. Grillmeier, art. 'Erlösung' in LTK III, 1016 to 1030; O. Procksch/F. Büschel, art. *'luo'* in TW IV, pp. 329-59.

[14]Cf G. Greshake, *Gnade als konkrete Freiheit. Eine Untersuchung zur Gnadenlehre des Pelagius* (Mainz, 1972).

[15]Cf J. Ternus, 'Das Seelenleben und Bewusstseinsleben Jesu. Problemgeschichtlich-systematische Untersuchung' in: *Das Konzil von Chalkedon,* Vol. 3, pp.81-237.

[16]Cf Barn V, II *(Patrum apostolicorum opera,* Fasc. I. ed., O de Gebhardt, A. Harnack, T. Zahn (Leipzig, 1875), p.20); 2. Clem 9.5 *(The Apostolic Fathers* I/II, ed,

J.B. Lightfoot (London, 1980), p.230); Ignatius of Antioch, Ephesians VII, 2 (Lightfoot, II/II/1, pp.47f); Polycarp VII, 1 (Lightfoot, II/II/2, p.918).

[17] Ignatius of Antioch, Smyrn IV, 2 (Lightfoot, II/II/1, pp.298ff).

[18] 1 Clem. 49,6 (Lightfoot, I/II, p.149)

[19] Irenaeus, *Adversus haereses* V, 1, 2 (W.W. Harvey II, p.325).

[20] Cf Tertullian, *De carne Christi* X (PL 2, pp.817f).

[21] Cf Origen, *De principiis* II, 6,5 (GCS 22, p.144).

[22] Cf Tertullian, *Adversus Praxeam* XXVII (PL 2, 213-6); *idem, De carne Christi* XIII (PL 2, 821f).

[23] Cf H. de Riedmatten, art. 'Apollinaris der Jüngere in: *LTK* I, p.714, and 'Apollinarismus' in: *LTK* I, pp.716f; A Grillmeier, 'Die theologische und sprachliche Vorbereitung der christologischen Formel von Chalkedon' *op. cit.*, especially pp.102 to

[24] Cf J.A. Jungmann, *Die Stellung Christi im liturgischen Gebet* (2nd ed., Münster, 1962), especially pp.151ff.

[25] Cf F.X. Arnold, *Seelsorge aus der Mitte der Heilsgeschichte. Pastoraltheologische Durchblicke* (Freiburg, 1956), pp.28-51.

[26] Cf Gregory of Nyssa, *Adversus Apollinaerem* XXI, XLI (PG 45 1163ff, 1217ff.)

[27] Cf Irenaeus, *Adversus haereses* V, 14, 1f (W.W. Harvey II, p.360); Tertullian, *De carne Christi* X (*loc. cit.,*); *idem, Adversus Marcionem* II, 27 (PL 2, pp.343ff).

[28] Origen, *Conversation with Heracleides* VII, p.5. (*Sources chrétiennes*, Vol. 67, p.70).

[29] Gregory of Nazianzen,*Epistola* CXXXVII, 3, 11 (PL 11, p.520); Epistola CXL, 4,12 (PL 11, 543); *De fide et symbolo* IV, 10 (CSEL 41, pp.13f).

[33] Cf Thomas Aquinas, *Summa Theologie* III, q.4 a.1; *Summa contra Gentiles* IV,pp.32-3.

[34] Cf John Damascene, *De fide orthodoxa* III, 6 (PG 94, 1001-1008); Augustine, *Epistola* CXXXVII, 8 (PL 33, p.519) and *De agone Christiano* XVIII (CSEL 41, pp.120f) Aquinas, *Super III lib. Sentarium*, d.2, q.2, a.1 and *Summa Theologiae* III, q.6, 1.a Origen has a very distinctive theology of the human soul of Christ; cf A. Grillmeier, 'Die theologische und sprachliche Vorbereitung der christologischen Formel von Chalkedon', *op.cit.*, pp.63-6; P. Smulders, 'Dogmengeschichtliche und lehramtliche Entfalting der Christologie', *op.cit.*, especially 418-22; cf also Chapter III/I.

[35] Cf J.P. Sartre, *L'existentialisme est un humanisme* (Paris, 1946); ET: *Existentialism and Humanism* (London, 1948).

[36] Cf M. Horkheimer and T.W. Adorno, *Dialektik der Aufklärung. Philosophische Fragmente* (Frankfurt am Main, 1969); ET: *Dialectic of Enlightenment* (New York and London, 1971-2).

[37] Cf G.von Rad, *Theologie des Alten Testaments*, Vol.I, pp.263ff; ET: *Old Testament Theologie* (Edinburgh-London, 1962), pp.262ff; W. Eichrodt, *Theologie des Alten Testaments* Vol.I, (6th ed., Stuttgart-Göttingen, 1959), pp.55f; ET: *Theology of the Old Testament* Vol.I, (London, 1961), pp.164-5).

[38] Cf J. Jeremias, *Neutestamentliche Theologie* I, pp.272ff; *idem, Pais '(theou)'* in the New Testament' in his *Abba*, pp.191-216; 'Das Lösegeld für Viele (Mk 10.45),' *ibid.*, pp.216-29.

[40] Cf E. Schweizer, *Erniedrigung und Erhöhung*, pp.7ff.

[41] This formula goes back to D. Bonhoeffer, *Widerstand und Ergebung* (Tübingen, 1900), pp.259; ET: *Letters and Papers from Prison* (enlarged edition, London, 1967), p.381.

[42] Cf H. Riesenfeld, art. *'huper'* in TW VII, pp.510-8; F. Hahn, *Hoheitstitel*, pp. 46-66; E. Schweizer, *Erniedrigung und Erhöhung*, pp.72-5; K.H. Schelkle, *Die Passion Jesu*, pp.131ff.

[43] Cf H.Urs. von Balthasar, *Die Gottesfrage des heutigen Menschen* (Vienna-Munich, 1956), pp.174-223.

[44] Cf. O. Cullmann, *Christus und die Zeit. Die urchristliche Zeit- und Geschichtsauffassung* (2nd ed., Zollikon-Zürich, 1948), pp.99-103.

[45] Cf W. Foerster, G.von Rad, art. *'Eirene'* in TW II, pp.398-418; H. Gross, *Die Idee des ewigen und allgemeinen Weltfriedens im Alten Orient und im Alten Testament* (Trier,

1956); W. Kasper, K. Lehmann, *Die Heilssendung der Kirche in der Gegenwart (Pastorale,* Vol.I) Mainz, 1970), pp.28-34.

[46] Cf H.F.von Campenhausen, *Die Jungfrauengeburt in der Theologie der alten Kirche* (Heidelberg, 1962).

[47] Cf J. McIntyre, *St Anselm and his Critics* (Edinburgh-London, 1954); H.Urs von Balthasar, *Herrlichkeit,* Vol II. (Einsiedeln, 1962), pp.217-63; F. Hammer, *Genugtuung und Heil* (Vienna, 1967); R. Haubst, 'Anselms Satisfaktions-lehre einst und heute', in *TThZ* 80 (1971), pp. 88-109 (bibliography); H. Kessler, *Die Heilsbedeutung des Todes Jesu,* pp.83-165; G. Greshake, 'Erlösung und Freiheit. Zur Neuinterpretation der Erlösungslehre Anselms von Canterbury' in *ThQ* 153 (1973), pp.323-45 (bibliography).

[48] Anselm of Canterbury, *Cur Deus homo* I, Chapter XV (ed. F.S. Schmitt [Munich, 1956]pp.48f) and elsewhere.

[49] Aquinas, *Summa theologiae* III, q.1 a.2; on the interpretation, cf H. Kessler, *Die Heilsbedeutung des Todes Jesu,* pp.167-226.

[50] On the different forms of the theory, cf F. Lakner, art. 'Satisfaktionstheorien' in: *LTK* IX, pp.341-3; on the historical development cf. J. Rivière, *Le dogme de la Rédemption. Essai d'étude historique* (Paris, 1950); *idem, Le dogme de la Rédemption au début du Moyen Age* (Paris, 1943).

[51] The following interpretation is largely based on G. Greshake, *Erlösung und Freiheit, loc.cit.*

[52] Anselm of Canterbury, *Cur Deus homo* I, Chapter XIV f (ed. F.S. Schmitt, pp.46ff).

[53] Cf E. Käsemann, 'Gottesgerechtigkeit bei Paulus' in: *idem, Exegetische Versuche und Besinningen,* II, pp. 181-93; ET: ' "The Righteousness of God" in Paul' in:*New Testament Questions of Today* (London, 1969), pp.168-82; P. Stuhlmacher, *Gerechtigkeit Gottes bei Paulus* (2nd ed., Göttingen, 1966).

[54] Cf the analyses of Dorothee Sölle, *Stellvertretung. Ein Kapital Theologie nach dem 'Tode Gottes'* (4th ed., Stuttgart, 1967); *idem, Leiden* (Stuttgart, 1973).

[55] Cf F.C. Baur's still indispensable presentation in *Die christliche Lehre von der Versöhnung in ihrer geschichtlichen Entwicklung von der ältesten Zeit bis auf die neueste* (Tübingen, 1838).

[56] Adolf von Harnack, *Lehrbuch der Dogmengeschichte,* Vol.III ('Die Entwicklung des kirchlichen Dogmas') (5th ed., Tübingen, 1932), pp.403-11; ET; *History of Dogma,* Vol.VI (London-Edinburgh, 1899), pp.54-83; A. Ritschl, *Die christliche Lehre von der Rechtfertigung und Versöhnung,* Vol I (Bonn, 1963), pp. 31-45. Similar criticism can be found in the recent work of such Catholic authors as J. Ratzinger, *Einführung in das Christentum. Vorlesungen über das Apostolische Glaubensbekenntnis* [Munich, 1968], pp. 186ff; ET: *Introduction to Christianity* [London, 1969], pp.172 ff), and H. Kessler, *Die Heilsbedeutung,* pp.153ff). See also R. Haubst, *Anselms Satisfaktionslehre, loc.cit.*

[57] Cf G.W.F. Hegel, *Grundlinien der Philosophie des Rechts* (ed. J. Hoffmeister) (4th ed., Hamburg, 1955), 4-32 etc.; ET: *Hegel's Philosophy of Right* (Oxford, 1952), pp.21-48.

[58] Marx, *Thesen über Feuerbach (Theses on Feuerbach)* in W II, Darmstadt, 1971, pp.2f.

[59] Cf. R. Affemann, 'Sunde und Erlösung in tiefenpsychologischer Sicht' in: L.Scheffczyk (ed), *Erlösung und Emanzipation* (QD, Vol.61) (Freiburg, 1973), pp.15-29.

[60] Cf M. Heidegger, *Sein und Zeit* (9th ed., Tübingen, 1960), pp.235ff; ET: *Being and Time* (London, 1962), pp.237ff.

[61] Cf E. Ritz, art *'Entfremdung'* in: *Historisches Wörterbuch der Philosophie* II, pp.509-25; for the theological application, cf especially P. Tillich, *Entfremdung und Versöhnung im modernen Denken* in the same author's W IV (Stuttgart, 1961), pp.183-99.

[62] Cf especially Immanuel Kant, *Grundlegung zur Metaphysik der Sitten,* BA 64-66 in W IV (ed. W. Weischedel), (Darmstadt, 1956), pp.59-61.

[63] Of the extensive literature, cf A. Grillmeier, 'Der Gottessohn im Totenreich' in *ZkTh* 71 (1949), pp.1-53, 184-203; *idem,* art. 'Höllenabsteig Christi' in *LTK* V, pp.450-5; K.H. Schelkle, *Die Petrusbriefe. Der Judasbrief* (Freiburg, 1961), pp.102-8; H. Vorgrimler,

'Fragen zum Höllenabstieg Christi' in *Concilium* 2 (1966), pp.70-5; ET: 'Christ's Descent into Hell; Is it important?' in *Concilium*, Jan., 1966, pp.75-81; J. Ratzinger, *Einführung in das Christentum*, *op.cit.*, pp.242-9; ET: *Introduction to Christianity*, *op.cit.*, pp.233-30; *idem*, 'Schwierigkeiten mit dem Apostolikum. Höllenbfahrt-Himmelfahrt-Auferstehung des Fleisches' in P. Brunner, G. Friedrich, K. Lehmann, J. Ratzinger, *Veraltetes Glaubensbekenntnis?* (Regensburg, 1968), pp.97-123; H. Urs von Balthasar, *Mysterium Paschale*, *loc.cit.*, pp.227-55; J.B. Metz, *Erlösung und Emanzipation*, *loc.cit.*, pp.131 f.

[64]Cf G.W.F. Hegel, *Phänomenologie des Geistes* (ed., J. Hoffmeister) (Hamburg, 1952), pp.398 ff; *idem*, *Grundlinien der Philosophie des Rechts*, *op.cit.*, Sect. 164 ff. ET: *Hegel's Philosophy of Right*, *op.cit.*, pp.113 ff; K.Marx, *Zur Judenfrage (on the Jewish Question)* in: W I (Darmstadt, 1962), pp.451-87; Especially the famous chapter on commodity fetishism in: *Das Kapital* W IV (Darmstadt, 1962), pp.46-63; ET: *Capital* (London, 1932, reprinted in 1972), Vol.I. pp.43-58.

[65]K. Marx, *Zur Judenfrage (on the Jewish Question)* in W I, p.479.

[66]*Ibid.*, p.459.

III. JESUS CHRIST — MEDIATOR BETWEEN GOD AND MAN

III JESUS CHRIST: MEDIATOR BETWEEN GOD AND MAN

1. THE PERSON OF THE MEDIATOR

The fundamental church confession of faith, as the Council of Chalcedon (451) formulated it, is that Jesus Christ is true God and true man in one person. The two previous chapters were devoted to the true Godhead and the true humanity; I must now turn to the third great Christological problem, which I have referred to repeatedly but always postponed: namely, the question of the unity of Godhead and humanity in the one person, or hypostasis.

At first sight it might seem that this is less a direct question of faith than a derivative theological problem which arises only as a consequence of the two fundamental truths of faith concerning the true Godhead and true humanity. Furthermore, the dogma of the Council of Chalcedon was formulated wholly in accordance with the intellectual and political assumptions of the situation at that time, and in rather technical philosophical terms. That being so, it might be considered an illegitimate anachronism to try to derive it directly from Scripture. Nevertheless, this dogma does concern a fundamental question of faith, even if in a limited historical perspective. What is at stake is the confession of faith that Jesus Christ in person is the mediator between God and man (cf 1 Tim 2.5) and the new Covenant (cf 1 Cor 11.25; Lk 22.20). Therefore this dogma is concerned with the fundamental question of salvation as well as the basic speculative problem of mediation between God and man.

(a) The testimony of Scripture and tradition
The unity of God and man in Jesus Christ is one of the fundamental Christological statements of Scripture. It is characteristic of the earthly Jesus that he speaks and acts as one who stands in God's place.[1] He is God's reign and God's self-communicating love in person. But God in his love does not act without regard to man or over man's head. The coming of God's reign is an expression of his fidelity as Creator and author of the Covenant. Consequently he comes in a humanly historical way, not eliminating man's freedom but involving it. For God begins to reign where he is acknowledged as Lord by man's obedient faith. Hence Jesus in person is both God's gift to man and man's response. His obedience marks his total origin from God and his utter self-giving to God. He lives so unreservedly by receiving from God, that he is in no way previous to, apart from or parallel to the obedient acceptance of that self-communication of God's love. Jesus lives God's giving of himself in a personal way.

Easter made unmistakably clear what Jesus' earthly life had really been. It was now expressed explicitly in a confession of faith. There are statements' of identity at the centre of the Easter message: He who has risen is the crucified, and the crucified is he who has risen.[2] The primitive Christian credal statements are identity statements as far as their formal structure is concerned: 'Jesus is the Christ'; 'Jesus is the Kyrios'; 'Jesus is the Son of God'. At first it might seem that the subject of these statements is the person of the man Jesus of Nazareth, whereas the title 'Son of God', for instance, functions simply as a predicate. But we have already seen that the credal statements must also be read in the converse sense. What and who the Son of God is, is interpreted by Jesus. The objective justification for such a reversal lies in the content of the Easter message, which says that henceforward the Crucified lives wholly and solely through the power of God's creative fidelity, in God's glory. The identity of the crucified and the risen Jesus is not, therefore, based on the enduring substrate of human nature, but solely on God's creative fidelity.

What the early Easter professions of faith suggest is explicit in some early hymns to and confessions of faith in, Christ. The Christ hymn of the Letter to the Philippians (2.6-11), for example, is of interest in this regard. Here, two different modes of existence are successively predicated of one and the same subject: he who before was in God's mode of existence enters into the mode of existence of human servitude to the cosmic powers. Similarly, the two-stage Christology in Romans 1.3 f speaks of two dimensions, the realm of *sarx* the 'natural' man, man as a bodily being, and the realm of *pneuma*, of spirit, through which the one Son of God passes. The Pauline mission formulas of Gal 4.4 and Rom 8.3 take up these paradoxical statements: It is the same one who as eternal Son is sent by the Father and who in time is born of woman and is condemned in sinful flesh. The soteriological meaning of these formulations finds clear expression in Paul. A great exchange takes place in the one divine-human history. 'Though he was rich, yet for your sake he became poor, so that by his poverty you might become rich' (2 Cor 8.9); 'For our sake he made him to be sin who knew no sin, so that in him we might become the righteousness of God' (2 Cor 5.21). The First Letter of Peter brings out the connexion of the two-stage Christology with this Christology of exchange: 'For Christ also died for sins once for all, the righteous for the unrighteous, that he might bring us to God, being put to death in the flesh but made alive in the spirit' (3.18). In the one history of the one Jesus Christ, therefore, the turning-point of all history takes place; God and man are reconciled with one another again. This universal scope of the two-stage Christology is once more brought out in 1 Tim 3.16, where once again what is plainly an older hymn is quoted:

'He was manifested in the flesh,
vindicated in the Spirit,
seen by angels,

preached among the nations,
believed on in the world,
taken up in glory.'

In the one Jesus Christ, heaven and earth, flesh and spirit are united.

Early patristic theology at first repeated the ancient *pneuma-sarx* Christology and developed its soteriological meaning. We are dealing here with the oldest Christological schema.[3] The most striking expression of this unity in duality is found in the Letter to the Ephesians (7.2) of Ignatius of Antioch;

	'There is only one physician who is at once	
fleshly	and	spiritual
generate	and	ingenerate
God		in man
true life	in	death
born of Mary	and	of God
first passible	then	impassible
	Jesus Christ our Lord.'[4]	

How realistically Ignatius understands the unity of the one subject, is shown by the fact that he can speak quite downrightly of the blood of God (Eph 1.1) and of God's suffering (Rom 6.3; cf. 1 Clem 2.1). The soteriological meaning of this unity is our participation in Jesus' spirit and immortality (cf. Eph 8.2; Magn 15; Barn 5.6, 14; 14.4; 2 Clem 14.3ff).

Pneuma-sarx Christology evidently became very soon liable to misunderstanding. It could easily be misinterpreted in an Adoptianist sense. It could give the impression that the Spirit merely operated or dwelt in Christ as in a particularly favoured man, and thereby made him the Son of God. There was another further factor: in the Stoic philosophy of those days the term 'pneuma' did not exclude materiality. As soon as Christianity entered into contact with the thought of the age, that term inevitably came to seem inappropriate to any clear denotation of Jesus' divine existence. What now seemed more helpful than the *pneuma-sarx* formula was another model, already pre-formed in Scripture but also found later to be liable to misunderstanding: the *logos-sarx* formula.

The biblical *locus classicus* of the *logos-sarx* Christology, is the sentence in the Prologue to St John's Gospel: 'and the Word *(logos)* was made flesh *(sarx)*' (1.14).[5] The subject of this sentence is the *Logos*. It is first said of him that from eternity he is with the Father; then, however, comes the unheard-of statement that he became 'flesh'. This 'became' does not mean a metamorphosis, or that a third entity arises from *Logos* and flesh. The *Logos* remains the subject of the event. Clearly the Gospel of John and the First Letter of

John are concerned above all to say two things: first, that it is the *Logos* himself, secondly, that he really appeared in the flesh, in our concrete history (1 Jn 1.2), that he has lived among us, and indeed that he 'became' flesh (Jn 1.14). Divine and human things are therefore asserted of one and the same subject. Consequently this passage contains all the premisses for later Christology, and Jn 1.14 rightly became the biblical theological basis for subsequent Christological development in the history of dogma. We can therefore consider it an essential and fundamental feature of New Testament Christology, that both divine and human predications are made of one and the same subject.

It would be historically mistaken, however, to seek the fully-developed two-natures doctrine in the Johannine writings. John is not yet concerned with two natures in a single subject, but with a succession of events in sacred history. He is concerned with the great turning-point of history. For the passage of the *Logos* down into the flesh and through the flesh up to glory, opens up to all who join him a new and final possibility of salvation, a way to truth and life (cf. 14.2,6). But where John's Gospel speaks expressly of the unity between Jesus and God, it is significant that he is concerned not with the unity between Jesus and the *Logos,* but with that between Jesus and the Father: 'I and the Father are one' (10.30). This unity between Jesus, as the Son, and the Father, is asserted in its soteriological significance: Anyone who follows the Son, may know that he is secure in the Father's hand (10.28f). Consequently the unity between Father and Son can become an exemplar and model of the unity which believers too must attain (17.21-23). Jesus' unity with the Father is to validate Jesus as the way to the Father (14.6) and as the mediator between God and man.

The Christological problem in the narrower sense, the question of Jesus' inner constitution, was only developed later when people reflected on the presuppositions inherently implied by the unity of Father and Son, and when the unique ontic, factual existence lived by Jesus was interpreted ontologically. As soon as people turned to this question, which had not been raised in the New Testament, they inevitably had to say – wholly in line with the fourth Gospel and the entire New Testament – that Jesus' dedication to the Father presupposes the Father's self-communication to Jesus. This self-communication, which constitutes the unity as well as the enduring distinction between Father and Son, is called by tradition the Logos, the second divine person. Inasmuch as Jesus lives wholly and entirely from this love of the Father and wills to be nothing of himself, Jesus is nothing but the incarnate love of the Father and the incarnate response of obedience. The unity of the man Jesus with the *Logos* is expressed in the New Testament only indirectly as the inner ground of the unity between the Father and Jesus.[6] We shall therefore have to understand the personal communion between Jesus and the Father as a communion in essence, but the community of essence as personal activity. It is the peculiarity of this community of essence that it is personal and relational.

The thesis just stated already indicates that the biblical statements inevitably gave rise to serious problems as soon as the scriptural concern with sacred history and soteriology was explicitly formulated as a question about Jesus' ontological status. Those problems, however, not only seriously preoccupied theology of the early centuries, but have continued to give cause for thought down to the present day. In what follows, only a few aspects can be suggested, and then only in a fragmentary way.[7] The first great Christological essay, so profound that it has scarcely been equalled since, was that of Irenaeus of Lyons. He starts from the paradoxical statements of Scripture and tradition; he contrasts birth from the Father and from Mary, glory and abasement, life and death.[8] His great theme in face of Gnostic dualism is, however, that of the unity in Christ. As against the Docetist distinction or, rather, division of Jesus from Christ, he strongly emphasizes that the two are one and the same *heis kai ho autos.*[9] The formula had thus been found which was to assume fundamental importance in later Christological controversies. In Irenaeus, too, the larger theological context of the Christological problem is apparent: the unity of Godhead and humanity in Christ also involves the question of the unity of creation and redemption, of God and world. Jesus Christ is not understood simply as a great exception, but rather as the new beginning. Consequently Irenaeus treats the Christological problem particularly from the soteriological point of view: 'factus est quod sumus nos, uti nos perficeret esse quod est ipse'.[10] 'For it was for this end that the Word of God was made man, and He who was the Son of God became the Son of man, that man, having been taken into the Word, and receiving the adoption, might become the son of God. For by no other means could we have attained to incorruptibility and immortality, unless we had been united to incorruptibility and immortality. But how could we be joined to incorruptibility and immortality, unless, first, incorruptibility and immortality had become that which we also are, so that the corruptible might be swallowed up by incorruptibility, and the mortal by immortality, that we might receive the adoption of sons?'[11] This Christology of exchange is still to be found in the Liturgy, in the offertory of the Mass: 'Grant that by the mystery of this water and wine we may be made partakers of his divinity who vouchsafed to become partaker of our humanity.'

The depth and breadth of Irenaeus' Christological ideas have never really been equalled. A conceptual command of the problem was of course still lacking in his work. That was achieved by Tertullian with such a touch of genius that here again it was a long time before his ideas and terminology were assimilated and surpassed. In his book against the Modalist Praxeas, for whom the Son is only a manifestation of the Father, so that it is possible to say that the Father suffered in the Son, Tertullian had to elucidate not only the distinction between Father and Son, but the distinction and unity of God and man in Christ. Therefore he supplemented the traditional pair of terms *spiritus-caro (pneuma-sarx)* by speaking of the two *status* and the two *substantiae,* which are not mixed but are nevertheless conjoined in the one person of the God-man Jesus Christ.[12] That anticipates the terminology of Chalcedon. But conceptual precision is achieved at the expense of the universal theological perspective of Irenaeus. The idea of exchange is lacking in Tertullian. Christology becomes a separate, special problem: 'In Tertullian and his circle the drama of the personal relation to salvation threatens to harden into an abstract structure of natures . . . Tertullian's strength lay in the analysis of what might be called the formal constitution of the God-man, not in thinking out the saving event. Hence his inheritance is a dangerous one. One can be led astray into an ever more refined definition of the "how" of the Incarnation, while losing sight of its saving significance. Then one forgets that the doctrine of Jesus' Godhead and humanity is a development of the original conviction of faith that this man is our divine salvation. Later Latin theology fell into this trap only too often.'[13]

Almost contemporaneously with Tertullian in the West, Origen in the East opened the way to a further Christological development. Unlike the West, the East only succeeded in clarifying its terminology after long struggles. On the other hand, it had more success in maintaining the inherent dynamism of the Christ-event. Unlike

Tertullian, Origen integrates his Christology into a vast pattern of descent and ascent in which even Irenaeus' idea of exchange finds its place. The *Logos* is the *imago* of the Father, Jesus' human body is the *imago* of the *Logos*. Hence the God-man Jesus Christ (an expression which is first found in Origen) opens up to us a way of ascent to the vision of God, but in fact a way on which Jesus' humanity is as it were left behind again. Mediation occurs through Jesus' human soul, which is united with the *Logos* in total obedience and utter dedication and love.

After Origen there were several possibilities. One was to elaborate his idea of the priest-hood and hegemony of the *Logos* and to place the entire emphasis on the divinizing power of the *Logos* who enters wholly into the flesh in order to permeate that flesh wholly with himself. That was the course followed by Alexandrine theology, and in particular by Cyril. Cyril was thus able clearly to exhibit the *Logos* as the ground of unity, and in general to safeguard Christ's unity, but he was not able to maintain quite as clearly the intrinsic significance of Christ's humanity and the continuing distinction between God and man. As a result, Cyril's Christology is still determined by the *logos-sarx* framework, although that had meanwhile become very liable to misunderstanding because of Arius and Apollinaris. The other possible line of thought after Origen led to the theologians of the Antiochene school with their emphasis on the human nature in Christ. They replaced the *Logos-sarx* by the *Logos-anthropos* framework. They were able to refer here to Origen's views on the significance of the human soul in Christ. But their problem now was to safeguard the unity of Godhead and humanity in Christ. Of course, the metaphors they use about the indwelling of the *Logos* in the man Jesus and about their mutual friendship need not be taken only in the sense of a moral unity. Nevertheless, they think of the unity as the result of mutual penetration and exchange betwen Godhead and humanity. The Antiochenes just as much as the Alexandrians were moved by soteriological concern.

In contrast to the West, both schools represented a dynamic Christology with a markedly soteriological interest. Whereas, however, Cyril with his idea of the *Logos* as the ground of unity represents the more impressive Christological idea, the Antiochenes have the merit of having furthered clarity of expression by their insistence on the distinction between Godhead and humanity. Nestorius[14] of the Antiochene school, who at once became a stumbling-block, found his way even before Chalcedon to the distinction between nature and person, and anticipated the Chalcedon formula of the one person in two natures. After long being accused in the history of dogma and theology of the gravest heresies, and having even been called a new Judas by the Council of Ephesus, he is now to a large extent being rehabilitated by historical scholarship. The pre-eminence of the *Logos*, which was Cyril's view, never, indeed, occurred to Nestorius; the unity of one person was, according to him, the result of the mutual penetration of the two natures.

The development of Christological doctrine in the early Church can only be understood in the light of this background of theological history. The controversies occasioned by the conciliar decisions were provoked by Nestorius who, as might be expected from the general character of his christology, would not speak of Mary as the 'mother of God' *(Theotokas)* but only as the 'mother of Christ' *(Christokos)*. This raised the fundamental question of the unity in Christ in connexion with a practical problem of theological language and usage. The question was whether the *Logos* is the one subject or whether the unity in Christ, (which, as we can see today in historical perspective, both sides acknowledged) constitutes a *tertium quid* made up of Godhead and humanity.

The Council of Ephesus (431) did not achieve even a common session, still less a doctrinal formula, so violent was the controversy. It was two years before the two sides struggled their way through to a common formula (DS 271-273). In Ephesus itself they acknowledged in principle only one Christological idea. As in Nicaea and Constantinople, the starting-point was the principle of tradition. They wanted to maintain the agreement of Cyril's basic Christological idea as expressed in his second letter to Nestorius (DS 250f), with the Nicene Creed. The creed of Nicaea-Constantinople speaks first of the eternal Son of God consubstantial with the Father, and then goes on: 'For us men and for our salvation he came down from heaven. He was made flesh and was made man' (DS 150; NR 250). According to the Council Fathers at Ephesus, this means that it is one and the same *heis kai ho autos* who is eternally begotten of the Father and was born of Mary, in time, as a man. The Council's concern here was exactly the same as had already been decisive in Nicaea, and which was in fact the fundamental contention of Scripture and of all tradition: It is God himself who meets us in Jesus Christ.

The only new thing in the Ephesus decision was that, from the basic Nicene Christological idea, conclusions were now drawn about correct ways of speaking theologically about Christ. Because of the identity of the one subject who from eternity is with the Father and who in time has become man, both what is divine and what is human must be predicated of Jesus Christ. Consequently we can and must say that Mary is the mother of God. A second and in practice probably even more important consequence concerned piety, namely, the question whether Jesus' humanity is to be worshipped. From the fact that the subject is one, it follows that we do not worship Jesus' humanity as if it were a different subject. *hos hetepon hetepo* only together with the Logos, but that both are glorified in one single worship *mia proskynesis* (DS 259). The question of orthodoxy was solved at Ephesus less in a theoretical, doctrinal way than in a practical fashion. Correct prayer and correct liturgical worship became the yardstick and criterion for correct belief. Even today a Christology will have to prove its orthodoxy by the fact that it not only regards Jesus as a model of true humanity and as the first and most perfect of many brethren, but as Lord *(Kyrios)* to whom divine dignity and divine worship are due.

However clear the decision regarding the fundamental Christological idea and the practical consequences for theological language and the practice of piety were, it was inevitably a disadvantage that the Council lacked a clear terminology which would have made it possible to conceive the inviolable distinction as well as the unity of Godhead and manhead in Jesus Christ. The problem once again became acute as a result of a heresy which sprang up on the basis of Cyril's position – the doctrine of the no doubt pious, but ignorant and stubborn monk Eutyches, that Christ did indeed consist of two natures before the union, but in only one nature *(mia physis)* after it. According to this 'Monophysitism', there is a transformation, mingling and complete compenetration of the two natures. Once again, in this lack of recognition of God's transcendence as against man, we are confronted with a hellenization of faith; God does not set man free here, but as it were absorbs him, so that the two form a sort of natural symbiosis. The soteriological sense of the distinction between God and man is therefore clearly recognizable. In fact, in a more complex way it was the same issue as in the controversy with Gnosticism and with Apollinaris: the reality and human character of the redemption.

This time clarification came from the West. Helped by the political circumstances, Pope Leo the Great, in his dogmatic letter of 449 to Patriarch Flavian, was able to introduce the distinction between nature and person which had been clarified in the

West since Tertullian. The decisive formula runs: 'salva igitur proprietate utriusque naturae et in unam coeunte personam' (DS 293). Leo also gives the reason why he maintains both the unity and distinction of the two natures: 'Non enim esset Dei hominumque mediator, nisi idem Deus idemque homo in utroque et unus esset et verus' (DS 299). This doctrinal letter was read out at Chalcedon (451) and was applauded: 'That is the faith of the Fathers, that is the faith of the apostles! That is what we all believe! . . . Peter has spoken through Leo! The apostles taught this! . . .' Nevertheless, after long resistance — they wanted indeed to confirm the ancient faith, but not a new dogma — they set about composing as it were a compromise formula out of the various existing ones.

The decisive passage in the doctrinal definition of the Council of Chalcedon runs: 'We confess one and the same *heis kai ho autos* Christ . . . in two natures *en duo physesin* without confusion, without change, without division, without separation, the difference of the natures having been in no wise taken away by reason of the union but rather the properties of each being preserved and both concurring into one person *(hen prosopon)* and one hypostasis *(mia hypostasis)*'[14a] (DS 302; NR 178).

The immediate sense of this definition is to teach, as against Monophysitism, the enduring distinction of the two natures ('in two natures'), without which Jesus' mediatorship would be illusory. At the same time, the intention is to go beyond Ephesus and not merely maintain the unity of the one subject in Jesus Christ but to give it conceptual expression as a unity in one person and hypostasis. Despite this aim, the theological legitimacy of which can hardly be questioned, the dogmatic formula of Chalcedon has met with not less, but even more criticism that the Nicene Creed. The most important objections raised may be summed up under two headings: (1) Chalcedon replaced the biblical and early church Christology which started from Jesus Christ in the concrete and regarded him from a double point of view, namely, according to the flesh *(sarx)* and according to the spirit *(pneuma)* by an abstract formula concerned with the unity and distinction of divine and human nature. (2) To speak of two natures is in any case problematic, because, on the one hand, the term 'nature' cannot be applied equally to God and man, and on the other, an ethical or personal relation is thereby misinterpreted in a physical sense.[15]

This criticism prompts us to inquire more closely into the objective theological meaning and import of the Chalcedonian definition. Two things may be noted: (1) The Chalcedonian dogma builds on the older Christology which said that Jesus Christ is 'one and the same, perfect in Godhead and perfect in humanity, true God and true man . . . consubstantial with the Father in Godhead, consubstantial with us in his humanity. . .'. The Council quotes the traditional Christology and then, because of misunderstandings that have arisen, interprets it more precisely by means of the abstract terms 'two natures' and 'one person or *hypostasis*'. The Council thus adheres to the principle of living tradition, according to which tradition and interpretation form a unity. It defines the traditional church doctrine in new terms appropriate to the changed state of the question. (2) With its distinction between nature and person or *hypostasis,* the Council safeguards the unity in duality, and duality in unity of God and man. That is not a hellenization of the Church's doctrine, but its de-hellenization in face of Monophysitism. For it insists that God and man do not form any natural symbiosis; in the incarnation God does not become a cosmic principle; he is not made spatial or temporal. God's transcendence is preserved, as are man's independence and freedom. It is true that the conceptual means are still inadequate to define precisely this idea of a union that posits freedom. The distinction between nature and person is first and foremost no more than a verbal expedient. And, above all, the terms 'person' and 'hypostasis' were not themselves defined at Chalcedon. Fundamentally, the Council had to express in the language of Greek philosophy something that shattered all its perspectives, and for which the intellectual resources were still lacking. The Council was content to mark the limits of the faith against errors to right and left. It was content to explain its formula by four negatives: 'without confusion, without change, without division, without separation'. The Council therefore does not express any metaphysical theory about Christ, but contents itself with a *christologia negativa* which safeguards the mystery.

In short, we may conclude that (1) the Christological dogma of the Council of Chalcedon constitutes, in the language and in the context of the problem at that time, an extremely precise version of what, according to the New Testament, we encounter in Jesus' history and what befell him: namely in Jesus Christ, God himself has entered into a human history, and meets us there in a fully and completely human way. The dogmatic profession of faith that Jesus Christ in one person is true God and true man, must therefore be regarded as a valid and permanently binding interpretation of Scripture. (2) Compared with the total Christological witness of Scripture, the Christological dogma of Chalcedon represents a contraction. The dogma is exclusively concerned with the inner constitution of the divine and human subject. It separates this question from the total context of Jesus' history and fate, from the relation in which Jesus stands, not only to the *Logos* but to 'his Father', and we miss the total eschatological perspective of biblical theology.[16] Even though the Christological dogma of Chalcedon is a permanently binding interpretation of Scripture, it nevertheless has to be integrated into the total biblical testimony and interpreted in its light.

From the fifth-century point of view, of course, another question was the focus of interest. The Chalcedon definition lies essentially within the framework of western Christology; there was no place for Cyril's dynamic Christological idea of the hegemony of the *Logos* within the apparently symmetrical scheme of two natures which meet in one person. That led to the first great schism in the Church, and to a long history of errors and confusions which are only now slowly being cleared up. At that time neither side succeeded in finding room in its own formula for the legitimate concern of the other. Yet each attempted to impose its own view and its own formulation. The Chalcedon dogma was primarily a more or less successful compromise which verbally linked what each side had at heart, but without making any conceptual connexion, and above all without further definition of the term 'person' and its ontological content. Consequently Chalcedon represented a reaching out towards a solution, and created as many problems as it solved.

In the first place room had to be found for the Christological concern of the East, Cyril's brilliant idea of the hegemony of the *Logos*, which had been brought into discredit by Monophysitism. After the preparatory work of the mediation theology of

Neo-Chalcedonianism,[17] that was done in extremely unfortunate circumstances by the Fifth General Council, Constantinople II (553). This stated that the one *hypostasis* is that of the *Logos* into which the human nature is assumed. Only now was the full concept of the hypostatic union attained *Kathypostasin* (DS 424 f; 426; 430). This decision prepared by Neo-Chalcedonianism is to some extent a subject of controversy even today. Fundamentally, however, despite all human and theological inadequacies, the aim was to maintain the fundamental Christological idea of Scripture and tradition, the identity of subject by which the eternal Son of God and the man Jesus are 'one and the same'. The Scythian monks expressed this in a phrase that is correct in itself but sounds odd: 'one of the Trinity suffered' (cf. DS 426; 432). In addition to the argument from Scripture and tradition, there is also an intrinsic reason in favour of this post-Chalcedonian development. Only within the idea of hegemony of the *Logos* is the possibility of a unity in distinction 'intelligible', for only God can be thought of as so 'supra-essential' and 'surpassingly free' that he can posit in itself with its own identity what is distinct from him, precisely by uniting it wholly with himself. Consequently, both on the ground of Scripture and tradition and on that of theological insight into the matter itself, the new interpretation of the Council of Chalcedon by that of Constantinople must be regarded as objectively legitimate and logical.

Once the fundamental decision had been taken by the Fifth General Council, the consequences this involved for a correct understanding of Jesus' human nature remained for subsequent reflection. It was inevitable that in the course of this increasingly complex inquiry, the problems inherent in the starting-point should become increasingly apparent. The Chalcedon-Constantinople formula was detached from its original theological context; instead of understanding it as an ontological interpretation of the relation between Jesus and the Father, they singled out the question of Jesus' inner constitution and drew out from it by purely logical deduction increasingly fine-spun conclusions.

Chalcedon and Constantinople had spoken rather abstractly of two natures, not going so far as Pope Leo who in addition spoke of each nature performing what is proper to it in communion with the other ('agit enim utraque forma cum alterius communione quod proprium est) (DS 294; NR 177). This conclusion from the two-natures doctrine was contested by the successors of Monophysitism, Monotheletism and Monergism, which assumed only one will and one operation in Christ. Accordingly, the Lateran Synod of 649 (DS 500 ff) and the Sixth General Council, Constantinople III (680-681) had to declare, in logical continuation of the Chalcedon two natures doctrine, that in Jesus Christ there are two wills and two operations, even though Jesus' human will is wholly subject to the divine will (DS 556 f).

Even with this elucidation, the problem of unity and duality in Jesus Christ did not cease to agitate men's minds. Whenever one aspect of the problem was clarified, the other aspect came up for discussion again in an ever more complicated form. The dialectical movement from Ephesus to Chalcedon, from Chalcedon to Constantinople and from one Council of Constantinople to the next, was now repeated once again. Once the duality of wills had been clarified, it was inevitable that the question would recur in the more subtle form of whether we can therefore assume that there are two subjects in Christ. The Spanish Adoptianism of the eighth and ninth centuries (not to be confused with the Ebionite Adoptianism of the early Church) represented that kind of subtle conception of two subjects, teaching that within the hypostatic union the man Jesus is assumed by God as his adopted son, whereas the *Logos* alone is the natural Son of God. In this way Godhead and humanity were distinguished not only as *aliud et aliud*, but also as *alius et alius*. After the Seventh General Council, Nicaea II (787) (DS 610 f), the Frankish plenary council in Frankfurt in 794 declared in logical continuation of tradition, that Jesus even as man is the natural Son of God (DS 612-615).

The question did not rest even during the whole of early Scholasticism.[18] Peter Lombard lists three opinions, the third of which, however, the *Habitus* theory, according to which Jesus' body and soul — separate in themselves — were each assumed by the *Logos*, was soon dropped, especially after its condemnation by Pope Alexander III in 1177 (DS 750) as incompatible with the doctrine of Jesus' true humanity. More important is the first-mentioned *Assumptus* theory, about which there is still some controversy even today. This holds that the *Logos* assumed not just a complete human nature, but a complete human being. Aquinas was the first, in his later works, to declare this doctrine to be in contradiction to the Church's teaching, and a heresy. He thus contributed to the acceptance of the subsistence theory, which now became the common opinion of theologians in the form that Jesus' human nature possesses no human *hypostasis* of its own, but subsists in the *hypostasis* of the *Logos*. With this theory, despite all precautions, the danger still remained either of the human nature being diminished or of the *Logos* being made a cosmic principle. As a result, the *Assumptus* theory in the more moderate form of the *Assumptus-homo* theology still found adherents even in the sixteenth and seventeenth centuries, especially among theologians of Scotist tendencies.[19] They were far from wanting to affirm two subjects in Christ. The essential question was, rather, whether the designation 'this man' or the title 'Christ' refers directly to the human nature and only indirectly to its bearer, the person of the *Logos*, or whether the concrete designation 'this human being' ('this man') in the proper sense can only be made of the one concrete subject, the person of the *Logos*, and only indirectly of the human nature. As long as we hold that the person of the *Logos* is the one and only ontological subject in Christ, this is more a question of theological usage and the ontology that it presupposes, and of Christological approach, than a question of the binding doctrine of faith. Consequently the Church's magisterium has come to no decision in the matter. While traditional scholastic theology in the overwhelming majority of its representatives has rejected the *Assumptus-homo* Christology, there is a certain tendency in that direction today in line with attempts at formulating a Christology 'from below'.

It is evident that behind the constant dialectical movement throughout the history of dogma and theology, which continues today, between emphasis on the unity or on the distinction between Godhead and humanity, there lies a still unsolved and perhaps insoluble problem, that of mediation between God and man. The attempt was made to master this problem by thinking it out mainly with the help of a distinction, quite unknown to Greek philosophy, between nature and person or *hypostasis*. The independence and originality of personal reality was only discovered and conceptually formulated in wrestling with the fundamental data of the history of revelation. This was one of the most important contributions of Christianity to human civilization, and meant the emergence of a new understanding of reality as a whole. The problem of traditional theology consisted to a large extent in having to discuss and express this new element within the intellectual framework of a different kind of conception of reality. Having elucidated the most important theological affirmations of Scripture and tradition, we must now try to gain a deeper understanding of them, together with an appropriate terminology to express that understanding.

(b) Philosophical and theological reflection

I shall proceed in three stages. I try first to throw some light on the concept of person in tradition by looking at the history of the word and at the classical scholastic theories based on it. I then try to carry the classical concept of person further against the background of the problems that have been raised in modern times and of a phenomenology of personal experience, in order finally with the help of this to attain a deeper understanding of the hypostatic union.

The lexiographical study concerns the two words *prosopon* and *hypostasis*. The term *prosopon*[20] originally meant 'face', 'countenance', and also the actor's mask and the rôle he plays. In the Septuagint it is often used to denote the face of God. Probably this theological usage influenced the early Church to some extent when it spoke of three *prosopa* in God. But the expression was obviously liable to misinterpretation in a modalist sense. Many scholars used to assume that this word or its Latin equivalent, *persona,* was given precise definition by the lawyer Tertullian, for *prosopon* also later on was a technical legal term for person. Recently, however, C. Andresen[21] has shown that Tertullian's terminology has an earlier history in the prosopographic exegesis of that age. This was a literary art-form in which an event is not merely narrated but is given dramatic form by introducing persons and assigning them various rôles. The concept of person thus by its very origin includes the feature of an event unfolding in dialogue and relations (rôles). The concept must, therefore, almost inevitably have suggested itself when it was a question of representing in concepts the mode in which God meets us in redemption history, especially in Jesus Christ. What for antiquity was an art-form, was now given real content.

To express this real content, it was possible in particular to use the term *hypostasis*[22] Originally this was largely the same as *ousia* or *physis* and meant 'reality', 'actuality'. In that sense Nicaea rejected the Arian doctrine that the Son was of another *hypostasis* or another essence than the Father (DS 126). Cyril still speaks of the one *hypostasis* (DS 250 f; 253) as well as of the *mia physis tou logou sesarkomene* (of the one incarnate nature of the *Logos*) and of the *henosis physike* (physical i.e. ontological union) (DS 254). But already for the Stoics *hypostasis* denoted realization, actualization, as well as reality and actuality; they were thinking of prime matter, formless and without qualities becoming real in concrete individual things. In neo-Platonism the word was used for the realization and manifestation of the One *(hev)* on ever lower levels of being, thus already serving to solve the problem of the one and the many. Whereas Origen still did not draw any clear distinction between reality *(ousia)* and realization *(hypostasis)* Athanasius at the Synod of Alexandria (362) accomplished a cautious change of mind and made it permissible to speak of God's three *hypostases* (expressions), provided the one essence *(ousia)* of God were safeguarded. What was new in this conception as compared with neo-Platonism, was that it abandoned the idea of hierarchy and did not subordinate, but co-ordinated the three *hypostases.* These clarifications amounted in principle to an advance towards a dynamic conception of being and of God, for *hypostasis* meant not a state but an act, not being static in itself, but being as happening. Thus the term corresponded to the relational sense of the concept of person, and it was not long before the divine hypostases could be thought of as relations, as happened with Basil in the East and Augustine in the West. The divine person is not essence and substance, but rather pure mutual regard, pure actuality in reciprocal giving and receiving, *relatio subsistens.*

The understanding of *hypostasis* as concrete realization, however, had the inevitable result of raising the question that was decisive for all further Christological discussion: In what does this concretion actually consist? The Cappadocians were the first to throw light on this.[23] For them, the *hypostasis* consists of a complex of *idiomata,* the individual and particularizing characteristics. These *idiomata* were conceived not as accidents but as constitutive features of the concrete entity. In that sense too, the term *hypostasis* once again closely approached the term *prosopon* and became identical with it; what was meant was the concrete perceptible unity. Conceptual definition was of course only given to this concept of person after Chalcedon by the lay theologian Boethius: 'persona est naturae rationalis individua substantia'.[24] Personality is here, therefore, still understood as individuality, though individuality understood as an ultimate reality, unique, irreplaceable, incommunicable. Almost contemporaneously another step forward was taken by Leontius of Byzantium, who regards being a person as 'being for oneself' (*to kath' heauto einai*), 'to exist for oneself' (*to kath' heauto hyparchein*).[25] Similarly, the deacon Rusticus defines person as 'remaining in oneself' *(manere in semetipso).*[26] This made it clear that the individuality of the person does not accrue to it accidentally from outside, but belongs to it intrinsically of itself. Precisely this, however, makes it possible for the divine person to take up the human nature into most intimate unity with itself and yet thereby to posit it to be precisely itself. This doctrine of *enhypostasis* developed by Leontius,[27] of the 'in-existence' of the human nature in the divine *hypostasis,* must therefore be seen in its dialectical character, whereby unity and distinction increase in direct, not in inverse proportion. At the very end of the patristic period, Maximus Confessor formulated this dialectical principle: 'For there is evidently a union of things in so far as their physical distinction is preserved'.[28]

What this dialectic means for the concept of person was first expressed by Richard of St Victor in the twelfth century; for him, person means 'naturae intellectualis incommunicabilis existentia'.[29] Person is irreplaceably unique, incommunicable, but it is so, not by being shut up in the self, but as *ex-sistentia,* as being from another and in relation to that other. Whereas Thomas Aquinas in essentials takes the same line as Boethius,[30] Duns Scotus took up and deepened the relational concept of person of Richard of St Victor.[31]

One gets the impression in all these scholastic definitions that while the terminology is that of antiquity, the conception of being that is implied is new and different. This is evident in the theories which the various traditional schools of thought worked out with the help of their respective ontological categories.[32] The fundamental question was whether and how it is possible to distinguish between person and nature. According to the Thomist theory, as represented above all by the Dominican Banez (+1604), the person is a *modus subsistendi* really distinct from the nature and to that extent added to it; in Jesus' human nature the human *modus subsistendi* is replaced by that of the second person of the Trinity. Furthermore, in accord with the Thomist real distinction between essence and existence, Jesus' human nature participates in the divine act of existence. According to this Thomist view, the human nature loses nothing by this subtraction not only of human personality but also of the human act of existence; in fact it receives a higher dignity than if it had possessed a human personality and existence of its own. This doctrine has the merit of seeing the hypostatic union as a close ontological unity; but it is open to the criticism that it does not recognize that the greater the unity, the more it means that a distinct reality is posited.

This is where the Scotist school develops its view that Jesus' humanity loses nothing by the hypostatic union with the *Logos,* since, it maintains, personality is not a positive but a negative determination: actual independence and absence of capacity for dependence (*independentia actualis et aptitudinalis*). In the hypostatic union, by God's omnipotence, the *potentia oboedientialis* of Christ's humanity, its relation to God, which is essential to personality, comes to fulfilment. In this way both God's transcendence and man's intrinsic reality are preserved, for it is clear that union with God does not concern a predicamental domain in man, but man's transcendental dimension, the orientation of his whole being towards God. This point certainly has to be retained. But the drawback of this theory is, of course, that it to a large extent empties the concept of personality of content, and what is the most perfect reality in the world, the person, is defined merely negatively, overlooking the fact that non-dependence is only the obverse of something positive: subsistence.

The Jesuit theologian Suarez accordingly attempted a certain mediation between Thomism and Scotism. For him, personality is something positive, a mode of existence of the nature, not of the accidental but of the substantial order; that is, an essentially necessary form in which the nature is manifested, but not a new ontological reality. This *modus per se existendi* is lacking in Jesus' human nature; in its place is a created *modus unionis* which links the two natures. This avoids affirming – with the Thomistic subtraction theory – that something is lacking in the humanity, which is replaced directly by God. And as opposed to the Scotist theory, it maintains that the bond of unity represents a positive ontological determination and, as this is of a created kind, a divinization of Jesus' humanity is avoided. But can a created reality be a bond of unity between God and man? This theory also leaves unexplained the term *modus substantialis*, which is not found elsewhere in scholastic usage. The question is, of course, whether Suarez is not trying to say that personality is realized not just accidentally but essentially, in certain relations. If Suarez' theory is open to such an interpretation, it would in a way link up with the question as it has been stated in modern times. Yet at the same time we must not lose Scotus' insight that the fundamental relation of the human person is the relation to God, so that the concrete essence of a person is determined in each case by the relation to God. Jesus' unique relation to God must in that case also constitute the concrete essence of his person. But before we can speak in this way, we must first examine how personality has been understood on the basis of the assumptions curnet in the modern period.

Corresponding to the move to subjectivity in modern times, the concept of person has been detached from the wider context of the concept of being. Since John Locke, the attempt has been made to define person on the basis of self-consciousness.[33] This first of all led to isolating the subject from the world of things. Although the attempt was repeatedly made to construct an ontology in the perspective of subjectivity, the problem of mediation between being and consciousness, substance and subject, act and being, remained a fundamental difficulty for modern thought, and persists in the still fashionable habit of opposing personalism and ontology. Yet it would be a mistake from the point of view of classical ontology in particular, to set up any opposition in principle between an ontological conception of personality and the modern concept based on consciousness. In the well-known axiom 'ens et verum convertuntur', being and consciousness had already been radically linked. Consequently it must be possible to move forward from a phenomenology of personal experience to the ontological essence of personality. However, if we seriously admit the irreversibility of the modern perspective, it will not be possible to determine the essence of personality on the basis of a general ontology, but, conversely, ontology will have to be determined on the basis of the reality of the person; in other words, we must think out ontology in personal terms and the person in ontological terms. With that kind of idea of personality and reality in mind, it should then be possible to attain a deeper understanding, with our present-day intellectual assumptions, of the Christological dogma of one person in two natures.

A number of such attempts have in fact already been made. In the nineteenth century those of A. Rosmini, A. Günther and H. Schell in particular deserve mention.[34] Their endeavours, however, were liable to misunderstanding or even came to grief because insufficient thought was given to the relation between being and consciousness. In contemporary theology, various attempts have been made to express the reality of the God-man in terms of consciousness. First the French Fransciscan Fr Déodat (+1937), called 'de Basly' from his birthplace in Normandy, provoked lively discussion.[35] In the

Scotist tradition he renewed the *Homo-assumptus* theory of the early Middle Ages. According to him, the God-man is a complex ontological whole, consisting of the two components the Verb and the man Jesus assumed by the Verb. Both, according to Déodat, are 'autre et autre Quelqu'un'; they are linked by a 'subjonction physique et transcendentale', on the basis of which a 'duel d'amour' exists between the two.

The encyclical *Sempiternus Rex*, on the 1500th anniversary of the Council of Chalcedon, expressly acknowledged the legitimacy of inquiring into Jesus' human reality, even psychologically, but clearly stated that the Chalcedon definition did not permit the supposition that in Christ there are two individuals so that as well as the *Logos* there is a fully autonomous *homo assumptus*. Consequently it is also impossible to postulate a double ontological subject in Christ. On the other hand, the encyclical leaves it open whether it is possible to recognize a relatively independent psychological human subject (self-consciousness).[36] A lively controversy subsequently arose among Catholic theologians on this question of Jesus' human self-consciousness.[37]

The fundamental issue in this discussion was whether consciousness belongs to person or nature. P. Parente reiterated once more very strictly the tradition of the Thomist school and, as an indirect consequence, that of Alexandrian theology: the divine I of the *Logos* is the sole centre of operations; there is in Jesus Christ, not only ontologically but also psychologically, only one I, and this one divine I is directly conscious of the human nature. The corresponding Scotist and Antiochene standpoint was represented by P. Galtier. According to him, consciousness belongs to nature, not to person. Consequently there is a proper human consciousness; it is, however, united with God by the supernatural beatific vision; by this, Jesus' human I is prevented from being ontologically and psychologically independent. M. de la Taille made an influential attempt at mediation, which has been taken up and carried further by Karl Rahner in particular. [38] The highest possible union means the highest possible realization of human nature in the man. From this principle it follows for Rahner that the rejection of Monophysitism and Monotheletism necessarily entails the rejection of Monosubjectivism. 'The Jesus of the Chalcedonian dogma, which was directed against Monophysitism and Monothelitism, likewise has a subjective centre of action which is human and creaturely in kind such that in his human freedom he is in confrontation with God the Inconceivable, such that in it Jesus has undergone all those experiences which we make of God not in a less radical but on the contrary in a more radical – almost, we might say, in a more terrible – form than in our own case. And this properly speaking, not in spite of, but rather because of the so-called hypostatic union.'[39] Schillebeeckx thinks along similar lines.

After this question of Jesus' human consciousness had been discussed for a long time in a very abstract way, it was a pleasant change when Schoonenberg abandoned this approach and tried a more concrete one. His starting-point is that, according to Scripture, Jesus is one person; hence he rejects Fr Déodat's theory of Jesus' person as a complex of relations.[40] But he goes on to add: Jesus is a human person.[41] This leads him to reverse the Chalcedonian dogma. 'Now not the human but the divine nature is anhypostatic in Christ . . . the divine nature is enhypostatic in the human person.'[42] Schoonenberg speaks of the presence of the Word of God or of God by his Word in Jesus Christ;[43] he calls his Christology 'a Christology of the presence of God',[44] for him it is both a Christology of Christ's human transcendence,[45] and of ultimate human fulfilment.[46] Subsequently he modified his position somewhat, so that Jesus is said to be maintained by God in the mode of being of the *Logos*. 'Consequently we may speak of an enhypostasis of Jesus in the *Logos* . . . and conversely of an anhypostasis of the *Logos* in the man Jesus.'[47] We have already indicated the inherent contradiction of this position as regards its Trinitarian doctrine. From the Christological point of view, Schoonenberg's account forces us to ask: Who is Jesus? Is he the eternal Son of God, or is he only a man in whom God is present in a unique way? Does Schoonenberg's theory safeguard the fundamental Christological affirmation of Scripture – the identity of subject of the eternal Son of God and of the man Jesus Christ?

Despite their efforts to bring the specific problems of modern times into the Christological debate, all these atttempts in fact still proceed in a thoroughly scholastic way. They move within the framework of the Chalcedonian dogma (even if they reverse it, as Schoonenberg does), and draw further inferences from it. I for my part shall consider the dogma as an interpretation of Jesus' historical reality and of his relation to the Father. For Jesus' human consciousness is turned not directly to the Logos, but to the Father. But we shall then have to ask what this must mean, not only for Jesus' consciousness, but also for his personality.

After this lengthy consideration of the history of the problem and its terminology, we are now in a position to ask how we at the present time can not merely understand theoretically, but actually assimilate and make our own as the supreme truth of our salvation, the defined dogma that God became man by assuming, without mixture and without separation, a human nature into the personal being of the eternal *Logos*. I shall move in two stages, first asking how such a statement of faith is to be understood from 'below', from the human side (*ex parte assumpti*), and then ask how this is to be understood from 'above', from God's side *(ex parte assumentis)*? In dealing with these questions, however, I am not going to start, like scholastic theology, from an abstract concept of human nature or of God's essence. Instead, I shall try to build on what has been established in the last two chapters, namely, that we know man and God only in and from history, ultimately in fact only from the history and fate of Jesus of Nazareth. Consequently my starting-point is the way in which God and man have been made known to us in Jesus' obedience to 'his Father' and in his service 'for us'.

In Jesus Christ we are faced with a new possibility and actual example of being human, that of living a human life for God and for others. In the course of history this new experience has been summed up and interpreted in the concept of essentially personal experience.[48] Two fundamental human experiences are comprised in the concept of person. A human being experiences himself on the one hand as a unique and incommunicable *I*, as this one here, an absolutely unique being who is responsible for himself and in his own charge. On the other hand, he finds himself in a world around him and in the society of his fellow men; he is not closed in on himself, he is a being that is already determined by reality and that opens out on all reality; he is mind, spirit, by his very nature, essentially of a kind to be *quodammodo omnia*. If we combine these two experiences, we are not far from the classical concept of person: Person is an individual in the intellectual order, *naturae rationalis (= incommunicabilis) substantia (= subsistentia)*. The person is the way in which that which is universal — being as the horizon of mind — is this concrete individual; the place where being is present to itself; the Being-there (as Heidegger terms it). The person is constituted by the tension between general and particular, definite and indefinite, facticity and transcendence, infinite and finite. It *is* this tension; its identity consists in permitting that which is different to be. It is Heidegger's 'ontological difference', Hegel's 'identity of identity and non-identity'. But it is all this not as a mere manifestation of a general law, but as its underivable, incommunicable, unique realization in each instance.

The traditional concept of the person which we have so far presented is still abstract; in the concrete, a person is only actually realized in relationships. The uniqueness of each individual *I* implies its demarcation from any other *I* and therefore a relation to him. Consequently a person only exists in threefold relation: to himself, to the world around, to his fellow men. A person is present to himself by having what is other than him present to him. In concrete terms, the essence of the person is love. Hegel clearly defined this fundamental law even before the personalism of our time (M. Buber, F. Ebner, F. Rosenzweig, and so on): 'It is in the nature or character of what we mean by personality or subject to abolish its isolation or separateness. In friendship and love I give up my abstract personality and in this way win it back as concrete personality.'[49] These relations on the horizontal plane, however, are so to speak crossed and supported by the all-embracing relation of man to God (here again we must go beyond the traditional concept). This applies both to the uniqueness and to the unbounded openness of the person. The uniqueness of each person demands absolute acceptance for their own sake; this is why the person is sacred and of inviolable dignity. Here in the conditioned, something absolutely unconditional shines out. In unbounded openness, the person points beyond everything limited into the infinite mystery of God. The uniqueness and openness both require a ground, consequently the person is not only a reference to, but also a participation in God's nature. The human person can therefore only ultimately be defined from God as ground and in relation to God; God himself has to be included in the definition of the human person. In this sense, Scripture speaks of man as the 'image and likeness of God' (Gen 1.27).

What was already evident in the traditional concept of personality is even clearer in this wider view. Personal being is essentially mediation. Because he is a person, a human being is placed on both horizontal and vertical planes; he is the being in the centre. Yet this centre is not inherently static, but one that is dynamically drawn out beyond itself. In this movement man never comes to rest. He is open to everything, fitted for society yet constantly thrown back on himself, orientated towards the infinite mystery of God, yet mercilessly bound down into his finitude and the banality of his everyday concerns. Consequently man is characterized by greatness and wretchedness. The two are not simply juxtaposed. Only because of his greatness is man aware of his wretchedness, but the consciousness of his wretchedness is also an index of his greatness. 'The greatness of man is great in that he knows himself to be miserable. A tree does not know itself to be miserable. It is then being miserable to know oneself to be miserable; but it is also being great to know that one is miserable.'[50] Pascal's fragment amounts to saying that the essential dignity of man consists in suffering. Suffering is the place where greatness and wretchedness meet, and man is aware of his absolute destiny by experiencing his questionableness, transitoriness and vulnerability.[51]

What follows from this? Is a man a mere torso, a fragment? Or is his very suffering a symbol of hope? He cannot answer this question himself. The infinite distance between God and man, Creator and creature, mediation between which is hinted at in the human person in his question and hope, cannot be bridged from man's side. By the very nature of the case it can only be done from God's side. Man in his personality is only the grammar, *potentia oboedientialis,* the purely passive potentiality, for this mediation. Its realization remains a *mysterium stricte dictum,* that is, we can grasp neither the That nor the How.[52] We cannot deduce that it will become a reality, because as men we have no control over God, and after it has happened we cannot understand how it does so, because we cannot in thought encompass the relation between God and man and so grasp it. What we can do as human beings is something purely negative, show that the mediation that has occurred in Jesus Christ is not in any way in contradiction to man's nature, but is its deepest fulfilment. Man as person is, as it were, the indeterminate mediation between God and man; in Jesus Christ this receives from God its specific form, plenitude and perfection. Consequently Jesus Christ in person is man's salvation.

A Christology purely 'from below' is therefore condemned to failure. Jesus himself understands himself 'from above' in his whole human existence. The transition from anthropological to theological viewpoint cannot therefore be carried out without a break. A decisive change of standpoint is required. We start 'from below' only to the extent that we reflect on the unity of God and man, even in what concerns God's side, on the basis of God's factual historical revelation in Jesus Christ. We can refer back here to what has already been said at various points, and therefore be brief.

What is new in Jesus' attitude to and preaching about God is twofold. Jesus announces God's reign, and gives an utterly radical sense to the first commandment. God's absolute independence, freedom, sovereignty and majesty are not only brought home in their full theoretical force, but are carried in practice to their ultimate conclusion. In face of God, man cannot even plead his highest works of piety; the only appropriate attitude to God is faith. Jesus' cross and Resurrection sealed this message about God. Yet they also definitely confirmed the second element in Jesus' knowledge of preaching about God: God's reign by love. God shows himself as man's God, a God who radically gives himself, communicates himself. 'God is love.' Each statement must interpret the other. This alone will prevent the statement that 'God is love' from turning into an intelligible principle meaning that it is God's essence of necessity to reveal and communicate himself. In that case, God would no longer be a mystery, and even his Incarnation in Jesus Christ could be seen to be necessary.[53] This is Hegel's road, and it is closed to us if we firmly maintain that God in his love is sovereign and free. God's love is not a calculable principle, but an unfathomable mystery of his freedom.

The two statements form a unique unity in the figure of Jesus. They are brought together in his personal obedience to the Father. His utter distinction from 'his Father' is expressed in it, and it is the most radical fulfilment of the first commandment, in this way the personal embodiment of God's reign. At the same time, however, his obedience is a response to God's turning in love to him. And so Jesus' radical unity with the Father is also shown here, in this way he is the Father's incarnate love. Because he is nothing as well as, apart from or before this obedience, he is also totally this self-communication of God. God's self-communicating love posits him freely in his own intrinsic human reality. Augustine coined the famous formula for this: 'ipsa assumptione creatur'.[54] The assumption of Jesus' humanity, the act of highest possible union, at the same time posits this in its own creaturely reality. Jesus' humanity is therefore hypostatically united with the *Logos* in a human way, and this means in a way which includes human freedom and human self-consciousness. Precisely because Jesus is no other than the *Logos,* in the *Logos* and through him, he is also a human person. Conversely, the person of the *Logos* is the human person. Aquinas had a firm hold on this dialectic: 'In Christo humana natura assumpta est ad hoc quod sit persona Filii Dei'[55]; 'Verbum caro factum est, id est homo; quasi ipsum Verbum personaliter sit homo'.[56] So we read too in Matthias Joseph Scheeben, that Jesus' humanity shares in the 'personal being of the *Logos*, inasmuch as in him and through him it forms a human person and thus subsists in him and through him and not through itself'.[57] Or even more clearly in J. Alfaro: 'Christ experienced himself in a human way as an 'I' who really is the Son of God'.[58]

Starting from our concrete and relational concept of person, we can take a step beyond these formal statements. We cannot merely say that nothing is lacking to Jesus' humanity because through the person of the *Logos* it is a human person. We must also say that the indeterminate and open aspect that belongs to the human person is determined definitively by the unity of person with the *Logos*, so that in Jesus through his unity of person with the *Logos*, the human personality comes to its absolutely unique and underivable fulfilment.

With this, we have reached the concept of the hypostatic union. Much would have to be said about its consequence for Jesus' human knowing and willing. There has been a good deal of discussion in the last few years about Jesus' psychology in this sense. In the light of our previous reflections we can be brief. For all considerations lead always to the same fundamental maxim: the greater the union with God, the greater the intrinsic reality of the man. Precisely because (and not despite the fact that) Jesus knew himself wholly one with the Father, he had at the same time a completely human consciousness, asked human questions, grew in age and wisdom (cf Lk 2.52). His consciousness of being one with the Father was therefore not a representational conceptual knowledge, but a sort of fundamental disposition and basic attitude which found concrete realization in the surprising situations in which Jesus became aware in the concrete of what God's will is.[60]

It follows that the same basic structure will apply to the relation between hypostatic union and Jesus' human freedom.[61] Dogmatic tradition sees Jesus' unity with God as the ground not only of a factual sinlessness but of essential sinlessness (cf Jn 8.46; 14.30; 2 Cor 5.21; Heb 4.15; 7.26; 1 Pet 2.22; 1 Jn 3.5).[62] Yet that does not mean the elimination or suppression of free will in Jesus, but rather his unconditional decision for God and men in conflict with the powers of evil in the world. 'Therefore he had to be made like his brethren in every respect. . . For because he himself has suffered and been tempted, he is able to help those who are tempted. . . For we have not a high priest who is unable to sympathize with our weaknesses, but one who in every respect has been tempted as we are, yet without sinning. . . Although he was a Son, he learned the obedience through what he suffered' (Heb 2.17f; 4.15; 5.8).

It is obvious that both ontological and psychological investigation of the mystery of God's incarnation of Jesus Christ, come up against an insuperable limit of thought, speech and sympathetic insight. It is not merely that thought suddenly breaks off and loses itself in the unfathomable. In faith this limit is, as it were, the obverse, the negative of something extremely positive, not darkness but excess of light, dazzling to our eyes. In contradiction to the mystery which dawns at the boundaries of philosophical thought, theology is concerned with a mystery of a certain character, the mystery of an unfathomable love, the very essence of which is to unite what is distinct while respecting the distinction; for love is, in an almost paradoxical way, the unity of two who, while remaining distinct and essentially free, nevertheless cannot exist the one without the other.[63]

The laborious attempts at an ontological approach to the mystery of God's incarnation in Jesus Christ, have finally led us to the distinctively theological plane of understanding, to which we must now finally turn. The doctrine of the hypostatic union is ultimately, as we have said, a conceptual, ontological expression of the biblical statement that God has manifested himself in Jesus Christ as love (cf 1 Jn 4.8, 16). And as this took place with eschatological finality in Jesus Christ, Jesus and God's loving self-communication in him belong to God's eternal being. In the last resort, the mediation of God and man in Jesus Christ can only be understood in the light of Trinitarian theology.[64] Jesus Christ as true God and true man in one person is the historical exegesis (Jn 1.18; *exegesato*) of the Trinity, just as the latter represents the transcendental theological condition of the possibility of the Incarnation. Furthermore, the mediation between God and man in Jesus Christ can be understood theologically only as an event 'in the Holy Spirit'. This leads us to a pneumatologically orientated Christology.

The connexion between Trinity and Incarnation is, of course, recognized in scholastic theology, but is considerably loosened. For Latin tradition, following Tertullian, Augustine and Peter Lombard, does not start from the revelation of the divine persons in sacred history, but moves in a more metaphysical way from the one divine essence as the principle of all operation *ad extra*.[65] Consequently the act of Incarnation (active

Incarnation) belongs in common to all three divine persons (cf DS 535; 801). Scholastic theology to some extent even goes so far as to maintain the thesis that passive incarnation would in itself have been possible to any of the three persons. This is a complete disjunction of sacred history and theological metaphysics, to the detriment of both; sacred history is ultimately evacuated of its theological reality, while theological metaphysics becomes historically meaningless and of no consequence. At the very least it should be said that the various divine persons are involved in the Incarnation each according to his personal distinctive character. A concrete approach from the standpoint of sacred history will therefore determine the distinctive features of the divine persons on the basis of their revelation in the Incarnation.

The starting point is the recognition that Jesus is in person God's loving self-communication. Yet he not only renders present what always was in God; he is also its radically new, historical realization. Consequently Christ is also the revelation of God's freedom in his love. This freedom, too, belongs to God's eternal being. That means that Father and Son are not limited as it were to their mutual love. This surplus and effusion of freedom in the love between Father and Son is the Spirit — at least if we follow the Greek theology of the Trinity.[66] As this 'extreme' in God, he is at the same time God's innermost essence, as one must say in the tradition of Latin theology of the Trinity.[67] In the Spirit, God's innermost essence, his freedom in love, impels him outwards. In him, as a love that is utterly free, God at the same time has the possibility of producing something outside, that is, a creature, and while maintaining its intrinsic creaturely independence, to draw it into his love. The Spirit is, as it were, the theological transcendental condition of the ɹry possibility of a free self-communication of God in history. In him, God can not only reveal but carry into effect his freedom in love in an historical manner. The Spirit as mediation between Father and Son is at the same time the mediation of God into history.

Scholastic theology was hardly able to give due prominence to the pneumatological aspect of the Incarnation, because of its unilaterally metaphysical approach based on the unity of the divine essence. It could do no more than attribute by 'appropriation' to the Holy Spirit the Incarnation as a work of God's love. As the Spirit expresses the grace-given character of the Incarnation, scholastic theology perfectly suitably expressed this by the term *gratia unionis*, or in the more metaphorical language of patristic theology by the image of 'unction', 'anointing'.[68] Usually, however, it ascribed both primarily to the *Logos* who, through his hypostatic union with human nature, endows this in the substantial order and, as it were, interpenetrates it like an ointment with its perfume (*perichoresis*). Through this interpenetration, Jesus' humanity is, in the words of many of the Fathers, actually divinized, without detriment to its own intrinsic reality. According to scholastic theology, this intimate union of the *Logos* with the humanity, entails the consequence that Jesus' humanity also receives the plentitude of the gifts of grace of the Spirit and is, in fact, wholly penetrated and filled with the Holy Spirit (cf Is 16.1f; Lk 4.21; Acts 10.38).

This traditional view is not simply to be contested, but needs to be freed from its onesidedness. For, in the first place, the thesis of the divinization of Jesus' humanity is only correct if at the same time it is added that the greater the proximity to God, the greater the intrinsic reality of the human being. By wholly filling Jesus' humanity, the Spirit endows it with the openness by which it can freely and wholly constitute a mould and receptacle for God's self-communication. The sanctification of Jesus by the Spirit and his gifts is, therefore, in the second place, not merely an adventitious consequence of the sanctification by the *Logos* through the hypostatic union, but its presupposition. The Spirit is thus in person God's love as freedom, and the creative principle which sanctifies the man Jesus in such a way as to enable him, by free obedience and dedication, to be the incarnate response to God's self-communication.

According to the testimony of Scripture, the Incarnation, like Jesus' whole history and fate, took place 'in the Holy Spirit'. Scripture sees the the Spirit at work at all stages of Jesus' life. Jesus is conceived by the power of the Spirit by the virgin Mary (Lk 1.35; Mt 1.18, 20); at his baptism he is installed in his messianic office by the Spirit (Mk 1.10 par.); he acts in the power of the Spirit (Mk 1.12; Mt 12.28; Lk 4.14, 18 *et passim*); on the cross, he offers himself in the Holy Spirit to the Father as victim (Heb 9.14); raised from the dead in the power of the Spirit (Rom 1.4; 8.11), he himself becomes a 'life-giving spirit' (1 Cor 15.45). The Spirit is, as it were, the medium in which God graciously acts in and through Jesus Christ and in which Jesus Christ by willing obedience is the response in personal form. Because Jesus is anointed with the Spirit (cf Is 61.1; Lk 4.21; Acts 10.38), he is the Christ; that is, the anointed, Furthermore, it is in the Spirit that Jesus is the Son of God. Luke expresses this with unusual precision: Because Jesus is in a unique way created by the power of the Spirit, 'therefore (*dio*) the child to be born will be called . . . the Son of God' (Lk 1.35). Jesus' conception by the Holy Spirit (virgin birth) and his divine sonship, are therefore much more closely connected than is usually assumed.[69] In an abstract theology of hypothetical possibilities, combined with a 'soulless' theological positivism, one can indeed say that God could have acted otherwise, he could have become man by way of a natural generation but in fact willed otherwise, so that we must believe in the fact of the virgin birth, although really it has merely the symbolic meaning of bearing witness to Jesus as the new beginning appointed by God, as the new Adam. In reality it is precisely in the Holy Spirit that Jesus is the new Adam through whose obedience we are saved (Rom 5.19), just as he is the Son of God because he is a Spirit-creation.

In this concrete consideration of Scripture in the light of redemptive history, many difficulties of scholastic theology evaporate, but the mystery of the Incarnation is not 'explained' for all that. The Spirit as the personal bond of the freedom of the love between Father and Son is the medium into which the Father freely and out of pure grace sends the Son, and in which he finds in Jesus the human partner in whom and through whom the Son obediently answers the Father's mission in an historical way. A Christology which does not start in a more or less Hegelian way from God's self-communication in the Son, but from the freedom and graciousness of this self-communication in the Holy Spirit, can solve the problem of mediation without thereby making the Incarnation either a logical necessity or an almost arbitrary fact to be taken as such positivistically. The freedom of love in the Holy Spirit has its own plausibility, power to convince, radiance, light and beauty, and by this it impresses man without coercing him.[70] This kind of pneumatological view of God's Incarnation has consequences, of course, for the understanding and practice of the Church. The Church's function in this perspective is not to take root in the world and its power-structures, 'according to the flesh', but to penetrate it spiritually. Only 'in the Spirit' will it succeed in determining the difficult mean between being 'in the world' but not 'of the world' (Jn 17.11, 14 f).

In these last remarks, the view has already moved out from the person of the mediator to his work of mediation. A pneumatologically defined Christology can in fact best convey the uniqueness of Jesus Christ and his universal significance. Pneumatology once more shows the universal horizons on which Christology opens. A double movement is set up. The Father communicates himself in love to the Son, in the Spirit this love is aware of its freedom; hence, in the Spirit, this love has the possibility of communicating itself outside the Trinity. In the Spirit, of course, an inverse movement also occurs. The creature filled with God's Spirit becomes in freedom an historical figure through which the Son gives himself to the Father. In this all-consuming dedication to the point of death, the Spirit as it were becomes free; he is released from his particular historical figure, and consequently Jesus' death and resurrection mediate the coming of the Spirit (cf Jn 16.7; 20.22). And thus Jesus Christ, who in the Spirit is in person the mediator between God and man, becomes in the Spirit the universal mediator of salvation.

2. THE WORK OF THE MEDIATOR

The person and work of Jesus Christ cannot be separated. Jesus Christ dedicates himself totally to his mission, is totally identified with it. He is the envoy, sacrificed for us, God's loving reign, God's self-communicating love in person. In speaking of his Godhead and his humanity, therefore, I indicated the significance for salvation of each, and it was possible to point out various aspects of one and the same redemptive reality: love, freedom, reconciliation, and so forth. At the end of the last section it had become clear that the doctrine of the unity of Godhood and humanity in one person does not simply represent a difficult topic for speculation, but makes possible the decisive statement which sums up all that has been said so far about the

Christian conception of salvation: Salvation is participation in the life of God in the Holy Spirit through the mediation of Jesus Christ.

Our reflections on a pneumatological understanding of the hypostatic union have led us back to the basic Christological statement: Jesus is the Christ: that is, the Messiah. In the Old Testament, the Messiah was in fact expected precisely as the bearer of the Spirit (cf Is 11.2).[71] Jesus is the Christ inasmuch as he is anointed with the Holy Spirit. As the Messiah, however, he is not just a private person but an 'official person,' that is, he makes a claim to general public importance and recognition. In the Old Testament, anointing of kings and high priests signified public authorization by God. Jesus' anointing with the Holy Spirit installs him as king and high priest and makes him the dispenser of the Spirit to all who believe in him. 'From his fulness we have all received, grace upon grace' (Jn. 1.16; cf Eph 4.15 f; Col 1.18 f). In the Spirit, Christ is Lord and head of the Church as his body (Rom 12.4 f; 1 Cor 12.4-13), head of the new humanity and Lord of history (Eph 1.22 f; Col 1.18-20). In the language of dogmatic tradition, the Spirit as the *gratia unionis* is not only his private endowment of grace, but is at the same time *gratia capitis,* which overflows from Christ the head into his body the Church and is transmitted by the Church to the world.

The confession of faith 'Jesus is the Christ', sums up Jesus' significance for salvation. This credo means first, that the person of Jesus is himself salvation; it therefore expresses the unique and irreplaceable character of the Christian Gospel. Secondly, it contains Jesus' universal and public claim and thereby excludes any false idea that salvation is only interior and private. Finally, it says how Jesus is the salvation of the world; he is filled with the Holy Spirit and we share in this plenitude in the Spirit. Salvation is therefore participation through the Holy Spirit in the life of God revealed in Jesus Christ.

With this thesis we depart from the scholastic distinction between the person of the redeemer and the work of redemption, Christology and soteriology. To speak of a separate work and effect of Jesus Christ, leads to a reification of salvation into particular saving benefits.[72] Because of this, the traditional soteriology makes a very fragmentary and disorganized impression; the extremely various biblical and traditional metaphors which are extremely difficult to bring together into a unity (ransom, redemption, liberation, sealing, forgiveness, rebirth, life, and so on) and theories of redemption (especially the physical theory of the Fathers, and Anselm's satisfaction theory), are simply juxtaposed, not developed systematically from a single point of view. This unifying centre can only be the person of the mediator, 'who became for us God's wisdom, righteousness, sanctification and redemption' (1 Cor 1.30). It is only from this central point that theology can correctly interpret the saving benefits referred to above. Soteriology must therefore explain the person of Jesus Christ as the enabling source and figure of authentic humanity, by interpreting it as God's love made man for us and permanently present for us in the Spirit. Our thesis, of course, separates us just as distinctly from the liberal parallel between Jesus as filled with the Spirit and our own endowment with grace by the Holy Spirit.[73] Jesus is not merely an exemplar of man filled with the Spirit, but the principle of our endowment with grace, not just our brother, but the head of his Church. This primacy of Christ (cf

Col 1.18) can only be grounded on his divine Sonship. Where this is not acknowledged, the question must inevitably arise, Why Jesus exactly? Why not Socrates, the Buddha, the Teacher of Righteousness in Qumran, Plato's just man who suffers, Che Guevara, or someone else?

In Scripture itself Jesus' one office is already described under many different aspects and very many different titles. Jesus is the prophet, high priest, shepherd, king, lord. The older tradition, including Luther, emphasized the *munus duplex*, the office of priest and king; it is only with Calvin that the doctrine of the threefold office is worked out, that of prophet (or teacher), priest and shepherd. By way of the Catholic theology of the Enlightenment period, with M. J. Scheeben this doctrine (following the precedent, it is true, of the Roman Catechism) became the common teaching of Catholic soteriology as well, and was even officially sanctioned by the second Vatican Council.[74] Yet the demarcation and order of the three offices is still in many respects obscure. In particular, Christ's teaching office includes many features of the priestly and pastoral offices. Furthermore, Barth has pointed out the problems created by placing the prophetic office first, before the other two.[75] Barth regards it as a mistaken definition of the relation between the revelation of Jesus Christ and his work; instead of advancing from the *extra me* of Christ's person and working to the *pro me* of his turning to me, Christ's being-for-us is made, in a sort of Christian Enlightenment fashion, to constitute the hermeneutical explanatory key to an existentialist interpretation of Christ's work. Barth therefore resolutely places the *munus propheticum* after the *munus sacerdotale et regale*, which it has to reveal and announce, namely, that Jesus is the light of life and that he himself is this life. Here, Barth has certainly correctly perceived possible dangers of the doctrine of the three offices, but one should not expect too much from such historically established systematizations of Jesus' redemptive significance. Basically it is a matter of bringing out the one significance of Jesus' person and work under a three-fold aspect, and of affirming that for the world he is truth and light, the way to life, liberation to service under his rule, and that he is all this in the one Spirit.

To establish positive grounds for the thesis that salvation consists in the participation in the Holy Spirit mediated by Jesus Christ in the life of God, we must move in three stages. First we must prove the thesis from Scripture and the history of dogma, and inquire into the meaning of the term *pneuma*. Then we can try to expound the single saving reality of Jesus in the Spirit, using as guidelines the three offices (prophetical, priestly and royal). Finally, a concluding summary will attempt to indicate how the Spirit mediates the unique work of Jesus with its universal significance, and why, therefore, Jesus in the Spirit is the recapitulation, culmination, reconciliation and mediation of all reality.

'Spirit' in western tradition usually means much the same as *logos, nous, mens, intellectus, ratio*: in other words, reason, understanding, thought, mind.[76] The Hebrew word *ruach*, on the other hand, like the Greek word *pneuma*[77] in its original sense, or the Latin words *animus, anima, spiritus*, points in another direction. What is meant is air in movement, wind, storm, breeze and, above all, breath. *Ruach/pneuma* consequently mean breath of life, vital force, vital principle. Not primarily the logical, but the dynamic and, in the original sense, the inspiring element is important. The term expresses the fact that man does not ultimately belong to himself, that he is not in his own power but beyond it, that he is as it were beside himself. Yet at this very point the early Greek and biblical conceptions diverge. For

254

Scripture, spirit is not an impersonal, vital force of nature, not Dionysian intoxication as opposed to Apollonian clarity (Nietzsche). According to the Bible, man does not belong to himself because he belongs to God and owes himself entirely to God. *Ruach* (spirit) as opposed to *nephesh* (soul) is never a principle which man has and which belongs to him. God alone has and is life. Spirit is God's living power, his living and life-giving presence in the world and in history; Spirit is God's power over creation and history.

The Spirit of God is in principle at work everywhere there is life and where life comes into existence. He is operative in the first place in the creation. It is the Spirit who according to the interpretation of the Fathers 'was moving over the face of the waters' (Gen 1.2), and makes a cosmos out of chaos. 'By the word of the Lord the heavens were made, and all their host by the breath of his mouth' (Ps 33.6). 'The spirit of God has made me, and the breath of the Almighty gives me life' (Job 33.4). 'If he should take back his spirit to himself, and gather to himself his breath, all flesh would perish together, and man would return to dust' (Job 34.14 f). The Spirit of God is not only at work in nature, however, but also in civilization, in agriculture, architecture, jurisprudence and politics; all human wisdom is a gift of God's Spirit. He 'comes upon' particular human beings and makes them instruments of God's plan. The Spirit is, as it were, the sphere in which such persons moved by him are placed. The Judges, Moses, Joshua, David, are therefore not described so much as bearers of the Spirit as men borne up by the Spirit. It is said both that the Spirit is in them and rests on them, and also that they are in the Spirit. Above all, it is expected of the Messiah who is to come that 'the Spirit of the Lord shall rest upon him' (Is 11.2). The same applies to God's Servant (42.1). It is the Spirit who will lead the work of creation and history to its fulfilment. The Spirit will be poured out like water on thirsty land (Is 44.3 f); God will give them a new heart and a new spirit (cf Ezek 11.19; 18.31; 36.27). Finally in the last days, God will pour out his Spirit on all flesh, and make all prophets (cf Joel 2.28; Acts 2.17). The Spirit is, therefore, the compendium of eschatological hope and eschatological salvation. He is the power of the new being (Paul Tillich).

The comprehensive description of this universal, creative and re-creative operation of the Spirit, is found at Rom 8.18-30.[78] We can distinguish three steps in the line of thought. Paul first speaks of the creation waiting, groaning and yearning. The creation is here viewed within the apocalyptic world-picture, as an historical phenomenon. It is journeying, groans, stretches out impatiently and seeks a glimmer of hope. Expressed concretely, it is orientated towards man, or rather to the new, transfigured man, the freedom of the sons of God. World and man are as it were interwoven in their destiny. The goal and fulfilment of the world is the perfect realm of freedom. The second stage represents the sighing of the creation as prolonged in those who already possess the Spirit of sonship, the Christians. Christendom here appears both as representative of all creation in travail, and as the great promise for the world. But Christians do not know what they should pray for; they, too, are still journeying, without actually knowing where everything is leading. Consequently the third stage speaks of the sighs of the Spirit himself. He comes to the aid of our weakness; he is the power of the future who guides everything for good; he directs and impels the creation in travail and with sighs towards its eschatological goal. He is the anticipated future of all the world.

Hardly any other term or any other reality could express the universality of God's action equally well as the word *pneuma*. The concept and reality of the *pneuma* was practically the obvious one to denote the universal saving significance of Jesus Christ. According to the New Testament, the universal historical operation of God's Spirit finds its goal and measure in Jesus Christ. He is different from other bearers of the Spirit not only in degree but in kind; he is not simply moved by the Spirit but conceived and formed by the Spirit: *conceptus de Spiritu Sancto ex Maria virgine* (cf Mt 1.18, 20; Lk 1.35). At his baptism in the Jordan he is anointed with the Spirit (Mk 1.10 par.); and thus all his activity stands under the aegis of the Spirit (Lk 4.14, 18; 5.17; 6.19; 10.21 etc.); the Spirit not only rests on him (Lk 4.18) but impels him (Mk 1.12). Above all, his miracles, as an anticipation of the new creation, are presented as the operation in him of the living Spirit (Mt 12.18-21, 28; Lk 5.17; 6.19). 'In the Spirit' he gives himself on the cross to the Father (Heb 9.14); in the power of the Spirit he is raised from the dead (Rom 1.4; 8.11; 1 Tim 3.16) and becomes a living spirit (1 Cor 15.45). The mode of existence of the *Kyrios* is the *Pneuma*; that is why Paul can actually identify the two (2 Cor 3.17).[79]

Just as Jesus Christ is, on the one hand, the goal and culmination of the presence and operation of the Spirit of God, so on the other he is also the starting-point for the sending, the mission, of the Spirit. In Christ the Spirit has, as it were, finally attained his goal, the new creation. His further task now consists in integrating all other reality into that of Jesus Christ, or in other words, to universalize the reality of Jesus Christ. Jesus Christ, who is conceived by the Spirit, bestows and sends him now as his own Spirit (Lk 24.49; Acts 2.33; Jn 15.26; 16.7; 20.22). The Spirit is now the Spirit of Jesus Christ (Rom 8.9; Phil 1.19) or of the Son (Gal 4.6). His function is to bring Christ to remembrance (Jn 14.26; 16.13f). The decisive criterion for the discernment of spirits accordingly lies in the fact that only the spirit which confesses that Jesus is the Lord, is of God. Conversely, of course, it follows that 'no one can say "Jesus is Lord" except by the Holy Spirit' (1 Cor 12.3). Thus the Spirit is the medium and the force in which Jesus Christ as the new Lord of the world is accessible to us, and where we can know him. The Spirit is the active presence of the exalted Lord in the Church, in individual believers and in the world. 'In the Spirit' and 'In Christ' are for Paul almost interchangeable expressions. This interiorization and rendering present of Jesus Christ by the Spirit, does not however take place by way of the law. For the Spirit is, of course, the power of what is eschatologically new. His function is therefore constantly to render Jesus Christ present in all his newness. He is therefore also the Spirit of prophecy, whose function it is to declare what is to come (Jn 16.13); he is the earnest of the glory that will only be revealed in the future (Rom 8.23; Eph 1.14).

Between the Council of Nicaea (325) and the first Council of Constantinople (381), these biblical contexts[80] led to the realization that the Spirit cannot be merely an impersonal force or a reality subordinate to Christ. When the divinity and consubstantiality of the Spirit with the Father and the Son is in question, Athanasius and Basil argue in the same way as in dealing with the question of Jesus' divinity: If the Spirit is not true God, consubstantial with the Father and the Son, then he cannot conform us to the Son and cannot lead the way to communion with the Father.[81] Against the Pneumatomachians, who contested (*machesthai*) the divinity of the Spirit and made him a servant (*hyperetes*), a function of Christ, the Council of Constantinople therefore defined: 'I believe in the Holy Spirit, the Lord (*kyrios*) and giver of life (*zoopoios*), who proceeds from the Father, who together with the Father and the Son is worshipped and glorified (*sunproskyvoumenos kai sundoxazomeros*)' (DS 150; NR 250). As in the development of Christological doctrine, motives of soteriology and of doxology, i.e. of the practice of liturgical prayer, were decisive criteria in the doctrinal formulation and pneumatology. What was at issue was that, conformed to Christ in the Spirit, we have communion with the Father, so that in the Spirit through Christ we can praise and glorify the Father.

The confession of faith of the First Council of Constantinople in the Spirit as 'Lord and giver of life', was not as precise as the corresponding Christological formulas of Nicaea. Even in later patristic theology the doctrine of the Spirit remained very open; in East and West different theologoumena took shape. Whereas the Greeks tended to speak of the procession of the Spirit from the Father *through* the Son, after Augustine the West came to speak of the procession of the Spirit from the Father *and* the Son (*filioque*). No one objected to this different mode of expression. The breach only came much later through an unfortunate accumulation of misunderstandings as well as through mutual incomprehension in face of the differences of mentality which lay behind the differences of formulation. Today we realise once more that in reality the two formulas are not very far apart at all.[82]

The starting-point of western Trinitarian doctrine since Tertullian, Augustine and, later, Peter Lombard, was not the different persons of the Trinity and their activity in the history of salvation, but the one essence of God which in itself is triune. The appropriate representational model for this conception is the circle: The Father begets the Son, the Spirit is the mutual love common to Father and Son (*filioque*).[83] In the Spirit, therefore, the circle of the interior Trinitarian life closes. The Spirit is, as it were, what is innermost and most hidden in God. All operation *ad extra* is in this view common to all three divine persons. This conception, however, led to the significance of the Trinity being shifted from the history of salvation into metaphysics. So it came about, as Joseph Ratzinger puts it: 'As a result, both teaching about the Church and teaching about the Holy Spirit were no longer interpreted from the angle of pneumatology and charisma, but seen exclusively – in an all too resolutely earthly way – from the standpoint of the incarnation, and finally expounded entirely on the basis of the power-categories of worldly thinking. In this fashion the teaching about the Holy Spirit also became homeless; in so far as it did not drag out a miserable existence in the realm of mere edification, it was absorbed into the general speculation about the Trinity and thus for all practical purposes had no function for the Christian consciousness'.[84]

It was different in eastern Trinitarian doctrine, where the starting-point is not the one divine essence, but the Father. He alone is *ho theos*. Not only the Son but also the Spirit proceeds directly from him, even if the procession of the Spirit is conditioned by that of the Son. The Spirit is, as it were, the excess, the overflow of the love manifest in the Son; so he is the revelation of the very being of the Son, just as the Son reveals the very being of the Father. In the Spirit, the love manifested in the Son again impels onwards and outwards to a further revelation of God. The Spirit is here, as it were, God's outermost and uttermost. Through him, therefore, God acts in creation and in history.

Both views have their own particular dangers.[85] The eastern view can lead to making the Spirit independent of the Son, to a mysticism which is not indeed hostile to the world and anti-institutional, but which often enough *is* indifferent to the Church as an institution and to the world. If the Roman Catholic Church is threatened with the danger of an earthly transfiguration, a secular *theologia gloriae*, the Eastern Church is threatened with that of a heavenly transfiguration, of a glory of heaven on earth. The eastern liturgy, consequently, is regarded not so much as the representation of the earthly saving work of Christ, as of the heavenly liturgy. Ultimately, this means that the Trinitarian doctrine of the Eastern Church threatens to be not thought of in terms of sacred history but supra-historically. The western systematic insistence on the *filioque* can lead to a one-sided Christocentrism. The Church is then viewed one-sidedly from the point of view of the Incarnation as *Christus prolongatus,* as 'le Christ répandu' (Bossuet), as Christ's continuing life (J.A. Möhler). Its goal, then, is to take root in the world and permeate the world even to the point of attempting to dominate it. The East, even today, makes the Latin *filioque* and the linking of the Spirit to the Son which it expresses, responsible for a one-sided western Christocentrism and the very markedly institutional ecclesiology which is inferred from it, including even the pope's claim to be the Vicar of Christ.[86]

The abstractly metaphysical mode of thought of Latin Trinitarian doctrine has led to failure to recognize the personal rôle and freedom of the Spirit in sacred history. Most theologians have ascribed to work of sanctification and indwelling of the Spirit to the Holy Spirit only by appropriation; only a few (Petavius, Thomassin, Passaglia, Scheeben, Schauf, among others) have by dint of considerable intellectual efforts spoken of a personal indwelling (not just by appropriation) of the Spirit.[87] Only if account is taken of the relative personal rôle of the Spirit in the work of sanctification by grace, is it also possible to preserve the truth that the Spirit in his bond with Christ, and in rendering present the person and work of Christ, does not enslave man under an alien law, but sets him free, does not put him in leading-strings by rigging him out with recipes and time-tables to consult, but releases him into the air of freedom.[88] Only if this charismatic element is taken seriously is it also realized that the Spirit is freedom in person, the superabundance of God's love, through whom God introduces his inexhaustible possibilities into history. His function is, therefore, not merely to render Jesus Christ present,[89] but to make him present as filled by the Spirit. The universalization of Christ's work thus takes place in a way that is spiritual, historical, determined freely and lovingly.

The abiding presence and significance of Jesus Christ in history can now be concretely described under three aspects by means of the traditional doctrine of the three offices. Jesus Christ through his Spirit is the way (pastor and king), the truth (prophet and teacher) and the life (priest) of the world (cf Jn 14.6). A comprehensive treatment of these three aspects would of course extend beyond Christology into the doctrine of revelation, theological anthropology (doctrine of grace) and ecclesiology, as well as into the theology of this world and of earthly realities; it would also require an account of the theology of the Church's magisterium or teaching office, and of the priestly and pastoral ministry. We cannot, of course, undertake so much in the present context. We must be content to glimpse at a few main perspectives in order once again to show the significance of the person and work of Jesus Christ for salvation.

1. The question of truth is a radical human question, especially of philosophy. Light, therefore, is one of the primordial symbols of mankind. For truth and light are not something adventitious, superimposed on reality and life; they are the medium in which reality and life can alone be human reality and humanly fulfilled life. Only where there is light and where things appear unconcealed (truth: *aletheia*), can man get his bearings in his world and find his way. Light is therefore a symbol of salvation, and darkness of perdition. But where is there a dependable light among the many will-o'-the-wisps and the deceitful glitter of the world?

The Old Testament speaks of Yahweh himself as light (Ps 27.1; 2 Sam 22.29; Is 60.19); his law is a lamp to the feet and a light to the path (Ps 119.105; cf. 19.9). The New Testament takes up this message. Jesus Christ is frequently designated as the eschatological prophet (Deut 18.15) promised in the Old Testament (Acts 3.22; Jn 1.45; 6.14). Similarly he is known as a teacher (Mk 1.22; 10.17; Mt 8.19; 23.10; Jn 13.13). The fourth gospel describes him as light of the world (Jn 1.9; 8.12; 12.46), as truth (14.6), the Letter to the Hebrews as the final revelation of God (1.1 f). He opposed lies and darkness, which are the consequence of sin (Rom 1.18 ff; Jn 1.5; 3.19; 8.44; 1 Jn 3.8). Consequently Christ's Spirit is called the Spirit of truth

(Jn 14.17; 15.26; 16.13), spirit of faith (2 Cor 4.13), of wisdom and of revelation, who enlightens the eyes of our heart, so that we may understand our vocation and inheritance (Eph 1.17 f).

It would be interesting to trace the long history of the symbolism of light in the Christian liturgy and its application to Jesus Christ, who is celebrated in the Easter Vigil as light, at Christmas and Epiphany as *sol invictus*.[90] Theologically it would be even more rewarding to study the metaphysics of light which dates back to Plato and Neo-Platonism, is introduced into Christian tradition by Augustine, reaches its culmination in the Franciscan theology of the thirteenth century with Grosseteste, Roger Bacon, Witelo and Bonaventure, and is given magnificent poetic expression in Dante. One would also have to mention the significance of light in modern nature-philosophy and in modern science. Finally we should have to go into the history of the idea of truth. To try to do so would, however, amount in practice to presenting a complete account of the whole history of western civilization and the western mind, which is obviously impossible. Yet only against that vast horizon can it become at all clear what it means to say that Jesus Christ is light, truth, prophet and teacher. In him the truth about God, man and the world has definitively become manifest, and his Spirit is for all who believe the *Lumen cordium* (Pentecost sequence, *Veni Sancte Spiritus*). Through him the meaning of existence has been definitively disclosed.

The eschatological finality of the coming of truth includes two things, the historical impossibility of surpassing its revelation in Christ, and the abiding presence of Christ's truth in the world through the Spirit, whose function it is to recall Christ's words and works and, by bringing them to remembrance, to keep them present (cf Jn 14.26; 16.13 f). Yet at the same time the Spirit is to declare the things that are to come. The truth of Jesus Christ can therefore not be rendered present in a rigid way, by mere repetition or by systematic logical explication, but only in a living and prophetic way. It is an essential feature of a prophet[91] that he does not occupy an absolute standpoint beyond history, but that his utterance is part of the events; he is subject to all the ambiguity and fragmentariness of the particular situation. But at the same time his message breaks through it, because it keeps awake the remembrance of faith and opens out a wider horizon of promise. It discloses possibilities which previously were covered or forgotten, and thus challenges decision and conversion. At the same time, the concrete historical meaning and the concrete historical realization of his message has to be manifested in the historical conflict of opinions. Jesus Christ is therefore the definitive truth inasmuch as again and again he proves himself to be truth, standing the test of historical situations. The finality of the truth which Jesus Christ himself is, is therefore the finality of God's fidelity which is demonstrated again and again in the historical course of the Church.[92]

2. Life too is, like light, a fundamental word. 'Scarcely any word with which philosophical thought has always been concerned, bears as many meanings as the word "life". Scarcely any term so eludes any attempt to

determine its use, without impoverishing its meaning, by defining it.'[93] For like light, life is not one object side by side with others, but 'the How, which characterizes all living beings as such'.[94] Vitality is event, self-movement, self-accomplishment, and is therefore not accessible to objective observation. 'The experience of life means the experience of something objective from which the subject cannot detach and distinguish himself . . . One of the basic features of the philosophical concept of life is the identification it involves of thought with what is other than itself, with what does not think. The concept of life is consequently opposed to the dichotomy of thought-matter.'[95] Life is therefore always more than the purely biological; life includes man and his question about life, about authentic, fulfilled, true life. Life longs for the light of life, and that light is an essential factor in life itself. But since life is constantly threatened by decay and death, the question of true life includes the question of abiding, eternal life.

The religious root-question about life is answered in the Old Testament with the confession of faith that God alone is the fount and Lord of life (cf 1 Sam 2.6; Job 12.9 f; Deut 32.39; Ps 104.29, etc.). His life has appeared in Jesus Christ (Jn 1.4; 5.26; 11.25; 14.6; 1 Jn 1.1; 5.11); he is sent to bring life to the world (Jn 3.15 f; 10.10). He who believes in him already has life (Jn 5.24; 1 Jn 3.14); similarly, he who loves his brethren has passed out of death into life (1 Jn 3.14; cf. 4.7, 12, 16). The life that has appeared in Jesus Christ is ultimately revealed in Jesus' sacrifice on the cross and in his resurrection from the dead (Rom 6.10; 14.9; 2 Cor 13.4, etc.). Death is finally defeated thereby (Rom 5.10), and life opened for those who believe (Rom 1.17; 6.8 ff; Gal 3.11; Heb 10.38, etc.). This life is bestowed on us in the Spirit. For he is God's vital creative power by which Christ was raised from the dead. The life of the risen Christ therefore dwells in believers through the Spirit given them in baptism (Rom 8.2, 10; Gal 6.8). He is the first fruits (Rom 8.23) and the guarantee (2 Cor 1.22; 5.5; Eph 1.14) of eternal life.

By giving his life, his self-sacrifice, Jesus is both sacrificial victim and sacrificing priest. This is already expressed in the Marcan-Matthean version of the eucharistic tradition (Mk 14.24; Mt 26.28), in the reference to the blood of the covenant with which the Israelites were sprinkled in Sinai (Ex 24.8). For that reason the Lord's Supper is contrasted with pagan sacrifices in 1 Cor 10.14-22. In John, Jesus' Last Supper is interpreted as a Passover meal (19.14, 36); Paul designates Jesus as paschal lamb (1 Cor 5.7; cf. 1 Pet 1.2, 19). He is the lamb which takes away the sins of the world (Jn 1.29, 36; cf. Rev 5.6, 12; 13.8). Finally, we read in Ephesians 5.2: 'He gave himself up for us, a fragrant offering and sacrifice to God'. An explicit theology of the sacrifice of the cross and of the high priesthood, is not found until the Letter to the Hebrews (3.1; 4.14 ff; 5.1 ff; 7.11 ff, etc.), where it is also said, of course, that Jesus has fulfilled and surpassed all the other sacrifices and so has abrogated them, but in the double sense of ending them yet raising them to a higher plane. The Letter to the Hebrews makes Christ say with Ps 39.7-9 when he comes into the world: 'Sacrifices and offerings thou has not desired, but a body thou hast prepared for me; in burnt offerings and sin offerings thou hast taken no pleasure. Then I said, "Lo, I have come to do thy will, O God," as it is written of me in the roll of the book' (10.5-7).

The talk of sacrifices, sacrificing priests and their intrinsic connexion with the question of the meaning of life, is not very easy to understand in our modern world where there is no counter-example of pagan sacrifices, and where people only speak of 'sacrifice' or of 'making sacrifices' in a secular sense. For what is a sacrifice? It is not a matter of the performance of a ritual. That is only a set form of expression of self-giving to God in order to attain communion with him. The external sacrificial gift stands as a symbol for the inner attitude of sacrifice, which denotes that the sacrificer is leaving the realm of sin in order to acknowledge God as true life, to be reconciled to him and to have communion with him. Sacrifice is therefore an objective symbol of praise, acknowledgement, thanksgiving and petition to God.[96] Hegel rightly defined sacrifice as the practical exercise of religion and faith.[97] To honour God in this way is not simply a private matter but a public concern. Consequently it requires a publicly appointed and authorized priest to offer the sacrifice in the name of the people. Against this background, to speak of Jesus' sacrificial death and of his high-priestly office becomes intelligible. What it means is, that in a public capacity he has opened out life for all and established reconciliation with God. Because he is in person the mediator between God and man, he was also in a position to perform the work of mediation. His sacrifice on the cross together with the resurrection, is therefore the highest exercise and definitive realization of his unity with God. Jesus Christ's function as priest and victim in one, gives expression once again, though in a way that is not easily understood by us today, to what the meaning of life is.

The eschatological turning-point which came with Jesus Christ, and the eschatological personal life made possible by him, thus become concrete reality in the Holy Spirit who dwells in the baptized as in a temple (1 Cor 3.16; cf 6.19; Rom 5.5; 8.11). Paul can actually define the Christian as one who is filled and impelled by the Holy Spirit. 'All who are led by the Spirit of God are sons of God' (Rom 8.14). What it means to be led by the Spirit in this manner is described by Paul through its contrast with life 'according to the flesh' (*kata sarxa*) (Rom 8.5 ff; Gal 5.16 ff). While the Spirit is God's vital power which is not under man's control, the 'flesh' is the sphere of the human being who thinks he can be master of his life by his own strength and power. The 'flesh' is the self-contained and cramped mode of existence of *homo incurvatus*, turned in on himself. Such fleshliness is expressed not only by 'sensuality' — Paul lists immorality, impurity, licentiousness, drunkenness and gluttony — but also by egotistical will to power — emnity, strife, jealousy, anger, selfishness, dissension, party spirit, envy, and finally, in refusal of God, idolatry, sorcery — which lead to fear and abandon man to futility and ultimately to death. The fruit of the Spirit, on the other hand, is love, joy, peace, patience, kindness, goodness, faithfulness, gentleness and self-control

(Gal 5.19-23; cf Rom 14.17). In short, one might say that the Spirit makes man open to God and his neighbour. It is the Spirit who causes man to come before God boldly and confidently and cry 'Abba! Father!' (Rom 8.15, 26; Gal 4.6); 'to walk by the Spirit' likewise means 'through love to be servants of one another' (Gal 5.13-15). Consequently love, according to 1 Corinthians 13, is the highest of all gifts of the Spirit; 'If I have not love, I am nothing' (1 Cor 13.2). So it is in the Spirit that the realization of the new humanity becomes possible: dedication to God and existence for others.

3. Consideration of the priestly office showed that life and salvation are not purely private matters, but have a public and to that extent political dimension. This thesis is based on the solidarity that links the freedom of one individual with that of all others. Freedom, life and salvation therefore presuppose an order of freedom, peace and justice. Consequently 'empire', 'city', 'state', have since long ago been not only political terms but also religious symbols. The king[98] counts as God's representative, indeed as a god, or son of God; he represented the sacred cosmic and political order within which alone salvation is possible. The ideal figure of the good king (*euergetes*) rules men like a god, and pastures them as a shepherd does his sheep. The shepherd and king motifs were closely linked in the ancient East. Behind both stood the question of sound and healthy order, which gives protection against the ruin of chaos, the question of leadership and guidance, security, tranquillity and peace.

The Old Testament answers the political question of salvation in an extremely exclusive way: Yahweh is King (Ex 15.18; Ps 145;11 ff; 146.10, etc.). Yahweh is Israel's shepherd (Ps 23; Gen 48.15; 49.24; etc.). Consequently it was only in face of the greatest resistance that it was possible to introduce an earthly kingship (1 Sam 8); the earthly kingship soon became a promise of the coming messianic King (cf 2 Sam 7). Jesus was reserved in regard to these messianic expectations; the cross destroyed them completely and made it clear that his rule was of a different order, that of service for the many. So he knows he is sent as a shepherd to seek out the lost sheep (Lk 15.4-7; Mt 18.12-14); he has compassion on the throng that is scattered and without a shepherd (Mk 6.34; Mt 9.36). Consequently he wants to gather together the lost sheep of Israel (Mt 10.6; 15.24). Under the image of the shepherd he sees his own death (Mk 14.27 f) as well as the last Judgment (Mt 25.32). The image of the shepherd, in fact, takes up Jesus' words about discipleship; Jesus goes before those who are his on the way. It therefore rightly belongs to the Christological statements of the primitive Church (1 Pet 2.25; 5.4; Heb 13.20; Rev 7.17; 14.4). The fullest treatment of Jesus as the good, that is, true shepherd, is found in the fourth gospel; he gives his life for his sheep, knows his own who know they are safe with him (10.11-16). 'Shepherding in the world is only an image and a pointer to the true proper shepherding which is shown in the rule of the Revealer'.[99] Jesus is the author, leader, pioneer (*'archegos'*) of life, salvation and faith (Acts 3.15; 5.31; Heb 2.10; 12.2). The shepherd statements, for the New Testament, imply royal majesty, sovereignty. Consquently the post-Easter community designated Jesus not only as Christ and Lord (*Kyrios*) but as king (*basileus*). Yet just as he is the crucified Messiah, so too he is a King on the cross (Mk 15.2, 9, 12, 18, 26). This *interpretatio christiana* of sovereign rule appears most clearly in the scene with Pilate where Jesus, mocked by the howling mob, streaming with blood, crowned with thorns, is asked by Pilate, 'Are you the King of the Jews?'. He then defines the kind of kingship that is his, in two ways: 'not of this world', 'witness to the truth' (Jn 18.33-37). His dominion is exercised by announcing his message and dispensing the sacraments, by faith and discipleship (Mt 28.19). Only in this sense is he 'King of kings and Lord of lords' (1 Tim 6.15; Rev 19.6). Christ's rule is ultimately at the service of God's. Just as we Christians belong to Christ as our Lord, so Christ belongs to God his Father (1 Cor 3.23). In the end, however, Christ will give up his Kingdom into the hands of his Father; then God will 'be all in all' (1 Cor 15.28). Christ's royal rule is marked by the two basic motives which characterize his whole being and work: dedication to God and service of human beings.

The statement that Jesus in the end will hand over his rule to the Father, has given rise to many speculations. It has often been compared with Rev 20.1-10, which speaks of a thousand-year messianic kingdom on earth which is to precede the final coming of God's reign and the general resurrection of the dead. In antiquity, Marcellus of Ancyra deduced that at the end of time Christ will lay aside his human nature and revert to God. It was in opposition to this opinion that the First Council of Constantinople (381) added to the Creed the words 'and of his kingdom there will be no end' (DS 150; NR 250). This safe-guarded the definitive, eschatological character of the person and work of Jesus Christ and his eternal reign (Lk 1.33). God's rule and kingdom does not mean the end of Christ's, but its accomplishment. The interval between the coming of Christ and the perfect accomplishment of God's reign, was imagined by Chiliásm[100] (*chilioi*=1000) in sometimes fantastic pictures. The most influential historically were the speculations of Joachim of Flora (died c. 1201), who foretold a coming age of the Holy Spirit and a spiritual interpretation of the Gospel, which would supersede the age of the Son, of the visible hierarchical Church. Modern philosophies of history and historical utopias have taken up this idea of progress in various secular ways; this is particularly true of the Marxist expectation of a qualitative change from the realm of necessity to that of free-dom. German National Socialism perverted to evil the dream of a third thousand-year empire. The eschatological character of the person and work of Christ is always misrep-resented in principle, whenever Christianity is incorporated into a secular pattern of progress. The Spirit is the Spirit of Christ; even if he constantly opens out the future afresh, he does not lead beyond Christ, but ever deeper into Christ's mystery. Therefore the transition from letter to Spirit has to be made continually anew, and the tension between the two in history has always to be endured.

Statements about Christ's royal office confront us with the burning question of the relation which Christ's rule bears to political rule in the world. And what is its relation to the Church? If talk of Christ's rule is not to be mere empty words and hollow emotion or the occasion for all kinds of fanatical or ideological misinterpretations, we must ask where and how Christ's sovereignty is actually exercised.

The answers given to this question in the course of church history display two tendencies. One is to identify the Kindom of God or rule of Christ either with the Church or with particular political or cultural forces or movements. Eusebius of Caesarea, the court theologian of Emperor Constantine, considered that the age of messianic fulfilment which began with Christ had come in Constantine's Christian Roman Empire: 'One God, one *Logos*, one Empire'. The dogma of Nicaea and the development of the Church's doctrine of the Trinity, inevitably appeared by contrast not only as sedition in the metaphysical world, but at the same time as sedition in the political order, subverting the very foundation of that political theology.[101] It was not by chance that Athanasius, the champion of the Christological dogma, also became, with Ambrose and Hilary, the champion of the Church's freedom from the Emperor. Christology thus founded a political theology of a new kind; the distinction between religion and politics became one of the essential bases of western ideas of freedom and tolerance. The mediaeval disputes between papacy and empire about the *libertas ecclesiae*, must therefore in justice also be regarded as part of the history of the western idea of freedom. It is true that it took the Church itself long enough, until Vatican II in fact, to recognize these consequences clearly and to overcome in principle any Integrism which would seek to impose a *potestas directa* of the Church in secular spheres,[102] even if in practice it still finds it difficult to accept this. Yet at the present time it is already having to defend this Christologically-based principle against neo-integralist endeavours which, developing certain ideas of the liberal Protestant theology of culture, seek on left-wing lines to make the Church itself form the advance guard of political liberation movements.

In contrast to the integralist tendency is the dualist conception of the relation between the reign of Christ and the Church or secular authorities. In Marcion's dualism of the orders of creation and redemption, there was also a radical identification of the kingdom with God or Christ: 'In evangelio est Dei regnum Christus ipse'.[103] On different principles there is a tendency to its spiritualization in some of the mystics and in many forms of the Lutheran two-kingdoms doctrine. To Gnostic dualism, Irenaeus already opposes his theology of the history of salvation, which makes it possible to safeguard both Christological unity and eschatological tension. The most important and historically influential, though often misunderstood synthesis, was that of Augustine in his City of God: *civitas Dei* and *civitas terrena* which from the beginning of history are in conflict, are not simply identical with Church and state. The line of division cuts across Church and state; each of them is mixed.[104] 'Fecerunt itaque civitates duas amores duo': self-love and the love of God,[105] life according to the flesh and life according to the Spirit. Consequently, the Church is only the dawn of the Kingdom of God. Many in fact who are outside are inside, while many who are in, are outside. The Church is only an effective and accomplished sacramental sign, not the reality of the Kingdom of God itself.

The sacramental and sacred-history viewpoint was renewed by the second Vatican Council: 'By her relationship with Christ, the Church is a kind of sacrament or sign of intimate union with God, and of the unity of all mankind'.[106] Fundamental in this definition is the concept of sacramental sign, which makes it possible to remain distinct from the neo-romantic idea that the Church is the continuation of the Incarnation, yet nevertheless understand the Church on the analogy of the hypostatic union: that is to say, as 'one interlocked reality which is comprised of a divine and human element'.[107] By this, the importance of the visible Church for salvation as well as its weakness and sinfulness, and the manifold Christian elements outside the Church, can be recognized. It can be maintained that the rule of Christ takes place in and through the visible Church and that nevertheless it is wider and more comprehensive than the Church; in the Church, as in the world, it is both visible and hidden in sign. The Church can therefore only fulfil its mission in correspondence with the 'signs of the times' which on the one hand it can interpret by faith, and through which, on the other hand, it is led more deeply into the meaning of faith.[108]

This conciliar view is often criticized for its one-sided Christocentrism and its neglect of the pneumatological dimension. It is said that according to the Council texts, the Spirit is only a function of Christ, that he only serves to bring Christ's words and work to universal effect and to bring about their subjective appropriation. Consequently the Church is viewed one-sidedly as Christ's foundation, the institutional aspect is in the foreground, while the charismatic and prophetic aspect is not given its full value. Yves Congar and others have shown that this criticism is too one-sided to be true.[109] Nevertheless, there is obviously still work to be done here. If what has been said is correct, we must concede that what Christ's rule means in actuality can ultimately only be expressed in prophetic signs. It is the saints who are the practical interpretation of Christ's will for any particular period.

The three aspects of the one activity of Jesus Christ in the Spirit brings us finally face to face with the same problem of mediation. On the one hand we had to consider the universal activity of the Spirit in the whole of creation, in nature and history; pneumatology was therefore a help to express the universality of the salvation that has come in Jesus Christ. On the other hand we had to hold strictly to the uniqueness of Jesus Christ, and define the Spirit as the Spirit of Jesus Christ. Consequently a double question arises: 1. What is the relation between the Spirit of Jesus Christ and the human spirit which is operative in the history of religions? 2. What is the relation between the Spirit of Jesus Christ and the Spirit which is active in the Church and in individual believers? In what way, therefore, is Jesus Christ the head of all men, and the head of the Church?

1. The biblical statements about the universal operation of God's Spirit throughout the history of mankind link up with anthropological statements about man's self-transcendence, his rising above and beyond himself, his longing for what is totally other, his hope for a new beginning, his question about salvation and redemption. For human existence is experienced as ex-sistence, ecstasy, exodus. This going beyond oneself has its ground in the

freedom of the human person; but it is nevertheless only possible by participation in the absolute creative force and power of all life.[110] Only where man opens himself in freedom to the Spirit of God, who comes to the aid of our weakness, can he find the meaning and fulfilment of his existence. That existence only succeeds if man allows himself in freedom, i.e. in faith, hope and love, to be led by the Spirit of God, in the dialogue of divine and human spirit. Everywhere, therefore, where men take upon themselves the risk of their existence, recognize the obligation to seek for truth and with evident seriousness accept responsibility, especially, however, where they abandon self and open themselves in love to God and their neighbour, the Spirit of God is at work. Wherever this happens in the religions and cultures of mankind, God's salvation is bestowed on men through them.

History also displays, of course, the other phenomenon, of human beings wanting to hold fast to their life, shutting themselves off and refusing the Spirit, and thereby failing to find themselves. Man can comfortably install himself in a humdrum philistine way among the trivialities and small joys of every day, and profess to be satisfied with what is and the way it is. Nietzsche described this refusal under the image of the last human being: 'There cometh the time when man will no longer launch the arrow of his longing beyond man — and the string of his bow will have unlearned to whizz! . . . Lo! I show you the last man. "What is love? What is creation? What is longing? What is a star?" — so asketh the last man and blinketh . . .'[111] But man can also presume, Prometheus-fashion, to be master of his life, without God, and to realize for himself the hopes that are in him. This, too, has been described by Nietzsche, in the superman, who wills God to be dead in order to become God himself.[112] This double refusal to accept the meaning and fulfilment of existence as a gift, marks the whole of history. Consequently the influence of God's Spirit appears in the history of mankind only in a disfigured and disguised, easily misunderstood and distorted way. The history of religions and cultures is profoundly ambivalent.

The Christian conviction is that there is only one instance in history where the Spirit found acceptance in a unique way, totally, undistorted and untarnished — in Jesus Christ. In the power of the Spirit he was wholly a mould and receptacle for God's self-communication through the Logos. He is this in an utterly unique way, so that he is God's love, the meaning of all reality, in person. The universal historical activity of the Spirit therefore reached its goal in him in a way that is ultimate. Light falls from Jesus Christ on the rest of history; Jesus Christ is for the Christian the measure and criterion for the discernment of spirits. Only through him and in him is it possible to share in the complete fullness of the Spirit. Conversely, it is also true that the plenitude and full riches of Christ in Christianity will only find realization when the Spirit-inspired riches of the nations have found entry into the Church and have been 'sublated' in the Church. The mission and conversion to Christianity are always both crisis and fulfilment.

A Christology in a pneumatological perspective is therefore what best enables us to combine both the uniqueness and the universality of Jesus Christ. It can show how the Spirit who is operative in Christ in his fulness, is at work in varying degrees everywhere in the history of mankind, and also how Jesus Christ is the goal and head of all humanity.[113] The Body of Christ, the Church, is greater and wider than the institutional boundaries of the Church; it has existed since the beginning of the world and to it belong all who allow themselves to be led by Christ's Spirit in faith, hope and love.

2. The unique and universal claim of Jesus Christ cannot be expressed merely in an interior and hidden way, but needs social and public attestation and representation. Because of the historical nature and solidarity of mankind, salvation, and that means Christ's Spirit, must be mediated in an historical and public manner. This happens in a fragmentary way through the religions of mankind. The unequivocal plenitude of the Spirit only finds its full effect and expression, however, where men explicitly confess Jesus Christ as the Lord, where they allow themselves to be laid hold of by his Spirit explicitly and publicly in faith, and submit to him as ground and measure, origin and goal. Where this happens through proclamation and the sacraments as signs of faith, there is the Church. It is the Body of Christ because in it the Spirit of Christ is present and vivifying in a public manner. And the Spirit produces in the Church both community with Jesus Christ and submission to him as head of the Church.

The Spirit is, therefore, in every respect the mediation, in freedom, of love, unity and distinction. This is shown once again in the relation between Church and world. The two cannot be either set in opposition in a dualist way, or absorbed in one another monistically. The Spirit of Christ is indeed at work everywhere where men seek to transcend their life towards an ultimate meaning of their existence and where, in the hope of being finally and absolutely accepted, they seek to accept themselves and their fellow men. But all these anonymous ways to Christ attain their ultimate clarity and fulfilment only in an explicit encounter with him. The Church cannot regard itself, therefore, as a closed system. It must enter on a spiritual exchange and an intellectual discussion with the world. In this, it must on the one hand pay heed to the external prophecy of the world, yet on the other bear witness that in Jesus Christ alone the hopes of mankind have been fulfilled in a unique and insurpassable way; and that he is the great Amen to all promises (cf 2 Cor 1.20).

Notes

[1] Cf *supra*, Pt II, ch. IV.

[2] See on this *supra*, Pt II, ch. VII.

[3] Cf F. Loofs, *Leitfaden zum Studium der Dogmengeschichte* (6th ed., Tübingen, 1959), pp. 69 ff; *idem, Theophilus von Antiochien Adversus Marcionem und die anderen theologischen Quellen bei Irenaeus* (Leipzig, 1930), (TU 46).

[4] Ignatius of Antioch, Eph VII, 2 *(The Apostolic Fathers* II/II/I, p. 47 f), and also Eph XVIII, 2 (*ibid.*, pp. 74 f); Smyrn I, 1 (*ibid.*, p. 289); 2 Clem 9.5 (*The Apostolic*

Fathers I/II, p. 230); Hermas, Sim. V, 6f (GCS 48,57f).
[5] Cf on this passage R. Schnackenburg, *Johannesevangelium* I, pp. 241-9. ET: *The Gospel according to St. John*, vol. 1 (London, 1968), pp. 265-57.
[6] See in particular on this, W. Pannenberg, *Grundzüge der Christologie* (Gütersloh, 1964), pp. 335 ff; ET: *Jesus — God and Man* (London, 1968), pp. 334 ff, and also D. Wiederkehr, 'Entwurf einer systematischen Christologie' in US III/1, pp. 506ff.
[7] For more detailed treatment, see A. von Harnack, *Lehrbuch der Dogmengeschichte*, vols. I and II (5th ed., Tübingen, 1931) ET: *History of Dogma*, 7 vols (New York, 1962); R. Seeberg, *Lehrbuch der Dogmengeschichte*, vols I and II (3rd ed., Leipzig-Erlangen, 1920-3); ET: *Textbook of the History of Dogma* (Grand Rapids, 1956); F. Loofs, *Leitfaden zum Studium der Dogmengeschichte* (6th ed., Tübingen, 1959); M. Werner, *Die Entstehung des christlichen Dogmas* (2nd ed., Bern-Tübingen, 1954); ET: *The Formation of Christian Dogma* (London-New York, 1957); A. Adam, *Lehrbuch der Dogmengeschichte*, vol. I, *Die Zeit der alten Kirche* (Gütersloh, 1965); G. L. Prestige, *God in Patristic Thought* (2nd ed., London, 1956); A. Grillmeier, 'Die theologische und sprachliche Vorbereitung der christologischen Formel von Chalkedon', in: *Das Konzil von Chalcedon*, vol. I (4th ed., Würzburg, 1973), pp. 5-202; *idem, Christ in Christian Tradition: From the Apostolic Age to Chalcedon* (London, 1965); P. Smulders, 'Dogmengeschichtliche und lehramtliche Entfaltung der Christologie', in: MS III/1, pp. 389-475. J. Liébaert, *Christologie (Handbuch der Dogmengeschichte, III/1)* (Freiburg, 1966).
[8] Irenaeus, *Adversus haereses* III, 19, 2.
[9] *Ibid.* III, 16, 2.3.8; 17, 4.
[10] *Ibid.* V praef.
[11] *Ibid.* III, 19, 1; ET: Anti-Nicene Library, vol. V, 1 (Edinburgh; 1868), p.345.
[12] Cf Tertullian, *Adversus Praxeam* 26 f (PL 2,212-216); 27 (215 B-C): 'Videmus duplicem statum non confusum, sed conjunctum in una persona, Deum et hominem Jesum. De Christo autem differo. Et adeo salva est utriusque proprietas substantiae, ut et spiritus res suas egerit in illo, id est virtutes et opera et signa, et caro passiones suas functa sit, esuriens sub diabolo, sitiens sub Samaritide, flens Lazarum, anxia usque ad mortem; denique et mortua est.' On the preparation of the formula in Melito of Sardis and Hippolytus, see Grillmeier, 'Die theologische und sprachliche Vorbereitung der christologischen Formel von Chalkedon,' *op. cit.*, pp. 38ff.
[13] P. Smulders, 'Dogmengeschichtliche und lehramtliche Entfaltung der Christologie', in: *op. cit*, p. 416.
[14] On recent scholarship, see A. Grillmeier, 'Das Scandalum oecumenicum des Nestorius in kirchlich-dogmatischer und theologiegeschichtlicher Sicht', in: *Scholastik* 36 (1961), pp. 321-56.
[14a] ET: R.V. Sellers, *The Council of Chalcedon* (London, 1953), pp. 210 f.
[15] See in this regard W. Pannenberg, *Grundzüge, op. cit.*, pp. 291-5; ET: pp. 291-6.
[16] Cf. J. Daniélou, 'Christologie et eschatologie', in: *Das Konzil von Chalkedon: Geschichte und Gegenwart*, ed. A. Grillmeier and H. Bacht (3 vols., Würzburg, 1951-4), vol. 3, pp. 269-86.
[17] On this, see C. Moeller, 'Le chalcédonisme et le neo-chalcédonisme en Orient de 451 à la fin du VIe siècle', in: *op. cit.*, vol. 1, pp. 637-720; A. Grillmeier, 'Vorbereitung des Mittelalters. Eine Studie über das Verhältnis von Chalkedonismus und Neo-Chalkedonismus in der lateinischen Theologie von Boethius bis zu Gregor dem Grossen', in: *op. cit.*, vol. 2, pp. 791-839.
[18] Cf L. Ott, 'Das Konzil von Chalkedon in der Frühscholastik', in: *op. cit.*, vol. 2, pp. 873-922; I. Backes, 'Die christologische Problematik der Hochscholastik und ihre Beziehung zu Chalkedon', in: *op. cit.*, pp. 923-39.
[19] Cf J. Ternus, 'Das Seelen—und Bewusstseinsleben Jesu', in: *op. cit.*, vol. 3, pp. 117-57.
[20] On this term and the history of its meaning, see in particular, E. Lohse, Art. *prosopon* in: TW VI, 769-781; S. Schlossmann, *Persona und prosopon im Recht und im christ-*

lichen Dogma, (Darmstadt, 1968); H. Rheinfelder, *Das Wort 'Persona* (Halle, 1928); M. Nédoncelle, *'Prosponon* et *persona* dans l'antiquité', in: *RevSR* 22 (1948), pp. 277-99; for a summary, A. Halder − A. Grillmeier − H. Erharter, Art. 'Person', in: LTK VIII, 287-92, with bibliography.

[21] Cf C. Andresen, 'Zur Entstehung und Geschichte des trinitarischen Personbegriffs', in: ZNW 52 (1961), pp. 1-39; and also J. Ratzinger, 'Zum Personverständnis in der Theologie', in: J. Ratzinger, *Dogma und Verkündigung* (Munich-Freiburg, 1973), pp. 205-23.

[22] Cf H. Köster, Art. *'hypostasis'*, in: TW VIII, 571-88 and in particular the study by H. Dörries, *Hypostasis. Wort- und Bedeutungsgeschichte* (Göttingen, 1955).

[23] Cf. H. Dörries, *De Spiritu Sancto. Der Beitrag des Basilius zum Abschluss des trinitarischen Dogmas* (Göttingen, 1956).

[24] A.M.S. Boethius, *Liber de persona et duabus naturis* III (PL 64, 1343).

[25] Leontius of Byzantium, *Contra Nestorianos et Eutychianos*, lib. I (PG 86, 1280 A); idem, *Solutio argumentorum a severo objectorum* (PG 86, 1917 D).

[26] Cf Rusticus Diaconus, *Contra Acephalos disputatio* (PL 67, 1239 B).

[27] Cf Leontius of Byzantium, *Contra Nestorianos et Eutychianos*, lib. I (PG 86, 1277 C-D).

[28] Maximus Confessor, *Opuscula theologica et polemica*, 8 (PG 91, 97 A).

[29] Richard of St Victor, *De Trinitate* IV, 22, 24 (PL 196, 945-947).

[30] On this see in particular, Thomas Aquinas, *Summa theol.* I, q. 29, a. 1-4.

[31] Cf J. Duns Scotus, *Ordinatio*, lib. I, dist. 23, q. 1, in: *Opera*, 5 vols, ed. P.A. Sépinski (Rome, 1959), pp. 355 ff, and on this, H. Mühlen, *Sein und Person nach Johannes Duns Scotus. Beiträge zur Metaphysik der Person* (Werl, 1954).

[32] On what follows, cf. the dogmatics textbooks of L. Ott, J. Pohle, F. Diekamp, M. Schmaus, and the account given in K. Adam, *Der Christus des Glaubens* (Düsseldorf, 1954), especially pp. 212 ff.

[33] Cf J. Locke, *Essay Concerning Human Understanding*, Bk II, ch. xxvii.

[34] Cf J. Ternus, *Das Seelen- und Bewusstseinsleben Jesu*, pp. 179-86 (on Schell), and pp. 199-206 (on Günther and Rosmini).

[35] *Ibid.* pp. 136-42.

[36] It is well-known that there is an interesting difference between the non-official text of the encyclical in the *Osservatore Romano* (13.9.1951, No. 212, p.2), and the official text in: AAS 43 (1951), p. 638 (DS 3905). Whereas in the non-official text theologians are criticized for assuming, even only psychologically, a human subject in his own right in Christ, this 'saltem psychologice' does not appear in the official text. Accordingly in the definitive text only Nestorianism and Adoptianism are condemned, but the question of Jesus' human self-consciousness is left open.

[37] Cf in this regard J. Ternus, *Das Seelen- und Bewusstseinsleben Jesu*, pp. 208-37; A. Grillmeier, 'Zum Christusbild der heutigen katholischen Theologie', in: FThH, pp. 277-96; R. Haubst, 'Welches Ich spricht in Christus?' in: TThZ 66 (1957), pp. 1-20.

[38] Cf in particular, K. Rahner, 'Reflections on the Knowledge and Self-consciousness of Christ', in: *Theological Investigations*, vol. V (London, 1966), pp. 193-215.

[39] Idem, 'The Position of Christology in the Church between Exegesis and Dogmatics', in: *Theological Investigations*, vol. XI (London, 1974), p. 198.

[40] Cf P. Schoonenberg, *Hij is een God van mensen; ET: The Christ* (New York, 1971), pp. 80 ff, and K. Reinhardt, 'Die menschliche Transzendenz Jesu Christ', in: TrThZ 80 (1971), pp. 273-89; A. Schilson & W. Kasper, *Christologie im Präsens* (Freiburg, 1974), pp. 115-22.

[41] In so many words, *loc. cit*, p. 79.

[42] *Ibid*, p. 92.

[43] For example, *ibid.*, p. 94, and cf. also p. 98 and note 18a on p. 98.

[44] *Ibid.* p. 98.

[45] *Ibid.*, p. 100.

[46] *Ibid.*, p. 104.

[47] P. Schoonenberg, 'Trinität – der vollendete Bund', in: *Orientierung* 37 (1973), p. 116.

[48] On the following, see in particular B. Welte, 'Zur Christologie von Chalkedon', in: *idem, Auf der Spur des Ewigen* (Freiburg, 1965), pp. 429-58. For the understanding of the concept of person I owe a good deal to M. Müller, *Erfahrung und Geschichte. Grundzüge einer Philosophie der Freiheit als transzendentale Erfahrung* (Freiburg-Munich, 1971), especially pp. 83-123; M. Müller – W. Vossenkuhl, Art. 'Person', in: *Handbuch philosophischer Grundbegriffe* II, 1059-70.

[49] G.W.F. Hegel, *Vorlesungen über die Philosophie der Religion* II/2 (ed. Lansom), p. 81; ET: *Lectures on the Philosophy of Religion*, 3 vols (London 1895), vol. 3, pp. 24-5.

[50] B. Pascal, *Pensées*, Fr. 397; ET: W.F. Trotter (London, 1932), p. 107.

[51] On this, see above, Part I.

[52] Cf. the official declarations of the magisterium on J. Frohschammer in DS 2851.

[53] Cf G.W.F. Hegel, *Vorlesungen über die Philosophie der Religion* II/2 (ed. Lanson), pp. 69 f, 77 ff.; ET: vol. 3, pp. 7-33.

[54] Augustine, *Contra sermonem Arianorum* (PL 42, 688); cf. also Leo the Great, *Epistola* XXXV (PL 54, 807). On the whole subject, see also F. Malmberg, *Über den Gottmenschen* (QD 9) (Freiburg, 1960).

[55] Thomas Aquinas, *Summa theol.* III, q. 2, a. 10 (according to the original reading).

[56] *Idem., Quaestiones disputatae* V., *De unione Verbi incarnati*, a. 1.

[57] M.J. Scheeben, *Handbuch der katholischen Dogmatik* V/1, *Gesammelte Schriften* VI/1 (Freiburg, 1954), p. 202.

[58] J. Alfaro, Art. 'Gott IV. Gott Vater', in: HThG I, p. 603.

[59] See bibliography in notes 37 f above, and in addition, E. Gutwenger, *Bewusstsein und Wissen Christi* (Innsbruck, 1960); *idem*, 'Das Wissen Christi', in: *Concilium* 2 (1966), pp. 45-52 (with bibliography); ET: 'The Problem of Christ's Knowledge', *Concilium* (1966) I/2, pp. 48-55; H. Riedlinger, *Geschichtlichkeit und Vollendung des Wissens Christi* (QD 32), (Freiburg, 1966).

[60] Cf K. Rahner, 'Reflections on the Knowledge and Self-consciousness of Christ', in: *Theological Investigations*, vol. V (London, 1966), pp. 193-215. What is, of course, open to question in Rahner's treatment is that he deals with the question of Jesus' consciousness and self-consciousness from the point of view of the relation of the human nature to the Logos hypostatically united to it. Scripture, on the other hand, speaks of Jesus' relation to the Father. The indirect character of Jesus' sonship which I deal with above is therefore not perceived in his treatment.

[61] Cf in this regard the survey and attempted solution in F. Malmberg, *Über den Gottmenschen*, pp. 115 ff.

[62] Cf the controversy between T. Lorenzmeier 'Wider das Dogma von der Sündlosigkeit Jesu', in: EvTh 31 (1971), pp. 452-71) and H. Gollwitzer ('Zur Frage der "Sündlosigkeit Jesu",' *ibid.*, pp. 496-506).

[63] Cf F.W.J. Schelling, *Philosophische Untersuchungen über das Wesen der menschlichen Freiheit und die damit zusammenhängenden Gegenstände*, in: *Werke* IV (ed. Schröter), p. 300.

[64] This important point of view has been repeatedly emphasized in modern theology by H. Urs von Balthasar in particular; for a summary, see *Herrlichkeit*, vol. III/2, Pt. 2 (Einsiedeln, 1969).

[65] Cf M. Schmaus, *Die psychologische Trinitätslehre des hl. Augustinus* (Münster, 1927).

[66] For a more detailed justification of this statement, see the following section of this third chapter.

[67] Cf H.Urs von Balthasar, 'Der Unbekannte jenseits des Wortes', in: *Spiritus Creator. Skizzen zur Theologie*, vol. III (Einsiedeln, 1967), pp. 97 f.

[68] Cf H. Mühlen, *Der Heilige Geist als Person. In der Trinität, bei der Inkarnation und im Gnadenbund: Ich – Du – Wir*, (2nd ed., Münster, 1966), pp. 180 ff, 206 ff.

[69] The difficult questions of biblical theology raised by the theme of the virgin birth cannot be dealt with here. See on this: H. Schürmann, *Lukasevangelium*, vol. I, pp. 60-4,

where at least it is shown that from the exegetical point of view the question is an open one and nothing is decided beforehand against tradition. But since the interpretation of Scripture of the ancient Church is completely unanimous, any contestation of the Church's teaching involves calling in question the principle of Tradition. Cf. also G. Delling, Art. 'parthenos', in: TW V, 824-35; K.S. Frank – R. Killian – O. Knoch – G. Lattke – K. Rahner, Zum Thema Jungfrauengeburt (Stuttgart, 1970); R.E. Brown, 'The Problem of the Virginal Conception of Jesus', in: ThSt 33 (1972), pp. 3-34; K.H. Schelkle, Theologie des neuen Testamentes, Vol. 2 (Düsseldorf, 1973), pp. 175-82. On the data of tradition: H. von Campenhausen, Die Jungfrauengeburt in der Theologie der alten Kirche (Heidelberg, 1962); H.J. Brosch – J. Hasenfuss (eds.), Jungfrauengeburt gestern und heute (Essen, 1969).

[70] I owe this point of view also to H. U. von Balthasar; see his Herrlichkeit, vol. I (Einsiedeln, 1961).

[71] R. Koch, Geist und Messias. Beitrag zur biblischen Theologie des Alten Testaments (Vienna, 1950); W. Grundmann and others, art. 'chrio', in: TW IX, 482-576; H. Mühlen, 'Das Christusereignis als Tat des Heiligen Geistes', in: Mysterium Salutis III/2, 513-44.

[72] Cf A. Grillmeier, 'Die Wirkung des Heilhandelns Gottes in Christus', in: loc. cit., 327-90.

[73] Cf in this regard, J. Ternus, 'Chalkedon und die Entwicklung der protestantischen Theologie. Ein Durchblick von der Reformation bis zur Gegenwart,' in: Das Konzil von Chalkedon, vol. 3, pp. 545, 557.

[74] Cf the summary accounts in M. Schmaus, art. 'Ämter Christi', in: LTK vol. I, 457-9; J. Alfaro, 'Die heilsfunktionen Christi als Offenbarer, Herr und Priester', in: Mysterium Salutis III/1, 649-708; H. Ott, Die Antwort des Glaubens. Systematische Theologie in 50 Artikeln (Stuttgart-Berlin, 1972), pp. 266-75. On the criticism of the doctrine of the three offices, see also W. Pannenberg, Grundzüge, pp. 218 ff; ET: pp. 212-25.

[75] Cf K. Barth, Die Kirchliche Dogmatik IV/3 (Zollikon-Zürich, 1959), pp. 13 ff; ET: Church Dogmatics, eds., G.W. Bromley and T.F. Torrance (Edinburgh, 1936-62, 12 vols.), vol. IV/3, 1 (1961), pp. 11 ff.

[76] Cf the comprehensive account in L. Oeing-Hanhoff, et al., art. 'Geist', in: Historisches Wörterbuch der Philosophie III, ed. J. Ritter (Darmstadt, 1974), 154-204.

[77] Cf H. Kleinknecht, F. Baumgärtel, W. Bieder, E. Sjöberg, E. Schweizer, art. 'pneuma' in: TW VI, 330-453.

[78] On the exegesis of this section, see O. Kuss, Der Römerbrief (2nd ed. Regensburg, 1963), pp. 619ff; O. Michel, Der Brief an die Römer (4th ed. Göttingen, 1966), pp. 200-12; H. Schlier, 'Das, worauf alles wartet. Eine Auslegung von Römer 8, 18-30', in: Das Ende der Zeit (Freiburg), pp. 250-70; E. Käsemann, An die Römer (Tübingen, 1973), pp. 219-34.

[79] Cf in this regard, I. Hermann, Kyrios und Pneuma. Studien zur Christologie der paulinischen Hauptbriefe (Munich, 1961).

[80] See also supra, Chapter I.

[81] Cf Athanasius, Epist. I ad Serapionem, 23 f (PG 26, 583-8); Basil, De Spiritu sancto 26 (PG 32, 185 f).

[82] Cf Y. Congar, Chrétiens Désunis (Paris, 1937). The difference between Eastern and Western doctrines of the Trinity was first brought out by T. de Régnon, Etudes de théologie positive sur la Sainte Trinité, 4 vols. (Paris, 1882ff). On the present state of the question, see in particular P. Evdokimov, L'Esprit saint dans la tradition orthodoxe (Paris, 1969).

[83] Cf on this M. Schmaus, Die psychologische Trinitätslehre des Hl. Augustinus. (Münster, 1927).

[84] J. Ratzinger, Einführung in das Christentum, pp. 276 f; ET: Introduction to Christianity (London, 1967), pp. 256-7.

[85] Cf E. Przywara, Logos. Logos, Abendland, Reich, Commercium (Düsseldorf, 1964), pp. 157 ff.

[86] Cf P. Evdokimov, L'Esprit saint dans la tradition orthodoxe, p. 70.

[87] Cf H. Schauf, *Die Einwohnung des Heiligen Geistes. Die Lehre von der nicht-approp-riierten Einwohnung des Heiligen Geistes als Beitrag zur Theologiegeschichte des neun-zehnten Jahrhunderts unter besonderer Berücksichtigung der beiden Theologen Carl Passaglia und Clemens Schrader* (Freiburg, 1941).

[88] This is brought out particularly by H. Urs von Balthasar, 'Der Unbekannte jenseits des Wortes', in: *Spiritus Creator. Skizzen zur Theologie*, vol. III (Einsiedeln, 1967).

[89] Cf H. Volk, 'Das Wirken des Heiligen Geistes in den Gläubigen', in: *idem, Gott alles in allem, op. cit.* pp. 89 f (especially note 3).

[90] For a fuller account, see J. Ratzinger, art. 'Licht', in: *HThG* II, 44-54 (with a bibliography).

[91] Cf M. Buber, 'Prophetismus und Apokalyptik', in: *Werke* vol. II, pp. 925-942; ET: Prophecy 'Apocalyptic and the Historical Hour', in: *Pointing the Way* (London, 1957), pp. 192-207. E. Fascher, *'Prophetes'* (Giessen, 1927); H. Krämer, R. Rendtorff, R. Meyer, G. Friedrich, art. *'Prophetes'*, in: *TW* VI, 781-833.

[92] On the biblical understanding of truth, see H. v. Soden, Was ist Wahrheit? Vom geschichtlichen Begriff der Wahrheit, in: *idem, Urchristentum und Geschichte*, vol. 1 (Tübingen, 1951), pp. 1-24; W. Pannenberg, 'Was ist Wahrheit?' in, *idem, Grundfragen systematischer Theologie* (Göttingen, 1967), pp. 202-220; W. Kasper, *Dogma unter dem Wort Gottes* (Mainz, 1965). pp. 58ff (with bibliography.

[93] J. Simon, art. 'Leben', in: *Handbuch philosophischer Grundbegriffe* II, 844.

[94] R. Bultmann, art. *'Zao'*, in: TW II, 833.

[95] J. Simon, art. 'Leben', *loc. cit.*

[96] K. Rahner, art. 'Opfer, V, Dogmatisch', in: LTK VII, 1174 ff.

[97] Cf G.W.F. Hegel, *Vorlesungen über die Philosophie der Religion* I/1 (ed. Lanson), pp.|227 ff; ET: *Lectures on the Philosophy of Religion*, vol. 1, pp. 299 ff.

[98] See in particular H. Kleinknecht, G. von Rad, K.G. Kuhn, K.L. Schmidt, Art.*'basileus'*, in: TW I, 562-95. On the problem itself, see H. Dombrowski,*Grundfragen der Christologie. Erörtert am Problem der Herrschaft Christi* (Munich, 1969).

[99] R. Bultmann, *Das Evangelium des Johannes*, p. 277; ET: *The Gospel of John* (Oxford, 1971), p. 364.

[100] Cf J. Michl, G. Englhardt, art. 'Chiliasmus', in: LTK II, 1058-62 (with bibliography). On the further history and effects of this expectation, see in particular R. Frick, *Die Geschichte des Reich-Gottes-Gedankens in der alten Kirche bis zu Origenes und Augustin* (Giessen, 1928); W. Nigg, *Das ewige Reich. Geschichte einer Sehnsucht und einer Enttäuschung* (Zürich, 1944); E. Iserloh, 'Das Reich Gottes', in: *Gottesreich und menschenreich. Ihr Spannungsverhältnis in Geschichte und Gegenwart* (Regensburg, 1971), pp. 51-72.

[101] On this see the important analysis by E. Peterson, 'Der Monotheismus als politisches Problem', in: *Theologische Traktate* (Munich, 1951), pp. 45-147.

[102] Cf Pastoral Constitution *Gaudium et Spes*, 36; *The Documents of Vatican II*, ed. W.M. Abbott (London, 1967), p. 233.

[103] Marcion, quoted in Tertullian, *Adversus Marcionem* IV, 33, 8 (CChr 1, 634).

[104] Cf Augustine, *De civitate Dei* 19, 26 (CSEL 40/2, 421).

[105] *Ibid.*, 14, 28; cf also 19, 24 and *Enarrationes in Psalmos* 64, 2 (CChr 39, 823 f).

[106] Vatican II, Dogmatic Constitution 'Lumen Gentium', 1; *The Documents of Vatican II*, p. 15. On this, see L. Boff, *Die Kirche als Sakrament im Horizont der Welterfahrung. Versuch einer Legitimation und einer struktur-funktionalistischen Grundlegung der Kirche im Anschluss an das II Vatikanische Konzil* (Paderborn, 1972).

[107] *Lumen Gentium*, 8; *The Documents of Vatican II*, p. 22.

[108] Cf Vatican II, *Gaudium et Spes*, 3 f, 10 f, 40, 42 f, 58 and *passim*.

[109] Cf Y. Congar, 'Pneumatologie et "christomonisme" dans la tradition latine', in: EThL 45 (1969), pp. 394-416.

[110] See the previous section of this chapter, pp. 230 ff.

[111] F. Nietzsche, *Also sprach Zarathustra, Werke* (ed. K. Schlechta), vol. 2, p. 284;

ET: *Thus Spake Zarathustra* (London, 1909), p. 11.

112 *Idem, Die Fröhliche Wissenschaft, op. cit.*, p. 127.

113 Cf Thomas Aquinas, *Summa theol*. III, q. 8, a. 3.

NAME INDEX

E

Ebeling, G. 33, 88, 99, 112, 132, 142, 143
Ebert, H. 136, 142
Ebner, F. 246
Eckhart, Meister 181
Eicher, P. 60
Eichhorn, J.G. 30
Eichrodt, W. 88, 227
Eisler, R. 71
Elert, W. 194
Engels, Friedrich 195
Englhardt, G. 273
Erharter, H. 270
Ernst, J. 111
Eusebius of Caesarea 265
Eutyches 236
Evdokimov, P. 272

F

Fabro, C. 60
Fascher, E. 38, 159, 273
Feiner, J.
Feld, H. 143
Feuerbach, Ludwig 23, 47, 60, 212
Fichte, J.G. 16, 54, 183, 184
Fiesler, P.
Fiorenza, Francis P. 226
Fischer, K.P. 60
Flavian 236
Flick, M. 226
Foerster, W. 153, 160, 227
Fohrer, G. 88, 112, 193, 195
Foucauld, Charles de 217
Francis of Assisi 28
Frank, K.S. 272
Frick, R. 273

Friedrich, G. 229, 273
Fries, H. 59, 99
Fuchs, E. 18, 33, 40, 111, 141
Fuller, R.H. 98
Furger, F. 141, 194

G

Gabler, J.P. 38
Galtier, P. 244
Geense, A. 141
Geiselmann, J.R. 9, 19
Gerken, A. 60
Gesché, A. 141
Gese, H. 122
Gewiess, J. 226
Geyer, H.G. 141
Gilg, A. 193
Gnilka, J. 159, 195
Goethe, Johann Wolfgang von 183, 195
Gogarten, F. 59
Gollwitzer, H. 271
Grässer, E. 71
Grass, H. 138, 140, 143
Gregory of Nazianzus 177, 212, 227
Gregory of Nyssa 177, 227
Gregory Thaumaturgus 179
Greiffenhagen, M. 59
Greshake, G. 194, 226, 228
Grillmeier, Adolf 193, 194, 226, 227, 228, 269, 270, 272
Gross, H. 111
Gross, J. 226, 227
Grosseteste, R. 260
Grotius, Hugo 221
Grünewald, M. 128
Grundmann, W. 71, 111, 112, 226, 272

K

Kähler, M.   32ff, 39
Käsemann, Ernest   18, 33ff, 39,
   99, 111, 112, 122, 132, 154,
   159, 160, 173, 199, 225,
   228, 272
Kaiser, G.P.   38
Kalthoff, A.   45
Kamlah, W.   45, 194
Kant, Immanuel   23, 37, 42f, 44,
   49, 54-5, 59, 61, 76, 182,
   228
Kasper, Walter   61, 142, 192, 193,
   194, 228, 270, 273
Kegel, G.   141
Kehl, M.   160
Keim, T.   30
Kertelge, K.   39, 99
Kessler, H.   71, 115, 122, 123,
   228
Kierkegaard, sren   183
Kilian, R.   272
Klappert, B.   141
Klausner, J.   71
Kleinknecht, H.   87, 193, 272,
   273
Knoch, O.   272
Koch, G.   160
Koch, R.   272
Köhler, W.   193
Köster, H.   270
Koester, W.   111
Kolping, A.   99, 141
Kottje, R.   122
Krämer, H.   273
Kramer, W.   111, 112, 160, 193
Kraus, H.J.   38
Kreck, W.   160
Kremer, J.   141, 159
Kretschmar, G.   225

Krings, H.   194
Kruijf, T. de   112
Kümmel, W.G.   76
Küng, Hans   19, 33, 99, 141, 142,
   160, 193, 194, 195
Künneth, Walter   141, 192
Kuhn, J.E.   39, 51, 60, 193
Kuhn, K.G.   87, 273
Kuss, O.   272

L

Lachmann, K.   39
Lakner, F.   226
Lamarche, P.   194
Lao Tse   26
Lattke, G.   272
Laurentin, René   70
Lehmann, Karl   138, 141, 142,
   143, 159, 228, 229
Lentzen-Deis, F.   70, 98
Léon-Dufour, Xavier   141
Leontius of Byzantium   242, 270
Leo the Great, Pope   236, 239, 271
Lessing, G.E.   29f, 39, 130, 141
Lewis, C.S.   99
Liébaert, J.   194, 269
Lightfoot, J.B.   194, 227
Locke, John   44, 243, 270
Loewenich, W. von   194
Lohfink, G.   159, 193
Lohse, E.   112, 122, 269
Lombard, Peter   239, 249, 257
Loofs, F.   36, 40, 193, 268, 269
Lorenzmeier, T.   271
Lucian of Antioch   176
Ludochowski, H.   141
Lübbe, H.   59
Luhmann, N.   38
Luther, Martin   22ff, 129, 180,194

279

S

SUBJECT INDEX

SUBJECT INDEX

D

E

F

G

H

I

J

K

L

M